Much of the so-called Age of Santa Anna in the history of independent Mexico remains a mystery – no decade is as poorly understood as the years from 1835 to 1846. In 1834, the ruling elite of middle-class *hombres de bien* concluded that a highly centralized republican government was the only solution to the turmoil and factionalism which had characterized the new nation since its emancipation from Spain in 1821. The central republic was thus set up in 1835, but once again civil strife, economic stagnation and military coups prevailed until 1846, when a disastrous war with the United States began, a war in which Mexico was to lose half of its national territory. This study explains the course of events and analyses why centralism failed, the issues and personalities involved and the underlying pressures of economic and social change.

CAMBRIDGE LATIN AMERICAN STUDIES

GENERAL EDITOR
SIMON COLLIER

ADVISORY COMMITTEE
MALCOLM DEAS, STUART SCHWARTZ, ARTURO VALENZUELA

73

THE CENTRAL REPUBLIC IN MEXICO, 1835–1846

For a list of other books in the
Cambridge Latin American Studies series,
see page 323

THE CENTRAL REPUBLIC
IN MEXICO, 1835–1846

HOMBRES DE BIEN IN THE AGE OF SANTA ANNA

MICHAEL P. COSTELOE

Professor of Hispanic and Latin American Studies
University of Bristol

CAMBRIDGE
UNIVERSITY PRESS

Published by the Press Syndicate of the University of Cambridge
The Pitt Building, Trumpington Street, Cambridge CB2 1RP
40 West 20th Street, New York, NY 10011–4211, USA
10 Stamford Road, Oakleigh, Victoria 3166, Australia

© Cambridge University Press 1993

First published 1993

Printed in the United States of America

Library of Congress Cataloging-in-Publication Data

Costeloe, Michael P.

The central republic in Mexico, 1835–1846 : *hombres de bien* in the
Age of Santa Anna / Michael P. Costeloe.

p.   cm. – (Cambridge Latin American studies : 73)

Includes index.

ISBN 0–521–44121–8

1. Mexico – Politics and government – 1821–1861.   2. Santa Anna,
Antonio López de, 1794?–1876.   3. Decentralization in government –
Mexico – History – 19th century.   I. Title.   II. Series.
F1232.C843   1993
972'.04 – dc20   92-33950
                                                                        CIP

A catalog record for this book is available from the British Library.

ISBN 0-521-44121-8 hardback

For Sarah Louise

Contents

Preface   *page* ix
Acknowledgements   xiii

1   An introduction: change and continuity in the Age
    of Santa Anna   1
2   The end of federalism   31
3   The transition to centralism: stage I   46
4   The transition to centralism: stage II   66
5   Las Siete Leyes   93
6   Anastasio Bustamante and the centralist republic,
    1837–1839   121
7   Santa Anna versus Bustamante: the end of the Siete
    Leyes, 1839–1841   149
8   'La dictadura disfrazada con el hermoso nombre de
    regeneración política'   184
9   Santa Anna and the Bases Orgánicas   213
10 'La revolución de tres horas'   239
11 Herrera and the rise of Paredes y Arrillaga   261
12 *Hombres de bien* and the restoration of federalism   284
13 Conclusion   298

Sources and works cited   307
Index   315

Preface

The origins of this book are both personal and academic. In 1975, I published a study of the first federal republic of Mexico which covered the years from 1824, when the republic was founded, to the middle of 1834, when it began to be dismantled. My interest in those years arose from a desire to know what were the politics, issues, personalities and, indeed, the events which had brought Mexico to the verge of political anarchy so soon after emancipation from Spain. After trying to guide undergraduates through the bewildering array of revolts and political factions, it was obvious that the existing literature was inadequate. Basically the same motives brought me to the following decade, from 1834 to 1846. Having tried a monarchist form of government with the short-lived Iturbide empire and then the federal republic, Mexicans chose to create a centralized republic with power firmly vested in national authorities located in the capital. Again, I wanted to know why they did so, who were the political and military leaders who brought about the change, what were their hopes, what pressures and tensions they faced and, in particular, why the chronic instability of the earlier decade continued unabated with the same myriad conflicting ideas, issues, factions and revolts. In short, my objective with the present work has been to write a reasonably detailed account of the centralist decade, a period which Professor Vázquez has correctly labelled recently the 'forgotten years' of Mexican history. Certainly, it has attracted very little scholarly attention, and apart from a handful of monographs by young Mexican historians on very specialized aspects, there has been no attempt to examine and explain the political parties, personalities, events or changes which took place.

My approach has been to provide a largely chronological framework because, as every other historian who has attempted to study these years has discovered, it is the most effective way to make sense of the inherent complexity of the people, issues and events of the time. The focal point is the national government and the problems and pressures it faced. The trend in recent Mexican historiography has been to concentrate on aspects of regional development, especially economic, and while that has provided welcome insights into how certain areas and industries developed, it is well not to forget, as is sometimes the case in such studies, that there was also a national government, however unstable and ineffective, and a national political scene. It was largely, although obviously not exclusively, at that level that there was constant conflict over the form of government, its nature and role, economic and commercial policy, the role of institutions such as the Church and army, social policy and a whole range of other issues which are the themes of this work and which I have sought to incorporate within the narrative framework.

Above all, I have placed much emphasis on the people involved in the turmoil. Known as the Age of Santa Anna, the three decades of that notorious Mexican's career from 1821 to 1855 have inevitably been overshadowed by his dominant, and it must be said remarkable, personality. But there were many other personalities who exercised considerable influence and about whom very little is known – men such as Anastasio Bustamante, Manuel Gómez Pedraza, Mariano Paredes y Arrillaga, Miguel Barragán, Gabriel Valencia and Francisco Manuel Sánchez de Tagle. It is with their careers that much of this book is concerned, although Santa Anna can never be, nor has been, neglected.

Finally, one strand which runs through every chapter concerns what was known to contemporaries as the *hombre de bien,* a term I seek to explain in the introduction. With the end of colonial rule in 1821, Mexico's population of 7 million people, composed largely of Indians and mestizos, came under the control of an elite of white, probably mostly creole, families and individuals. Their social and economic status at the pinnacle of wealth and power seemed secure. They hoped to consolidate and improve that control using the opportunities which followed the abolition of the colonial regime of corporate and inherited privilege, discrimination, trade and industry monopolies and the opening of Mexico to the international world of commerce and industrial development. They saw as the vital first step in that process the construction of a political system which would guarantee and protect their own interests. Rightly or wrongly, however, they came to believe that their new-found pre-eminence was tenuous and subject to threat not just from external aggression but also from extremists who attempted to mobilize for their own purposes the impoverished masses with promises of genuine equality, civil rights and the redistribution of wealth. Furthermore, they believed that their personal and religious values, the accepted norms of social conduct and especially the relationship between one class and another were under immense pressure of change from both within and without the country. If the end of Spanish rule had brought them political opportunities, it had also initiated significant social change which jeopardized their status, and this has been one of the central themes incorporated in several chapters.

Indeed, in many respects, in my view, it is in the field of social change that we must look to find many of the tensions and pressures which brought about much of the turmoil of the Age of Santa Anna in general and of the decade of centralism in particular.

Acknowledgements

Grateful acknowledgement is made to the many scholars and the staff of archives and libraries in Mexico, Great Britain and the United States without whose generous assistance and cooperation the research for this book would not have been possible. I am particularly indebted to Josefina Vázquez and Jan Bazant for their hospitality and help during my various stays in Mexico. Jane Garner, Asunción Lavrin, Jaime Olveda, John Coatsworth and Barbara Tenenbaum, to name only a few, kindly helped with books, photocopies and microfilm. Special thanks are due to Julie Sheppard, who patiently and efficiently helped prepare the typescript. Both the British Academy and the University of Bristol provided essential financial support.

1

An introduction: change and continuity in the Age of Santa Anna

Over the past forty years, impressive progress has been made in our knowledge of the history of Mexico; historians on both sides of the Atlantic have written many important books and articles which have cast new light on the way the country has developed. Looking at the broad sweep of Mexican historiography from the sixteenth to the twentieth century, it is evident that the colonial era and the 1910 Revolution and its aftermath have found most favour. Since the seminal work of Tannenbaum and his generation, the Revolution in particular has been subjected to intense scrutiny. There have been many studies of major and minor personalities and dozens of well-researched investigations into political, social, economic and cultural aspects. Almost a whole generation's work culminated in 1986 with the publication of Knight's monumental two-volume work, more than one thousand pages long, which brought together and analysed, supported or rejected, the myriad interpretations of one of the major events of the twentieth century.[1]

The colonial period has been equally well, if not even better, served. Borah, Gibson, Hanke and others in the United States, Zavala and Miranda in Mexico, Chevalier and Ricard in France, to name only a few, examined early colonial institutions, society and religious life with unprecedented skill and attention. With archival research in national and state depositories becoming increasingly possible as Mexicans themselves realized the value of safeguarding their historical patrimony, younger scholars moved to the eighteenth century, where the efforts of Brading, Hamnett, Lavrin, Florescano and many others have given us a much broader and deeper appreciation of the Bourbon age.

There remains, however, one substantial gap in the historiography. The nineteenth century – above all, the three decades between independence in 1821 and the midcentury Reform, has attracted comparatively little scholarly interest. The so-called Age of Santa Anna remains, to use Van Young's words in a recent article, 'one of the great unexplored

1 A. Knight, *The Mexican Revolution* (Cambridge, 1986).

territories of Mexican history' and compared with the colonial and modern eras, concerning which there is a voluminous and ever-expanding literature, it is almost virgin territory for the historian.[2] This neglect, of course, is not total, and in the past few years monographs have appeared on Church–State relations, fiscal policy, industry and trade and diverse other aspects, as have a number of accounts of prominent family dynasties. The emphasis has been, and continues to be, on economic topics, with the political sphere and the lives of those who participated in it comparatively untouched. Few of the many men who rose to dominate the young republic have been deemed worthy of serious biographical study, and there remains no satisfactory explanation of why the country, after three centuries of relative stability under Spanish rule, descended so rapidly into political turmoil. Mexicans at the time had no doubts as to the cause of their problems. For them, it was their inability to find a stable constitutional basis for self-government, to create political structures which would ensure both individual and institutional rights and liberties. They were firmly convinced that social and economic progress could and would be achieved only when a permanent political framework had been devised. They failed in their aims and priorities, and as a result, Mexico was to suffer almost fifty years of political ferment and economic difficulty until the iron hand of Porfirio Díaz was able to impose order in the name of economic progress.

A main feature of the Age of Santa Anna, therefore, was chronic political upheaval and Mexicans' apparent incapacity to establish a stable and enduring system of self-government. As both cause and effect of the turmoil, no president save the first managed to retain office for his full elected or appointed term, and governments changed with bewildering frequency. An incalculable number of revolts, or *pronunciamientos,* took place, and military action by ambitious army officers became the normal method of expressing dissent or pursuing policy change. The constitutional basis of the nation fluctuated: monarchy, federal and central republicanism, dictatorship and variants of all four systems were tried from time to time. Political parties came and went to re-emerge under different guises as the ideologies of liberalism and conservatism fragmented into dozens of divergent sects. From 1824 to 1857, there were sixteen presidents and thirty-three provisional national leaders, for a total of forty-nine administrations. The Ministry of War changed hands fifty-three times, that of Foreign Affairs fifty-seven times, Interior sixty-one times and Treasury no less than eighty-seven times.[3] In the provincial and

2 E. Van Young, 'Recent Anglophone Scholarship on Mexico and Central America in the Age of Revolution (1750–1850)', *Hispanic American Historical Review,* 65 (1985), 725–43.
3 Statistics from D. F. Stevens, 'Instability in Mexico from Independence to the War of the Reform', Ph.D. diss., University of Chicago, 1984, p. 182.

municipal bureaucracies, there was an unending stream of momentarily favoured or disgraced officials in and out. Representative congresses of various types were elected or appointed more or less every two years, but often only to have their deliberations abruptly halted by the rise of a general-president who saw no need for a legislative assembly.

The list of such tangible symptoms of political instability and of the economic difficulties which accompanied them is almost endless, and their origins lie in many respects in the pressures released and problems that arose when Mexico won the ten-year-long war of independence. One feature of recent Mexican historiography is that the traditional periodization of history into colonial–independence–modern is no longer considered convenient or apt. Recent works on institutions, economy and society have begun to advocate the continuity of history and to argue that although the separation from Spain was undeniably a traumatic and disruptive event, it could not and did not represent a sudden break in every respect with the past.[4] The generation which survived the war faced economic difficulties, as well as social, cultural and to some extent ideological issues which had been germinating long before Hidalgo's *Grito de Dolores* in 1810. Hence, to explain many aspects of the instability of the post-independence years, we must look to the tensions of late colonial times and seek connections with the early republican era.

It is not my intention to enter into this debate except to say that it seems to me that the concept of continuity has considerable validity. In many respects, it may even be said to be self-evident inasmuch as the personal problems, social values and opinions of merchants, shopkeepers, artisans, landowners, peasants and all the other groups and individuals which made up Mexico's population obviously did not disappear overnight. Also, to quote Van Young again, 'Modes and social relations of production, family and gender relationships, certain characteristics of state structure and action, and so on, appear to have been substantially in place by the middle of the eighteenth century and to have altered more between 1700 and 1750, or between 1850 and 1900, than between 1750 and 1850'.[5] But, and it does seem to me a serious qualification of the current continuity thesis, it would also be wrong to underestimate or diminish the effects of independence. Change certainly did follow in many spheres when the political, institutional, judicial, social and economic structures

4 For example, see L. Arnold, *Bureaucracy and Bureaucrats in Mexico City, 1742–1835* (Tucson, Ariz., 1988); B. Hamnett, *Roots of Insurgency: Mexican Regions, 1750–1824* (Cambridge, 1986); G. P. C. Thomson, *Puebla de los Angeles: Industry and Society in a Mexican City, 1700–1850* (Boulder, Colo., 1989); L. B. Hall, 'Independence and Revolution: Continuities and Discontinuities', in J. E. Rodríguez O, ed., *The Independence of Mexico and the Creation of the New Nation* (Berkeley and Los Angeles, 1989), pp. 323–9.
5 Van Young, 'Recent Anglophone Scholarship', pp. 728–9.

of the colonial era began to break down as a result of both emancipation and changes on the broader international scene. When Agustín de Iturbide and his supporters entered the gates of the city of Mexico on 27 September 1821, they indeed faced a new world with new problems, pressures and unforeseen difficulties. It is with these new problems and pressures that I am mostly concerned in this introduction. Added to those inherited from the past, they were to be the cause of much of the turmoil which persuaded many Mexicans that their nation required a centralized form of government. In accordance with their conservative but, they thought, progressive attitudes, they hoped to preserve those values and practices they esteemed from their past and to reconcile them with the new circumstances and changing ideas of their own time.

Some of the problems were certainly predictable. The war had caused immense damage to the economy with the widespread destruction of property, commerce and industry, notably mining, and, most important of all, the flight of capital. The lack of capital, especially the shortage of Gsilver coin, was not a new phenomenon – large amounts of specie had gone to Spain in the final decades of the viceroyalty – but the situation was seriously exacerbated during the war when vast quantities left the country. Economic recovery, if it did take place (and that is also a matter of current debate among economic historians), was definitely patchy and slow, and with one or two notable exceptions, such as the growth of the textile industry, from the 1830s onwards there was little tangible evidence of it as far as contemporaries were concerned. No government was able to generate sufficient revenues with which to meet its obligations internationally, a situation that led to war with France and many years of dispute with the United States. Internally, the fiscal situation hovered on the edge of national bankruptcy, and governments resorted to desperate measures to make even token payments to state employees, including the military, pensioners, widows and many others dependent on the public purse. A vicious circle of mortgaging present and future income to secure loans from speculators at ever-higher rates of interest reduced the net revenues available for daily needs, and a futile attempt to increase the amount of currency in circulation by issuing copper coin led to increased poverty and hunger as the new money rapidly lost much of its face value.[6] After defaulting on foreign loans obtained in the early 1820s closed the possibility of any large-scale international capital investment, there seemed no solution to the fiscal crisis. Governments responded with ad hoc measures of forced loans, confiscation and sale of assets, including

6 M. Gayón Córdoba, 'Guerra, dictadura y cobre: Crónica de una ciudad asediada (agosto–diciembre 1841)', *Historias*, 5 (1984), 53–65.

those of the Church, and increased taxation of every kind and at every level.[7]

Much of the financial crisis, and the general political instability accompanying it, was attributable to the demands of one institution, which, although it absorbed a major proportion of the revenues, at the same time was never provided with enough to meet its claimed needs. The Mexican army assumed control in 1821 and was to dominate the executive branch of government for the next 125 years. A military caste, at the officer level, with its own traditions and conceptions of the role and status of an army, had existed under Bourbon rule, but the institution which emerged in 1821 was essentially new in Mexican society.[8] The officer corps, with its love of parades and colourful uniforms, consisted almost entirely of men who had made their reputations and acquired their ranks while fighting on either side during the war. Led by Iturbide, they reached a consensus to separate from Spain, and they became immensely popular as a result. Because of their decision, and in some cases heroic careers in the insurgency, they were the natural and popular leaders of the new country, and they were given the esteem and privileged status which they, and it must be said the public at large, thought they deserved. It was from their ranks that every president, with a couple of interim exceptions, before Benito Juárez was to be drawn, and despite the subsequent rise of powerful civilian politicians and political parties that opposed the pre-eminence of a military caste, they successfully defended their status and their privileges.[9]

They were able to do so for a number of reasons. Most important was the fact that the emancipation achieved by Iturbide was believed to be both insecure and vulnerable. For the next thirty years, if not longer, many Mexicans thought that the recolonization of their country was always possible, if not probable, and events were to bear out their fears when Napoleon III imposed Maximilian as their emperor. The more immediate threat, to persist until 1833, came from Spain and Ferdinand VII, who, it was well known, had vowed never to sacrifice his claims to his former colony. Throughout the 1820s, and in the full knowledge of the Mexican

---

7 For the best analysis of the fiscal crisis, see B. Tenenbaum, *The Politics of Penury: Debts and Taxes in Mexico, 1821–1856* (Albuquerque, N.M., 1986). On the more general economic problems, see J. H. Coatsworth, 'Obstacles to Economic Growth in Nineteenth Century Mexico,' *American Historical Review*, 83 (1978), 80–100. On the foreign loans, see J. Bazant, *Historia de la deuda exterior de México (1823–1946)* (Mexico, 1968).

8 C. Archer, *The Army in Bourbon Mexico* (Albuquerque, N.M., 1977). There is no satisfactory history of the Mexican army after independence.

9 Between 1821 and 1851, fifteen generals occupied the presidential office, some on an interim basis and some, notably Santa Anna, on several occasions. During the same period, six civilians were acting or interim president but three of these for only a few days. For the full list, see F. N. Samponaro, 'The Political Role of the Army in Mexico, 1821–1848,' Ph.D. diss., State University of New York, 1974, pp. 394–6.

government, he plotted and planned reconquest, seeking aid in the courts of Europe and concocting all manner of schemes to fund an invasion force. His efforts culminated in 1829 with an attack on Mexico by an army dispatched from Cuba. Even after the humiliating defeat of that force, Ferdinand continued to believe that reconquest was possible and even wanted by most Mexicans.[10]

The death of Ferdinand in 1833 removed the Spanish threat, but several years before another potential source of foreign aggression had become clear. From 1825, with the arrival of the first U.S. ambassador, Joel R. Poinsett, the desire of the United States for territorial expansion was obvious, particularly with regard to Texas. Relations between the two countries quickly deteriorated, and with almost constant friction on the northern border, soon compounded by disputes in California, open conflict became probable rather than possible. After the Texas war of 1836 and the Mexican defeat, the United States was viewed as a permanent threat to the future territorial integrity of the republic, and every government proclaimed its intention to resist militarily any further aggression as well as to reconquer Texas.

Mexicans feared the United States as the greatest potential foreign aggressor, but they also had strong suspicions of British and French intentions, notably when France invaded and occupied the port of Veracruz in 1838 on the pretext of collecting debts owed to French citizens. The insecurity they felt was the main factor in their sustaining, at least in theory, a large standing army and in ensuring that the military retained its status, privileges and popular acclaim. The generals themselves were very conscious of the value of emphasizing their own importance, and they saw to it that military victories and heroes of the war of independence were celebrated with public holidays and other forms of recognition. Santa Anna, above all, was a master of the personality cult and of glorifying the virtues and indispensability of the military, and he constantly re-minded the public of his own successes on the battlefield, few and far between though they actually were.

The army and the associated cult of the military caste were, therefore, one new feature of the years after independence, and yet the extent of the army's public esteem was hardly justified by its condition or achievements. The senior officer level, which so carefully and successfully cultivated its own prestige, does seem to have had a certain esprit de corps and sense of duty, even if that did include the right and obligation to intervene in political affairs and act as the ultimate arbiter of the national good. But the regular army as a whole was a shambles and in no sense a coherent,

10 See my *Response to Revolution: Imperial Spain and the Spanish American Revolutions, 1810–1840* (Cambridge, 1986), pp. 96–100.

disciplined body. An impressive array of legislation to create a well-regulated military force was certainly enacted. There were ordinances, an administrative framework, command structure and all manner of directives flowing from the Ministry of War, but it was the unofficial, irregular practices which became the norm. Promotions, for example, came to depend not on rank, service or deeds but on the patronage of individual officers, and the quickest route to the much sought after general's insignia was soon known to be via the *pronunciamiento,* or at least by declaring support for the winning side. As one contemporary put it, 'The rebellions are speculations in which one risks nothing and can gain a lot.'[11]

The lower ranks were notoriously ill-equipped, housed and trained, and given the methods of recruitment, their condition was not surprising. Although national conscription of all adult males was decreed from time to time in moments of crisis, real or assumed, the usual methods of finding men to fill the numerous infantry regiments were forced levy or lottery together with regular round-ups of vagrants. If the victims failed to escape the chains which bound them together as they were marched to the barracks, their destitute women and children had little option but to follow them.[12] Desertion became the common means of escape, and when the deserters were unable to disappear into the rural communities from which they were often taken, they joined the hordes of bandits and thieves who infested the highways and urban centres. Desertion was so rife that the official statistics of the size of the army are meaningless, and it was a rare occasion when more than a few thousand men could be said to be under arms. But it was in the interests of the officer corps to inflate the number of those needed to defend the nation in order to justify the ever-increasing expenditure. Thus, in several years, more than half the national budget went towards the army, and yet the men lacked uniforms, weapons and ammunition and often went for months without pay.[13] Not surprisingly, they were reluctant to fight foreign enemies in return for glory but only too willing to follow an ambitious officer planning a revolt who promised them promotions and money in return for their support.

In contrast, the affluent life-style of nouveau riche generals with their city mansions and country estates became a matter of public scandal. Santa Anna is the most obvious example, becoming a millionaire owner of extensive lands in the Veracruz region, but he was by no means the only successful general to seek the social status which landownership undoubtedly conferred. Indeed, most of the top generals, despite low official

11 *El Siglo XIX,* 19 August 1845.
12 A vivid picture of a bedraggled army with its camp followers is given in F. Calderón de la Barca, *Life in Mexico* (London, 1970), p. 426.
13 For a summary of the annual military budget, see Tenenbaum, *Politics of Penury,* pp. 180–1.

salaries and little or no inherited wealth, promptly acquired substantial rural holdings.

The structure of the army was based on a series of general commands located in about twenty strategic points scattered across the immense area of the country from Yucatán in the south to Coahuila in the north. Each of these units was in the charge of a commander general, and it was from their ranks that most of the rebellious officers were to appear. Although in theory controlled by central command, the Minister of War and, ultimately, the president, in practice the commander generals enjoyed virtual autonomy in their respective regions, and when in the 1830s authority over civilian affairs was combined with their military powers, they were tantamount to provincial autocrats. This was particularly the case in the distant peripheral regions to the north and south such as Sonora, Durango, Chihuahua, Coahuila, Nuevo León, Yucatán and Chiapas. In those areas nearer the capital – Veracruz, Puebla, Oaxaca, Michoacán, Jalisco, San Luis Potosí, Querétaro and so on – to which it was practical, although rarely possible, to march an army to castigate a dissident officer, their power was more directly supervised. Even within these nearer areas, however, the central government was often powerless to impose its will, and local military caudillos like General Juan Alvarez, who ruled Acapulco and its hinterland for more than thirty years, were independent of all national authority. Similar locally based chieftains – in some cases incipient family dynasties – emerged in most provinces, and like their contemporaries in the River Plate and elsewhere in the southern continent, they were able to rule their domains for many years, acquiring extensive landholdings for themselves and sufficient powers of patronage or influence to be able to manipulate the political sphere regardless of the wishes or orders of the central government. Furthermore, proximity to the capital worked both ways; most of the successful revolts began in areas in the central cone. More often than not, rebellions consisted of an initial declaration by a local commander, who would usually have obtained promises of support from neighbouring commanders. If the central provinces – that is, their military garrisons – united behind the call to arms, the regime in Mexico City knew that its time was limited and that resistance would be futile. Occasionally, doubting the strength of the rebel movement, they refused to capitulate, and the result was bloody and destructive conflict in and around the capital with rebels marched in from the surrounding regions.[14]

The apparently almost endless series of *pronunciamientos* must nevertheless be kept in proportion. The division of the military commands reflected

14 See e.g., my article on the July 1840 revolt, 'A *Pronunciamiento* in Nineteenth Century Mexico: 15 de julio de 1840', *Mexican Studies/Estudios Mexicanos*, 4 (1988), 245–64.

the regional character of independent Mexico, which did not exist as a single, unified nation. 'Many Mexicos' is an apt phrase to describe the diversity, isolation and virtual autonomy of many provinces regardless of the constitutional framework of federal or central republic, military dictatorship, or, in due course, monarchy. Hence, of the hundreds of revolts which took place – so many that nobody has yet counted them – relatively few can be described as nationally oriented, that is, having as their objective the overthrow of the national government. Most were concerned with purely local issues or rivalries between competing factions, and if they were centred in places where there was a ready flow of cash, for example, in or near a major port like Tampico or Veracruz, often the purpose was financial, as the winner took possession of the customs house revenues. The regional diversity of Mexico's economy was also at times a contributory factor in the *pronunciamiento* syndrome as local interest groups strived to protect their position. Tobacco and cotton farmers in Veracruz, textile manufacturers in Puebla, miners in Zacatecas did not hesitate to seek the support of their local military commander in their efforts to influence national economic policy, and merchants in several regions on at least one occasion combined to encourage and finance a revolt.[15] Mexico remained a nation of very loosely connected parts; the national government based in the capital had little effective control over the central cone and almost none over the periphery, where Texas had little difficulty in achieving independence and Yucatán was easily able to break away to set up a separate state on more than one occasion.

Just as the central government was unable to control the provincial military, its influence on regional economic life was also minimal. Economic policy – for example, on the terms of trade and particularly the free trade versus protectionism debate – was dictated in Mexico City, but the decisions were rarely enforceable and often ignored by local interests. Recent research suggests that, in some areas, certain aspects of economic activity made a fairly rapid recovery after the devastation of the war in spite of the political chaos or policy dictates at the national level.[16] The impact of the war varied, of course, according to region. In response to changing markets and trade patterns inevitably disrupted by the separation from Spain and technology, adjustments were made by industrial and agricultural producers, and the image of the typical absentee landowner, blind to commercial criteria and innovation, has long since been dispelled.

---

15 See my article, 'The Triangular Revolt in Mexico and the Fall of Anastasio Bustamante, August–October, 1841', *Journal of Latin American Studies*, 20 (1988), 337–60.
16 M. Chowning, 'The Contours of the Post–1810 Depression in Mexico: A Reappraisal', unpublished conference paper. Chowning gives an excellent analysis of recent work by economic historians in this paper, and on the basis of her study of Michoacán, she concludes that economic recovery started much earlier than hitherto thought.

Clearly, areas as far distant from the centre as the Californias were to all intents and purposes independent and left to their own devices to implement national policy as and when it suited them. Other frontier areas, like Chihuahua and Sonora in the north, were also largely cut off from central control and again were left to depend on their own resources when it came, for example, to defending themselves against the constant incursions of hostile nomadic Indian tribes, or *bárbaros* as they were known. Such areas, in political, military and economic matters, were largely autonomous, and while they paid lip service to the concept of national unity, they remained on the margin of national affairs, contributing little or nothing in taxation or military conscription, which were always the two main demands of central government.

Regional interests were certainly prominent, therefore, in the postindependence period, but it would be wrong to depict Mexico as nothing more than a disparate collection of autonomous provinces, each developing its own economic and political structures. A national government existed, made policy and enacted legislation which was applicable, even if not enforceable, in all regions. Every government was well aware of the tensions which threatened territorial disintegration, and conscious efforts were made from the time of Iturbide onwards to promote a sense of national identity. The victory over Spain had instilled a sense of national pride and patriotism, and while certain very marginal groups of Indians and isolated, self-sufficient rural communities were largely immune to the significance of monuments, national holidays and celebrations of past Mexican victories and heroes, a sense of loyalty to the nation as well as to locality or region was developing. Above all, within the literate middle class, which I will discuss later in this introduction, there was a marked sense of national pride, regardless of place of birth or residence. Sharing common social and cultural values, they tended to differ only on the political means whereby they could best defend their privileged status. Alamán, among many other politicians, was to try to use this feeling of class solidarity precisely to overcome regional differences and rivalries.

Nevertheless, despite the many efforts to create a sense of national identity and unity following independence, the characteristic feature of the Age of Santa Anna was undeniably regional diversity and tension. Regionalism and diversity of economic and other interests had, of course, existed in colonial times, when methods of transport, roads and communications were even more primitive, but in the highly regulated colonial society, the two great unifying forces of Crown and Church had been sufficient to hold the pieces together. The end of the monarchy, which came to be looked on by some Mexicans as a mistake, loosened the bonds of unity and gave way to incessant demands for a federal form of government which reflected regional interests and aspirations. The decline in the power and influence of the Roman Catholic Church after independence was an equally important factor in the erosion of the former appearance of cohesion, and the clergy's attempts to protect their status, wealth, privileges and influence were to be a source of much of the political turmoil. Clearly an institution in decline as a result of the reformist zeal of Bourbon monarchs and the substantial losses of revenues, assets and personnel during the war of independence, the Church in 1821 was still, somewhat paradoxically, the most influential corporation in the country. It alone had the structural organization, the revenues and, above all, the unquestioning obedience of the great majority of the population sufficient to enable it to resist any serious challenge from the divided power of the State. This clerical influence, and subsequent power, were to be seen in almost all spheres of life and at all social levels. The Church was a major owner of both urban and rural property and was probably landlord to a majority of the population in the towns and cities. It also had huge investments in real estate, and few property owners were not in some way indebted to a clerical institution. Church schools and colleges often remained the only ones available, and universities in Mexico City and elsewhere continued to be subject to clerical control. Many social welfare organizations such as orphanages, poorhouses and homes for foundlings were managed and financed by clergy, and public hospitals in urban areas were administered by the bishop and chapter. In short, Mexico remained a nation in which both the spiritual and temporal power of the Church pervaded all aspects of life.

The Church, however, although protected as representative of the official and only religion allowed in the country, was not immune to the forces of change. As the poverty of the national Treasury increased and sources of credit dried up, its apparent wealth appeared more and more an intolerable anomaly, and even proclerical, conservative administrations found that they had no alternative but to turn to the clergy for financial aid. Unlike the radical anticlericals who advocated the nationalization of all Church assets on economic, ideological and political grounds, the conservatives resorted to less drastic measures, such as taxation or the use of clerical real estate as security for loans. But the fact that the once sacrosanct wealth of the Church became such a hot political issue after independence reflected more than the fiscal crisis. It was the result of underlying pressures and changes which surfaced in Mexican society once emancipation was achieved. A process of secularization which was both cause and effect of the declining prestige of the Church is clearly evident as Mexicans of all classes gradually lost their once unquestioning obedience to the dictates of their clergy. The more progressive considered the Church's economic, social and political influence, the innate and in some cases reactionary conservatism of the senior hierarchy and, above all, the religious fanaticism of the masses an offence to their rationality. For them, the emphasis on external piety, the daily religious pomp and ceremony and the exaggerated prestige in secular life of a small, nonelected social class were relics of a bygone theocratic age and had no place in the modern, progressive society they were intent on creating. Naturally, the forces of conservatism disagreed. In their eyes, the Church was the embodiment of the only true religious faith and the guardian of the values, morality and attitudes they considered essential for the stability of society and the avoidance of profound social upheaval.

The agents of change which brought the spread of secular as opposed to religious values were many and varied. The spread of freemasonry; the expansion of urban-based population; the improvement in transport and communications with the arrival of regular coach and postal services; the general increase in Mexican contact with the rest of the world which travel, trade and diplomacy entailed – all of these factors enabled Mexicans to view their own society and traditions in a new and more objective light. Above all, independence brought freedom of the press, and polemical journalism became one of the most decisive factors in political life. Thousands of broadsides and pamphlets appeared, and sooner or later every leading personality, and countless minor ones, took up their pens to defend themselves or attack their enemies. Daily, twice-weekly and weekly newspapers were established in every city, the more successful being circulated throughout the country, and although few survived more than a fleeting existence, some continued for several years.[17] They became the main organs of political debate, and they had, or were certainly believed to have, significant influence on public opinion, as is illustrated by the fact that almost every government tried to suppress those in opposition to it.

We have few statistical data on circulation – the leading daily of the 1840s printed 2,200 copies a day[18] – but even though perhaps fewer than 5 per cent of the population were literate, the demand for news and opinion within that minority was insatiable. The papers, especially in the capital, provided the main topics of debate and discussion in the numerous cafés and societies. As one contemporary recorded, 'There were not many newspapers around the café but those that were there were very popular'.[19] While much of the content concerned domestic political matters – for example, government legislation and the record of congressional sessions –

17 In 1844, for example, there were at least twenty-three newspapers being published in provincial cities; see the list in *El Siglo XIX*, 25 June 1844. For a very incomplete listing of the press, see J. Bravo Ugarte, *Periodistas y periódicos mexicanos* (Mexico, 1966).
18 Article in *El Siglo XIX*, 17 April 1845. By comparison, the *New York Daily Herald* was said in the same article to have a daily circulation of 23,500.
19 G. Prieto, *Memorias de mis tiempos* (Mexico, 1948), vol. 1, p. 79.

editors were also careful to include sections on international events, regularly reprinting items from papers published in Britain, France, Spain, the United States and elsewhere in the world.

Another new pressure evident after 1821, which was to be a considerable source of tension, arose from immigration. Religious intolerance prevented a flood of immigrants from settling permanently, but it did not stop the entry of a substantial number of foreigners from Britain, France, Germany, the United States and elsewhere. The newspapers from the 1820s onwards carried frequent advertisements from newly arrived residents offering instructions or services in myriad skills and occupations. These independent entrepreneurs, ranging from teachers of foreign languages, fencing and dancing, to booksellers and those skilled in haute coiffure, were soon evident in all the main urban centres. Mexico City, once a relatively closed Hispanic society, was soon a cosmopolitan home for people of many different nationalities. Even more conspicuous and new were the many foreign merchants, businessmen and speculators who were initially attracted by the legendary, if illusory, wealth of the country. By 1833, for example, there were at least 21 wholesale and 438 retail businesses with a value of 30 million francs owned by French immigrants, and by 1838 about 4,000 French citizens were living in Mexico.[20] In one list of commercial companies in Mexico City in 1842, almost half were owned or managed by foreigners, and of the 15 most important enterprises in Puebla in 1852, 6 belonged to people with English, French or German surnames.[21] Foreign businessmen were also resident in Veracruz, Jalapa, Tampico, Guadalajara and all the other main trading centres, and groups of Cornish miners had been imported in a vain attempt to revive one area of the decadent mining industry.[22] These merchants, together with the large diplomatic corps which defended and promoted their interests, and the many visiting travellers, came to form an integral, though sometimes temporary, part of the social elite of the country.

Of all the changes brought by independence, however, none had a greater impact than the most obvious, namely, the opening of the world of politics. Freedom from colonial rule gave Mexicans for the first time 'realistic political possibilities' to change their own society, to reorder the political, social, economic and cultural structure imposed on them by the all-embracing union of Crown and Church.[23] They accepted the oppor-

20 N. N. Barker, *The French Experience in Mexico, 1821–1861: A History of Constant Misunderstanding* (Chapel Hill, N.C., 1979), pp. 44, 57, 58.
21 M. Galván Rivera, *Guía de forasteros* (Mexico, 1842), pp. 113–68; J. Bazant, *Alienation of Church Wealth in Mexico: Social and Economic Aspects of the Liberal Revolution, 1856–1875* (Cambridge, 1971), p. 45.
22 R. W. Randall, *Real del Monte: A British Mining Venture in Mexico* (Austin, Tex., 1972).
23 B. R. Wilson, *Religion in Secular Society: A Sociological Comment* (London, 1966), pp. 36–7.

tunity with perhaps surprising vigour, considering that public political action and debate had been virtually unknown activities in their previous history. Yet in another sense, the dominance of politics after independence was not surprising. The generation which assumed control with the end of Spanish rule had spent its formative years in a time of unprecedented political ferment in the international arena, and again, despite the rigours of Spanish censorship, it was fully imbued with the ideological trends of the Napoleonic age. The members of this new generation were heirs to the Enlightenment, and they were familiar with the democratic creed of the United States and its constitution. They had a detailed knowledge of the French Revolution, both its ideology and effects, and some had attended the Cortes of Cádiz, where they participated in the debates which led to the liberal constitution of 1812. Others learned their trade and gained their experience of politics at the Spanish Cortes of 1820 and then returned home to participate in the new political arena which had opened up to them.[24]

In other words, despite the absence of any tradition of political debate, there was no shortage of men who sought a political career or the political power to enact or prevent change. The adoption of the federal charter in 1824, based on an elected representative system, opened up endless opportunities for the committed or the ambitious, and over the next thirty years, literally thousands of men sought places on the numerous elected representative assemblies. With the national Congress renewed approximately every two years and eighteen or more state legislatures being regularly summoned, the chance of occupying public office exerted a powerful appeal. In addition, there were the thousands of posts in the national and provincial bureaucracies to attract a never-ending flow of *aspirantes*. *Empleomanía* became just as dominant a phenomenon as it was in Spain at the time, but election or appointment to office came at once to depend on political patronage.[25] Hence, in addition to any ideological motives, there was a real incentive to join one or more of the many political parties which quickly appeared on the scene. A new vocabulary developed as Mexicans scoured their lexicon in search of names to label the dozens of different factions; almost a separate glossary would be needed to understand the meaning of the epithets of the time. Apart from the obvious, such as federalists, centralists, liberals and conservatives, there were, to cite only a sample, *yorkinos, escoceses, imparciales, bustamantistas, santanistas, aristócratas, anarquistas, demagogos, sansculottes, puros, ultras* and *innovadores*. While not parties in the modern sense – the contemporary

24 N. L. Benson, ed., *Mexico and the Spanish Cortes* (Austin, Tex., 1966).

25 *Empleomanía* was often denounced as one of the 'funestas herencias' of the Spanish era: see, e.g., 'Honores y distinciones', *El Siglo XIX*, 19 August 1844, and J. M. L. Mora, 'Discurso sobre los perniciosos efectos de la empleomanía', in *Obras sueltas* (Mexico, 1963), pp. 531–7.

word always used was *partido* – they were often coherent and organized groups quite capable of waging election campaigns over a wide area or of mounting propaganda attacks through their newspapers. The freemasonry movement at times and particularly up to 1834 provided a framework of organization, and even in later years, although less public in their activities, the masonic societies continued to be influential.

The fact that every president was a general, and in some years military dictatorship prevailed, did not inhibit political activity or debate. In the first place, as Professor Carr has pointed out in respect of Spain, the military–civilian distinction at this time was blurred, and many senior army officers devoted most of their time and energies to political intrigue rather than military manoeuvres.[26] Living in the towns and cities, they served as cabinet ministers or state governors, or in the Congress and legislatures. Some were active businessmen or estate owners, and their ranks and uniforms were little more than symbolic but visible reminders of their status. In most cases, their military experience after independence consisted almost entirely of a rare and occasional campaign to defend their political power or privileges threatened by fellow, rebellious officers. Amid the apparent praetorian world of the Age of Santa Anna, one of the most notable characteristics was not so much militarism as the development and persistence of a largely civilian political scene. Thus, while the military dominated the route to executive authority at both national and state levels through the *pronunciamiento,* the generals, including Santa Anna, were never able to suppress or control the national Congress, which was always composed largely of civilians. Attempts to achieve control by electoral manipulation and even to suppress by force the civilian-dominated legislative power were invariably short-lived, and every military president found himself in conflict with the representative assembly, even when he had personally appointed most of the members.[27]

But who were the politicians who participated in this intense world of political action, debate and conflict? There is little information concerning the social origins, education and personal relationships of the mass of still largely anonymous men who sought public office. The only study – the recent work of Professor Stevens – of a reasonably significant number of the more prominent who achieved office or notoriety provides some indications.[28] Radicals tended to come from the more rural, peripheral provinces and conservatives from the more urbanized centre, and 'there was a statistically significant division between radicals, moderates and

26 R. Carr, *Spain, 1808–1975* (2d. ed., Oxford, 1982), p. 217.
27 For one illustration of the civilian–military conflict, see my 'Generals versus Presidents: Santa Anna and the 1842 Congressional Elections in Mexico', *Bulletin of Latin American Research,* 8 (1989), 257–74.
28 D. F. Stevens, *Origins of Instability in Early Republican Mexico* (Durham, N.C., 1991).

conservatives on the basis of rural or urban birthplaces'.[29] On the other hand, there was no distinct regional bias, no northern dynasty of the early twentieth century type. Nor was there any predominant occupational background, for example, of landowners, industrialists, miners or merchants, and while occupational characteristics reveal a large proportion of lawyers, most other professionals, including the clergy, were also well represented.[30]

Mexico's politicians, therefore, were drawn from a wide range of backgrounds and places, but they also shared important characteristics. Independence brought decisive social change, and the society, particularly of the capital, so brilliantly described by Kicza, if it did not disappear overnight, was subject to profound pressures of change.[31] The long supreme Spanish, or *gachupín,* sector was destroyed, not just with the loss of its political and economic domination but also with the emigration during the years of war of many Spaniards and their families to Europe or North America. Those who remained survived for a time, but within a few years in 1827 and 1829, several thousand were expelled from the republic.[32] Some did escape the blanket expulsion, and after 1836, when Spain finally recognized independence, immigrants from Spain returned.[33] Nevertheless, Spaniards became just one relatively small group of foreigners who resided largely in the cities among the English, French, German and other foreign residents. The old aristocracy also suffered a marked decline, and with the abolition of hereditary and other privileges, the status of nobility brought little political reward or advantage. Indeed, the very word *aristócrata* became a term of abuse in the political lexicon of the day, applied by radicals to those who in their view represented the forces of reaction and regression.

In place of the old upper classes, another group came to dominate political life. Sometimes *gente de orden, gente decente* or *gente de frac,* but most commonly, *hombre de bien* was the epithet given throughout the 1820s to the late 1840s to this distinct social and political type. In every political context and polemic, the *hombre de bien* was held up as the ideal citizen, the sort of person the electorate was always urged to vote for by all parties in every election campaign. Again, the question must be asked,

29 Ibid., pp. 82–5.
30 Ibid., pp. 49–50.
31 J. E. Kicza, *Colonial Entrepreneurs: Families and Business in Bourbon Mexico City* (Albuquerque, N.M., 1983).
32 H. D. Sims, *The Expulsion of Mexico's Spaniards, 1821–1836* (Pittsburgh, Pa., 1990).
33 The Spanish ambassador calculated that 2,319 young Spaniards migrated to Mexico in the four years after 1836. He considered the number large enough to be of concern at Spain's loss of talent. Many of the migrants went into the retail trade; P. P. de Oliver to Secretary of State, 8 October 1842, in *Relaciones diplomáticas hispano-mexicanas,* Serie I, Despachos Generales, vol. 2, 1841–1843 (Mexico, 1952), pp. 130–2.

what was an *hombre de bien?* The first immediate answer is, of course, that
he was a gentleman. But that answer tells us nothing because we need
to know how to define and recognize a gentleman or rather, how Mexicans
in the years after 1821 came to define the archetype. What were his ideas,
values, attitudes, prejudices and life-style? What occupational groups were
included, what, if any, wealth or income level was required? Such questions had preoccupied some Spaniards in the eighteenth century and
European prototypes were being considered, but as far as Mexicans in the
Age of Santa Anna were concerned, the *hombre de bien* was from the middle
sector of society, neither aristocrat nor proletariat, but from what they
increasingly described after the late 1820s as *la clase media,* or middle
class. He could not be recognized by his political stance, for both radicals
like Valentín Gómez Farías and conservatives like Alamán were undoubtedly *hombres de bien* and accepted as such. In fact, according to Alamán,
the *hombre de bien* was a 'man of faith, honour, property, education and
virtue'.[34] In other words, he was a believer in the Roman Catholic faith,
with a strong sense of honour and morality, and of sufficient financial
means to maintain a certain life-style. Alamán did not use the word *property*
to mean only real estate, for although property owners were considered
hombres de bien, it was equally acceptable to have an income derived from
invested capital or professional employment. The liberal José María Luis
Mora agreed. According to him, an *hombre de bien* was a man 'who has a
job which provides him with the necessities of life, or has some productive
skill, or some invested capital, or some property'.[35]

This distinction between income and property or assets was particularly
important in two respects. In the first place, individual private ownership
of property was comparatively rare, especially in the cities. In Mexico
City, for example, where there was a greater concentration of wealth and
thus of *hombres de bien* than in the provincial urban centres, little more
than 1 per cent of the estimated 200,000 population, or in numerical
terms, a mere 2,242 people, were property owners.[36] While the proportion
may have varied in other towns and cities where the Church, which owned
almost 40 per cent of the property in the capital, was less dominant, it
is unlikely that the number was much greater. Second, both Alamán and
Mora, together with many other conservatives and liberals, believed that

34 L. Alamán, 'Defensa del ex-ministro de Relaciones don Lucas Alamán, escrita por el mismo ex-
   ministro quien la dirige a la nación' (Mexico, 1834), in *Obras: Documentos diversos* (Mexico, 1946),
   vol. 2, p. 45. Alamán refers throughout his writings to the importance of political power being
   in the hands of *hombres respetables, clase propietaria,* etc. See, e.g., his letter to Santa Anna of 23
   February 1837, cited in J. C. Valadés, *Alamán, estadista e historiador* (Mexico, 1938), pp.
   362–8.
35 J. M. L. Mora, *Ensayos, ideas y retratos* (Mexico, 1964), p. 45, cited in M. Gayón Córdova,
   Condiciones de vida y de trabajo en la ciudad de México en el siglo XIX (Mexico, 1988), p. 41.
36 Gayón Córdova, *Condiciones de vida,* p. 31.

election to political office should be restricted to *hombres de bien* who were either property owners or above a certain income level. Mora put the amount of income at 1,000 pesos per annum, and Alamán was directly involved in producing electoral regulations which specified a minimum income of 1,200 pesos for congressional candidates (the exchange rate was approximately 5 pesos to the £1 sterling and parity with the U.S. dollar). Those who earned less than that, as many of the middle class did, were not thereby excluded from the *hombre de bien* category but were restricted to lesser office, for example, local councillor, which required 500 pesos annual income in the 1836 electoral law. An income below 500 pesos, however, while not automatically implying proletariat status, was inadequate for a true *hombre de bien* and insufficient for a candidate for public office. Indeed, it was said in Congress in 1836 that anyone with an income of less than 40 pesos a month must be a vagabond. Even the ardent radical Gómez Farías was at times reluctant to allow the lower-income groups to be directly represented in Congress. Writing in 1846 to Santa Anna, whose actions on the franchise in an 1841 electoral law mark him as more of a democrat than many of his rivals, Gómez Farías advised him against unrestricted access to Congress: 'You would want all the classes in our society represented in congress; in my opinion, that has a serious drawback because the classes are so varied and diverse and very few of them have people of sufficient aptitude and understanding to be able to carry out the arduous and difficult task which has to be entrusted to their care'.[37]

Hence, the *hombre de bien* was considered to be of the middle class. He retained his respect, if not ambition, for honours and distinctions and continued to have the traditional Spanish disdain for manual labour, 'that horror of work', as one writer put it in 1837. He was not impressed by the small-scale artisan of any sort, whom he regarded with 'some disdain and indifference',[38] and he did not yet have the materialistic, capitalist values of the Marxist bourgeois. On the contrary, as Knapp puts it, 'Business pursuits remained somewhat stigmatized with a medieval disdain'.[39] On the other hand, he was impressed by public office, by employment in the civil or military bureaucracy, by the law and by other professions.

Finally, it is noticeable that in none of the contemporary definitions of an *hombre de bien* is there any reference to ethnic origin. Historians have assumed that it was the white creole who took over the country after the

37 V. Gómez Farías to Santa Anna, June (n.d.) 1846, in N. L. Benson Library, University of Texas at Austin, Gómez Farías Papers, no. 1427. I have used a microfilm copy of this archive in which the numbers given on the manuscripts do not always correspond to the printed guide; see P. M. Ynsfran, *Catálogo de los manuscritos del Archivo de Don Valentín Gómez Farías* (Mexico, 1968).
38 *Diario del Gobierno*, 4 July 1837; *El Siglo XIX*, 19 August 1844.
39 F. A. Knapp, *The Life of Sebastián Lerdo de Tejada, 1823–1889* (New York, 1968), p. 9.

defeat and expulsion of the Spanish rulers, and although it is rare to find any use of the colonial terminology of creole, mestizo, *casta* and so on after independence, when such legal distinctions were abolished, there are signs that racial prejudice remained a significant, if unspoken and unwritten, factor. Vicente Guerrero, who was a half-caste, is one example of a successful insurgent leader who was said to be resented by the social elite of the capital, especially the ladies, on the grounds of his colour.[40] In the 1840s, the U.S. diplomat Waddy Thompson remarked that 'at one of those large assemblies at the President's palace, it is very rare to see a lady whose color indicates any impurity of blood'. On the other hand, he went on to say that while the same was true to a great extent of the gentlemen, 'there are a good many exceptions'.[41] It seems, in other words, that racial prejudice was still important but at the same time probably of declining significance for the mestizos, and it did not prevent someone of mixed or non-European blood from entering the ranks of *hombres de bien*, always provided that he met all the other requirements – Benito Juárez is one obvious example.

Just as we do not know to any extent the nature or influence of racial prejudice in terms of *hombres de bien*, there are many other aspects about which we know little. For example, we do not know if regional origins or accent were factors in determining class, nor if there was any urban– rural discrimination, although there are signs that city dwellers, notably those born in the capital, felt some metropolitan superiority over their rural counterparts. Those with aristocratic origins, especially Spanish – for example, Spain's first ambassador, Calderón de la Barca – retained respect among the socially ambitious. Finally, mode of dress was an important mark of social class.

This preliminary sketch indicates some of the characteristics of the *hombre de bien*. To explain his life-style, however, requires a degree of imagination, the invention, if you will, of a fictional *hombre de bien*.[42] Let us assume that he was born towards the end of the eighteenth century into a reasonably affluent family. He would have been educated at home in his early years and then have entered one of the colleges run by the Church, perhaps the highly respected Colegio de San Ildefonso, where his fellow pupils might well have included Mora or the future Minister of War and Santa Anna loyalist José María Tornel. There he would have acquired a thorough grounding in theology, civil and canon law, juris- prudence and possibly the French language. After leaving the college, he may have gone to the University of Mexico to specialize in law and graduate

40 L. de Zavala, *Obras* (Mexico, 1969), p. 353.
41 W. Thompson, *Recollections of Mexico* (New York, 1846), p. 168.
42 The following portrait of an imaginary *hombre de bien* is based on an analysis of several such men of the time together with, where indicated, specific details from various contemporary sources.

with the prized title of *licenciado*. After the war of independence, he would have practiced law, which together with the rent from some small inherited rural property would have provided him with an income of more than 1,000 pesos per annum.

That sum of 1,000 pesos would have enabled him to live very comfortably with his family in the capital, where he would probably have rented the upper floors of a Church-owned house near the central square, or plaza de la Constitución (now the Zócalo). He would have had domestic servants to cater to his daily needs and possibly a carriage, which he could have purchased or rented from one of several suppliers in the city. Always keen to adopt the latest in European fashion, he would have bought his best clothes from one of several French tailors, his frock coat costing 34 to 42 pesos, his trousers, 14 to 16 pesos and a good-quality pair of boots, 7 to 8 pesos. He would have subscribed to a newspaper, possibly *El Siglo XIX,* costing 20 reales a month (8 reals = 1 peso), and he might also, if he were ambitious socially, have belonged to one of the many literary societies of the city. If his interests were nonliterary, he might have spent his leisure time in one of the billiard halls, 'indulging himself in the moderate exercise of a game of billiards',[43] or at the bull-fight, and almost certainly he would have been a regular attender at one of the three theatres, where a good seat cost 12 reales. He would have debated controversial issues of the day with his friends in the café of the city's best-known hotel, La Gran Sociedad, 'meeting place of the well-to-do',[44] and he would occasionally have bought a lottery ticket, which might bring a top prize of 6,000 pesos but more likely one of 100 or 200 pesos. He would have often dined out at one of the new restaurants, perhaps La Sociedad del Progreso with its ladies' room upstairs or the Fonda de la Amistad, which would offer him for just 1 real a meal of 'broth, soup, stew, entrée, beans, sweets and bread'.[45]

He would also have spent some time browsing in his personal library or in one or more of at least eleven bookshops where he would find works on theology, political science and history as well as Spanish versions of many of the novels of Walter Scott.[46] As he walked around the city, avoiding the open sewers and persistent hawkers while keeping an eye open for the beggars, thieves and pickpockets who infested every street, he would have noticed the growing presence of foreign-owned businesses

---

43 A. Gilliam, *Travels in Mexico during the Years 1843 and 1844* (Aberdeen, 1847), p. 90.
44 Prieto, *Memorias,* 1, 80.
45 These and following details of prices are taken from newspaper advertisements throughout the 1830s and 1840s.
46 There also seem to have been some very large private libraries at this time. When the estate of a lawyer, José Antonio López García de Salazar, was settled in 1838, his possessions included 13,754 volumes, which were offered for sale in *Diario del Gobierno,* 24 January 1838.

such as the Guiard, Lance y Cía garden centre with dahlias at 2 pesos a plant, the sadlery of Carlos Johansson, the daguerrotype portrait service of R. W. Holt, at least four dentists of French, German or British origin and an English brewery owned by R. and A. T. Blackmore, where a barrel of ale (*cerveza blanca*) could be had for 10 pesos.

In common with most of his compatriots, he would have been a regular church-goer and probably a member of his parish confraternity (*cofradía*), to which he would have made generous contributions. His main vice, shared by most of his friends and considered eminently respectable, would have been gambling, especially at the regular cock-fights or perhaps at home in his 'gaming room, which is always crowded, and not to play is to render yourself unfit for polite society'.[47] One of the highlights of his year would have been the very popular and well-attended Whitsuntide cock-fights at San Agustín de las Cuevas (now Tlalpan), where a box cost 4 reales in the afternoon and 6 in the evening.

At Tlalpan, he would have rubbed shoulders with the nation's leading personalities, including President Santa Anna or Bustamante, ministers like Tornel or generals like Gabriel Valencia, as well as with many lesser luminaries who were seeking favours or advancement in their careers.[48] If he made the right contacts, he might have been offered a job in a government department and become a civil servant. The pay might be modest, and often unpaid, but the work would not have been onerous and the prestige considerable.[49] Alternatively, if he were known to be a person of strong political ambition or conviction and had perhaps written a few articles in the press on controversial topics of the day, he would perhaps have been asked by one of the political factions to be a candidate in the city council or congressional elections.

By now, it is clear that the typical *hombre de bien* was seen at the time to belong to the upper echelons of the middle class, defined in 1838 as 'well-off people whose education, assets or connections, jobs or important posts, separate them to a certain extent from the class which has none of those attributes'.[50] As already indicated, his precise political views were not significant in the social environment in which he moved, and in any case his opinions were likely to be fluid, changing to some extent in accordance with experience and the prevailing circumstances. He might

---

47 Gilliam, *Travels in Mexico,* p. 90.

48 The best contemporary description of the scenes at the Tlalpan cock-fights appear in Calderón de la Barca, *Life in Mexico,* pp. 201–8, 376–90.

49 The pay of *empleados* ranged from 500 pesos per year for a scribe to 3,000 per year for a chief accountant. An office boy received 100; *El Siglo XIX,* 30 April 1845.

50 *Diario del Gobierno,* 8 January 1838. I am, of course, concerned here with the public persona of an archetype. The private, including sexual, mores of the middle class remain ill-defined, although it is noticeable that several of the prominent personalities of the time fathered illegitimate children and were known to have done so.

disagree strongly with his friends on some issues – for example, on the merits of central or federal republicanism – but such disagreements never jeopardized his social standing. 'Social assumptions', to use Hale's words, 'ran deeper than the liberal–conservative conflict'.[51] At the same time, he shared many attitudes with his peers. Most notably, he always saw politics and society in terms of social class, and he firmly believed that his own, the middle class, was the 'most solid pillar of our society'.[52] Equality might for him be a desirable ideal, but those who preached its virtues had to recognize that 'there is always an inequality of condition, needs, abilities, climates, way of life and of many other things'.[53]

Class distinctions, therefore, were very important for him, and his greatest fear in the face of all the political chaos that existed around him was what he would call 'social dissolution' (*disolución social*). This was a phrase used constantly by *hombres de bien*. Extremists like Lorenzo de Zavala who advocated radical policies such as the redistribution of wealth or a more or less unrestricted suffrage were always denounced as anarchists, sansculottes or demagogues and were accused of bringing the nation to the brink of social dissolution. What was implied by the phrase is not entirely clear, but it was certainly related to the fear of a class war in which the impoverished masses might get out of control and destroy the existing social and economic structure. Every *hombre de bien* was well aware of what had happened in France during and after the Revolution, and the conservative press in particular repeatedly warned of the dangers of a Mexican 'Terror' and the 'dreadful assembly, known as convention'.[54] The history of the French Revolution 'must never be allowed to fall from the hands of our statesmen', and it was not to be forgotten that 'those who were seduced by brilliant theories released the torrent of demagogy and were afterwards its victims'.[55] Nothing good came of revolution, and the inevitable consequence of Mexico's political instability was 'to loosen the ties which bind society together more and more'.[56] The moderate *hombre de bien* wanted change but only gradually and without violence, and he could not accept that the uneducated and impoverished lower orders were ready for the full privileges of citizenship. Those radicals who advocated unrestricted freedom for what Zavala called the 'low democracy' were misleading the populace, who would soon discover that 'the extreme liberty which they proclaimed was a pipe dream'.[57] Extremism in any

51 C. Hale, *Mexican Liberalism in the Age of Mora, 1821–1853* (New Haven, Conn., 1968), p. 298.
52 *La Voz del Pueblo*, 2 August 1845.
53 *Diario del Gobierno*, 22 July 1838.
54 *El Independiente*, 2 October 1839.
55 Ibid., 2 and 23 October 1839. See also *Diario del Gobierno*, 26 May, 16 and 25 June 1837.
56 *Diario del Gobierno*, 11 May 1837.
57 Ibid., 21 July 1838.

form or sphere could only lead to violence and destruction. All social progress was slow and that fact was an 'invariable law of nature'.[58]

It was not just the French Revolution and the Terror which caused some Mexicans to fear what one general-president described as the 'dreadful and pernicious proletariat'.[59] During the war of independence, the wholesale destruction of property and the massacres of the 'rich' which had occurred in the early stages of the Hidalgo insurrection were never forgotten. Then, in the early years after emancipation, there had been signs of unrest among the populace, and in 1828 anarchy had reigned in the capital for several days as the poor rioted and looted in what became known as the Parián riot. The memory and fear of what they witnessed during those few days long haunted *hombres de bien* like Carlos María Bustamante.

The attitude of the middle class towards the populace was also somewhat ambivalent. Another recurrent theme of the time is expressed in the phrase *voluntad popular* or *voluntad del pueblo*. Political parties of all persuasions, not to mention the generals, always claimed to be acting to fulfill or represent the will of the people. They had read their Jovellanos and accepted the concept that society was the sum of individual wills and that it was the function of government to meet the wishes of the majority. The more radical politicians tried to mobilize popular support with their promises of equality and redistribution of wealth, and the more conservative claimed that in their uneducated and apathetic condition, it was not possible to ascertain the 'will of the people', at least not by counting votes. When we talk of the majority, wrote the editor of the official daily in 1835, 'we are not speaking precisely of a numerical majority' but rather of the majority view of 'citizens who are influential because of their integrity, service, wealth, education, eloquence, age, experience, usefulness, connections, opinion, employment, impartiality'.[60] In between the two extremes stood the moderate *hombre de bien*, who accepted the existence of a popular will but believed that until primary education and literacy were widespread, it was the right and duty of his social class to interpret what that will was. The 1836 constitution even went so far as to create a fourth branch of government known as the Supreme Conservative Power, one main function of which was precisely to 'declare what is the will of the nation' in times of conflict or dispute.[61]

This long-held, traditional, paternalistic colonial mentality towards the

58 Ibid.
59 M. Paredes y Arrillaga to J. M. Tornel, 10 May 1842; published in G. García, *Documentos inéditos o muy raros para la historia de México* (Mexico, 1974), vol. 56, p. 25.
60 *Diario del Gobierno*, 2 September 1835.
61 Leyes constitucionales, segunda, art. 1, sec. 8, in F. Tena Ramírez, *Leyes fundamentales de México, 1808–1971* (Mexico, 1971), p. 211.

populace, a mixture of fear of social revolution and a sense of benevolent duty, reflected the manifest and growing economic inequalities. The great majority of the population lived in abject poverty; emancipation from Spain had brought for many a deterioration in their already depressed living conditions. Perhaps in the rural areas, in the pueblos and haciendas where a certain self-sufficiency had always prevailed, the change was only gradual, for there was little sign of popular protest in the countryside. Indeed, Tutino suggests that 'the long era of agrarian decompression from 1810 to 1880 took some economic pressure off the rural poor',[62] and certainly those scholars who have investigated rural rebellion have been hard-pressed to find any examples before the 1840s.[63] In the cities, however, the situation was very different. The many foreigners who visited the capital and provincial towns described vividly the poverty, filth and widespread scenes of decay which they found.[64] An underclass – known as *léperos* – infested the streets of every neighborhood, where drunkenness, prostitution, unemployment and vagrancy were rampant. Violence and robbery were everyday occurrences, and crime was virtually out of control with both national and municipal authorities powerless to stop it. Describing the situation in Mexico City in 1837, one observer wrote:

> Its streets are no longer worthy of the name; they are chasms, precipices and filthy sewers. Its suburbs are heaps of ruins, horrific dungheaps, centres of corruption and pestilence. Its avenues are now no more than remnants of what they once were. Its most public thoroughfares are places of scandal and indecency and there is a tavern, vice and prostitution on almost every street. Nowhere is safe from crime.[65]

Poverty, according to one report in 1843, had become the only topic of conversation: 'Conversations in the home, in the newspapers and everywhere are about nothing else but poverty and more poverty'.[66]

In contrast to the majority, who lived in squalid poverty, a small minority, including the nouveau riche generals, financial speculators and

---

62 J. Tutino, *From Insurrection to Revolution in Mexico: Social Bases of Agrarian Violence, 1750–1940* (Princeton, N.J., 1986), p. 356.

63 Stevens gives a good statistical summary of the findings of the several scholars who have investigated rural unrest and notes that 'from 1825–1844, insurrections in rural areas averaged fewer than one per year'; Stevens, 'Political Instability', p. 146. His conclusions are confirmed by one of the few regional studies, on Jalisco, which found evidence of only one minor rural disturbance between 1825 and 1844; see D. F. Deaton, 'La protesta social rural durante el siglo XIX en Jalisco', in C. Castañeda, ed., *Elite, clases sociales y rebelión en Guadalajara y Jalisco, Siglos XVIII y XIX* (Guadalajara, 1988), pp. 97–121. See also the various essays in F. Katz, ed., *Riot, Rebellion, and Revolution: Rural Social Conflict in Mexico* (Princeton, N.J., 1988).

64 There are many useful accounts by foreign visitors. Among the best are H. G. Ward, *Mexico in 1827* (2 vols., London, 1828); W. Bullock, *Six Months' Residence and Travels in Mexico* (London, 1824); Calderón de la Barca, *Life in Mexico;* and Gilliam, *Travels in Mexico.* For an excellent recent study of the poor in the capital, see F. J. Shaw, 'Poverty and Politics in Mexico City, 1824–1854', Ph.D. diss., University of Florida, 1975.

65 *Diario del Gobierno,* 5 August 1837.

66 *El Siglo XIX,* 16 April 1843.

corrupt politicians, enjoyed seemingly immense fortunes. Some displayed their wealth in an ostentatious fashion or 'with an Asiatic lavishness',[67] living in expensively furnished mansions, riding around the city in imported carriages and gambling away large sums at cock-fights. Their behaviour was provocative and dangerous, and it persuaded some *hombres de bien* to warn of an explosion of anger among the poor against the rich unless a more equitable distribution of wealth could be achieved: 'A levelling of incomes is absolutely indispensable if the ruin of society is to be avoided'.[68]

When the *hombres de bien* saw what was happening around them – the political chaos, poverty, collapse of law and order on the streets and rural highways – some, not surprisingly, began to look back with growing nostalgia at the colonial era. Certainly none, not even the most pro-Hispanic, favoured a return to colonial status, and there was never any kind of reactionary movement in that direction. Nevertheless, they began increasingly to compare their impressions or memories of what they fondly recalled as the comparative peace and stability of colonial times. They remembered, rightly or wrongly, that criminals were punished and justice was done and that things were generally more efficient under the rule of the viceroys. Even food supplies were regular and plentiful and cheaper. Meat, bread and pulque had never been better or less expensive than in colonial days, according to one resident in the capital in 1843.[69]

Even more important than the rising cost of food, they believed that the declining prestige of the Church was at least partly the cause and effect of changing social values and a growing lack of respect for authority within and outside of the home, especially among the young. They recalled a society in which personal and public values were universally accepted, a society in which the relationship between the classes was fixed and in which every man knew his place. Although a lack of research in this area precludes firm conclusions, there is no doubt that one of the principal preoccupations of the *hombres de bien* concerned changing personal morality and what they called the 'morality of society'. In their sermons and pastoral letters, bishops often warned of the corruption of the nation's youth by foreign and, for them, heretical ideas. It is interesting to note that Gómez Farías himself was also preoccupied with the question of individual and social morality. In his personal archive, and in what seem like jottings recorded in a moment of reflection, he wrote his own definition of 'morality'. As one would expect from a committed Roman Catholic, he emphasized all the Christian virtues of honesty, integrity, help for the

67 Ibid.
68 Ibid. The radical newspaper *El Cosmopolita*, 24 August 1842, predicted a class war 'entre los pudientes con los de medianas fortunas y con los pobres'.
69 *El Siglo XIX*, 25 September 1843.

poor and disadvantaged, hard work for six days a week and rest on the Sabbath and respect for authority and the law. As a politician, he went on to express the belief of every *hombre de bien* that 'without good customs, laws serve no purpose; morality should be the basis and complement of all legislation'.[70]

This nostalgia for the past, in the light of the present with all its difficulties, gave rise to an intensely frustrating sense that Mexico's natural inheritance was being wasted. The *hombre de bien* firmly believed that his country had been divinely endowed with sufficient natural resources which, if a satisfactory constitutional and political system could only be devised, were destined to make it one of the most advanced and prosperous nations on earth. As one writer put it in 1845, Mexico was 'a beautiful, uncut diamond' prevented from realizing its potential only by the failure to find a secure constitutional framework and by the political instability and economic stagnation which that failure engendered.[71]

The political instability, however, and its symptoms of revolts, rapidly changing governments, ideological conflict and so on were the immediate concern of only a small minority of Mexicans. It was in the homes and clubs of the *hombres de bien,* or middle class in the broadest sense of the term, where the debates were heard and the conspiracies planned. Those involved and affected were the military officers, clergy, merchants, shop-keepers, large and small landowners, lawyers, doctors and all manner of other professionals who saw the world of politics as the sphere in which to fulfil their ambitions. The great majority of Mexico's estimated 7 million population was never involved in either the intellectual debate or the military conflict. Even the scale of the latter has to be kept in pro-portion, for despite the inflated number of military, it was rare indeed for any general, including Santa Anna, to be able to mobilize more than a few thousand men and none of the many so-called revolutions attracted any mass popular support.

For the landless rural masses and the urban proletariat, therefore, the daily struggle for survival took precedence, and they watched events passively and without any visible interest. As Tornel commented: 'The people were silent and obedient as they have always been. Nothing could stir them from the cold indifference with which they saw revolt after revolt come and go and in which they neither took part nor derived any benefit'.[72] Some political factions and their leaders did try on occasion to rally popular support for their cause, particularly in the poor neighbour-hoods of the capital, but they failed. Hence, the few large-scale popular

70 Gómez Farías Papers, nos. 1059–60.

71 *La Voz del Pueblo,* 5 February 1845.

72 J. M. Tornel y Mendívil, *Breve reseña histórica de los acontecimientos más notables de la nación mexicana desde el año de 1821 hasta nuestros días* (Mexico, 1852), p. 12.

protests that did occur – for example, the riots in 1838 and the demonstrations by five thousand tobacco factory workers in 1839 – were always
related to a specific grievance, mostly to do with food prices, wages and
conditions of work.[73] Similarly, in the rural areas there was little sign
before the 1840s of mass peasant movements inspired by demands for
land reform or better treatment by landowners, and as already noted,
rural-based rebellions or protests are notable for their absence. Of course,
the economic consequences of the endless conflict did affect both directly
and indirectly the poorer classes (e.g., the copper money crisis of the late
1830s), but the deterioration in their living standards never seems to have
been such as to provoke the mass rebellion and social dissolution so feared
by the *hombres de bien*.

Governments came and went, constitutions were promulgated and revoked, parties rose and fell, and yet this picture of chronic instability,
or anarchy as the *hombre de bien* considered it to be, is in one respect
misleading. Throughout all the turmoil, there was a remarkable degree
of human continuity in the sense that the people involved did not change.
Partly because of a tradition of leniency towards defeated opponents –
Iturbide and Guerrero were the exception rather than the rule – rebel
military and civilians were able to live to fight another day and mostly
did so. Santa Anna is the most obvious example, rising and falling from
power and in public esteem continuously and yet always having the good
luck or ability to survive. His case was by no means exceptional, for the
majority of those in his age group who emerged into the limelight around
the time of independence remained leading figures on the political scene
for the next thirty years. Tornel, Alamán, Nicolás Bravo, José Joaquín
de Herrera, Manuel Gómez Pedraza, Gómez Farías, Anastasio and Carlos
Bustamante were just a few. These well-known names recur throughout the decades between independence and the Reform, as do hundreds
of lesser personalities in Congress, legislatures, army, Church and
bureaucracy.

The continuity of this generation of people, in and out of office and
power over thirty years, and the relatively narrow confines of the social
and political elite which they constituted, had important consequences
which are not always obvious. For example, many knew each other personally, and there were numerous marital and professional ties as well as
political alliances. Until we have more studies of regional elites, particularly at the provincial and local levels, we will continue to know little
of the dominant families or clans who emerged in the years after independence to impose themselves on localities or wider regions. Neverthe-

73 D. W. Walker, 'Business as Usual: The Empresa del Tabaco in Mexico, 1837–1844', *Hispanic
American Historical Review*, 64 (1984), 675–705.

less, in addition to the successful military caudillos like Bravo, Alvarez and Gordiano Guzmán, some families were exceptionally influential in their own areas, and there were a large number of brothers and other relatives prominent in the political sphere. The Tornels, José María and José Julián, of Orizaba, allied to their brother-in-law, Manuel Díez de Bonilla, are one obvious example. The Canalizo brothers of Monterrey are another, as are the Cortazar brothers from Celaya, the Haro y Tamariz brothers of Puebla, the Furlong family, also of Puebla, the Fagoaga family of the capital and the Sánchez Navarros of Coahuila.

At times on opposite sides of the political spectrum, and as rivals in the struggle for personal advancement, these families incurred personal debts as well as insults to be avenged at a later date. For example, Santa Anna was humiliated and disgraced at the end of 1844 following a rebellion initiated by his one-time loyal supporter, General Mariano Paredes y Arrillaga (henceforth referred to as Paredes). His hostility was at least partly motivated, according to Santa Anna, by an incident which had taken place some three years before. Similarly, Paredes blamed a fellow officer of harbouring a personal grudge against him for almost twenty years.[74] Mora and Tornel's mutual dislike was said to have its origins in their schooldays or 'schoolboy rivalries'.[75] In other words, personal friendships and enmities, family loyalties and rivalries, memories of past actions and events all became significant factors in the political ferment. As Mora commented in trying to explain the bitter differences among men of similar social background and ideas, 'They were not yet over the antipathies caused between them by the mutual attacks on each other which earlier revolts had brought about'.[76]

Nevertheless, there was loyalty to their class, a social solidarity which allowed bitter rivals to maintain respect for one another and, it must be added, to switch their allegiances whenever it suited them. Gómez Farías was more than once the beneficiary of material help from his political enemies. After his defeat in 1834, in a gesture of goodwill to a fellow *hombre de bien,* Carlos Bustamante wrote to wish him luck in exile, saying that, although they differed in opinions, he hoped they remained good friends.[77] Again facing foreign exile in 1840 after the failure of an attempted *golpe de estado,* Gómez Farías was given 4,000 pesos that had been raised by political rivals to help him on his way.[78]

These, then, are issues and features which characterize the Age of Santa

---

74 For details, see Chapter 9.
75 *El Mexicano,* 1 June 1839.
76 Mora, *Obras sueltas,* p. 10.
77 Both letters in Gómez Farías Papers, nos. 303 and 326.
78 The main fund-raiser for Gómez Farías seems to have been the financier Antonio Garay; see the several accounts in the Gómez Farías Papers, nos. 745 and 750.

Anna. Some clearly had their origins in the colonial era, when, for example, regional rivalries and social tensions were prominent, while others such as the destruction of the economy were caused during the years of insurgency. Several, however, while perhaps present in earlier times, certainly came to the fore after emancipation was achieved. It was in the 1820s when the status and privileges of institutions like the army and the Church, especially the latter's relationship with the State, economic and commercial policy, the function and purpose of politics and parties, social relationships, the role of the press and all manner of other issues became the subject of often heated debate and at times violent action. In short, seeking to adapt their society, its economy and institutions to their new-found liberation, Mexicans asked themselves two fundamental questions: what was the best form of government for their country, and who should govern it?

In answer to the first question, and after the brief imperial interlude of Iturbide, the firm majority consensus was that a federal system was the most appropriate, and strongly influenced by the growing prosperity of the United States, which they attributed directly to its republican constitution, they formally created the first federal republic in 1824. Unfortunately, none of the hopes of political harmony, social order and economic growth were realized and instead, within a couple of years, Mexico was plagued by factionalism, economic difficulties and rising conflict with the Church and its influential senior clergy. *Pronunciamientos* became commonplace, the representative process was discredited and constitutional rule collapsed as the first two vice-presidents led rebellions against the governments of which they were members. And then, it can never be forgotten, there was Santa Anna, whose long career of arbitrary conspiracy and intervention properly began in 1828 when he successfully rebelled against the results of a presidential election he did not like.

The answer to the second question was equally difficult and controversial, preoccupying many throughout the 1820s, but it is clear that, by 1830 and probably before, most *hombres de bien* of both liberal and conservative convictions had concluded that Mexico was not ready for genuinely popular, representative government and that the idea and practice of such things as universal male franchise and other democratic rights advocated by radicals had to be resisted, if not suppressed entirely. They concluded that economic growth and prosperity, law and order, social progress and harmony and, above all, political stability could and would be achieved only if the responsibility for government was vested firmly and exclusively in their own social class. That could not be guaranteed under the federal structure with its electoral procedures, unrestricted freedom of the press aaand distribution of powers to twenty-four separate and disparate states or territories. Their first priority, therefore, was to change the form of government to concentrate political power in the centre and to ensure that, in future, change in every sphere would be under the control of *hombres de bien*. It is to the collapse of federalism and the transition to the centralized republic of the *hombres de bien* that we now turn.

2

The end of federalism

The collapse of Mexico's first radical government in the spring of 1834 was swift and dramatic. Throughout their year in power, from April 1833 to April 1834, radical reformers led by Vice-President Valentín Gómez Farías had attempted to transform Mexican society. They had imposed or signalled fundamental changes in the political, social, economic and cultural life of the nation, and their ambition, or hope, was clear. The colonial society inherited after three centuries of Spanish domination, its privileged institutions and classes and its divisive social values were to be destroyed and replaced by a new order based on civil equality before the law, freedom of expression and eventually of belief and democratic representative government in which individual rather than corporate liberties were guaranteed. Major institutional reforms were thus enacted or promised in education, the army and above all the Roman Catholic Church, whose removal as an all-pervasive influence was, for liberals, a prerequisite of the dynamic, secular society they foresaw on the horizon. The reform of institutions by legislation, however, was only part of the process of change. Gómez Farías and his supporters were fully aware that laws did not change opinions and that their new society would not be consolidated unless the people who benefited from and defended the status quo could be removed from positions of influence and power. Thus, parallel with their programme of legislative change of institutions, the liberals sought to quell reaction by conducting a wholesale purge of their opponents from public office.[1]

From the national to the local level hundreds, if not thousands, of people were deprived of their jobs and, perhaps more important, of their status in society. Throughout the republic, senior and junior officials in the judiciary, local and state bureaucracies, town councils and a wide range of other publicly funded occupations were unceremoniously dismissed and replaced by liberals and their clientele. A similar purge was

---

1 For a detailed analysis of the ideology of the liberal reform, see J. Reyes Heroles, *El liberalismo mexicano* (3 vols., Mexico, 1961) and Hale, *Mexican Liberalism*.

conducted in the army; generals and senior officers believed hostile to the reform policies were dismissed, demoted, deprived of their pensions and humiliated. Nobody, regardless of his record of service or public prestige, was immune. Former vice-president Anastasio Bustamante and generals Felipe Codallos, Manuel Rincón and Miguel Cervantes were some of the many stripped of their military rank; members of the Supreme Court were charged with malpractice and suspended; Alamán and other former cabinet ministers in the Bustamante government of 1830–2 were accused of complicity in the murder of Vicente Guerrero; Bishop Pablo Vázquez of Puebla was ordered into exile for his opposition to the reforms and his public attempts to foment rebellion against them.[2]

This kind of personal, individual retribution was not without precedent in Mexican political life. Similar purges of those defeated in the political battle had taken place in earlier years, particularly in 1830–2, but the difference now was one of scale. Most of the well-known victims were active politicians accused of specific offences but demands soon appeared in the radical press for the sacking of all those antiliberals, or aristocrats as they were labelled, who were still employed by state or federal authorities. Broad catch-all decrees began to appear in several states, in San Luis Potosí, for example, where the legislature ordered that supporters of several earlier unsuccessful revolts be disenfranchised. A renewed campaign for the expulsion of Spaniards still in the country was waged, and several states issued blanket expulsion orders against all supporters of the defeated Bustamante regime. In June 1833, the federal government issued the *ley del caso,* according to which fifty-one named persons, all prominent figures, were summarily sentenced to six years of exile, apparently because of their political beliefs and, in some instances certainly, for reasons of personal vengeance. A few months later, the nation's bishops and senior clergy were threatened with expulsion unless they accepted the ecclesiastical reforms.[3]

The intention and effect of this purge were to enable the liberals to gain control of the national, provincial and local bureaucracies to which their own loyalists were duly appointed.[4] The federal executive power was already in their control and Congress was dominated by the party of progress, to use Mora's phrase.[5] New elections had been ordered in those states likely to resist the reform, and the new governors and legislatures

2 For further details of the liberal administration of 1833–4, see my *La primera república federal de México (1824–1835)* (Mexico, 1975), chaps. 13–15.

3 For details of the Church issue, see my *Church and State in Independent Mexico: A Study of the Patronage Debate, 1821–1857* (London, 1978).

4 Among these liberals was a young Benito Juárez, who was appointed an acting judge in Oaxaca in January 1834, only to lose the post a few months later with the fall of the liberal administration.

5 Mora, *Obras sueltas,* pp. 46–53.

were now in sympathy with national policy. Likewise, Mexico City's council and those of other important urban centres were appropriately renewed, and domination of the Supreme Court was ensured by the appointment of progressive judges. The military commands around the country were reshuffled, and commanders presumed to be at least obedient to the supreme government were designated. Recent experience had amply demonstrated, however, that the loyalty of the military could not be guaranteed, and the liberals knew that they needed some form of counterweight which could be used as a deterrent if not defence against ambitious or disloyal officers. Hence, strong support was given to the expansion of a civic militia which could, and would in due course, be used to sustain the liberal authorities. Large sums of money were spent, matériel was acquired and in some states, notably Zacatecas, the militia was soon numerically superior to and better equipped than the federal army.

Simultaneously with their take-over of the organs of state, however, the radicals' propaganda had sought to increase and broaden the basis of their popular support. Day after day their press denounced the aristocrats. Newspapers argued the case for the abolition of all property and income qualifications for the franchise; they promised equality for all and an end to the privileged classes of colonial society. The struggle, warned *La Verdad Desnuda,* was between the haves and the have-nots in society.[6] The *Fénix de la Libertad* repeatedly stressed the gulf between rich and poor, and the *Columna de la Federación* interpreted the situation as a class war. On 6 July 1833, the *Fénix* contained the following:

Let their possessions be divided among the villages; let us give them something to eat; let them have lands to cultivate for their own benefit; and let them be armed to defend their lands and pass them on to their children.

Absentee landlords were condemned and the government urged to implement a more equitable distribution of land with owners being obliged to cultivate it.

Thus, within a few months of taking office, radicals seemed to have consolidated their position and to be firmly entrenched in all the corridors of power. They controlled the executive authority at both the national and state levels; they enjoyed a large majority in Congress and the legislatures; their supporters had taken over many of the municipalities; their reform programme was rapidly being implemented; their propaganda was daily pouring forth from their several newspapers; and their opponents were in disarray. Yet in less than one month, the entire liberal edifice

6 *La Verdad Desnuda,* 24 April 1833.

was to collapse with its leaders retreating into foreign exile and almost all their legislation suspended, if not repealed.

There are many reasons for the failure of this first attempt at radical reform. Clearly, those powerful and influential institutions, notably the Church and the army, whose privileged status and financial interests were directly threatened opposed the government and its policies, and they did everything they could to bring about a military reaction against them. The purge of officials, high and low, throughout the national and provincial bureaucracies had created a pool of discontented and hostile opponents who saw a change of regime as the only hope of rescuing their reputations and their careers. Then, there is no doubt that despite their attempts to mobilize the populace with promises of education, land, the redistribution of wealth and an end to the hated tithe tax, the radicals were unsuccessful in generating any significant popular support.[7] But more than anything else, the reform failed because it alienated the *hombres de bien*. Regardless of their political creed, moderate liberal and conservative *hombres de bien* had a common fear of extremism and of the social upheaval which their own daily press warned them was inevitable if the radicals had their way. Some might have tolerated, even supported, the reform of the Church establishment and the army, even the purge of people, but the talk of a class war, of enfranchising the masses and allowing power to fall into the hands of the *baja democracia*, that was too much, too risky to contemplate. In their eyes, what the radicals were after was clear:

All they want is to take other people's wealth in the name of equality, to seize the honours and jobs which should be reserved for those with knowledge and virtue. The lack of equality in every level of society created by the Author of all nature to form a scale of communications and services has been used by these instigators of the populace to make them aware of the difference of their own situation, to arouse their self-interest against the rigours of fortune, and to encourage them to conquer it through crime and pillage in the name of 'sacred equality'.[8]

Moreover, it was far more than their social and economic pre-eminence that was at stake. Their moral values, their belief in the sacrosanct nature of legally acquired private property, both individual and corporate, in the Roman Catholic faith, in the family and in traditional education – all seemed threatened by the extremists, the sansculottes of Gómez Farías and his cohorts.

Not for the first time since independence, therefore, *hombres de bien* united in the face of extremism from below, and they turned for help to the one man Gómez Farías and his colleagues almost literally seemed to

7 See Shaw, 'Poverty and Politics', pp. 315–49.
8 *El Telégrafo*, 11 July 1834.

have forgotten: Antonio López de Santa Anna, president of the republic. Santa Anna had made one of his frequent tactical retreats to his country estate at Manga de Clavo (Veracruz) in December 1833, thus disassociating himself at least publicly from the actions of his own government. During the early months of 1834, opponents of Gómez Farías told him that political chaos and social anarchy were imminent because of the liberal policies. By way of letters and numerous personal envoys, they implored him to intervene, to save the nation and its faith from the radicals, to depose them and repeal the hated laws of reform.

It seems that it took a long time for Santa Anna to make up his mind, but more and more rumours that he had decided to break with his own government emerged in the closing weeks of March. Then on 16 April, letters from Santa Anna to General José Antonio Mejía were read in Congress, and these seemed to prove the truth of the rumours. By the third week in April, Gómez Farías and his colleagues were convinced that Santa Anna was about to desert them, so it came as no surprise when they learned that he was preparing to return to the capital. He arrived on the evening of 24 April and over the next few days and weeks the carefully constructed liberal edifice which had seemed so entrenched in the corridors of power collapsed. A process of reconstruction, or reaction as liberal historians would have it, was begun whereby the *hombres de bien* reasserted their dominance. What they were to impose was in many respects as fundamental as the liberal reform because it soon became evident that it was their intention to suppress not only the liberal ideology but also its constitutional creed, federalism.

The dismantling of the federation and the transition to a centralized republic in effect began as soon as Santa Anna returned to the capital. Within twenty-four hours, the resignation of two Ministers, Antonio Garay and José Joaquín de Herrera, of Finance and War respectively, was announced. Then on 29 April, Santa Anna issued a proclamation in which he made it clear that he would not sanction the liberal reforms. Faced with his opposition, Gómez Farías resigned himself to his fate and early in May rumours that he had asked for his passport were confirmed. The liberal executive thus capitulated rapidly and without resistance, but the radical majority in Congress was not so easily pressured into submission. A complex drama of defiance ensued in which the congressmen tried to sustain the independence of the legislative branch. Eventually Santa Anna imposed his own solution to the impasse that had developed by simply ordering soldiers to close the congressional building and telling the representatives that their services were no longer required.[9]

It is clear that Santa Anna had prepared his ground carefully, and

9 For a detailed account of the dispute with Congress, see my *La primera república federal*, chap. 15.

although we lack specific evidence, we may assume that he had obtained prior commitments of financial and military support from the Church and army if he required it. But Santa Anna always liked to be seen as a populist and he had no wish to be branded a tyrant. He wanted an apparently popular mandate for his actions, and hence during his dispute with Congress, a series of antiliberal *pronunciamientos* was announced. Plans were proclaimed at Puebla, Orizaba, Jalapa, Oaxaca and finally, on 25 May, Cuernavaca. Santa Anna had been in direct contact with at least four of these places, and it was generally assumed that the *pronunciamientos* were coordinated in advance. The Cuernavaca document became the charter under which Santa Anna justified his actions.[10] In brief, it stated that the people did not want and would not tolerate the liberal programme of reform, and Santa Anna was asked to ensure that the recent legislation was repealed as unconstitutional. Furthermore, all legislators and officials who had sanctioned the laws were called upon to resign. Within days, support for this plan came in from around the country, and in due course it was adopted as an authentic reflection of the national popular will.[11]

Santa Anna had his mandate, and during the next few weeks of June and July, having extracted a promise of a substantial loan from the clergy, he proceeded to dismantle the liberal administration.[12] On 17 June, Gómez Farías' principal advisers – José Bernardo Couto, Manuel Crescencio Rejón, Mora, Manuel Eduardo Gorostiza, José Espinosa de los Monteros and Juan Rodríguez Puebla – were dismissed from their posts. On 23 June, Andrés Quintana Roo resigned from the Ministry of Justice and other posts he held, and he was replaced as Minister two days later by Juan Cayetano Portugal, bishop of Michoacán. Also on 21 and 23 June, the *ley del caso* and other liberal measures were suspended until such time as a new Congress could revise them. Then the expulsion order against Bishop Vázquez was lifted, a papal bull appointing José María Guerra to the bishopric of Yucatán, which Congress had refused to accept, was admitted, the order for the arrest of Alamán was cancelled, charges against the Supreme Court judges were dropped and they were returned to office and, finally, the university and several of the recently closed clerical colleges were reopened. Accepting its own inevitable closure, the editors of the main liberal newspaper, *Fénix de la Libertad,* ceased pub-

10 The full text of the Plan of Cuernavaca is in *Planes de la nación mexicana* (Mexico, 1987), book 2, p. 214.
11 Texts of several supporting plans are in ibid. Bocanegra maintains that the Cuernavaca proposals were genuinely popular: J. M. Bocanegra, *Memorias para la historia de México independiente, 1821–1841* (Mexico, 1892–7), vol. 2, pp. 547–8. Bustamante describes how the movement in support in Mexico City was organized by General Tornel and General Gabriel Valencia; C. M. de Bustamante, *Continución del cuadro histórico de la revolución mexicana* (Mexico, 1963), vol. 4, p. 313.
12 The Church duly announced a 'voluntary' loan of 40,000 pesos a month for six months; see *El Telégrafo,* 3 June 1834.

lication on 4 June with these words: 'Caesar has crossed the Rubicon and has already declared himself a tyrant'.

For the liberal press, there was no doubt that Santa Anna aspired to autocratic rule and intended the abolition of the federal system. Several states shared this view, and while they were willing to accept, if not welcome, the end of the liberal reform, they would not countenance the destruction of their sovereignty. Michoacán, Jalisco, San Luis Potosí and others had already taken steps to form a defensive coalition, and on 10 June, Zacatecas informed Santa Anna of its determination to defend its rights.[13] In San Luis Potosí, Jalisco and Puebla, the authorities decided to take immediate defensive action, and Santa Anna was obliged to send large detachments of troops to subdue them, a process which in the case of Puebla involved a protracted and bloody siege of the city until August.[14] In other provincial cities, local reactions, some supported by the military, forced the incumbent authorities from office. In Guadalajara, for example, a mob of about sixty to eighty men, through intimidation and threats, persuaded the authorities to resign and then installed their own nominees as governor and in the local bureaucracy.[15] In some instances, legislatures and municipal bodies simply resigned and military commanders like Brigadier-General Antonio de León in Oaxaca assumed provisional executive power 'because of the inescapable demands of the circumstances'.[16]

Throughout June, July and August 1834, therefore, the liberals were removed from public office in a purge just as extensive as they themselves had conducted in 1833. In several instances, as at least a temporary expedient, previous incumbents were simply reinstated to fill the vacancies. In Yucatán and other states, for example, the legislatures which had been overthrown in 1832 were reinstalled. In Mexico City, members of the council dissolved by Gómez Farías in 1833 were reinstated and the same occurred in many other institutions such as the Academy of Law and the Colegio de Abogados. Judges of the Supreme Court who had been suspended were reinstated and the liberal appointees on the newly established Board of Public Education were removed and replaced by Santa Anna's own nominees. In some states – for example, Oaxaca, San Luis Potosí and Puebla – the blanket expulsion orders were lifted and those in the judiciary and civil bureaucracy sacked by the liberals restored to their posts. In the army, many officers who had lost their posts under

---

13 Zacatecas legislature to Santa Anna, 10 June 1834, in *El Telégrafo*, 22 June 1834. For the states' coalition plan, see *La Lima*, 24 May 1834.
14 Details of the siege of Puebla are in V. Riva Palacio, ed., *México a través de los siglos* (Mexico, 1962), vol. 4, p. 348; Bustamante, *Cuadro histórico*, vol. 4, pp. 322–3.
15 'Pocos quieren centralismo y los más federalismo, o sea representación que el pueblo de Guadalajara dirije al Excmo. Sr. Presidente de la República para que se restablezca el orden constitucional en el estado de Jalisco', Impreso de Guadalajara; reprinted in *La Oposición*, 22 October 1834.
16 Decree of Antonio de León, Oaxaca, 16 July 1834, in *El Telégrafo*, 2 August 1834.

the liberal regime had them returned, and long lists of promotions and retirements soon appeared in the official government press. Those who expressed their opposition were demoted.

The destruction of the liberal edifice was thus rapid and thorough, but the full implications of the new situation were by no means clear. On a superficial level all that had happened was that the incumbent government had fallen, Congress and legislatures closed, legislation suspended or repealed and public officials purged. The same process had occurred, in other words, as when the liberals had removed the Bustamante regime in 1832. The real significance, however, was more profound. Moderate politicians of all shades of opinion had reacted in 1828 and 1829 against the extremism of the radicals, then known as *yorkinos,* and they had formed an alliance with the aristocrats to restore their version of an ordered society.[17] Now these same men, including many former supporters of the liberal programme, moderate progressives in outlook like Manuel Gómez Pedraza, Guadalupe Victoria, Vicente Romero and even the ardent federalist governor of Zacatecas, Francisco García, agreed with and accepted the need to end the reform.[18] Confronted with what they saw as the threat of social dissolution being fomented by extremists in Congress and elsewhere, they joined with conservatives in defence of order, property and privilege.

The bond which produced the united front against the so-called demagogic liberals was based on mutual social and economic interests and on the conviction that political power should be controlled and exercised by the property-owning classes, or *hombres de bien.* But the problem of how to ensure that power stayed within the acceptable social classes against the pressures of ambitious military and fanatical reformers remained. For one group, the solution was evident. It lay in changing the political system, which was, they believed, the root cause of the country's many problems – in other words, to abandon the experiment in federalism and create a centralized republic in which access to political power would be firmly restricted to the literate, salaried and affluent classes. The respective merits of federalism and centralism as forms of political organization had been debated at length in many forums after independence, but following the adoption of federalism in 1824, the intellectual argument had faded into the background until 1830, when Bustamante and his political mentor, Alamán, had risen to power. Alamán in particular was a well-known believer in centralism, and without changing the constitution, he had in effect begun the process of concentrating power in the hands of the *hombres*

17 See my *La primera república federal,* chaps. 14 and 15.
18 In a series of private letters in the summer of 1834, Santa Anna repeatedly reassured Francisco García that he had no intention of destroying the federation; see García Collection, University of Texas at Austin, folder 36, Archivo de Francisco García Salinas, 1829–1847.

de bien. He did this by reforming the electoral system, by controlling the press, as well as the state executive and legislative authorities, and by protecting and strengthening what he considered to be the main pillar of a civilized society, the Roman Catholic Church. The reaction against the Alamán administration, led by Santa Anna in 1832, had been caused partly by fear among federalists that the next stage in Alamán's design was indeed to change the constitution. His fall had opened the way for the Gómez Farías government, and thus radicalism and federalism became closely associated. After the experience of the 1833 reforms, Alamán's ideas on society, on the economy, and on the centralization of power and the groups who should exercise it regained support, and it began to be argued that the way to eradicate extremism was first to remove the people concerned and then to change the political structures which enabled them to achieve power.

From approximately March 1834, the first signs of the re-emergence of the centralists were to be seen. On the 14th of that month, a new twice-weekly newspaper entitled *El Mosquito Mexicano* made its appearance in the capital. Its editorial policy was promptly evident from the denunciations of the liberals that filled almost every issue. The country was depicted as being under the rule of a vicious tyranny, hated by the people and by the 'useful classes' in society. The *ley del casso* was constantly cited as proof that personal liberty no longer existed and no individual was safe from the arbitrary whims of the vice-president. Gómez Farías was described as evil, a 'scourge sent from Heaven against the Mexican republic'. Congress, legislatures and everything associated with liberalism were subjected to similar scathing attacks.[19] Gradually, the purpose of this publicity campaign in the newspapers, accompanied as it was by the ever-sensational pamphlets, became apparent. The centralists were out to convince their readers and everyone else that the country was in chaos and on the verge of anarchy, of domination by the populace and by demagogues. But the solution was no longer, as it had been in 1829, presented mainly as that of restoring order in society and re-establishing the control of the property-owning classes. First by implication but soon openly, the paper began to campaign against the form of government and to attribute all the ills of the nation to the federal system. An alternative mode of government, it was suggested, must be found if the very existence of the republic was to be saved:

It is things which have changed, not men nor words. The constitution ended some time ago and, in consequence, the political system which the nation adopted disappeared. All that remains in its place is the confused chaos of unrestrained demagogy.[20]

19 *El Mosquito Mexicano*, 18, 21 and 25 March, 1 and 29 April 1834.
20 Ibid., 2 May 1834.

The effectiveness of this campaign is revealed by a report the U.S. ambassador, Butler, made to his government. 'My impressions decidedly are', he wrote, 'that the next *pronunciamiento* will include among its objects a modification of the present system of government – what that modification may be – what change may be attempted – is now nothing but mere speculation'.[21] Butler's impressions were even more significant than he realized, for although the demand for change was given more and more publicity, the *Mosquito Mexicano* was deliberately imprecise as to what the new system should be. It was assumed by the profederal press that the whole campaign was the work of centralist republicans. In fact, although this may well have been the case, the centralists did not openly declare their aims, because they were unsure of the attitude of one man, and one man alone, Santa Anna. It was by no means certain that he would look kindly on a central republic in which economic, social and political power was vested in pressure groups such as the clergy, landowners and other conservative-minded people. Hence, it was important in the first few months of 1834 for the centralists to leave open and obscure the precise nature of the form of government they envisaged. Their strategy for the time being was to depict the nation as rushing headlong into anarchy because of the federalist system, which allowed demagogues like the radical liberals to gain power.

The strategy, of course, worked and with the aid of Santa Anna the liberals were overthrown, but all that was left after the purge was a political vacuum. Centralists, federalists, conservatives and moderate reformers remained, and each group now engaged in intrigue to attract the support of the still uncommitted Santa Anna. Not for the first time in his career, he managed to do the unexpected. Contrary to the persistent rumours and private impressions, he insisted in every public declaration that he would not initiate or allow any attack on the constitution or the federal system. The purpose of his actions, he maintained, had been to restore order.[22] This he had done and would continue to do until such time as a new Congress could be elected. As if to emphasize this determination, he issued a law in July calling for state and congressional elections to be held for the new assemblies, which in the case of the national body were to open on 1 January 1835.[23]

Santa Anna's failure to declare his hand, at least in public, left the way open for the competing factions to press their own interests. The moderate liberals or progressives, according to Mora, concerned themselves with preserving some of the reform programme.[24] They were able to persuade

21 A. Butler to L. McLane, 8 March 1834, Justin Smith Papers, University of Texas, III, 66.
22 See, e.g., Santa Anna's proclamation of 1 June, published in *El Telégrafo*, 3 June 1834.
23 Decree of 9 July 1834, ibid., 11 July 1834.
24 Mora, *Obras sueltas*, p. 157.

Santa Anna to accept some of their ideas on education, and although at least one state, Puebla, reimposed unilaterally the civil enforcement of tithes and monastic vows, the federal laws were not revoked.[25] Even more important, he was persuaded to accept at least a neutral position in respect of ecclesiastical patronage and the nation's claim to it, a decision which led to the rapid resignation of Bishop Portugal from the Ministry of Justice.[26]

In contrast, the centralists seemed at first unable to extract much from Santa Anna. Because their political aim of changing to a centralist system appeared to be making no progress, they adopted another, ultimately more successful tactic, which was to concentrate their efforts on the elections Santa Anna had ordered. The constitutional position regarding the election of all the representative assemblies was extremely confusing. The federal Congress had been closed by presidential dictate and Santa Anna had decided that a new one should be elected to begin in January 1835. The election of the lower house was by indirect popular vote, but senators were chosen by the state legislatures and in this respect nobody quite knew what the legal position was. In a few states, some legislatures remained in office, in others they had ended prematurely and elsewhere provisional bodies had replaced the deposed liberals. The position was chaotic, especially over the proper timing of the state elections, and the solution to be adopted was duly floated in the government newspaper. There it was suggested that the constitutional timetable for the renewal of the legislatures should where necessary be ignored and the elections brought forward as a matter of urgency to permit the reunion of temporary bodies which could choose the national senators and then dissolve themselves as and when the constitutional period required.[27] Santa Anna issued on 9 July an appropriate decree in which the state authorities were told to arrange elections in such a way that senators could be selected on 1 September. The governors were empowered to vary electoral procedures and, significantly, to broaden the powers to be conferred on those elected.

The intention of these elections was quite clear. It was to wipe the slate clean of all traces of the radicals and to ensure that future legislative bodies at the national and state levels were dominated by *hombres de bien*. Liberals returning to their own regions who might have sought re-election were left in no doubt of the dangers of doing so. For example, Deputy Pedro Celestino Pérez and Senator José Mariano de Cícero both returned to their home state of Yucatán after Santa Anna closed the Congress. On arrival they were abused, threatened and forced to embark immediately

25 The text of the Puebla state law, dated 15 December 1834, is in *La Oposición*, 20 December 1834. Oaxaca also reimposed payment of tithes; *El Telégrafo*, 9 August 1834.
26 Details of the dispute over ecclesiastical patronage are in my *Church and State*, chap. 6.
27 Editorials in *El Telégrafo*, 23 June, 1 July 1834.

for Veracruz by the local military authorities under the command of Santa Anna's brother-in-law, Francisco de Paula Toro.[28] In Puebla, Deputy Joaquín Bazo, who was also a parish priest, found on his return that he had been suspended from his parish by Bishop Vázquez because he had spoken in favour of some of the liberal legislation.[29] José María Troncoso, one of Puebla's senators, felt it necessary or prudent to issue a public statement denying that he had ever supported any 'schismatic or anti-canonical law'.[30] Bishop Guerra, in his first pastoral letter, gave unequivocal advice to his congregation:

> Flee, flee from those seducers. Slaves of corruption and avarice, they are the ones who promise freedom. Flee, flee from those seducers. They are the ones who under the pretext of the public good want to introduce reforms which, if carried out, would bring upheaval to Catholic unity, casting us headlong into calamitous consequences.[31]

The intimidation of the liberals, together with the suppression of much of the radical press, meant that there was little campaigning for the elections. Government writers and supporters nevertheless felt it necessary to explain to the electorate what was required, and their main theme, constantly repeated, was that henceforth the ownership of property must be an essential qualification for any representative. The editor of the *Telégrafo* put this succinctly:

> Property is the only barrier capable of containing the force of excessive desires, of dangerous innovations, of the ardent enthusiasm of extremism. It is only in those countries where the basis of representation is property that one finds rational liberty.[32]

With frequent reference to Edmund Burke, he insisted that the English Parliament was the ideal model and was successful because it included the principal landowners and merchants, leaders of the army, navy and legal profession as well as private individuals publicly known for their industry, knowledge and eloquence. The radicals' demand that all groups in society but particularly the 'useful classes' be represented was nonsense. How, he asked, could you expect tavern-keepers, coachmen, water carriers, tailors, shoemakers and all the infinite variety of tradesmen and manual workers to be represented? Utility to society was not what was important: property, income, education and religious belief were the essentials.[33] The same message was preached in the states. In San Luis

---

28 Letter from Pérez and Cícero to Santa Anna, published in *La Oposición*, 4 October 1834.
29 See report in *El Telégrafo*, 28 October 1834.
30 J. M. Troncoso to editors, 21 November 1834, *La Lima*, 27 November 1834.
31 Pastoral letter dated 26 July 1834, in *El Telégrafo*, 27 July 1834. For a similar clerical attack on the liberals, see the pastoral of Bishop Vázquez (Puebla), dated 15 October 1834, in ibid., 22 October 1834.
32 *El Telégrafo*, 23 June 1834.
33 Ibid., 7 July, 17 and 20 November 1834.

Potosí, the unemployed were banned from voting, and the people were urged to vote only for *hombres de bien*.[34] In Querétaro, the governor José Rafael Canalizo insisted on the election of honourable, educated men.[35]

The three-stage (primary, district and state) electoral process was held in the summer of 1834, and while there were occasional reports of public disorder, destroyed ballots and the corruption that always accompanied elections, in general they passed without major incident. Despite all the exhortations to voters to use their vote and detailed regulations and attempts to compile proper registers, there was little interest among the electorate as a whole. From Toluca, for example, it was reported that the voting booths were empty, and in some, officials did not bother to turn up to count the votes.[36] The election day scenes of earlier years when rival factions had taken boisterously to the streets were replaced by ones of complete apathy. The same situation prevailed in the Federal District. For voting purposes, it was divided into 262 blocks, each of which was supposed to choose one elector in the primary stage. When the returns were in, it was found that in 104 of the blocks, no election had been held. The people, it was said, had simply lost all faith in the ballot box because of the blatant fraud that had occurred on previous occasions.[37]

The results began to emerge from September onwards, and it was soon clear that in terms of their socioeconomic background, the 'right' men had been chosen. The editor of the *Telégrafo* celebrated the fact that the new Congress would be composed of men 'who do not need to depend for their livelihoods on public sector jobs', and from Veracruz and elsewhere it was reported that *hombres de bien* had triumphed.[38] As the full list became known, other significant features were at once prominent.[39] The clerical campaign in defence of Church interests was reflected in the number of clergy who were elected. At least fifteen were to be deputies; these included five parish priests and five canons, two of the latter being future bishops – Pedro Barajas and José Luis Becerra. The Church was also well represented in the Senate, with at least seven, or about 20 per

---

34 Proclamation by Juan J. Domínguez, San Luis Potosí, 1 August 1834, in ibid., 9 August 1834.
35 Proclamation by José Rafael Canalizo, Querétaro, 1 August 1834, in ibid., 8 August 1834.
36 Report in ibid., 10 October 1834.
37 Ibid., 25 and 27 September 1834.
38 Ibid., 17 July, 17 September 1834. Sordo Cedeño found in his analysis of the Congress that there was 'un equilibrio de fuerzas entre una clase alta y una de clase media en desarrollo'; R. Sordo Cedeño, 'El congreso en la primera república centralista', Ph.D. diss., El Colegio de México, 1989, cited in J. Z. Vázquez, 'Iglesia, ejército y centralismo', *Historia Mexicana*, 39 (July–September 1989), 229.
39 The following analysis of the election results is based on my own list of those elected and that given in *Catálogo de la Colección Lafragua, 1821–1853* (Mexico, 1975), pp. 909–11. Personal details are from my own records from many sources, including *Semblanzas de los representantes que compusieron el congreso constituyente de 1836* (Mexico, 1837). Sordo Cedeño's work gives slightly different figures.

cent of the membership, being canons and *curas,* including the future bishop of Guadalajara, Diego Aranda y Carpinteiro. In all, ten states included one or more serving clergy among their representatives. The direct clerical lobby would thus amount in due course to almost 30 per cent of the national Congress and in addition, there were a number of nonordained members of the Church who were very proclerical in their views. Although not all of the results of the state legislature elections are available, those that are indicate a similar pattern of strong direct clerical presence, for example, in Querétaro, where one-third of the new assembly were clerics, and Puebla, with approximately one-fifth, or three of a total of sixteen.

The army also provided a significant group in both houses of the Congress. Among the deputies were a dozen serving officers, including four generals, and in the Senate there were at least five, again including generals and other senior-ranking officers. The legal profession, as ever, was well represented with twenty-four lawyers, and there were several *hacendados,* or large landowners, sixteen bureaucrats and nine from other professions in what may be called the civilian sector. Far more notable than any of these groups was the number of those who had been deputies or senators in earlier Congresses. About half of the total had served previously, some – for example, Horcasitas and Huarte – for several consecutive years. This group had one particularly significant feature. Approximately thirty, or not far short of half of those who were to be regular attenders, had been in Congress during the Bustamante regime of 1830–2. They included such well-known centralists as Alamán, Manuel Sánchez de Tagle, José Berruecos and Demetrio Castillo, and they had participated in the centralizing process of those years which had given rise to the federal/liberal reaction. Their re-emergence in such strength left little doubt that the end of the federal system was merely a matter of time. *Hombres de bien* were once again dominant, and they would now proceed to change the constitution in an attempt to ensure their dominance.[40]

As so many of those re-elected were known centralists, it was no surprise that the pressure to change the constitution intensified. In September, plans and *pronunciamientos* demanding the change appeared, but once again Santa Anna refused to cooperate. He repeated that he would suppress, as he had been doing, any movements to change the form of government. Faced with mounting pressure from the centralists and with more and more election results confirming that they would control the next Congress, he issued a statement on 15 October which purported to be a declaration of his government's political principles. He reaffirmed that

---

40 Sordo Cedeño calculates that of the twenty most active congressmen, fourteen were centralists.

he would not himself countenance any change in the federal system. Constitutional reforms, he said, were permissible only if they did not affect the political structure, the division of powers, religion or freedom of the press.[41]

The political parties were perplexed, especially the centralists, who were amazed and irritated by Santa Anna's apparent continued opposition to their aims. In fact, the mystery was quickly resolved. Having assessed the new-found strength of the centralist supporters, Santa Anna decided not to oppose them. In his inimitable way, he seriously offered as an explanation of his circular that he could not permit or enact any changes in the constitution as a result of the pressure of rebellions, because to do so would be illegal and unconstitutional. The question of centralism was not a matter for him. Only the next Congress could decide, and he would abide by any decisions reached by that body when it assembled and debated the matter in the coming months of 1835. In other words, knowing as he did that the centralists would control the next Congress, and as everybody at the time realized, Santa Anna had chosen to desert the cause of federalism. The end of the federation was thus inevitable.

41 The text is in *La Oposición,* 25 October 1834.

3

The transition to centralism: stage I

When the newly elected deputies and senators began to assemble in Mexico City for their preparatory sessions beginning on 14 December 1834, the first problem they encountered was the condition of their respective chambers, which had been closed since the previous May. Thieves had removed lead from the roof, rain had poured in and, with the carpets ruined and rotting papers scattered about the floors, there was an atmosphere of dampness and decay.[1] Santa Anna's apparent hostility to constitutional reform had deterred many from travelling to the capital, and by the beginning of January, the Chamber of Deputies was barely quorate and the Senate still inquorate. Within a few days, more representatives had arrived, and Santa Anna duly performed the opening ceremony on 4 January 1835. In his address, he adopted the mantle of statesman and patriot, and in what was becoming his archetypal hyperbolic and bombastic style, he proclaimed that his government had conquered the 'monster that is anarchy'. Extremists – 'men without morals' – had attacked the fundamental beliefs of the people, rooted in three centuries of tradition, but they had been soundly defeated. Their factions had been suppressed, their laws suspended or repealed, bishops had returned to their flocks and priests to their parishes. The doors had been closed forever to political fanaticism, and his government, having steadied the faltering ship of state, had opened the way to reason and progress.[2]

In fact, the situation was by no means as stable nor the future as clear as Santa Anna claimed. Certainly, the liberals and their reform programme had been defeated, but there remained major national issues to be resolved. The most important was the form and nature of the political system to be adopted. Most *hombres de bien*, both moderate liberal and conservative, agreed on the need for an increased centralization of power to enable the national government to impose its authority and keep control in the

---

1 Bustamante, *Cuadro histórico*, vol. 4, pp. 345–6.
2 The full text of Santa Anna's speech is in *México a través de los informes presidenciales: Los mensajes políticos* (Mexico, 1976), pp. 33–4.

regions, but there was no consensus on exactly what form that centralization should take. Convinced centralists like Alamán, Sánchez de Tagle and Francisco Lope de Vergara were strongly represented in Congress, and there was no doubt that their ideas on restoring and restricting political power to the hands of the property-owning classes to which they belonged found favour with most senior clergy and army officers. But there were also many other *gente de orden,* including clergy and military, who still believed that federalism was the most appropriate form of government, and they were to argue not for the abolition of the federation but for the reform of the 1824 constitution which had created it. Furthermore, it was clear that any attempt to destroy the federation would provoke military resistance in some regions, and even if that could be overcome, there were many practical problems in dismantling federal institutions and legislation. Then there were the thousands of legislators, councillors, state and municipal officials across the country as well as local chieftains and others who had personally benefited from the devolution of powers and whose status and careers would be at least jeopardized by change. In short, the transition to a centralized republic was to be neither peaceful nor unopposed, and those who supported it knew that they still had to persuade many groups and individuals of the virtues of change.

One man who seemed yet unconvinced was Santa Anna, and his own future status was the most critical problem to be resolved. Aged 41 in 1834, he was described by a contemporary as a man of 'ordinary stature, 160 pounds weight, gracious aspect, of lustrous black hair, white complexion, wide forehead, small square nose, round, black eyes'.[3] Although one of the younger generation of army officers who had taken control of the country in 1821, he was already an experienced veteran of political intrigue, and he was clearly not content with his present status as president of the republic. For several years rumours had circulated that he aspired to some kind of autocratic power, and his behaviour after defeating Gómez Farías seemed to confirm the rumours. A master of propaganda and apparently sensing the wish of Mexicans, most of whom never set eyes on him, to have a hero to worship, he set about developing and promoting a personality cult of himself. Using all the propaganda devices available to him – portraits, parades, statues, press eulogies, titles and honours – he promoted his own image as the Napoleon of the West, a man who had risen above the hurly-burly of the political maelstrom to become a statesman-general, always ready to give his life in defence of independence and the true faith. On the occasion of his birthday, supposedly 13 June,

3 Cited in O. L. Jones, *Santa Anna* (New York, 1968), p. 73. Santa Anna is one of the few Mexicans of this time to have attracted the attention of biographers. Callcott's study remains as good as any; W. H. Callcott, *Santa Anna* (Hamden, Conn., 1964). For a more recent and more interpretative study, see A. Yañéz, *Santa Anna: Espectro de una sociedad* (Mexico, 1982).

he hosted opulent dinner dances attended by up to eight hundred guests from the capital's political and social elite, and mass demonstrations by the populace were arranged to show their 'sincere outpouring of affection'. As the crowds filled the central square, they wore in their sombreros 'a white or blue ribbon with the words "Long live religion and the noble Santa Anna" ', and the reluctant hero made an appearance on the palace balcony. The churches rang their bells and a service of thanksgiving was held in his honour in the cathedral.[4]

For the defeated liberals and their supporters, there was no doubt what Santa Anna was seeking. In their view, he aspired to some kind of dictatorial power, even to be king or emperor, and it may be that he did hope that the unofficial title of Protector which he enjoyed after May 1834 might be given at least some form of permanent status.[5] From May to December, in the absence of the federal Congress which he had closed and with only one active minister remaining, he did in practice rule single-handedly, presiding in somewhat regal fashion over a public audience from 12 noon to 2 p.m. each Monday, Tuesday, Thursday and Friday.[6] Nevertheless, he must have soon realized that while he might be able to manipulate popular opinion, several other important factors militated against any Napoleonic ambitions. First, it was obvious that he would have to overcome the opposition of some of the states, which, although the radical liberals had been removed, were still controlled by determined federalists. Zacatecas, above all, had devoted substantial resources to building up its civic militia, and its suppression could be achieved only by what would doubtless be a long and bloody campaign which it was not certain that Santa Anna would win. Furthermore, in order to conduct such a campaign, although Santa Anna could presume to count on the backing of at least part of the regular army, it was essential that he attract the acquiescence, if not the support, of a majority of those groups which controlled the economy and many of the finances of the country. Their opposition, allied to that of the federalists, would mean his almost certain defeat.

It was in this area of political support that Santa Anna faced his greatest problem. Throughout his career to date, he had never fully sided with any one political group but had preferred to surround himself with a small clique of friends and admirers from both civilian and military circles. It is difficult to penetrate his entourage, which was to change over time, particularly the junior officers he used as his personal escorts, but some

---

4 *El Telégrafo*, 15 and 16 June 1834. Santa Anna's exact date of birth is not known, but he seems always to have celebrated it on 13 June, which was also his saint's day. For a summary of various supposed dates, see Jones, *Santa Anna*, p. 165, n. 2.
5 See the editorials in *La Oposición*, 24 and 27 September 1834.
6 Decree of 20 October 1834, in *El Telégrafo*, 27 October 1834.

of the senior figures were at his side or within the group he trusted for many years. The most loyal was Tornel, the 'bashaw of General Santa Anna', as the U.S. ambassador put it.[7] General Tornel, a devoted supporter for more than twenty years, served as his personal spokesman during his absences in the countryside or on campaigns and as his link with the army. Among the generals, he could usually rely on Gabriel Valencia and always on his brother-in-law, Francisco de Paula Toro, commander general of Yucatán. Until his death in 1836, General Juan Arago was his 'constant companion' on all his campaigns[8] and Ciriaco Vázquez, commander general of the strategically vital Veracruz port and region was, according to Carlos Bustamante, the 'faithful agent of the capricious will of Santa Anna'.[9] For raising money and supplies, Santa Anna could count on the services of another relative, the financier and speculator Ricardo Dromundo, and his personal affairs were looked after for many years by his friend and lawyer, Lic. Ignacio Sierra y Rosso.[10] To keep him in touch with the political mood, there was Tornel's brother-in-law, Manuel Díez de Bonilla, and as his private secretary, to whom at least some of the stylistic features of his oratory are attributed, there was Ramón Martínez Caro. Finally, there was his regional power base in the department of Veracruz, where there seems to have been a 'brotherhood of the Santa Anna order'.[11] Over his long career, he was always careful to place his friends, perhaps as a reward for services rendered, in various government offices, notably the customs service at Veracruz, and there were the countless *jarochos* of the rural areas who could always be relied on to support their local patron and hero.

With his home base secure and surrounded by his inner circle, which tended to expand or contract according to the circumstances of his career, Santa Anna was largely isolated from all the main political factions, and nobody knew definitely what, if any, his political principles were. One can look in vain at his entire career for any sign of ideas on economic or social policy. His actions since 1821, if not before, had generally shown him to be an opportunist who determined his attitudes on the basis of the individuals concerned rather than on any ideology. But this was a two-way process, for just as he had not adopted any party, so no political group had adopted him as its leader. From one point of view, he had used the politicians to promote his various projects from the overthrow

---

7 A. Butler to J. Forsyth, 8 February 1836, in Justin Smith Papers, file 22.
8 J. R. Malo, *Diario de sucesos notables* (Mexico, 1948), p. 114.
9 Bustamante, *Cuadro histórico*, vol. 4, p. 399.
10 Dromundo was soon to get the contract to supply the army for Texas from which, according to Bustamante, a great deal of money was made; ibid., p. 410.
11 F. Díaz y Díaz, *Caudillos y caciques* (Mexico, 1972), pp. 149–53. Díaz gives the names of various other politicians and military officers who were generally associated with Santa Anna over his career.

of Iturbide in 1822–3 to the defeat of Gómez Farías in 1834, but from another view, the politicians and others, especially the many equally ambitious generals, had used him to further their own careers. The result was that whereas he always posed as the champion of the army and defender of its privileges, few politicians, by no means all generals and no party were ready to trust him. Moreover, while his public image with the masses was assuming its regal proportions, politicians and the social elite in general were well aware of his love of money and his corruption in arranging financial deals and contracts to his own personal advantage. Although he was by no means alone in this respect, his personal life-style and obvious affluence, his liking for the ladies, and his extravagant use of public monies to further his own image and interests were looked on with distaste and resentment.[12]

At the beginning of 1835, Santa Anna had to take these factors into account, and he knew that his support for any bid for personal autocratic power had declined rather than increased during the previous six months. Even his faithful among the clergy who earlier had treated him as a demigod could no longer be counted on in the light of his neutrality over the patronage issue and his refusal to repeal all the detested anticlerical legislation. The centralist republicans were likewise disillusioned and had noted with alarm his equivocation over the question of the future form of government. Hence, it came as no surprise when, within a couple of weeks of the opening of Congress, it was announced that Santa Anna had decided to take one of his frequent extended rests at his country estate, Manga de Clavo. For the sake of appearances, he offered to resign the presidency. Congress refused to accept and instead, on 28 January, granted him leave of absence to restore his health.

Before departing for Veracruz, Santa Anna appointed Tornel Minister of War to keep an eye on the military and to keep his patron informed of any developments in the capital. As his successor in the presidency, he named General Miguel Barragán, who was to hold the office until ill-health obliged him to retire on 27 February 1836. Before we examine the Barragán government, it will be convenient to follow Santa Anna's movements. Although he did not know it, his decision to leave the presidency was to lead to the most humiliating moment of his career on the battle-fields of Texas and to his political ostracism until another foreign venture provided him with an opportunity to restore his disgraced reputation.

During the months that Santa Anna spent on his country estate, February and March of 1835, it became clear that changing the constitutional system was not going to be easy. Federalists around the country began a

---

12 Santa Anna acknowledged five illegitimate children in his will.

series of revolts, and while these caused the government some difficulty, far more serious was the confirmation that two states were preparing to resist, namely, Zacatecas and Texas.[13] Informed of everything that was happening by Tornel, Santa Anna decided early in April to return to the centre of the action. In a letter to Congress of 3 April, he told the deputies that although he had not fully recovered his health, he realized that he must once again sacrifice his personal well-being for the sake of the nation. He would, therefore, resume command of the army, which he would lead to suppress the federalist revolts 'with the most inflexible severity'.[14] A few days later, 18 April, he left to travel north to take command. He travelled quickly, and by early May he had brought his army north to the state of Zacatecas. There, on 11 May, in a battle which lasted some two hours near the town of Guadalupe, his men routed those led by the governor of Zacatecas, Francisco García.[15] Having defeated García, he and his men ransacked the city of Zacatecas and, in particular, the rich silver mines at Fresnillo, where Santa Anna arranged various contracts from which he and, it is said, Tornel derived personal profits of several hundred thousand pesos.[16] Following his victory, he went on a triumphant tour of Jalisco, Michoacán and Querétaro, where he was feted by the authorities and the social elite scrambled to pay their respects to the all-conquering hero.

Towards the third week in June, he returned to Mexico City to receive the acclamation of the capital's population. Dinners, dances, receptions, military parades, church services, a bull-fight and three days' public holiday in his honour were held, and Congress bestowed on him the supreme honour of 'Hero of the Fatherland' (Benemérito de la patria), to add to his already glowing collection of medals and titles.[17] The adulation was extreme, even for Santa Anna, and soon there was talk again that he was to be granted the dictatorship he coveted. The opposition press warned that an Asian-style 'omnipotent power' was being prepared and that tyranny was about to be imposed.[18] There were even rumours of plans afoot to offer him a crown, which brought one writer to recall the fate of Iturbide: 'The party of a king is now appearing and liberal institutions are begining to have many enemies. Padilla, Padilla. Let no Mexican ever forget that memory.'[19] The strength of the rumours was such that the

---

13 The most serious revolt, at least potentially, was at Texca, where General Juan Alvarez rebelled against the government; for details, see *El Sol,* 31 March 1835.
14 Santa Anna's letter is published in ibid., 10 April 1835.
15 E. Amador, *Bosquejo histórico de Zacatecas* (2d. ed., Zacatecas, 1943), vol. 2, pp. 411–22.
16 For details, see *El Anteojo,* 5 August 1835; Amador, *Bosquejo histórico,* vol. 2, pp. 423–5.
17 For a description of Santa Anna's reception in the city, see *El Sol,* 20, 22 and 23 June 1835; *La Oposición,* 23 and 25 June 1835.
18 *La Oposición,* 23 June 1835; *La Enciclopedia de los sansculottes,* 24 May 1835.
19 *El Anteojo,* 19 July 1835. Perhaps significantly, there was much in the press at this time about

government daily, *Diario del Gobierno,* felt it necessary to issue a formal denial that Santa Anna had regal ambitions or that he considered himself the equal of Napoleon.[20]

For his part Santa Anna, who did nothing to stop the press speculation, was left in no doubt by the Congress that it would not consent to any kind of autocracy. Hence, while basking in the glory of his military success, attending the banquets and theatres as well as his favourite cock-fights, he was making little progress in his political objective. Then, as often seems to have happened in Santa Anna's long career, an external event appeared to come to his rescue. The history of the movement for the independence of Texas has been thoroughly studied, and it would be superfluous to detail it here. Suffice to say that the Texans had watched the destruction of the liberal regime with concern and with even greater alarm when it became evident that they would lose their virtual autonomy with the ending of the federation. From the Mexican viewpoint, their hold on the distant state was well known to be tenuous at best and U.S. ambitions to acquire it by purchase or by force had been a cause for concern since the early 1820s, if not before. Hence, it came as no surprise when on 22 June 1835 the Texans rebelled in defence of the federal system.[21]

For Santa Anna, already bored with the social scene in the capital, the Texas revolt was another opportunity to add to his laurels and perhaps to persuade the doubters and dissenters among the *hombres de bien* that he was fit to wear a crown. He hastened to make preparations for the campaign and again set out for the north, arriving at San Luis Potosí on 5 December. With little or no support from the central government, which simply had no money, and with few units of the army in a fit state for war, he was forced to rely on his own ingenuity and skill at finding men and resources. He took mortgages on some of his own properties, arranged loans, found supplies and equipment and eventually persuaded some 6,000 men to join him. The march into Texas was, however, fraught with difficulties involving food supplies, climatic conditions including snow, desertion and the problems caused by some 2,500 women and children who accompanied the army.[22] Nevertheless, at first there were some successes on the battle-fields, and although progress was slow, by early March Santa Anna had reached the outskirts of San Antonio de Béjar, to be confronted with the last-ditch resistance of the defenders of the Alamo. The massacre at the Alamo took place on Sunday morning, 6 March.

a bust of Napoleon presented to Congress by Dr. F. Antoinmarchi; see, e.g., *El Sol,* 19 June 1835.

20 *Diario del Gobierno,* 7 November 1835.

21 The text of the Texas *pronunciamiento* was published in ibid., 12 November 1835.

22 Jones, *Santa Anna,* pp. 65–6.

For Santa Anna, it provided the further opportunity he had hoped for to portray himself as the invincible, all-conquering hero of the nation. In military terms, the engagement was relatively minor and the Mexican victory inevitable given the disparity in the strength of the two sides, but Santa Anna immediately put a very different gloss on the event. In his report to the government in Mexico City, dictated at 8 a.m. on 6 March, just a few hours after the fighting had ended, he declared that a total and glorious victory had been won by 1,400 Mexican soldiers who, overcoming fierce, well-armed resistance, had taken the Alamo fort. More than six hundred rebels, he claimed, had been killed, and a so far unknown number of others in the surrounding countryside had been dispatched by the cavalry. Mexican casualties were seventy dead and three hundred wounded. The army would never permit foreigners to insult or seize national territory, and it had shown its willingness to make any sacrifice, including the ultimate, in defence of the nation's rights.[23]

The news of the victory, based on Santa Anna's highly exaggerated description, reached Mexico City around 20 March. The first press report appeared on 21 March in *El Nacional,* an antifederalist paper which carried the following headline: 'IMMORTAL GLORY TO THE ILLUSTRIOUS GENERAL SANTA ANNA; ETERNAL PRAISE TO THE INVINCIBLE MEXICAN ARMY'. The next day, two more papers, both antiliberal, picked up the story. The headline in *El Mosquito Mexicano* read, "Long live the fatherland, long live the valiant Mexican army, long live the brave general SANTA ANNA!!!' The success at the Alamo, it said, gave rise to the hope that peace would now be re-established across the republic. The Texas rebels had lost everything, and Santa Anna had sent their 'insulting flag' to the capital. Over the following days other papers bestowed ecstatic praise on the 'Invincible Liberator'. There was no triumph in history to compare with what Mexico's intrepid leader had achieved. The Alexanders, Caesars, Pompeys, Hannibals, even Napoleon, were not his equal: 'Our pen is incapable of describing your heroism; we can only admire you.'[24]

This outburst of hero worship of Santa Anna was not confined to the capital. In Oaxaca, for example, a paper whose stance is indicated by its name, *El Santanista Oaxaqueño,* published daily panegyrics on his personal qualities and leadership. Patriotic marching songs in his honour were hurriedly composed in order to be sung in the local theatre and then printed in the paper. Again, he was openly and favourably compared with Napoleon.[25] At Veracruz, similar eulogies were published in the local

23 Together with other documents relating to the Texas campaign, Santa Anna's report was published by the *Diario del Gobierno* in a special supplement on 20 March 1836, but I have not been able to locate the supplement.
24 *El Mosquito Mexicano,* 22 March 1836; *La Lima de Vulcano,* 22 and 24 March 1836.
25 *El Santanista Oaxaqueño,* 26 March, 1 and 9 April 1836.

press, and in Mérida, Yucatán, it was proclaimed that Santa Anna was a 'father of Anahuac, a liberator of Mexicans'.[26]

This almost hysterical adulation of Santa Anna naturally began to worry his political opponents, and the proliberal and profederal press soon began to cast doubts on the accuracy of his account of the battle at the Alamo and on its military significance.[27] Of even greater concern to them was a renewal of the campaign to give him dictatorial powers. One paper referred to him as the 'pretender', saying that his supporters were intriguing to have him crowned,[28] and throughout April and early May 1836 there were persistent rumours of a plot to stage a *golpe de estado* with the objective of making him 'supreme dictator'.[29] The profederal press responded again with warnings of the dangers of dictatorship and despotism. Santa Anna's allies, it was said, were people who 'preach a liberator in order to enthrone a sultan'.[30]

It was almost precisely at the height of the speculation over Santa Anna's possible elevation to monarch or dictator that the first news arrived in Mexico City of his humiliating defeat and capture by Sam Houston on the banks of the San Jacinto River. On 19 May, the news was reported briefly,[31] and over the next few days and weeks as word spread of his traitorous deals with the Texans, and later the U.S. government, to save his own skin, the reputation of the 'immortal hero' fell into headlong descent.[32] The government publicly disowned him, refusing to recognize any agreements which he signed, and the press took the opportunity to ridicule and mock the 'little Napoleon'.[33] Far from being the great hero of the nation, he was now a 'monster, pilferer and cheat, traitor, perjurer'.[34] Santa Anna's fall was indeed rapid, sudden and unexpected, and although he was after a time able to slip back into Mexico, his career in national life seemed over. He returned to the rural tranquility of Manga de Clavo in 1837, a disgraced and humiliated man, to tend to his cattle and his fighting cocks and to await the next twist in his fortunes.

When Santa Anna had withdrawn from the presidency in January 1835,

---

26 Article from *El Censor* (Veracruz) reprinted in ibid., 15 April 1836; article from *El Cometa* (Mérida) reprinted in *La Lima de Vulcano*, 30 April 1836.

27 See, e.g., the article in *El Cosmopolita*, 2 April 1836. I have examined the Mexican press reaction to the Alamo in 'The Mexican Press of 1836 and the Battle of the Alamo', *Southwestern Historical Quarterly*, 91 (April 1988), 533–43.

28 *La Luz*, 16 December 1835, 11 March 1836.

29 *La Lima de Vulcano*, 14 May 1836; *El Cosmopolita*, 18 May, 4 June 1836.

30 *El Cosmopolita*, 9 and 12 March, 20 April 1836; *Proceso del General Santa Anna* (Mexico, 1836).

31 The news was released on 19 May in a formal announcement by the government; *Diario del Gobierno*, 19 May 1836.

32 *El Cosmopolita*, 1 June 1836, reported rumours of Santa Anna's deals with the Texans.

33 Ibid., 18 June 1836.

34 *Proceso del General Santa Anna*.

he had left General Miguel Barragán as his interim successor.[35] Barragán was a career army officer who enjoyed a considerable reputation as a military tactician and as a man of integrity, although the U.S. ambassador described him as 'worthy and amiable but indecisive, and intellectually feeble'.[36] He was born at Valle de Maíz (San Luis Potosí) in 1789, and after some years of fighting for the royalists in the war of independence, he joined Iturbide and participated in the final defeat of the Spanish forces. He was imprisoned for his opposition to Iturbide's rise to the monarchy, but in 1824, after the empire had ended, he was made commander general of Veracruz. There he acquired national fame by organizing and achieving the defeat of the last Spanish garrison on Mexican soil, which had occupied the island fortress of San Juan de Ulúa. Two years later, in 1827, he participated in the unsuccessful Tulancingo revolt against the presidency of Guadalupe Victoria, and after some months of imprisonment, ironically in San Juan de Ulúa, he was sentenced to foreign exile. On his return, Santa Anna appointed him Minister of War, a post he occupied briefly from November 1833 to February 1834.

His record, therefore, was in most respects typical of many army officers of the time, but in terms of his political views he had been perhaps unusually consistent. In the 1820s he was an active and prominent member of the Scottish Rite freemasons, the *escoceses,* whose Grand Master, Nicolás Bravo, had led the Tulancingo revolt. The *escoceses* attracted those with moderate, conservative and in some cases, but not all, procentralist views. They favoured a strong but not dominant Church and army as the main safeguards of social stability, and they wanted to retain many of the moral and social values of the colonial era. Barragán certainly shared these attitudes and opinions, and he was given the presidency, if Mora is to be believed, because Santa Anna had decided for the time being to throw his weight behind the *escocés* faction.[37]

Barragán took over the presidency on 28 January 1835, and although it was said that he never made a decision without first consulting Santa Anna, it was his job to supervise the ending of the federation and the introduction of its replacement.[38] There were several stages in the process of change. The first was negative in the sense that it required the removal or defeat of the remnants of the liberal regime and then the remaining suppression of federal opposition in the states. The most important liberal to be dealt with was Gómez Farías, who was still the legally elected vice-

35 Barragán was technically elected by the states with 13 votes against 1 for Nicolás Bravo and 1 for Luis Quintanar; *El Sol,* 3 February 1835.
36 A. Butler to J. Forsyth, 8 February 1836, Justin Smith Papers, file 22.
37 Mora, *Obras sueltas,* pp. 157–9.
38 H. H. Bancroft, *History of Mexico* (San Francisco, 1887), vol. 5, p. 143; F. de P. Arrangoiz, *México desde 1808 hasta 1867* (Mexico, 1968), p. 368.

president. A vilification campaign directed against him personally as well as against his administration quickly filled the pages of the newspapers.[39] Predictably, in the light of such abuse, on 15 January Senator Ramón Pacheco introduced a proposal that Gómez Farías be declared 'morally unfit' to carry out the duties of his office. A week later, after normal referral to committee, the proposal was approved in the Senate by a vote of 21 for to 2 against and a few days later by the lower house with a vote of 31 for and 15 against.[40] Gómez Farías prepared to leave for exile.

As already indicated, Santa Anna assumed the task of suppressing the federalists in Zacatecas, but as a prelude to that campaign and as a sop to the army, the first major initiative in Congress was directed against the civic militia. Much to the anger of senior army officers, since 1827 the states had been developing their own militia, which were controlled by the governors. The regular army saw these irregular forces as a threat to its own status and role and also as a waste of scarce resources. With the notable exception of that in Zacatecas, however, where twenty thousand men had enlisted and four thousand were ready for active service, the militia were more important as a symbol than for their military power.[41] In the eyes of conservatives, they offered a fertile recruiting ground for rebels, and they had become associated with radicalism. They were also a visible symbol of the sovereignty of the states and a first line of defence against any aggressor. Hence, it was no surprise that one of the first initiatives the executive sent to Congress recommended abolition. Discussion, always in closed session, began on 15 January, but news of it soon leaked out and comments began to appear in the press. One of the main platforms at this time for conservative opinion was *El Sol,* and it began to put the case, if not for outright abolition, certainly for reform and reduction. The militia, it said, was a 'cruel servitude for the people, a focus of corruption and immorality and a harmful distraction for industrious people'. Thousands of artisans were taken from their families and their workplaces, which had dire effects on local economies, and with desertions endemic, recruits quickly joined the ranks of thieves and murderers to become the 'worst plague of society'.[42]

The appearance of such articles was accompanied, as it always was when government was sponsoring controversial legislation, by representations from regional authorities which were intended to show that the proposed

---

39 *La Lima de Vulcano,* 17 January 1835.
40 Details from congressional sessions in *El Sol,* 2, 10 and 14–18 February 1835; M. Dublán and J. M. Lozano, *Legislación mexicana* (Mexico, 1876), vol. 3, p. 15. The vote against Gómez Farías was overwhelming – 31 to 15 in the Chamber of Deputies and 21 to 2 in the Senate.
41 Amador, *Bosquejo histórico,* p. 411.
42 *El Sol,* 26 and 28 February 1835.

change enjoyed widespread support. The Jalisco legislature sent an initiative calling for abolition, and this was quickly followed by a similar plea from Querétaro.[43] The publication of both these documents provided further opportunities for the case to be made in the conservative press, as did news that the Zacatecas gazette was strongly defending the militia. It was obvious, the editor of the latter wrote, that the campaign against the militia was merely a prelude to a full-scale assault on the federal system.[44] This charge was angrily denied by the procentralist *El Mosquito Mexicano*. The government's aim, it insisted, was thoroughly justified and was to reform the militia which had become 'hirelings of the sansculottes, to install and remove governments at their whim, to take revenge on anybody they chose, to start a religious schism'.[45] Against the background of the public debate, Congress discussed the issue, and although the Zacatecan deputies, led by Pedro Ramírez, argued against the proposal, they were heavily outnumbered. A law was approved on 31 March by which the militias were to be reduced to one recruit per five hundred inhabitants.[46]

Backed by the army and the conservative press, the success of the move to reduce the militia to impotence was clearly inevitable, and it was widely seen as a preparatory step in the process of dismantling the federation. The centralists, however, were well aware that there was still powerful opposition to their aims in several quarters. They realized that they needed to make and justify their case, and during the early months of 1835 they set out what amounted to their political manifesto. Countless newspaper articles and pamphlets analysed the advantages and disadvantages of federalism, and promises and pledges, some public and some private, were made in an attempt to demonstrate that there was a better alternative. The initial plank of their platform was negative – there were more aversions than principles, as Mora puts it – in that it consisted of an attack on the federal system on the grounds of its unsuitability as a form of government for the country in its current state of development and, more important, on its failure to fulfil the expectations aroused on its adoption in 1824.[47] The decade or so of experience of federalism in operation provided the centralists with numerous practical rather than ideological targets for criticism. Hence, their attacks on the system embraced the whole range of political, social and economic problems facing

---

43 'Iniciativa de la legislatura del estado de Jalisco sobre extinción de la milicia cívica', Guadalajara, 20 February 1835, in *La Lima de Vulcano*, 5 March 1835; for the Querétaro initiative, see *El Sol*, 28 March 1835.
44 Article from the Zacatecas gazette, in *El Sol*, 24 February 1835.
45 *El Mosquito Mexicano*, 3 April 1835.
46 Dublán and Lozano, *Legislación mexicana*, vol. 3, p. 38.
47 Mora, *Obras sueltas*, p. 152.

the republic, almost all of which they attributed to or blamed on the form of government.[48]

The condemnation of the practical effects of federalism was expressed in representations from state legislatures, local authorities and other public bodies as well as in almost daily editorials in some sections of the press. Citizens of Toluca, for example, said that federalism had been adopted in a desire to imitate the United States but without any real understanding of how the system worked and without any account being taken of the very different customs, traditions and level of civilization in Mexico. None of the federalists had foreseen the consequences of dividing what had been for centuries a homogenous and compact mass into so many heterogeneous parts.[49] But the consequences were now evident to everyone, according to the Guadalajara town council. The federal system had not brought economic prosperity but poverty and recession. It had caused political and factional division, which in turn had led to the constant rebellions and *pronunciamientos* that inhibited all progress. Provincial and local politicians had never properly understood the concept of state sovereignty, with the result that some states believed themselves to be totally independent of all national authority. The enormous increase in state bureaucracies had caused a huge rise in administrative costs; whereas in the colonial era Jalisco had been administered for 45,000 pesos a year, by 1834 the cost had risen to more than 1 million pesos. Taxes had, therefore, risen to an intolerable level. Federalism had brought no benefits. On the contrary, 'fortunes, properties, individual freedom, public morality, law, religion, everything has been destroyed'.[50]

Federalism was similarly criticized again and again in the centralist press. According to *El Sol*, which carried a series of editorials on the subject throughout the early months of 1835, the states had rarely if ever made their due financial contributions to the national Treasury, and the 'frenzy of provincialism' had led to the creation of excessive and wasteful bureaucracies.[51] The rush to create public-sector jobs had stimulated *aspirantismo*, which sowed the seeds of revolutions as people were willing to support anyone who promised them employment or promotion. There were far too many overpaid legislators with retinues of advisers and officials who were more often than not an ostentatious luxury. With so many of the nation's scant resources being consumed by the ever-expanding number

48 The argument in the 1834–6 years also differs from that in the earlier period in that there is markedly less reference to European writers.
49 M. Díez de Bonilla to Minister of War, Toluca, 30 May 1835, in *El Sol*, 31 May 1835.
50 'Representación del muy ilustre ayuntamiento de la capital del estado de Jalisco, dirigida al honorable congreso del estado para que inicie ante las cámaras de la unión la variación de la actual forma de gobierno, en república central', Guadalajara, 1 June 1835, in *El Mosquito Mexicano*, 30 June 1835.
51 *El Sol*, 12 February 1835.

of officials, commerce and industry were being starved of investment and economic progress was impossible.[52]

The Orizaba municipality and the Querétaro legislature made similar points.[53] The strife and political rivalry caused by the federal system were now such that even the independence of the nation was in jeopardy. The religion of the people had been threatened, clergy proscribed, Church goods alienated and monasteries closed. There was no justice, no personal security, no protection of property.

These attacks on federalism, although seemingly independent and spontaneous expressions of opinion from diverse sources around the country contain many similarities both in the points made and in the language used. It seems that they were coordinated centrally, presumably from the capital, and it gradually became evident that certain themes were being emphasized as the centralist case for change was being constructed in the public mind.

Possibly the most prominent of these was the problem of law and order. Rural banditry and crimes of violence against persons and property had long been a serious problem, especially on the highways, but although we lack statistical evidence of crime rates, according to centralist propaganda general lawlessness and violence had significantly increased in the years following independence and the effective breakdown of the Spanish judicial code and policing system. They were no longer a danger only in the remoter rural areas. According to the Minister of Justice and numerous newspaper reports, theft and murder were almost daily events in the cities.[54] Muggings and robberies were commonplace in broad daylight in the main thoroughfares of the capital, and the people went about their affairs in fear of their lives and their property. There was no personal safety anymore in Mexico, one newspaper declared. People, especially honourable citizens, were obliged to buy guns to protect themselves, but 'nobody is safe on the streets even in broad daylight, nor in their homes at any time'.[55] Demands for tougher sentences were heard in Congress and in the press, and the government promised that increased penalties for crimes of theft and violence would be introduced.

Violence against the person and against property was not restricted to the level of common criminality. According to the centralists, it was a reflection or extension of officially sanctioned violence against the individual. One of the most bitter complaints against the liberal regime of Gómez Farías and the federal authorities in the states was their alleged persecution of political opponents. This issue attracted probably more

52 Ibid., 24 March 1835.
53 Representations in ibid., 28 March, 24 May 1835.
54 *Diario del Gobierno*, 20 November 1835.
55 Ibid.

hostility and hatred of the liberals than any of their anticlerical legislation, and no single act was more condemned than the so-called *ley del caso* of June 1833 and its arbitrary expulsion of fifty-one leading *hombres de bien*. Similar laws against individuals enacted in the states were depicted as sanctioning unjustified acts of state violence against the individual, as crimes on a par with those of common criminals. The many confiscations of property of corporations and individuals were also portrayed as symptomatic of the liberals' contempt for the accepted standards of political and personal conduct. In short, the liberals had broken the rules. They had threatened the social cohesion of the *hombres de bien* by not accepting the unspoken convention that class allegiances were more important than political differences. The only result would be anarchy and social dissolution.

This breakdown of law and order and of the standards of civilized political conduct were attributed to the effects of federalism. The 'plague of thieves' was said to include those who 'as they commit their robberies, defend liberty and the divine system'.[56] The crime wave was also a product of a more general malaise, a 'torrent of immorality' which federalism had caused.[57] Respect for law and order, for property and for the person had disappeared in the corruption now endemic in all areas of life. The nation's traditional values were being undermined by the new ideas and those who advocated them. Immoral literature was flooding into the towns and cities, and demoralization and despair pervaded all of the social classes. The once strong commitment to public service had been replaced by unrestrained personal ambition and a spirit of insubordination. Laws were abused, discipline in the army was lax, corruption and theft by public officials commonplace, and criminals escaped with impunity because of protection by their political patrons. Education was being prostituted and youth perverted as parents struggled in vain to protect their families.[58]

One cause of this decline in public and private moral standards was the damage done to the Church and to religious faith by the federalist sansculottes. They had consistently decried the value of the established Church, attacking its temporalities and ridiculing its clergy. Religion itself had been profaned by Gómez Farías and his cohorts, and as a direct result standards of behaviour had declined. The cancer of impiety had to be stopped before it was too late and the social fabric of the nation destroyed. Respect for religion, the Church and its ministers had to be restored because it was precisely attacks on their prestige which brought civil disorder in any society.[59]

56 *El Mosquito Mexicano*, 24 April, 8 May 1835.
57 *Diario del Gobierno*, 8 November 1835.
58 *El Mosquito Mexicano*, 30 June 1835; *El Sol*, 1–3 February 1835.
59 *La Lima de Vulcano*, 14 March 1835, supplement.

The restoration of public morality, respect for the government, for law and order and for religion could be achieved only by removing the radical federalists from power and replacing them with *hombres de bien*. The latter would restore the lost values of earlier years. Employees would be paid on time, the public highways made safe and crimes justly punished. Order and stability would again prevail, and the nation would grow prosperous once the infinite 'little congresses' and anarchic factions had been defeated. The only social group which could achieve these things were the men of property.[60] The 'chimerical equality' preached by liberal extremists was their pretext to deprive honourable citizens of their goods, and their hostility towards the propertied classes was intended to stir up popular hatred against them. It was essential, therefore, to reform the electoral system in order to ensure that *hombres de bien* were elected, and the only secure way to do this was to make property ownership the basic qualification for voters and candidates. Property owners would restrain the wild extremism and 'dangerous innovations' of radicals, and with such men in control of national affairs, economic progress would be rapidly achieved because it would be in their own interest. Under the new regime, industry, agriculture and commerce would be encouraged and Mexico's neglected natural resources fully exploited. The taxation system would be revised, and with more efficiency and less corruption, revenues would increase and public investment in roads, communications and other services expanded.[61]

These, then, were the general themes of the manifesto which conservatives offered to the Mexican public in the final months of 1834 and early part of 1835 as they tried to win support for the constitutional change to centralism. The politics of nostalgia was a powerful force after the decade of chaos experienced under the federal system, and centralist propaganda was always careful to remind the property-owning classes of the peace and order of colonial times, when, it was suggested, social values were accepted and every man knew his place.[62] A new form of government would restore national unity and end the factional divisions and multiparty politics which had caused so much instability and administrative corruption. Law and order would be guaranteed, and above all, the traditional values of the family, respect for the nation's once venerated institutions, the spirit of public service and public morality in general would prevail. The precepts of the only true faith would again be taught

60 *El Sol*, 7 April 1835.
61 *El Telégrafo*, 23 June, 7 and 17 July 1834.
62 In many respects, the transition to centralism was a rerun of the events, people and ideological propaganda of the Bustamante–Alamán regime of 1830–2, and those years were also held up as a model of the beneficial effects of centralizing the political system; see the editorial in *El Sol*, 16 March 1835.

in the schools and the corruption of youth by the modern heresies of the day stopped. Men of property would reoccupy their rightful position in the corridors of power, and their presence would ensure that reforms, when needed, would be made without the radical upheaval of society and all the dangers of social and economic equality as preached by the demagogic, federalist sansculottes. The Church and the army would once again be the twin pillars of social order.

This manifesto was clearly designed to persuade *hombres de bien* of the potential benefits of ending the federation, and if we are to accept contemporary opinion, excluding that of liberals like Mora, it would seem that it was singularly successful. The word *federalism* as one writer put it, had lost its magic appeal and the experience of the past decade had brought disillusionment and a desire for change.[63] In a private letter to the duke of Terranova, Alamán, whose ideas certainly inspired much of the manifesto, wrote that the change to centralism would be easily achieved because the people were tired of the present situation.[64] Carlos Bustamante also maintained that the change was popular because the people were tired of the 'excesses of those in power, especially the little congresses and state governors', and even the staunch federalist José María Bocanegra implied the same opinion in his description of the situation.[65] In the words of the editor of *El Sol* on 26 March 1835, 'A new constitution, a new constitution, ABOVE ALL ELSE, is what the country wants'.

Although the federalist press had mounted a vigorous counterattack on the centralist manifesto, by the early summer of 1835 the intellectual and political battle on behalf of centralism had been won. There remained, however, a number of problems. First, there was Santa Anna and his desire for autocratic power. It was still not certain whether he would countenance the replacement of federalism with anything other than himself. The solution came in late May or early June. It was then that *pronunciamientos* demanding a centralist republic began to be announced from Orizaba, Toluca, Cuernavaca, Zacatecas and dozens of other places in all parts of the country.[66] In the first two weeks of June, the pressure mounted daily, and on 13 June the people of the capital, armed with flags bearing the slogan 'In Revolt for Popular Government' took to the

63 Ibid., 2 February 1835.
64 L. Alamán to Duque de Terranova, 28 July 1835, in *Obras: Documentos diversos*, vol. 12, pp. 286–90.
65 Bustamante, *Cuadro histórico*, vol. 4, p. 370; J. M. Bocanegra, *Memorias*, vol. 2, pp. 610–15. Henceforth, I refer to C. M. de Bustamante as Carlos Bustamante to distinguish him from his namesake, Anastasio Bustamante.
66 More than four hundred petitions for change were presented to Congress, apparently coordinated centrally. Bustamante says that they came directly from the cabinet; *Cuadro histórico*, vol. 4, pp. 370–1. The texts of many of the *pronunciamientos* appeared in the press and have more recently been included in the collection *Planes en la nación mexicana*, book 3.

streets. Public meetings were held, which led to an emergency meeting of the city council and the overwhelming view, taken formally to the government, that the people wanted centralism.[67] A couple of days later, Santa Anna summoned leading members of both houses of Congress to discuss the situation and to try to turn it to his own advantage. We do not know in detail what was said, but Carlos Bustamante, who was present, recorded that he and his fellow congressmen let Santa Anna know that 'we would not allow him to use us as a stepping-stone to create under our auspices a Mexican autocrat'.[68] Faced with this opposition and another mass demonstration in the capital in favour of centralism, Santa Anna chose once more to withdraw from the scene, soon to head for Texas.

As these several developments were preparing the way for the new conservative and centralized republic, the Barragán government began to implement a number of changes which though minor in themselves were intended to be practical evidence that the promises in the manifesto would be fulfilled. Most, but not all, the outstanding reform laws were repealed, especially those concerning the clergy.[69] Alamán was absolved of all charges of involvement in the death of Guerrero, and the law ordering memorial services in his memory was repealed. To demonstrate that henceforth legally acquired, privately owned property would be respected, the properties belonging to Hernán Cortés' heir, the duke of Terranova, whose representative in Mexico was Alamán, were returned and the liberal law by which they had been confiscated repealed. The army was restored to favour, with the demotions imposed by the liberals cancelled and a new round of promotions announced. Laws which had seemed to persecute individuals were abolished, exiles were allowed to return and on 6 May a general amnesty for political offences since 1821 was declared. All employees in both civil and military sectors who had lost their jobs or had been demoted for political reasons were to be reinstated. Iturbide's family was allowed to return, and it was promised that the 1 million pesos and other benefits he had been awarded at the height of his fame would be paid when circumstances permitted. As evidence of the new fiscal probity and the regime's determination to put the nation's finances on a sound footing, the states were ordered to pay a proportion of what they owed to the central Treasury. Also, new contracts were awarded to improve coach and postal services.[70]

As already indicated, one of the major areas of criticism of the federal

---

67 See the reports in *El Sol*, 30 May, 2, 3, 6 and 14 June 1835.
68 Bustamante, *Cuadro histórico*, vol. 4, p. 366; Malo, who was also present at the meeting, lists those who attended (*Diario*, 101).
69 A number of anticlerical measures were not repealed; these will be discussed in the next chapter.
70 For these various decrees, see Dublán and Lozano, *Legislación mexicana*, vol. 4, and *El Sol*, 14, 19, 20 and 22 March, 26 and 30 April, 6 May, 1 June 1835.

system was the lack of law and order. Perhaps the most prominent policy commitment in the centralist manifesto was to improve the judicial system and stop the growth of violent crime. Property owners were quickly assured by the Minister of Justice that the judicial code would be thoroughly overhauled, with new legislation, penal, civil and commercial, introduced. The chaos in the courts and in legal proceedings, caused, he said, by the fact that the legal system had been devised for a colony rather than a free republic, would be improved.[71] More immediate, specific measures were also introduced. The governor of the Federal District ordered the withdrawal of all licenses to carry firearms and declared that future applications would be granted only if supported by two financial guarantees. Penalties for carrying weapons without a license were increased to a fine of 25 pesos or one month in jail.[72] Penalties for theft were also made much more severe, with nonviolent theft of goods to the value of up to 1,000 pesos liable to three to four years' imprisonment. Robbery with violence brought a minimum sentence of ten years, and if serious physical injury or death resulted, the penalty was capital punishment, as it was for murder. Finally, to emphasize the government's determination to reduce crime, it was decided that serious cases of theft or murder would in future be tried in the military rather than civil courts. Henceforth, the commander general of each military district would be the final judge of appeal, and the delays endemic in the civil judicial system, it was hoped, would be eliminated.[73]

Property owners and *hombres de bien* in general were encouraged to contribute to their own protection. An earlier measure which had created a kind of middle-class militia for the Federal District was reintroduced, and all householders and businessmen were ordered to enlist, or nominate a substitute who was competent in the use of firearms.[74] In addition, householders were urged to pay for guards to patrol the streets where they lived. The nightwatchmen, or *guarda-serenos,* who were already employed by some were not, it was suggested, to be trusted, for they were not all '*hombres de bien* in the full meaning of the word'. New recruits should be carefully selected and paid 10 reales a night by residents.[75] The municipal authorities were asked to improve their own security patrols, and a constant theme in all the press was the need to set up a properly organized and well-funded police force.

Educational and cultural initiatives were also introduced. The liberals' reforms of the education system were cancelled and the University of

71 *Memoria de Justicia* (1835).
72 Decree of 23 November 1835, in *Diario del Gobierno,* 25 November 1835.
73 Decrees in *Diario del Gobierno,* 8 November 1835.
74 *El Sol,* 8 May 1835.
75 Editorial in *Diario del Gobierno,* 26 November 1835.

Mexico and other colleges reopened. New regulations for the university were quickly produced in an attempt to stop the spread of so-called heretical ideas in all fields. Professors were told that their courses must reflect 'our situation and customs' and be illustrated with 'ancient and modern classical authors, omitting those points which are not in accord with the religion, customs and politics of our country'.[76] The Institute of Geography and Statistics, formed in 1833 but inactive because of the political situation, was reconstituted. The Academies of History and Language were founded, and the list of members illustrates not only that there was social cohesion among *hombres de bien* regardless of their political affiliations but that intellectual interests and achievements were considered necessary attributes of successful politicians. Thus, the names of conservatives like Alamán, Sánchez de Tagle and Basilio Arrillaga, a former Jesuit priest and passionate defender of Church prerogatives, appear alongside those of radicals like Mora and Zavala and, finally, Tornel, a founding member of both academies and currently Minister of War.[77]

With the propaganda battle won, Santa Anna side-tracked in Texas and Congress firmly in the control of conservatives, it seemed that all that remained in the transition to a centralized republic was the production of a new constitutional charter. But already other problems had begun to appear. What sort of constitution was it to be, what was the relationship to be between executive and Congress, what were to be the powers of institutions such as the Church and army, what role were the states to be given, how was the sacred sovereignty of the people to be safeguarded and expressed? These and many other issues were still to be resolved before the centralized republic could be created.

76 The new *reglamento* for the university was published on 16 February 1835; the full text is in Dublín and Lozano, *Legislación mexicana*, vol. 3, pp. 20–2.
77 The full list of members of both Academies and the Institute of Geography and Statistics is in ibid., pp. 13–14, 35–7.

4

The transition to centralism: stage II

On 6 February 1836, José Bernardo Couto, senator for Veracruz, wrote to his exiled friend, Mora, who had retreated to Paris after the fall of the Gómez Farías administration.[1] Couto, together with other friends, took the trouble to write often to keep him up to date with the political and other changes that were taking place during his absence. He explained the latest developments and his own sense of disillusion, which had reached the point that he no longer bothered to attend the Senate. In 1834, he wrote, a coalition of people and opposing interests had been formed to bring about the downfall of the radicals but that had been the only common objective. Once it was achieved, it became clear that there were no firm ideas or plans for the future, and when discussion began on what was to replace the radical programme, 'everyone has a plan of his own'. Hence, when the issue of the form of government arose and the destruction of the federal charter became certain, many people abandoned the coalition to form a 'mass of deserters who are wandering about, not knowing what to join'.

When Mora received this letter from Couto, he was in the process of writing his own analysis of the political situation which he was to publish in Paris the following year.[2] Using the information from Couto and other correspondents, he summarized the party political situation as follows. There were four main groups or classes. First, there were the clergy and military, the largest and strongest group, whose objective was to establish within a representative framework something akin to the colonial system. Second, there were the defeated federalists, whose political programme was much the same as that of Gómez Farías. Third, there were the moderates, including the former *escoceses* who favoured retaining a modified version of the federation. Finally, there were Santa Anna and his sup-

---

1 García, *Documentos inéditos,* vol. 60, 'Papeles inéditos del Dr. Mora', pp. 525–7.
2 Mora, *Obras sueltas,* pp. 5–172.

porters, who were mostly ambitious army officers with no known programme and whose sole ambition was personal advancement and fortune.[3]

Mora's work has become the basis of most liberal interpretations of the Age of Santa Anna, but while the general lines of his analysis seem to be accurate, his assessment of the situation is an oversimplification and, in several respects, misleading. His insistence that a military/clerical oligarchy had taken control of the country is by no means correct. The strongest political force certainly appeared to be the clergy, and given that the campaign against the liberals had been fought under the slogan 'Religion and Privileges', it was not surprising that the bishops and their supporters confidently expected that the Church would once again be restored to its position of privilege and influence. Their confidence also reflected the fact that the clerical group was the most prominent in Congress and included the highly articulate and active former Jesuit Basilio Arrillaga. In addition, there were lay deputies and senators who were very much proclerical and who believed in the need for a strong Church as the essential regulator of social customs and practice. Among the latter was Carlos Bustamante, who was always ready to defend the clerical interests. Other powerful figures who had personal reasons to support the Church included President Barragán, who early in 1836 asked for and was granted a personal loan of 4,000 pesos from the Church's finance office, or Juzgado de Capellanías.[4] In the country at large, the main Church spokesman was the bishop of Puebla, Pablo Vázquez, who was said to have considerable influence in the corridors of power, even on the appointment of cabinet ministers.[5]

The Church, therefore, was exceptionally well represented in the political sphere and expected to use its strength to influence the new constitution in its favour and to halt the all too evident decline it had suffered since independence. A steady decrease in its revenues since the beginning of the century had left it short of ready cash, and with the liberal law of 1833 abolishing the civil obligation to pay tithes, it looked as if its financial situation would deteriorate even further. Even more serious, and in part a consequence of the declining revenues, was a severe shortage of clergy. By 1835, four of the ten dioceses in the country – Mexico, Oaxaca, Guadalajara, Chiapas – were vacant and in a fifth – Sonora – the incumbent bishop was gravely ill. The cathedral chapters had been decimated – the archdiocese of Mexico had only four canons out of an establishment of

3 Ibid., pp. 158–9.
4 The documents on Barragán's loan are in Archivo General de la Nación (Mexico), Papeles de Bienes Nacionales (henceforth referred to as AGN, PBN), leg. 685.
5 Marcos de Esparza to Luis G. Gordoa, 8 December 1840, Correspondencia de Luis Gonzaga Gordoa, García Collection, folder 27A (3).

more than twenty – and in some cases had almost ceased to function. At the parish level, several regions, for example, Sonora and Durango, had almost no priests, and even in the more populated central areas, many parishes were vacant. In Puebla there were almost 10 per cent fewer priests than there had been in 1830, and in Michoacán the reduction was almost 30 per cent over the same period. The same picture of decline was to be seen in the religious orders, where the number of monks and nuns had fallen by almost 25 per cent since 1829.[6]

The immediate political aims of the clerical group were obvious: to stop the decline in the number of Church personnel and to increase the Church's revenues, especially with the restoration of the tithe. Neither aim, however, was to be achieved because of a long-standing dispute over the question of ecclesiastical patronage and the view which moderate conservatives held of the future role and status of the Church in a central republic. The controversy over patronage had begun soon after independence, and the essence of the dispute is summarized by Mecham: 'Do the republics inherit the patronal rights previously exercised by the Spanish Crown? The regalists said Yes, the canonists said No'.[7] The canonists, or ultramontanists, argued that the patronal rights of the Spanish Crown over the Church ended the moment Mexico became independent, whereas the regalists maintained that either as sovereign heir to the Spanish Crown or as sovereign in its own right, Mexico possessed patronal rights over all its churches and related ecclesiastical institutions. This is not the place to elaborate on the intellectual arguments in favour of or against either view.[8] What mattered in 1835 was the key aspect of patronal rights, namely, the right of presentation to ecclesiastical benefices or, to put it more simply, the appointment of priests. The Church claimed that with the end of the colonial patronage, the process of appointment reverted entirely to itself, whereas the regalists insisted that the final decision on appointments rested with the State.

As already indicated, in the aftermath of the fall of Gómez Farías, Santa Anna had adopted an ambivalent posture towards the liberals' laws on clerical appointments and the issue of national patronage. In what he called a 'Memoir to Posterity', an anonymous canon in the metropolitan cathedral recorded that he and his colleagues sought an interview with the president and asked him to restore to their posts those prebendaries who had been dismissed as a result of the liberal legislation.[9] Santa Anna

6 *Memoria de Justicia* (1835).
7 J. L. Mecham, *Church and State in Latin America* (rev. ed., Chapel Hill, N.C., 1966), pp. 3–4.
8 For a more detailed discussion of the patronage issue, see my *Church and State*.
9 'Memoria que un individuo del cabildo eclesiástico de la catedral de México presenta a la posteridad', 1834, AGN, PBN, leg. 200, exp. 2.

had replied that he would consider their request but he had done nothing. The chapter renewed its pressure on him, sending on 10 August a strongly worded representation, and other bishops and chapters submitted similar demands. While in some states the deposed canons were restored to their posts by the new civil and military authorities, Santa Anna still equivocated and would not commit himself on the general point. As the canon noted, 'For reasons of high politics, the government did not accede to the wishes of the churches or the people, leaving the matter pending for the deliberations of the general congress'.

Santa Anna maintained this policy of equivocation throughout the final months of 1834. Although he had revoked sanctions against individual clergy and suspended the effects of some of the liberal laws, he insisted he would not repeal them on the grounds that he lacked the constitutional power to do so. The clerical lobby had to await the assembly of the new Congress, and once that was in session, attention was soon given to the question of clerical appointments. Carlos Bustamante, described as a 'very pious man, much attached to the ecclesiastical estate',[10] promptly proposed that those canons who had been dismissed should be restored to their posts, and after committee reports were made his proposal was approved by the deputies by a vote of 46 in favour to 3 against. After approval in the Senate by a similar margin, the appropriate law was issued on 1 April 1835.[11]

Other liberal measures affecting the Church were also soon repealed, and it seemed that the Congress with its large clerical presence was allying itself to the clerical viewpoint. It was soon evident that the executive did not share this attitude. Its views at first seemed contradictory. On 7 January 1835, it forwarded an initiative to Congress through the senior clerk and acting Minister of Justice, Joaquín de Iturbide, calling for the derogation of the two liberal laws on clerical appointments of 17 December 1833 and 22 April 1834.[12] In due course, again on 1 April, the laws were declared null and void, and until a concordat was negotiated the bishops and senior clergy were to appoint parish priests in accordance with an earlier law of 22 April 1829 whereby the civil authorities retained only the right to exclude candidates.[13] This apparently pro-Church attitude of the executive on the matter of clerical appointments was soon belied by its actions in private. Again the anonymous canon in the cathedral recorded the details. By January 1835, the metropolitan chapter was administering the Sonora diocese because the recently consecrated

10 Ibid.
11 The law was published in *Diario del Gobierno*, 3 April 1835.
12 The text of the initiative is in B. Arrillaga, *Examen crítico de la memoria del Ministerio de Justicia y Negocios Eclesiásticos leída en las cámaras de la unión el año de 1835* (Mexico, 1835).
13 *Diario del Gobierno*, 3 April 1835.

bishop, Angel Morales, was ill. The acting governor of the see died in December 1834, and news of this reached the capital about the middle of January. After private consultations with Bishop Morales, the metropolitan chapter agreed to appoint José Nicolás Quirós y Medina as the new acting governor. A few days later, the government learned of these events and strongly urged the chapter to appoint another person. Various notes were exchanged, with the government insisting that the appointment proposed was unacceptable because it had been made without its approval. The chapter refused to give way and eventually the government dropped the matter.

This insistence in private on its patronal power of presentation contradicted the executive's position implied in the initiative calling for the repeal of the liberal laws on the appointment of parish priests. The confusion was soon resolved on 4 February when Iturbide presented to Congress the annual report of his department.[14] He proceeded to make a detailed defence of national patronage, which, he claimed, had long since been recognized. The government's desire to revoke the liberal measures reflected its acknowledgement that the laws were 'impolitic and inopportune', but he wanted to remind the public and the clergy that the possession and exercise of national patronage had been established. At the same time, he did not want it to be thought that the government considered papal authorization to be useless or unnecessary. On the contrary, Congress had ordered the government to seek such an authorization in 1827 and that instruction would be obeyed. A new envoy to Rome would soon be appointed, but even so, the government expected the clergy to recognize its right to make ecclesiastical appointments.

According to one eye-witness, the reaction of the deputies to Iturbide's speech was one of astonishment and disbelief.[15] Taken completely by surprise by such a hostile attitude to the Church and its claimed status, they decided not to allow the customary publication of the report until it could be given further consideration. News of what had transpired, however, soon leaked out. On the next day, 5 February, an anonymous letter in a newspaper criticized the attacks made on the report and denounced the decision not to publish it as tantamount to a return to absolutism. Two days later, Basilio Arrillaga promised in the same paper to produce a refutation of everything that Iturbide had alleged.[16] Meanwhile, the debates on the repeal of the liberal legislation began in secret sessions of Congress, and Iturbide, although he had been replaced as

14 *Memoria de Justicia* (1835).
15 Arrillaga, *Examen crítico*, p. 8.
16 *El Sol*, 5 and 7 February 1835. The letter in the issue of 7 February is unsigned, but Iturbide named Arrillaga as the author in a letter published in the same paper on 11 February 1835.

minister, continued to oppose any attempts to renounce the principle of national patronage.[17] His views were supported in a series of editorials in the official government newspaper.[18] Then, despite congressional opposition, he was able to have his report published in May and the government paper printed extracts of it in July.[19]

Iturbide's arguments, of course, did not go unanswered. Arrillaga duly produced a long essay in which he presented the ultramontanist case, but despite the strength of the clerical group in Congress and a vigorous propaganda campaign to put its case, the Church lost the battle over the patronage.[20] The government did not renounce its claims, and Iturbide's premise that de facto patronage had been established became official policy and was steadfastly maintained in the future. Similarly, there was no restriction on the extent of the powers claimed. The full patronal attributes formerly held by the Spanish Crown remained the national objective.

The Church also lost the next battle to be fought over the issue of the tithe. A tax of approximately 10 per cent on agricultural produce, the tithe had for generations been a rich source of income for the dioceses, in particular the bishops and chapters, who took half the total yield between them. Since the early years of the sixteenth century, payment of the tax had been enforced by the civil authorities, and although it was an extremely unpopular tax with landowners and others, no government had taken any steps to abolish or restrict its collection. Then Gómez Farías, while not abolishing the tax, removed the civil coercion to pay, and henceforth it was left to the conscience or other motives of the faithful whether to hand it over to the Church collectors. In other words, it became a voluntary contribution. The bishops knew perfectly well that most people in future would not pay and that what was in effect the main source of income for the Church would disappear, as indeed happened. While the issue of the patronage was a matter of principle, the tithe was an urgent practical matter which had to be resolved. Pressure to have it reinstated as an obligatory tax was immediately applied, and in some states it was successful; in both Puebla and Oaxaca, for example, the governors repealed the liberal law. At the national level, however, the government consistently refused to initiate legislation to revert to the status quo.[21] The tithe law became the one major piece of liberal legislation

---

17 'Memoria a la posteridad'. Bustamante said that debates on Iturbide's report lasted many days and that Iturbide was so harassed by the attacks on him that he resigned as acting minister; *Continuación del cuadro histórico*, vol. 4, 377.

18 *Diario del Gobierno*, 22–6 March 1835; *El Sol*, 2 April 1835.

19 *Diario del Gobierno*, 6 July 1835.

20 Arrillaga, *Examen crítico;* C. Portugal, *Pastoral*, 2 February 1835.

21 *La nación no quiere diezmos* (Mexico, 1835).

to remain on the statute book, and all the efforts of the clerical party in and out of Congress failed to have it removed.

There are several reasons why Santa Anna, Barragán and their successors refused to meet the Church's demands. As indicated, the tax was very unpopular, and just as the conservatives were presenting their manifesto and promises of better things to come under a centralist regime, they had no wish to alienate the country's landowners. Even more important, however, was another, more subtle and at the time secret reason related to the patronage issue. The government's position, always rejected by the Church, was that national patronage had been established, but as a kind of compromise, it declared that it would not use the patronal powers until authorized to do so by the Papacy. Iturbide had indicated that a new envoy to Rome would soon be appointed and in September 1835, Díez de Bonilla, Minister of State from July to October, was appointed to the post. His instructions included the following: to negotiate a concordat in which the Papacy 'should authorize in the nation the exercise of the patronage with the same powers as used by the kings of Spain'; to obtain a reduction in the size of the tithe to half or less of what it had previously been, extending its collection to all kinds of produce to spread the burden of payment more widely; and to establish that the tithe revenue would be used for the general costs of worship so that parochial fees could be abolished. If agreement on these points could be reached, the government in return would give the protection needed for the collection of tithes.[22]

In short, the main reason the government did not revoke the liberal law on tithes was that it intended to use the reimposition of civil coercion as a bargaining counter in negotiations with the Papacy over the patronage. Bonilla went to negotiate on that basis, and at first the talks in Rome appeared to make some progress with the Cardinal Secretary of State 'very disposed to accede to the point, if he could be sure of the guarantee for their effective collection'.[23] After more protracted discussions, the talks stalled largely over patronage, which the Papacy refused to authorize, and the government eventually instructed Bonilla to withdraw the offer to reimpose the tithe. Thus, the liberal law remained in force, and as the clergy had predicted, most former payers refused to pay and Church revenues suffered another major blow.

The clergy and their supporters had lost on the two major issues of patronage and the tithe. It was clear that while a respected and privileged Church would continue and Roman Catholicism would remain the ex-

22 These details are taken from an unsigned memorandum written on official Ministry of Justice paper and almost certainly by the Minister, dated 18 October 1845 and addressed to the Council of State. The manuscript is in AGN, Justicia Eclesiástica, vol. 15, fols. 242–51.
23 Letter published in J. Ramírez Cabañas, *Las relaciones entre México y el Vaticano* (Mexico, 1928), pp. 169–71.

clusive religion of the State, the conservative forces now in power did not intend, as Mora alleged, to create a priestly oligarchy. What Alamán, Sánchez de Tagle, Juan Manuel Elizalde and other conservatives sought was to centralize power in their own social class throughout the country. In essence, they wanted a return to what they fondly remembered as the social stability of colonial society, but in that society the Church had been a subordinate institution subject to the will of the secular head of State. In the minds of the more moderate conservatives, that was to continue to be the clerical status in their centralist republic, and despite the fury of senior clergy and their ultramontanist supporters in Congress, they kept to the regalist principle of State supremacy. Although on many issues diametrically opposed to them, the *escoceses* and moderate federalists led by José María and José Francisco Fagoaga, Gutiérrez Estrada, Felipe and Rafael Barrio, Manuel Gómez Pedraza, Sebastián Camacho and others shared the same opinions on Church matters. Finally, Santa Anna and his supporters in the military likewise had no wish to see the Church as a rival power to the army or to have an entirely unfettered clergy able to use their pulpits and still profound influence on the population as a whole to intervene too actively and openly in the political sphere.[24]

There was, therefore, a coalescence of interests among the rival political groups on the role and future status of the Church, and the clerical lobby found that despite its strength in Congress and its influence in the country at large, it was isolated in the ranks of the *hombres de bien*. Hence, when the new centralist constitution was eventually published on 30 December 1836, it was at once clear that in most respects its clauses on Church affairs were very similar to those of its federal predecessor. For example, Congress retained the right to approve concordats, and the government still had the power to admit or refuse entry to papal bulls.[25] The clergy did retain their own judicial *fuero* and Roman Catholicism remained the exclusive faith, but there was one new and significant clause.[26] Among the specific attributes of the president was that of presenting candidates for all 'bishoprics, dignitaries and ecclesiastical benefices which may pertain to national patronage'. Although the exercise of this power was to

24 All governments tried to use parish priests to influence public opinion; sometimes the clergy cooperated and sometimes not. In a circular to his parish priests on 11 February 1835, Bishop Vázquez urged 'que en el confesionario, en el púlpito y en sus conversaciones privadas' – they should persuade their parishioners not to take part in a revolt; for the text of the circular, see *La Lima de Vulcano*, 24 February 1835. The metropolitan chapter similarly promised to instruct priests to make sure that their parishioners understood that the Texans were rebels; see *Diario del Gobierno*, 25 November 1835.

25 The clause on the *pase real* caused a heated debate in Congress, where the clerical deputies acted in unison in a vain attempt to defeat it; *El Nacional*, 20 April 1836; *El Cosmopolita*, 14 May 1836.

26 Cuarta ley, art. 17, sec. 25. I have used the text of the constitution given in Tena Ramírez, *Leyes fundamentales de México*, pp. 202–48.

be 'subject to the concordat with the Holy See', there is no doubt that
the legislators intended this clause to be an assertion of the national rights
of patronage over the Church. Finally, one other article was ominous for
the clergy. On the basis of an article of the 1824 charter but now much
more specific, the government was given the right, if national need could
be established, to confiscate property, including that owned by ecclesiastical corporations.[27] With the national Treasury empty, the implied
threat to the wealth of the Church, soon to become a reality, was obvious.

The Church, therefore, did not do particularly well under the new
conservative regime, and the same ambivalent attitude was soon seen
towards the army. At least fifteen officers, including seven generals, served
as deputies or senators, and Congress quickly approved a number of
measures favourable to the military. Commander generals were authorized
to intervene in the distribution of Treasury funds in their areas to ensure
that army pay was given absolute priority over all other commitments.[28]
In some cases, civil and military authority was combined in the hands of
the local commander, and a whole range of orders were issued to improve
recruitment, discipline and administration.[29] The civic militia, of course,
was effectively suppressed, and then with the Zacatecas and, more important, the Texas campaign imminent, the army had and used the opportunity to promote its own interests even further. While his reputation
was still intact, Santa Anna used the Texas situation to heap praise on
the army and to demand more men and resources. Permission was duly
given to recruit an additional four thousand soldiers, and more promotions
were announced, including two new brigadier-generals in the persons of
Colonel Ignacio Mora y Villamil and Colonel Eulogio Villaurrutia.[30] Santa
Anna also ensured that officers he thought loyal to himself were placed
in strategic commands. General Vázquez continued at Veracruz, Toro
stayed on at Yucatán and a rising newcomer on the national scene, Paredes,
was given the command at Jalisco. Knowing or believing that they were
indispensable in the political and military circumstances of the time, the
commanders took full advantage of their renewed prestige. Opponents of
the government were subjected to summary arrest, and distinguished
political leaders found they were not immune from the whims of the local
commander. For example, Manuel Crescencio Rejón, a prominent member
of several previous Congresses and ardent federalist *escocés*, had to endure
a forced entry and search of his home by soldiers at 1 a.m.[31] At Veracruz,
Vázquez ruled in such an arbitrary fashion that the wives and families of

27 Primera ley, art. 2, sec. 3, Tena Ramírez, *Leyes fundamentales*, p. 205.
28 Decree of 29 January 1835 in Dublán and Lozano, *Legislación mexicana*, vol. 3, pp. 16–17.
29 *La Oposición*, 22 June 1835.
30 *El Sol*, 18 February, 3 May 1835.
31 *El Cosmopolita*, 23 January 1836.

men he had jailed waged a public campaign to have him removed, and after the fall of Santa Anna, they were successful.[32] At Zacatecas, it was reported that the military were acting like conquerors: 'The difference established between the military and the other classes is very noticeable, so much so that it seems that the military class consists of individuals who are not Mexican'.[33]

Ironically, the favoured status of the army was strengthened even further by Santa Anna's defeat in Texas because all political parties (and the Texas issue was one of the few on which there was some degree of unity) agreed that the state must be reconquered. It was recognized that despite the large expenditure and the theoretical number of soldiers, the army was nevertheless weak and incapable of mounting a sustained campaign in the north. Hence, an array of new taxes, largely on property, was announced, always on the pretext of re-equipping the army. Contracts for uniforms and matériel were signed, ships and supplies were bought from the United States and munitions were purchased from England. Military expenditure rose rapidly and soon exceeded the Treasury's revenue. The Minister of Hacienda reported to Congress that income was running at 430,000 pesos a month, while normal expenditure on the army amounted to 600,000 pesos a month, to which an additional 200,000 pesos monthly had to be raised for the proposed Texas campaign. There were also large sums due on contracts Santa Anna had signed as he prepared his expedition. The Minister concluded, 'I leave the political and economic influence of the present state of affairs to the perceptive consideration of the august congress'.[34]

The predominance, political and financial, and the favoured status of the military did not mean that the army was exempt from criticism. The opposition press was always quick to point out the discrepancy between expenditure and results.[35] There were, it was frequently said, far too many officers both serving and retired – there were thirteen divisional generals and eighteen brigadier-generals whose official pay cost a total of 159,000 pesos per year – and as for all the additional expenditure on the Texas campaign, where was it all going? 'How many units are there in Texas?

32 'Representación que varias señoras de la ciudad de Jalapa elevan al señor gobernador, quejándose de los excesos del comandante general de Veracruz, D. Ciriaco Vázquez', 17 January 1836, in ibid., 23 January 1836.
33 Cayetano? [illegible] to V. Gómez Farías, 4 July 1836, García Collection, Gómez Farías Papers, no. 384.
34 Memorandum of Ministry of Hacienda to Congress, 12 April 1836, in *El Cosmopolita,* 20 April 1836.
35 To improve its image, the army began its own periodical, which seems to have had four issues in 1835 and 1836. Entitled *Aurora, Periódico Científico y Militar,* it was edited by Colonel Ignacio de Mora. The opening article was 'Necesidad del Ejército'.

How much is the monthly budget?'[36] The arbitrary actions of the commander generals around the country were denounced, and when Colonel Francisco García Conde, already a deputy in Congress, was appointed governor of the Federal District, it was asked, 'Is it only among military and clerical deputies that there are men worthy to fill this post?'[37] Even the Minister of War, Tornel, was not reluctant to voice criticism. In May 1835, he reminded the army that its role did not include intervention in political affairs, and later, arguing the case for primary education facilities to be set up in all military units, he insisted that the level of literacy in recruits was unacceptably low and the cause of much public contempt.[38] In the annual report of his Ministry, he was even more critical of recruitment practices. The army, he said, had been used as a prison to which the authorities, ignoring the correct practice of selection by lottery, had conscripted criminals, vagabonds and the dregs of society. Military discipline and morale had inevitably suffered and desertion was an ever-growing problem.[39]

In several respects, it is difficult to explain Tornel's criticism of the army. A general himself, although in reality a full-time politician for most of his career since independence, he was, as already noted, Santa Anna's most loyal ally and as such it was presumed that he spoke with his approval. Certainly, he favoured a strong and privileged army, and he promoted many changes in its organization and administration, again presumably with no objection from Santa Anna. But Tornel was no mere puppet, and throughout his earlier career, he had used his powers and influence as governor of the Federal District or as a deputy in Congress to promote reforms in several areas. He was also an *hombre de bien* in his more general social attitudes, and from his provincial origins at Jalapa, he had quickly risen to become an accepted member of the social elite in the capital. Thus, although a senior army officer, he seems to have shared the views of the civilian majority in Congress and in the political sphere at large that a military oligarchy or dictatorship was undesirable. He was to change his opinions within a few years, as so many others were to do, but for the time being, he was quite willing to warn Congress that 'the military aristocracy is the most dangerous of all'.[40]

Just as the conservatives and centralists, therefore, were unwilling to see an ecclesiastical oligarchy in their new republic, so they were opposed

---

36 The number of generals is given in *Diario del Gobierno*, 3 November 1835. The questions were asked in *El Cosmopolita*, 4 May 1836.

37 *El Cosmopolita*, 19 October 1836.

38 Decrees of 31 May and 3 September 1835, Dublán and Lozano, *Legislación mexicana*, vol. 3, pp. 54–5, 66–70.

39 *Memoria de Guerra* (1835), also published in *El Sol*, 12–27 April 1835.

40 Ibid.

to undue power being given to the army. But they were pragmatists, and they recognized that sudden reductions in military expenditure, personnel or privileges were dangerous and, especially after the defeat in Texas, politically impossible. On the other hand, they opposed Santa Anna's attempt to manoeuvre himself into a dictator's chair, and when the question of the military *fuero* was debated in the context of the new constitution, there was a serious attempt to restrict it. A congressional committee proposed that the special higher military court be abolished and that henceforth cases involving persons entitled to the military *fuero* be heard in the higher civil court.[41] The generals at once reacted angrily and menacingly. Melchor Múzquiz, president of the military tribunal, submitted a lengthy memorandum opposing the idea, and Valencia, commander general of Mexico, warned that it was a blatant attack on the rights of the army.[42] It was extremely dangerous, he added, and could well open the door to a 'devastating anarchy'.[43] Once again, it was left to Tornel to advise Congress of the government's view. He defended the *fuero* as a necessary and justified privilege earned by the army in the long war of independence, and he repeated his earlier view that neither the time nor circumstances were appropriate for any change. What the government wanted established in the constitution was a new Supreme Military Court staffed by senior military personnel which would enforce the *fuero*.[44]

The executive's opposition, allied to that of the generals, was enough to ensure that no innovations were made in the military *fuero,* and in the new constitution, both it and its ecclesiastical equivalent were clearly confirmed. Article 32 of the fifth law states, 'There will be no personal *fueros* except the ecclesiastic and the military', and when this clause was debated in Congress, it was overwhelmingly approved by a vote of 61 in favour and only 3 against.[45]

It is tempting to think that the election of José Justo Corro as interim president on 27 February 1836 was a reflection of the general mistrust of the army. Corro was a lawyer by training and the first civilian to be elected to the office since independence.[46] His election was occasioned by

---

41 *Diario del Gobierno,* 12 September 1836.
42 M. Múzquiz, 'Exposición del supremo tribunal de guerra y marina sobre los inconvenientes que resultarían de la adopción del art. 14 del proyecto de la quinta ley constitucional, presentada por su respectiva comisión al soberano congreso de la república sobre erijirse en corte marcial la suprema actual de justicia, suprimiendo el tribunal militar', 22 August 1836, in *Diario del Gobierno,* 12 September 1836.
43 G. Valencia to J. M. Tornel, 1 September 1836, in ibid.
44 J. M. Tornel to Secretaries of Congress, 7 September 1836, in ibid.
45 Congressional record 25 September 1836, in ibid.
46 The minor exception was José María Bocanegra, who served as president for about six days from 18 to 23 December 1829.

the resignation of Barragán, who died shortly afterwards, and with Santa Anna still away in Texas a second interim president was required to serve the remainder of the term until April 1837, or until Santa Anna himself returned. As always, a number of possible candidates were floated in the press, including Alamán, Valencia, Tornel, Bravo, General Joaquín Parres and General Manuel Rincón. Since Barragán's illness was unexpected, there seems to have been no time for any campaigning, and when Congress met for the election, the main dispute was over voting procedures. In the end, there were three serious candidates – Corro, Bravo and Parres – and when the votes were counted, Corro won with 51 votes against 18 for Bravo and 12 for Parres.[47]

Corro was aged 42, from Guadalajara and a relatively unknown figure on the political stage. He had been Minister of Justice since May 1835 and was apparently very devout and proclerical in his views. Bancroft describes him as a 'man of excessive piety and timidity and utterly ignorant of military affairs'.[48] According to Mora, his election was a triumph for the clerical faction in Congress, although as already explained, it does not seem to have brought much benefit to the Church.[49] For the press, he was an acceptable choice, and even the opposition papers acknowledged, at first, that he enjoyed a reputation as an honest and honourable public servant.[50] He was also, however, alleged to be weak and indecisive, and throughout most of his year in office the man believed to be in control of the government was Tornel, who continued in his post as Minister of War.[51]

Unusually, Corro made no cabinet changes. His own replacement as Minister of Justice was again Joaquín de Iturbide, whose advocacy of national patronage had previously cost him the job. José María Ortíz Monasterio continued as Minister of State for Internal and Foreign Affairs, and Rafael Mangino, who had been appointed on 3 February, was confirmed in office. Mangino was a native of Puebla and had long experience of fiscal matters in various posts since 1821, including a spell as Minister from 1830 to 1832. During that period, he had acquired a reputation for fiscal conservatism, and much of the credit for the relatively successful economic policy of the government at that time was accorded to him.

Mangino's appointment was evidently made in the hope of finding a

47 Details from *El Cosmopolita*, 27 February 1836. Rafael Mangino also received one vote.
48 Prieto, *Memorias*, vol. 2, p. 209; Bancroft, *History of Mexico*, vol. 5, p. 178. Bancroft was probably quoting Mariano Chico, who in a letter published in *El Cosmopolita*, 18 March 1837, described Corro as 'timorato católico, débil político y nulo militar'.
49 Mora, *Obras sueltas*, pp. 160–5.
50 *El Voto Nacional*, 9 March 1836; *El Cosmopolita*, 16 April 1836. Sierra describes him as 'un abogado circunspecto y de buenas intenciones'; J. Sierra, *Evolución política del pueblo mexicano* (Mexico, 1948), p. 216.
51 Mora, *Obras sueltas*, p. 165.

solution to a rapidly worsening fiscal and economic situation which was becoming increasingly intrusive on the political scene. In the often long and detailed accounts of this time by such contemporaries as Carlos Bustamante, Malo, Arrangoiz, Mora, Alamán, Tornel and Zavala, there is scant reference to economic policy. To a large extent, this reflects the fact that political and constitutional affairs had hitherto been given priority, but now with the fall of the radicals, their replacement by *hombres de bien* and the end of federalism, the state of the national economy and especially the fiscal crisis at both national and provincial levels assumed much greater importance. Furthermore, dramatic changes were taking place in some industries, notably textiles, with the advent of mechanization, and for the first time on any scale, 'merchants, shopkeepers, public officials and clerics became directly involved with the manufacturing process'.[52] This change of priorities had been emphasized in the conservative manifesto throughout 1835, which had promised that one of the main benefits of centralism would be an improved and, above all, consistent economic policy. Presenting his annual report to Congress on 22 May 1835, Minister of Hacienda José Mariano Blasco declared, 'The need for reforms is, therefore, beyond question' and he pledged that the government would make changes. Administrative costs would be brought under control; no more public-sector jobs would be created; restrictions on industry and commerce would be removed; public income and expenditure would be brought into balance; the nation's credit-worthiness would be restored.[53]

The national fiscal situation was deteriorating almost daily, and as the Minister informed Congress, revenues were far short of what was needed to meet current expenditure. The normal demands of the army and the additional costs arising from the Texas campaign meant that other government commitments could not be met. Public-sector salaries were not being paid, pensioners were being left destitute and dividends on the foreign debt could not be honoured. An added complication was the continued issue of copper money, which was depreciating rapidly. The minting of copper coins had been started in 1814 by the Spanish viceroy, Félix María Calleja, in response to a growing shortage of gold and especially silver currency caused by the export of up to 75 per cent of the output of the Mexican mints.[54] The remaining years of the war of independence saw the continued haemorrhage of coins, and with the virtual destruction of the mining industry during the war, the early independent governments had little option but to continue to issue copper. In addition, as Thomson has pointed out, after independence most silver that was

52 Thomson, *Puebla de los Angeles*, p. 239.
53 'Memoria de Hacienda', in *Diario del Gobierno*, 24 November 1835.
54 For a good discussion of the copper coinage problem, see M. Gayón Córdova, 'Guerra, dictadura y cobre', pp. 63–5.

produced was minted close to the mining areas in the north and north west, and Guanajuato, Durango, Zacatecas and San Luis Potosí became the principal minting centres.[55] With many of the large-scale foreign import–export merchants basing themselves in the peripheral ports and provincial cities where the attraction was greater access to the limited silver supplies, the centre and south of the country were starved of silver coin. Counterfeiters promptly took advantage of the situation and flooded the market with the easily forged copper coins, and what had initially been a relatively small discount of 5 or 6 per cent rapidly rose by 1835 to more than 70 per cent. New issues of official coins had no effect, and demands in Congress in February 1835 to stop the minting did nothing to help as fears grew that the coins might be withdrawn.

The government failed, or was unable, to respond, and in the financial year from July 1834 to July 1835 the face value of coins issued amounted to more than 1 million pesos, or almost double the amount of the previous twelve months.[56] With something like 5 million to 6 million pesos worth of copper in circulation, public discontent mounted and manifested itself in various ways, sometimes violently. In Querétaro, for example, workers rioted and people were killed in fights over money.[57] In Mexico City, tenants refused to pay rents except in copper, arguing that that was all they received for their salaries and in their businesses, and when the government decreed that landlords must accept one-third of rents in copper, most tenants still refused to pay any silver.[58] Retailers such as butchers and bakers petitioned Congress for relief, saying that they could not pay taxes in silver because they received none from their customers.[59] Prices in the shops increased, and popular resentment of those speculators who managed to get hold of silver was heightened. The government was besieged with complaints, and eventually a committee was formed to see if a solution could be found. Alamán, who chaired the committee, wrote that a report had been concluded but that the government had done nothing and was unlikely even to suspend the issue of copper money. Meanwhile, he warned, the commercial and property-owning classes were being ruined.[60]

55 Thomson, *Puebla de los Angeles*, pp. 227–8.
56 Figures given in *El Cosmopolita*, 13 July 1836. This contains a table of the amounts issued each year since 1829.
57 L. Alamán to Duque de Terranova, 3 March 1837, in *Obras: Documentos diversos*, vol. 4, pp. 371–2.
58 Ibid., 28 June 1836, p. 344, and 3 August 1836, pp. 349–50.
59 *Representación que los dueños y administradores de las casas de matanza hacen al Soberano Congreso pidiendo que se derogue la ley que previene se paguen los derechos de la Hacienda Pública con dos terceras partes de plata y una de cobre* (Mexico, 1836).
60 L. Alamán to Duque de Terranova, 5 September 1836, in *Obras: Documentos diversos*, vol. 4, pp. 352–3. The Alamán committee report is in *Diario del Gobierno*, 28 August 1836. The

In fact, the government did react to the crisis early in 1837. On 17 January it ordered that no more copper coins were to be minted anywhere in the republic, and at the same time it announced the creation of a Banco Nacional de Amortización de moneda de cobre. The new Bank was allocated various state-owned assets and tax revenues and was authorized to raise a foreign loan of up to 4 million pesos. It was to use these assets to redeem the existing copper coins, whose owners were to be offered in exchange silver, new copper coins or bonds, depending on the Bank's liquidity. Three days later, a further decree announced regulations for the selection of a board of directors.[61]

On the same day the Bank was established, 17 January, Congress elected as its first president Pedro José Echeverría, a former senator and member of a wealthy landowning and merchant family. A few days later, the other directors were chosen: José Fernández de Celis (merchants), Ignacio Cortina Chávez (landowners), Manuel Posadas (Church), Francisco Fagoaga (miners).[62] The board began its work immediately but inspired no confidence in the public at large or in those who had copper money. Rumours began to spread that copper coins were to be devalued and by early March panic began to set in. Producers refused to bring their food supplies into the capital and shopkeepers kept their doors shut.[63] Government orders that shops be opened were ignored, and basic foodstuffs, particularly bread and meat, became almost unobtainable. On 8 March the rumours proved to be well-founded when a 50 per cent devaluation was decreed.[64] Prices immediately soared and the poor took to the streets in protest. A mass demonstration in the central square denounced foreigners for causing the crisis, but to the alarm of the authorities the demonstrators also began to shout, 'Long live federalism'. Troops that were called out to disperse the crowds opened fire, causing untold casualties.[65] Meetings of more than five persons were banned and no one except the military was allowed to ride on horseback. Shopkeepers were again ordered to open and to accept copper or risk a fine of 200 pesos, and butchers and bakers were urged to reduce their prices to the levels at which they had been before the devaluation.[66] Similar events occurred in some other prov-

committee recommended the immediate end to all minting of copper money and the amortization of the estimated 6 million pesos in circulation within four years.

61 Decrees in Dublán and Lozano, Legislación mexicana, vol. 3, pp. 260–5.
62 Congressional sessions in Diario del Gobierno, 15, 23 and 24 January 1837.
63 Anon., 'Diario político y militar', 1836–7, 9 March 1837 entry, García Collection, p. 441.
64 Dublán and Lozano, Legislación mexicana, vol. 3, p. 302.
65 'Diario político y militar', 9 March entry.
66 Orders of Luis Gonzaga Vieyra, governor of Mexico department, in Diario del Gobierno, 12 and 13 March 1837. El Mosquito Mexicano, 21 March 1837, reported massive public reaction against the devaluation and accused the government of deceit.

inces.[67] Alamán summarized the situation in a private letter on 3 April: 'Public poverty, therefore, is extreme'.[68]

The copper money crisis simply added to the government's growing problems, not just with the poor, who were hard hit by their loss of purchasing power and the rise in the prices of their basic foodstuffs, which was not helped by drought and poor harvests in 1836, but also with the middle-class *hombres de bien*. They too suffered from the shortage of silver and from the fact that the civil list salaries and pensions were rarely paid in cash, if at all. Even more damaging to all property owners was a series of new taxes and forced loans which the government introduced in an attempt to increase revenues both for the war effort in Texas and for general use. On 21 November 1835, all urban property owners were required to pay 1 per cent of the purchase price of their properties as an emergency war tax.[69] In theory, the payments were to be loans which would earn 6 per cent interest, and the government promised that the money would be repaid from revenues of a new tax to be levied on urban and rural property as well as on commercial establishments. A few months later, a direct tax on urban property was announced at the rate of 2 pesos per 1,000 value. This was followed by an equivalent levy on rural property at the rate of 3 pesos per 1,000 value, and two days later it was the turn of commerce.[70] Henceforth, all businesses of any type, both wholesale and retail, had to purchase a licence or permit in order to operate. The rates payable varied according to the nature of the business and its size. Wholesalers, for example, were assessed at 300 pesos, clothes shops at 100, cafés at 25, cakeshops, booksellers and ironmongers at 6, and for every table in the popular billiard halls, the levy was 15 pesos.

These new taxes failed to resolve the government's financial problems, yielding only 582,940 pesos, or 4.5 per cent of total tax receipts in their first year of operation.[71] Property owners and businessmen refused to pay or found ways of not doing so because, as the Minister of Hacienda remarked, of 'the custom established by our predecessors of not having citizens contribute directly to the public Treasury'.[72] With a long tradition of indirect taxation, particularly sales taxes and levies on trade, the concept of direct taxation of privately owned assets or private income was not something the *hombres de bien* expected from the conservative administra-

---

67 E.g., at Orizaba and Querétaro. See also the anonymous letter in *El Mosquito Mexicano*, 31 March 1837.
68 L. Alamán to Duque de Terranova, 3 April 1837, in *Obras: Documentos diversos*, vol. 4, pp. 373–4.
69 Dublán and Lozano, *Legislación mexicana*, vol. 3, pp. 102–5.
70 Decrees of 5 and 7 July 1836, ibid., pp. 176–85.
71 Tenenbaum, *Politics of Penury*, p. 48.
72 Quoted in ibid.

tion they themselves had put into power.[73] Moreover, one of the groups hardest hit was the clergy. As the largest single property-owning institution in the country, especially in the towns and cities, the Church had to bear the brunt of the new taxes. The convents, monasteries and other ecclesiastical bodies found that they were doubly penalized. This was because the laws allowed those with mortgages – and the Church was by far the largest mortgage lender – to deduct some of what they paid in taxes from the interest payments on their mortgage debts. Tenants of Church-owned houses, if they were military personnel or government employees whose salaries were not being paid, were excused from paying rent altogether, much to the annoyance of the clerical administrators.[74]

The propertied and commercial classes, therefore, found that even before their new centralist constitution was completed, there was a price to pay, and they soon discovered that taxation was not the government's only solution to the crisis. Even more controversial was the practice of securing loans, initially on a voluntary basis from financial speculators and entrepreneurs, and later as forced loans on everybody who was thought to have ready cash. Raising revenue by means of short-term loans was not a new practice. Governments from the 1820s onwards had begun to offer high-interest-bearing loans by which the lenders provided a proportion in cash and the rest in government credits. A very active market had developed in these pre- and postindependence bonds, and when public employees began to be paid in promissory notes, they entered the market, where they were exchanged for cash at whatever discount was offered. Prosperous merchants, both national and foreign, who had access to cash on their own account and to substantial sums in silver generated by the import–export cycle, quickly found that there was more money to be made in dealing with the Treasury than in the normal world of commerce. These men, who were known popularly as *agiotistas,* became the government's bankers, and as Tenenbaum has put it, 'the man with money to lend was king'.[75] A small group of *agiotistas* began to assume inordinate influence and prominence in the corridors of power, and public anger against the large profits some appeared to be making was soon manifest in the press and elsewhere.[76]

Some examples will illustrate what were very complex financial trans-

---

73 Previous administrations, beginning with Iturbide, had also tried to tax the property-owning classes heavily but with similar scant financial return; see T. E. Anna, *The Mexican Empire of Iturbide* (Lincoln, Neb., 1990), pp. 131–6.
74 Mayordomo de Santa Teresa la Antigua to Vicario de Religiosas, undated, 1837, AGN, PBN, leg. 648, exp. 16.
75 Tenenbaum, *Politics of Penury,* p. 61.
76 One periodical was largely devoted to exposing and attacking the activities of the *agiotistas* – *El Cardillo de los Agiotistas* (Mexico, 1837). For further details of the *agiotistas,* see Tenenbaum, *Politics of Penury.*

actions. In April 1835 a loan of 200,000 pesos per month for a maximum of six months was announced, and this was followed in November by another of 1 million pesos, again at 4 per cent for a term of five months.[77] As security, the government pledged its revenues from the Fresnillo silver mines. Thirty-five shareholders responded, including Manuel Escandón, who, although only 23 years old at the time, was emerging as one of the leading entrepreneurs and speculators.[78] Two weeks later another loan of 500,000 pesos was authorized, and on 8 February 1836 one of 600,000 pesos at 3 per cent per month.[79] The *agiotistas,* of course, were not philanthropists, and when offered participation in these loans, they wanted not only a high return in interest but also some firm assurance that their money would be returned. In April 1835, the government had insisted that in future lenders must offer at least 55 per cent in cash, but the lenders needed a carrot to persuade them to cooperate. To assure them that they would get their funds back, the government set up what was labelled the 'Fifteen Percent Fund' whereby 15 per cent of the customs revenue, not already allocated to repay previous debts, was earmarked to redeem the loans. Those *agiotistas* with influence and connections among the social and political elite were given priority; their credits were repaid first and often in cash.

Taxation and large-scale, expensive loans from speculators were still insufficient to meet the rising demands on the public purse. There were two other possibilities. The sale of assets was one, and the government began to look with increasing attention at the apparently enormous wealth in land and property of the Church. Expropriation of ecclesiastical holdings was for the time being politically impossible; even Santa Anna knew that any move in that direction would provoke instant retaliation by the clergy. Also, it was always possible, as long as the Church owned assets, to use them as collateral for loans and that would soon become a common practice. For the time being, the government was restricted to the sale of properties which had already been appropriated. The possessions of the Philippine missionaries, for example, were sold, with several of the best haciendas being acquired by General José María Cervantes, who had, coincidentally, loaned the government 50,000 pesos.[80]

The final option open to the government was to impose a general forced or obligatory loan on the affluent classes, and on 16 June 1836 such a measure was announced to the dismay and anger of *hombres de bien* in

77 Decrees of 27 April 1835, in *El Sol,* 3 May 1835 and 5 November 1835, in Dublán and Lozano, *Legislación mexicana,* vol. 3, pp. 95–6.
78 For information on the Escandón family and their business, see C. F. S. Cardoso, ed., *Formación y desarrollo de la burguesía en México* (Mexico, 1978), pp. 33–45.
79 Decrees in Dublán and Lozano, *Legislación mexicana,* vol. 3, pp. 106, 130.
80 Bazant, *Alienation of Church Wealth,* pp. 28–9.

general and conservative supporters in particular. The loan was to amount to 2 million pesos, consisting of four rates of payment according to means: 1,000 pesos, 500 pesos, 250 pesos, 100 pesos. The maximum of 1,000 pesos was payable by those with assets worth 50,000 pesos or more. Commercial establishments and, once again, ecclesiastical corporations were liable for assessment.[81]

In the capital, several hundred businesses and individuals were placed in the 1,000 peso category and the list provides a perhaps unique gallery of the city's wealthy residents.[82] Included were the leading families and merchants, such as Francisco and José Francisco Fagoaga, Felipe Neri del Barrio, Miguel Garibay, Antonio Garay, Francisco Iturbe and General Cervantes. Also, there was the metropolitan chapter, six *conventos* and four *cofradías*. Protests promptly followed. Manuel Escandón and his partners, who operated a recently established carriage company, complained that their business had been charged 1,000 pesos while at the same time most of the shareholders in it had also been assessed individually at that sum, meaning in effect that they were being taxed twice.[83] Foreign businessmen, notably British and French, complained bitterly, urging their respective ministers to protest.[84] José Francisco Fagoaga, a member of one of the wealthiest families in the country, announced that he would not pay unless forced to do so because he challenged the right of the executive to levy such an imposition. He also picked up a point already made in the opposition press that certain apparently favoured persons who were known to have money had not been included and, therefore, the tax was unfair and discriminatory. He queried the fact that neither the president nor any of the ministers were being asked to contribute.[85] The editor of *El Cosmopolita* had already noted the same inconsistency. On 6 July, he had asked for reasons for the exclusion of such obviously rich people as Santa Anna, Díez de Bonilla, General Ormachea, canons Madrid and Mendiola and presbyters Teodoro and José Orihuela, who owned several bakeries and other businesses.

The taxes on real estate and commerce, loans from speculators and the forced loan on individuals and businesses all reflected the critical situation facing the national Treasury, and that in turn was a reflection of widespread economic difficulties. As already noted in the introductory chapter, the impact of these, of course, was variable: the problems of the peripheral regions like Yucatán in the south and the Californias and elsewhere in

81 Dublán and Lozano, *Legislación mexicana*, vol. 3, pp. 166–7.
82 Lists of those required to pay were published in the press; see *El Cosmopolita*, 25 and 29 June 1836.
83 M. Escandón et al. to Minister of Hacienda, in *Diario del Gobierno*, 31 August 1836.
84 Tenenbaum, *Politics of Penury*, p. 61; Barker, *The French Experience in Mexico*, pp. 60–1.
85 J. F. Fagoaga to editors, 30 November 1836, in *El Cosmopolita*, 3 December 1836.

the north were different from those of the more central and more populated areas. Most of the agitation and complaints about the economy were to come from those involved in commerce in general and from particular industrial and agricultural producers such as mining, sugar, cotton, textiles and tobacco, and from those areas where these activities were important – Veracruz, Puebla, Oaxaca, Querétaro, Jalisco, Guanajuato and Zacatecas. In other distant or more remote and largely self-sufficient rural communities in which most Mexicans lived and which had never been integrated in the north–south networks of exchange or in the trade cycle between the pastoral and mining north and the manufacturing and grain-producing centre and south east, the recession seems to have had a much less direct impact. Nevertheless, although variable according to region and particular activity, for most contemporaries there was a general consensus that overall industrial and agricultural output was in decline and commerce was stagnant. Coatsworth has calculated that per capita income and productivity were falling relative to those of other nations and that colonial income levels were not to be surpassed until well into the Porfiriato.[86] Population growth was negligible, transport and communications remained primitive and, although companies were formed to promote railway construction, no real progress was made. The effects of rising prices and unemployment were most visible in the cities, where every foreign visitor commented on the enormous number of vagrants and the extreme poverty of the working class.

Excluding silver, which still represented 70 per cent of the value of the country's exports, little was produced that was exportable. Cochineal dyes amounted to about 7 per cent of the total, and a range of other primary products such as Tabasco pepper, sugar, coffee, tobacco, vegetables and animal products made up the remainder.[87] All but the largest producers were forced to rely on local markets or at best, if roads existed, on regional ones, and with many of the large rural estates self-sufficient in basic necessities, demand for both agricultural and industrial products was weak. Furthermore, with little capital to invest in mechanization, industrialists found themselves unable to compete with the cheaper imports which flooded into the country once trade barriers were removed with the abolition of the colonial monopoly system.[88] Above all, textiles – more than 250 products – poured in and quickly amounted to more

86 Coatsworth, 'Obstacles to Economic Growth', pp. 81–3. Coatsworth's figures and his interpretation are challenged in R. Salvucci and L. K. Salvucci, 'Crecimiento económico y cambio de productividad en México, 1750–1895', *HISLA*, 10 (1987); see Chowning, 'The Contours of the Post–1810 Depression'. See also E. Cárdenas, *Some Issues on Mexico's Nineteenth Century Depression* (Mexico, 1983).

87 I. Herrera Canales, *El comercio exterior de México* (Mexico, 1977), pp. 25–113.

88 Trade with Spain virtually collapsed in the early years after independence and was slow to recover.

than 50 per cent of total imports. Alcholic beverages also increased rapidly to between 4 and 10 per cent of the total, and with the supply of mercury, essential for the mining industry, controlled by the House of Rothschild, the price almost doubled between 1825 and 1835.[89]

The economic situation surprised most Mexicans, who had believed that once the restrictions imposed by Spain had been removed, it would be easy, if not inevitable, to develop the country's natural resources. Disillusion soon set in, and by the early 1830s there was general concern at the lack of progress, which centralists blamed on the federal system, federalists on corruption and inefficiency, and everybody on the political instability caused by the numerous revolts and changes of regime. Merchants, farmers, industrialists, shopkeepers, artisans and producers in general also found that in the absence of the highly regulated and centralized control of the Crown, they had to reorganize to compete for official favour and to promote their own interests. The abolition of *gremios* and *consulados* was followed by the formal or informal creation of producer or trade-related associations together with all manner of societies for the promotion of industry. Most of the retailers in the capital, for example, pulque sellers and wine merchants, butchers, bakers, shoemakers and tobacconists, were sufficiently organized to present signed petitions to Congress. Wholesalers and the larger import–export merchants met at their private club or exchange, La Lonja, where they at times coordinated their response to a particular government action and groups of merchants had at least informal associations in all the principal cities in the regions. A distinct class of entrepreneurs including a number of foreigners became an important 'social force' on both the social and the political scene.[90]

Many of these groups, directly affected by the economic difficulties and the increasing tax demands of the State, began to lobby the new Congress and executives after the fall of Gómez Farías. For example, demands were soon heard for the reintroduction of a monopoly on the production and sale of tobacco. The Spanish monopoly had been abolished by Gómez Farías in May 1833 in accord with the liberal belief in a free market, but within a couple of years, several groups involved in the tobacco business began to press for the decision to be reversed. The tobacco producers, located mostly in the Veracruz region, were well organized in a *común de cosecheros,* and the Veracruz legislature, together with those of Mexico and Michoacán, asked Congress to create a new monopoly.[91] They argued that

---

89 Herrera Canales, *Comercio exterior,* pp. 27–48.
90 The phrase *fuerza social* is used by M. Urías, 'Militares y comerciantes en México, 1830–1846', in E. Florescano, ed., *Orígenes y desarrollo de la burguesía en América Latina, 1700–1955* (Mexico, 1985), pp. 73–103.
91 'Proyecto de ley sobre restablecimiento del estanco de tabaco', Morelia, 25 May 1836, in *Diario*

the industry had long been a fruitful source of tax revenues, which had dropped drastically since the end of the monopoly. The planters' association of Orizaba and Córdoba, the only places where the cultivation of tobacco had been allowed in the colonial era, joined in with their own petition.[92] They too were disillusioned with so-called free trade and had found that Mexican consumers, when given a choice, preferred imported Cuban and Virginian tobacco to their products. With a glut in the market caused by imports and new production elsewhere since 1833, prices had fallen and their area, they claimed, was being impoverished.[93]

Congress responded to these pressures with a committee that reported in favour of bringing back the monopoly, which, it noted, should be easy to do because 'under the present order of affairs, there is now little or no difficulty in centralizing the revenue, unifying the administration throughout the republic, and sytematically pursuing smugglers'.[94] A government monopoly, however, was not practical in view of the poverty of the Treasury. Hence, the committee recommended that a private one be established with a contract negotiated with entrepreneurs, perhaps the planters of Orizaba and Córdoba. Santa Anna had close connections with the tobacco and other producers in his home region around Jalapa, but because of his disgrace in Texas this offer was not made, and a few months later, in a law of 12 January 1837, the national government resumed control of the monopoly, assigning responsibility for it to the newly created Banco de Amortización.

The tobacco planters, administrators and others involved in the industry were one powerful lobby whose influence on the political scene was to be felt again in future years. They were by no means the most powerful. That distinction must go to the textile industry, whose workers, planters, manufacturers and merchants were to become the most vociferous of all economic interest groups. In the euphoria accompanying emancipation and the end of Spain's commercial monopoly system, Mexico had opened up its ports to foreign trade. Few goods were prohibited, and although some – for example, industrial, mining and agricultural machinery – were exempted from all taxes, most had to pay a basic 25 per cent ad valorem duty.[95] Mexican manufacturers and artisans soon found, however, that free trade was not the panacea they had hoped it would be, and over the next few years the government reluctantly responded to their complaints

del Gobierno, 7 May 1836. The representations from the Veracruz and Mexican legislatures are also in this issue of the *Diario*.

92 'Exposición de los cosecheros de las villas de Orizaba y Córdoba', 31 October 1835, in ibid.
93 Details from Walker, 'Business as Usual'.
94 The *dictamen* is in *Diario del Gobierno*, 7 May 1836.
95 G. Garza Villareal, *El proceso de industrialización en la ciudad de México (1821–1970)* (Mexico, 1985), pp. 76–80.

by increasing the number of banned articles and raising the levy on others to 40 per cent. Among those whose industry was most affected by the imports, which despite the duties were still cheaper, of better quality and certainly much preferred by the *hombres de bien,* were textile industry workers, especially cotton plantation owners. In response to pressure from the cotton bloc, to use Potash's phrase, the Guerrero government decreed on 22 May 1829 a ban on cotton textile imports, together with a further fifty other articles, but with Guerrero's defeat soon afterwards, the May law was not put into effect.[96]

All governments to that time had been very reluctant to adopt a protectionist trading policy because the customs duties provided the Treasury with most of its revenue. Then in 1830, largely at the inspiration of Alamán, a national industrial promotion bank was set up – the Banco de Avío – and its capital was to be raised from a levy on duties collected on imported cotton goods. The Bank had quickly approved several loans to potential entrepreneurs in various industries, including cotton and woollen mills, and although its activities and revenues were curtailed during the Gómez Farías interlude, it was soon clear that the conservative government was again concerned to promote its work. At the same time, the cotton producers and artisans in the domestic textile industry saw the advent of the new regime as a further opportunity to campaign for a ban on foreign imports. Thus, between January and April 1835, initiatives to Congress came from Puebla, Jalisco, Mexico, Oaxaca and Veracruz, all pleading for protective legislation, and several deputies promoted bills of their own. The farmers and artisans were joined by some cotton factory owners who hitherto had sought to keep their access to the cheaper and better-quality foreign products.

The government was in a dilemma, not wishing to alienate the 'cotton bloc' but at the same time wanting to sustain revenues. It decided to resist the protectionist pressures by lauding the potential benefits for industrial development of the Banco de Avío. Its capital base was raised from 1 million pesos to 1.5 million pesos, with the money again to be raised from import dues on foreign cottons. The directors of the Bank promptly approved several grants totalling 152,000 pesos to four individuals, including Alamán, whose projects involved both a paper mill and a cotton factory.[97] Later in 1835, a further 476,000 pesos were promised, and among the fortunate recipients were such influential figures as Tornel, Escandón, Guadalupe Victoria, General Mariano Arista and General Manuel Barrera. Barrera was already a large-scale textile manu-

96 R. A. Potash, *Mexican Government and Industrial Development in the Early Republic: The Banco de Avío* (Amherst, Mass., 1983), p. 128.
97 These and following details on the Banco de Avío are from ibid., chap. 8.

facturer, and for years he had had a lucrative contract to supply the army with uniforms which were made in his own workshops in the capital and elsewhere.[98] Payment from the Bank was made not in cash but in drafts and, it seems, a loss of face value of between 30 and 40 per cent. Personal favouritism and political connections undoubtedly influenced the distribution of the Bank's credit, especially since the chairman of the board was Tornel's brother-in-law, Díez de Bonilla.

Meanwhile, in the Chamber of Deputies support for the protectionists was growing, and the industry committee concluded in a report of 27 March 1835 that 'the unrestrained freedom of trade is a public evil'.[99] The deputies accepted this report and soon approved a draft bill which in effect banned the import of cotton textiles, but when the bill reached the Senate, it was stalled and no action was taken before the end of the session.

The cotton lobby, against the wishes of the executive, seemed to have won the argument even though no law had yet been enacted. The deputies had responded to its pressure, but they had also been lobbied by other groups demanding restrictions on imports. Brandy producers, for example, warned that imports were destroying their industry and that sales of by-products were also badly affected. Sugar plantations in Veracruz, Querétaro, Guanajuato and elsewhere were being ruined, and unemployment in those areas was rising.[100] In the capital, even the tanners' association appealed for protection against the competition from tanned leather imports.[101]

The protectionist clamour increased, notably from Puebla, where several of the new textile factories had been or were being set up.[102] As Thomson states, 'No other region projected such articulate protectionist propaganda or maintained such persistent political pressure in favour of a protectionist and autonomist model of economic development'.[103] The pamphleteers and newspapers provided the essential propaganda forum, and behind the scenes Alamán and many of the country's leading figures used their influence. By the summer of 1836, the executive gave in, and following more representations from the cotton-growing areas of Veracruz and Oaxaca, Congress resolved to ban the import of foreign-grown cotton in both

98 M. Barrera, *Exposición que acerca de la contrata de vestuarios para los cuerpos del ejército hace el que suscribe* (Mexico, 1837).
99 'Dictamen de la comisión de industria sobre prohibición de hilazas y tejidos de algodón del extranjero, presentado en la cámara de diputados, el día 27 de marzo de 1835', in *A Collection of Dictamenes*, British Library, L.A.S. 515. 8.
100 Representation by 'un destilador mexicano' in *El Sol*, 14 March 1835.
101 Senate session of 15 January 1835, in ibid., 10 February 1835.
102 The Puebla legislature asked for a blanket ban on the import of 'efectos y manufacturas extranjeras que perjudican a las del país'; ibid., 5 May 1835.
103 Thomson, *Puebla de los Angeles*, p. 218.

the ginned and seeded state.[104] A few months later, the government confirmed that trading policy under centralism was to be highly protectionist. In March 1837, a general tariff revision was introduced and all the various industrial lobbies had their demands met.[105] For the 'cotton bloc', imports of raw cotton were banned at once and all types of foreign yarn and coarse cotton textiles were to be prohibited one year from the date of the decree. Clothing of all types, including ecclesiastical vestments, was banned, the only exceptions being handkerchiefs, gloves, hats and stockings. For the tobacco trade, both foreign tobacco leaf and cigars were henceforth excluded, and for sugar producers and the alcohol business, there were to be no more imports of sugar or sugar-cane brandies. Finally, for the tanners, such leather goods as shoes and boots for men and women were prohibited.

Many other items were placed on the prohibited list – among them rice, coffee, flour, soap, toys, playing cards, timber and salt – and the government approved a number of other measures to stimulate domestic production and commerce. Responding at times to pressure from representatives in Congress who sought benefits for their own states, taxes were reduced or even abolished – for example, on cochineal, which was exempted from all taxation. Administrative reforms were also introduced in the customs service in the hope of making it more efficient and to reduce the endemic corruption among the officials. Contraband was a major problem, and again partly to counter it, some of the smaller ports were closed to overseas trade and new customs posts were set up in Chihuahua.

Changes were made in several other areas, for example, the postal service and education, but however positive and welcome such measures were, the transitional phase from federalism to centralism had proved a trying time for the middle-class *hombres de bien*. The defeat in Texas and the escalating cost of the army, the crisis in the Treasury with the increase in taxation on property and commerce and the forced loan, and the general economic malaise were far from what had been predicted would follow the defeat of the radicals and the end of federalism. The conservative and centralist leaders knew that even before their constitutional system had been fully enacted, disillusion among their supporters, especially the moderate *hombres de bien,* was spreading. They attempted to counteract this with appeals for patience and class solidarity.[106] Property owners were urged not to complain about the tax burden they had to bear and to come forward in defence of their government and their own interests: 'The

104 Potash, *Banco de Avío*, p. 129.
105 Dublán and Lozano, *Legislación mexicana*, vol. 3, pp. 303–22.
106 *Diario del Gobierno*, 30 July 1836.

property owners of the republic must come forward, both for the honour of the nation and for our own self-interest'.[107]

Such appeals to middle-class self-interest do not seem to have raised morale or expectations. Couto had written to Mora in February 1836 that he no longer bothered to attend Congress, and he was by no means the only one to lose hope that the country's situation would improve. Felipe Neri del Barrio, the financier-entrepreneur and deputy for Mexico, also wrote in March 1836 to his fellow federalist at Zacatecas, Luis G. Gordoa, that he had not bothered to attend Congress recently because there seemed little point: 'They do not want an opposition'.[108] Even Alamán was very pessimistic; in a series of letters throughout 1836, he portrayed the country as being on the verge of collapse. 'Everything', he wrote, 'offers a very gloomy and uncertain prospect'.[109] By early 1837, Congress was frequently unable to hold its sessions because it was inquorate. One newspaper, condemning the deputies and senators for failing in their duties, summed up the public mood in these words: 'total discontent throughout the republic with no hope of improvement'.[110]

107 Ibid., 26 August 1836.
108 F. N. del Barrio to L. G. Gordoa, 12 March 1836, Correspondencia de Luis Gonzaga Gordoa, García Collection, 27 A(3).
109 L. Alamán to Duque de Terranova, 28 June 1836, in *Obras: Documentos diversos*, vol. 4, p. 343.
110 *El Mosquito Mexicano*, 14 February 1837.

5

Las Siete Leyes

Our imaginary typical *hombre de bien* must have been confused, not to say depressed, when he surveyed his country at the end of 1836. He had been glad to see the back of Gómez Farías and his sansculottes, who had seemed to threaten his moral, social and religious values, and he had welcomed the election of the new Congress, dominated as it was by men of his own social class. The conservative and centralist politicians had promised him progress with order, political calm and social stability in which his own standing as a respectable member of society would be protected and consolidated. Instead, he had seen Santa Anna defeated and the nation humiliated in Texas. His salary was not being paid, and the purchasing power of the money he had was declining as prices in the shops rose and even his basic food supplies became scarce and expensive. His taxes had been raised, and he had been required to contribute to the forced loan. He could no longer buy the foreign-made brandy and cigars he preferred or the European clothes and footwear, and even the cost of his occasional game of billiards had gone up. Although he no longer had to pay tithes on the vegetables grown in his garden or on his small rural retreat, the Church collector still came and appealed to his conscience and that disturbed him. The environment in which he lived remained both dirty and dangerous, and despite all the talk by politicians, crime of every sort was just as much a worry as it had always been. Even the Swedish consul, M. Mairet, had been murdered, and he had only recently read of the brutal killing of a congressional deputy, Manuel Muría, who had been stabbed to death in a frenzied attack by his own wife at 8 a.m. on 27 September.[1] Nothing had been done to stop the spread of what his priest told him was an 'invidious flood of perverse books'.[2] It was no wonder that moral standards were declining when a priest, said to be the rich owner of three disreputable taverns, was caught shoplifting; when the notary Covarrubías

---

1 Reported in *La Lima de Vulcano*, 24 March 1836; *Diario del Gobierno*, 1 October 1836; Malo, *Diario*, p. 109.
2 D. Aranda, *Carta pastoral*, 2 January 1837 (Guadalajara, 1837).

had returned home to discover his wife in a compromising situation with Colonel Tomás Requena, a deputy for Yucatán; and when even a nun had been found with her lover.[3] He was reluctant to take his family to the theatre any more because there had been scandalous, sacrilegious goings-on there; the place had become the 'main source of the most impious and sacrilegious morality'.[4] He became even more depressed when he read in the newspaper repeated warnings of a 'revolution like that of France', which was sure to bring about the destruction of the 'social edifice' and his place in it.[5]

Observing and experiencing all the political, social and economic problems of his *patria,* however, our *hombre de bien* found himself with perhaps one last ray of hope. The politicians were devising a new constitution which they promised him would guarantee that the sansculottes would never again have control and which would safeguard all the interests of all *hombres de bien.*

The constitutional change from the federal to the centralized form of government took almost two years to achieve, and there are several reasons why the process took so long. Within the Congress, even among the conservatives and centralists and no doubt reflecting the large number of lawyers in their ranks, doubts were soon raised as to their legal authority to enact constitutional change. There were, as we have seen, differences of opinion over such issues as the Church and the army and, of course, the few federalists among the deputies and senators did all they could to prevent the destruction of the federation. Even more significant for the future, there were major areas of disagreement between the Congress and the executive, and until his defeat in Texas, there was the menacing shadow of Santa Anna and his autocratic ambitions. Finally, in the country at large, there were the untold numbers of provincial politicians, bureaucrats and others who owed their livelihoods to the opportunities the federal system had created. Their concerns had to be taken into account, and the government hastened to reassure them that their jobs were safe.

The first serious difficulty arose in Congress over the nature of its powers to reform the federal charter of 1824. Soon after the sessions began in 1835, a committee was set up to advise on the extent to which the representatives had been empowered by their electorates to make constitutional changes. Chaired by the indefatigable Carlos Bustamante, the committee conducted an exhaustive investigation into the credentials of all the deputies, seeking to ascertain what, if any, restrictions had been placed on their powers at the time of their election. It was found that

---

3 *El Cosmopolita,* 5 November 1836; Malo, *Diario,* p. 110.
4 *Diario del Gobierno,* 27 September 1835.
5 Ibid., 28 December 1836.

some states, Chiapas, for example, had forbidden their representatives to make any changes to the 1824 charter. Others had made no mention of constitutional reform, and some had authorized change only in certain areas, which did not include the form of government. Oaxaca and Puebla had given broad powers to change but excluded the clerical and military *fueros,* while Jalisco, Tamaulipas, Durango, Guanajuato, Yucatán and several others had given what seemed to be unrestricted authority. Finally, a significant number had given permission for broad changes to anything in the 1824 charter with the one crucial exception of article 171. That article reads as follows:

> No reform shall ever be made to those articles of this constitution and the constituent acts which establish the liberty and independence of the Mexican nation, its religion, form of government, freedom of the press and division of the supreme powers of the federation and the states.

The legal position, therefore, was by no means clear, and it was left to Bustamante to argue in the preface to the committee report that popular opinion was demanding constitutional reform. More than 6.5 million of the 7 million Mexicans, he insisted, were in favour of change because the federal system had brought rising crime, lack of security for the person and for property, attacks on religion, economic decline and poverty. Bustamante signed his report on 2 March, and two days later the committee issued its recommendations.[6] The first stated that the existing Congress enjoyed all the necessary extraconstitutional powers to make those changes to the 1824 constitution which it thought were for the good of the nation. The second recommendation, however, proposed that Congress accept that its powers did not extend to changing article 171.

This insistence on article 171 is curious – Bustamante offers no explanation in his other writings – because it prevented any change in the form of government, which Sánchez de Tagle, Lope de Vergara and Becerra, who were members of Bustamante's committee, clearly wanted. When the report passed to the floor of the Congress, they argued strongly in favour of change, although in their speeches they did not openly promote the centralist alternative. A few speakers, notably Pedro María Ramírez (Zacatecas), defended the 1824 constitution and Felipe Neri de Barrio tried the delaying tactic of demanding that a states' convention be held to discuss the matter before any decision was taken.[7] In the profederal press, it was argued that the petitions cited by Bustamante as evidence of the popular will were fraudulent. *El Sol* responded to the charge of undemocratic procedures by insisting that popular consultation on a wide

---

6 *Dictamen de la comisión revisora de los poderes conferidos a los Sres. diputados al congreso general de la unión para reforma de la constitución federal* (Mexico, 1835).

7 Congressional sessions in *El Sol,* 5–17 May 1835.

scale was an impossible dream and that the only way to consult the people was through institutions and their representatives.[8]

When the final vote was taken in Congress on 28 March, Bustamante's first proposal was approved by 42 votes to 15, and the second, relating to article 171, was approved by 43 to 8. The two proposals then passed to the Senate, where again they were hotly debated.[9] Couto led the federalist opposition, but Portugal, Garza Flores and Pacheco all argued that the legal niceties of constitutional law were irrelevant in the circumstances and that the popular will had to be obeyed, because if the wishes of the majority were ignored, the people would have no choice but to resort to revolution. Both articles were duly approved by a large majority and an appropriate decree was issued on 2 May.[10]

The position was, therefore, that Congress had decided it was empowered by the electorate to make changes to the existing federal constitution but not to the actual form of government. In other words, the federation would continue. Within days after the decision was published, hundreds of petitions and *pronunciamientos* openly calling for a change to centralism were announced.[11] These so-called demonstrations of public opinion from what Bocanegra says was an 'incredible number of citizens' were allegedly co-ordinated from the capital by Tornel, and they were used as a pretext to put pressure on Congress to respond.[12] Tornel, and later Santa Anna himself, met with groups of congressmen and other notables but quickly realized that bullying tactics were not going to work. It was at this point that Carlos Bustamante says they made it quite clear to Santa Anna that they were not willing to give him autocratic powers. Realizing they were not going to get what they wanted from the present deputies and senators, Santa Anna and Tornel tried another tactic; this was to argue that the Congress should be *convocante*, in other words should exist only as a body to prepare the ground for a new assembly which they assumed they would be better able to control. Again, the congressmen refused to co-operate.[13]

By the end of June a kind of stalemate had been reached between the executive and legislative branches. Then, on 23 June, a new session of Congress was summoned by the Council of State to open on 19 July, the principal business on the agenda being to consider the 'public demonstrations regarding change in the present form of government'.[14] Within two days of opening, Sánchez de Tagle and Arrillaga tabled a proposal

8 Ibid., 22 March 1835.
9 Ibid., 16 and 17 June 1835.
10 Dublán and Lozano, *Legislación mexicana*, vol. 3, p. 43.
11 For the texts of some of these plans, see *Planes en la nación mexicana*, book 3. Many of them were published in the press at the time.
12 Bocanegra, *Memorias*, vol. 2, p. 611; Mora, *Obras sueltas*, p. 319; *La Oposición*, 24 June 1835.
13 Bustamante, *Cuadro histórico*, vol. 4, pp. 366, 371–4.
14 Dublán and Lozano, *Legislación mexicana*, vol. 3, pp. 58–9.

that a committee be formed to report first on whether Congress should reform the constitution or summon another assembly and, second, if the former were decided, on whether the two houses of Congress should unite or continue separately. It was agreed that the committee should be established. Obviously dominated by Sánchez de Tagle, it reported that more than four hundred petitions in favour of change had been examined and that the people were indisputably disillusioned with federalism. It recommended, therefore, that Congress declare itself fully empowered to change the form of government; that the bicameral arrangement continue; that in cases of disagreement, the two houses unite and settle issues by a majority vote.[15]

These recommendations were quickly approved and passed to the Senate, where its committee severely criticized the federal system, arguing that 'the most cursory examination of our present institutions is enough to convince us that in them lies the origin of public disasters'.[16] With 20 state legislatures, 295 legislators, a multitude of subordinates and countless officials to be supported, taxation had inevitably risen and public discontent had followed. The choice facing Congress was not whether to have a new constitution but whether to have any constitution, because the 1824 charter was in such disrepute that it in effect no longer existed. Hence, they supported the deputies' proposal that Congress be empowered to change the form of government, but they also thought that the two houses should be united in a single chamber.

When this report came to the floor of the Senate, the federalist minority made what turned out to be their last stand against what was now a centralist bandwagon. Couto tried in vain to persuade his colleagues to refer the whole matter to the regular committee on constitutional questions, but the most impressive and informed speech came from former president Guadalupe Victoria. Like those of many politicians of the time, Victoria's political views fluctuated, and even during his presidency from 1824 to 1829 it was never clear whether he favoured federalism or centralism. On this occasion, he voiced his disagreement with the idea that federalism had caused all the nation's difficulties. Certainly, the 1824 constitution had its faults, but they could be remedied and there was no case for abolition. Furthermore, he rejected the basis of the centralist case, namely that it was the popular will. Public opinion, in his view, should not determine the actions of legislators but only influence them. Otherwise, there would be 'pure democracy, which is the worst of all imaginable systems'. Citing Constant, Watel and others, he went on to

15 *Dictamen de la comisión especial de la cámara de diputados, nombrada para darlo sobre las manifestaciones relativas al cambio del sistema de gobierno* (Mexico, 1835).
16 *Dictamen de la comisión especial de la cámara de senadores sobre cambio de la forma de gobierno y voto particular del señor Couto* (Mexico, 1835).

postulate that the so-called popular will, to which so many of his contemporaries referred, could never be properly ascertained, and thus it was
the duty of the ruling class to guide the nation along the path of prudence
and responsibility.[17]

Victoria's at times impassioned speech, which also contained suggested
reforms to the 1824 constitution, failed to sway the senators, and the
report in favour of change and a single chamber was approved. The
deputies accepted the amendments, and on 9 September 1835 a law was
promulgated by which Congress was empowered to draw up a new constitution and, henceforth, to meet as a single chamber.[18]

It had been a long and at times bitter procedural battle, but with the
juridical obstacles now out of the way, the centralists led by Sánchez de
Tagle, Pacheco Leal, Anzorena and Cuevas began to dismantle the federal
system and at the same time to discuss the basic principles on which their
new form of government was to rest. On 3 October, again following a
committee chaired by Sánchez de Tagle, it was announced that state
governors would continue in post for the time being but their tenure of
office and powers would in future be subject to the central government.
State legislatures were to be dissolved immediately, their final act being
to nominate a temporary departmental junta of five persons who would
serve as an advisory council to the governor. If the legislatures were not
in session, the local council was to choose the members of the junta. State
judiciary personnel were to remain in post for the time being, as were
public employees, although no vacancies were to be filled and central
government assumed control of all offices and revenues. Officials were
required to compile inventories of all furniture and equipment in state
offices and buildings, prepare up-to-date accounts of assets and liabilities,
revenues and expenditure and remit all the information via the governor
to Mexico City. In future, governors were obliged to consult with the
Minister of Hacienda on all matters of finance and taxation, and until
their powers were defined in a new law, they were forbidden to dispose
of any properties or enter into any contract without prior approval.[19]

This law of 3 October began the actual process of centralizing power
in Mexico City, especially over the appointment of personnel and fiscal
policy. Three weeks later, on 23 October, the principles, or *bases*, of the
new constitutional framework were published, and once again the same
five people – Sánchez de Tagle, Pacheco Leal, Cuevas, Anzorena and
Valentín – were responsible for the initial drafting. The principles were
set out in fourteen clauses beginning with the confirmation of religious

17 *Voto particular del senador Guadalupe Victoria sobre el proyecto de ley en que se declara que las actuales
   cámaras tienen facultad para variar la forma de gobierno* (Mexico, 1835).
18 Dublán and Lozano, *Legislación mexicana*, vol. 3, p. 71.
19 Ibid., pp. 75–8.

intolerance in favour of Roman Catholicism as the only permitted religious faith.[20] The government was to be republican, representative and popular, with the supreme power divided into three branches of executive, legislative and judicial, which under no circumstances could be united. A new method would be devised to ensure that none of the three branches could exceed its powers. The legislative power would be exercised by a popularly elected bicameral congress, and a new electoral law would be issued. Executive power would be vested in a president chosen by indirect popular election, and judicial power in a supreme court, the nature and attributes of which would also be specified in a forthcoming constitutional law. The national territory was to be divided into departments based on population and other factors, and they would be governed by governors appointed by the national executive power and popularly elected departmental juntas. The procedure for the appointment of all public officials and members of the judiciary at the departmental level would be indicated in an appropriate law, as would new arrangements for fiscal practice and policy.

Federalism thus officially ended with the publication of these *bases* on 23 October 1835, and as Cuevas puts it, 'with this change, the 1824 constitution was buried'.[21] There remained, however, two final stages in the transitional phase. The first was the implementation of the practical changes which followed directly from the legal base and, in particular, the formation of the new temporary juntas in the departments. For the most part, these were formed without difficulty and the incumbent legislatures accepted the inevitable, voting themselves out of office after choosing the new five-man juntas. In several areas, the legislatures had already closed and town councils elected the new bodies, most of which seem to have been in place by the end of November. Only at Veracruz, where Tornel's brother José Julián was put on the junta, does there seem to have been any resistance to the demise of the legislature. This was led by Sebastián Camacho, a former member of the federal Congress and long-standing partisan of the *escoceses*. He refused to participate in the naming of a departmental junta and released a long statement challenging the idea that popular opinion favoured constitutional change.[22] He demanded to know who had signed the four hundred and more petitions cited as evidence of the popular will and asked how representative were those who had signed. His protest, of course, was in vain, and after some delay, the junta was chosen and the legislators retired.

The final stage in the creation of the centralized republic was the writing and enactment of the constitutional laws promised in the *bases*. Although

20 Ibid., pp. 89–90.
21 M. Cuevas, *Historia de la nación mexicana* (Mexico, 1967), p. 600.
22 *El Cosmopolita*, 23 December 1835.

Sánchez de Tagle assured Congress that he and his committee were meeting daily from 5 p.m. to 10 p.m. to draft them, it was to take the whole of 1836 for the eventual seven laws to be completed. Their inspiration, and probably author, was Sánchez de Tagle himself. Born in 1782 at Morelia to an aristocratic family, he had enjoyed a long career in public affairs, occupying various posts during the final years of the viceroyalty and then as deputy or senator for Michoacán, and later Mexico, and as governor of the Federal District. A man of many talents, including the writing of poetry, and a founder member of the Academies of Language and History, he was an *hacendado* who owned the hacienda de Goicoechea (now San Angel Inn) and an established and well-respected member of the political and social elite of the capital. In terms of his political views, he was, together with Alamán, the unofficial leader of conservatism, and having steered the centralist cause through Congress throughout 1835, it was largely his ideas which were incorporated in the new constitutional laws. He had been educated at the Colegio de San Juan de Letrán in the capital, where he studied theology, philosophy and jurisprudence, and he subsequently acquired a knowledge of several foreign languages such as Latin, French, Italian and English. His main intellectual interest, however, seems to have been political theory, and he was thoroughly conversant with the works of Locke, Montesquieu, Jovellanos, Blackstone, Constant, Bentham and many others. As Noriega has shown, from these writers he derived ideas on the nature of individual rights, sanctity of property, separation of powers and tyranny which he was to bring to the debates on the constitutional laws.[23]

The first law concerned the rights and obligations of Mexicans.[24] They were guaranteed security of their property and possessions, although as previously noted, the State could confiscate property, including ecclesiastical, in the public interest. Those arrested on suspicion of criminal activity could not be held for more than three days before being brought to court, and there were no restrictions on travel within the country or on emigration. Much to the annoyance of Basilio Arrillaga, who opposed the clause in Congress, complete press freedom was allowed for political ideas, and there was no reference to prior censorship of works on religion. The significant innovation, however, concerned the qualifications for citizenship and the rights which went with it. Henceforth, full citizenship was restricted to men with an income of at least 100 pesos per annum derived from employment or invested capital. The right to vote in popular elections was thus restricted by this income qualification. Citizenship

23 A. Noriega Cantú, *Las ideas políticas en las declaraciones de derechos de las constituciones políticas de México (1814–1917)* (Mexico, 1984), pp. 109–45.
24 For the full text of the Siete Leyes, see Tena Ramírez, *Leyes Fundamentales de México*, pp. 204–48.

rights were also suspended for various categories of people – for example, vagabonds, unemployed and domestic servants and, notably, those who were still illiterate by the year 1846.

At this point, it is appropriate to defer any summary or analysis of the second law, which was to prove the most controversial. The third concerned the legislative power, its membership and role in the formation of laws. There was to be a bicameral congress with a chamber of deputies and a senate. Deputies were to be elected on the basis of population, with 1 per 50,000 inhabitants, and half of them renewed every two years. The qualifications to be a deputy included being a citizen, being at least 30 years of age and having an income of at least 1,500 pesos per annum. Twenty-four senators would be chosen through a dual process whereby the deputies, the cabinet, and the Supreme Court would each elect by majority vote one candidate for each vacancy, and this composite short list would then be sent to each departmental junta to make the final choice. One-third of the Senate was to be re-elected every two years, and the qualifications for election included being a citizen, being at least 35 years of age and having an income of at least 2,500 pesos.

Congressional sessions were to be daily and to begin on 1 January and 1 July, with the second session devoted exclusively to budgetary matters. Fifty per cent attendance constituted a quorum, and votes would be determined by a simply majority. All legislation was to be initiated in the lower house, with the Senate acting as a revising body. The executive and deputies could initiate laws on any matter, while the departmental juntas could make proposals relating to taxation, industry, commerce, education and municipal administration. Any citizen had the right to make proposals through his town council or elected representative, who in turn could submit them to the departmental junta for consideration as formal initiatives. A law approved in Congress required the sanction of the president of the republic, who could refuse it unless two-thirds of those present in both chambers twice voted in its favour. Congress was given powers to legislate on all matters of public administration and expenditure and to approve, reject or reform any measures taken by the departmental juntas. The annual budget of each ministry was subject to its approval, and it had the right to determine the size of the national army and navy. It could authorize the executive to contract debts, approve all treaties with other nations, including the Holy See, and it could declare war. Finally, the Senate retained the right to admit or refuse papal bulls.

The fourth law concerned the executive power. This was to be vested in a president for eight years, or double the previous term under the federation, and there was to be no vice-president. The method of election was indirect. The cabinet, Senate and Supreme Court were each to draw up a short list, and the three lists were then passed to the Chamber of

Deputies. It in turn was to choose three names from the lists, and this final short list was sent to the departments. They would each choose one name, which was to be returned in a sealed envelope to the deputies, who would count the votes and announce who had obtained most votes and victory. Re-election of an incumbent president was permitted if the cabinet and other bodies voted for him in the first stage and if he obtained three-quarters of the votes of the departmental juntas.

To be elected president required being a citizen, native born, and 40 years of age, as well as having an annual income of at least 4,000 pesos and experience in high public office. Presidential powers and attributes included the limited sanction of congressional decrees, personal immunity from prosecution, appointment of cabinet ministers, regulation of public administration, initiation of laws, suspension of taxation, command of the armed forces and the appointment of departmental governors, military officers and all senior ecclesiastical dignitaries which pertained to national patronage, subject to a concordat with Rome. The main restrictions were that the president could not take command of the armed forces without the approval of Congress, could not alienate national territory and could not directly impose any form of taxation.

The president was to be assisted by an advisory council – Council of Government – consisting of thirteen members chosen by him from a list of thirty-nine names submitted by Congress. Membership on the council was permanent, and the personal qualifications were the same as those for a deputy. The function of the council was to advise the president on all matters he referred to it. There were also to be four ministries – Internal Affairs, Foreign Affairs, Treasury, War and Navy. Ministers were appointed by the president, and in all serious State affairs, decisions had to be reached in a cabinet of ministers chaired by the president.

The fifth law detailed the formation and attributes of the judicial power. The Supreme Court was to have eleven permanent ministers and one fiscal, who were to be at least 40 years of age and with a minimum of ten years' experience as practising lawyers. They were to be chosen by the same method used for the election of the president. Each departmental capital was to have a high court, and there were several lesser tribunals whose range and functions were much the same as those under the federation. The various clauses regulating the whole judicial system provoked little controversy, except, as already noted, the futile attempt to challenge the legal immunities granted the clergy and the military in article 30.

The sixth law was rather more innovatory. It concerned the territorial division of the republic into departments rather than states, although the actual division was deferred to a future congressional law. The departments were to be administered by a governor appointed by the central government from a short list submitted by the departmental junta. Each governor would serve eight years, and qualifications for office included citizenship, being at least 30 years of age, and having an annual income of at least 2,000 pesos. His powers included the appointment of public officials, execution of laws and orders from the central government, suspension of town councils, intervention in the election of councillors and suspension of Treasury officials. Each department was also to have a junta of seven members elected by the same electorate as chose the deputies and for a term of four years. Personal qualifications were the same as those for the deputies, including an income of 1,500 pesos. The juntas could initiate legislation, and it was their responsibility to establish primary schools in all villages, levying 'moderate' taxes for the purpose, if necessary, and also to improve roads within their department, again establishing 'moderate' tolls where required to cover costs. They had to participate in the election of the president, senators and other national officers as well as providing a short list for the governorship. Neither the junta nor the governor could impose taxes except where indicated or recruit any armed forces unless authorized to do so by the central government. Finally, at the municipal level, in the main town in each district, there was to be a prefect appointed by the governor but subject to confirmation by the central authorities. Personal qualifications included birth or residency in the department, being at least 30 years of age and having an income of at least 1,000 pesos per annum. Prefects were responsible for public order and keeping an eye on the activities of town councils. There was also to be a deputy prefect, who had to have an income of 500 pesos. All departmental capitals and major population centres like ports were to have a town council, popularly elected according to a law to be issued. The minimum age for election to a council was 25 and the minimum income was 500 pesos. Among the responsibilities of the councils were policing, prisons, hospitals, public primary schools, roads, bridges, promotion of agriculture, industry and commerce and, in general, the preservation of public order.

The seventh and final constitutional law was brief, stipulating that no changes were to be made to the constitution until at least six years had elapsed and reserving the right of Congress to interpret the meaning of any article. Various transitional clauses were added in which Congress was authorized to make ad hoc arrangements, especially for the imminent presidential and congressional elections, which in future had to be held in accordance with the schedule and dates set out in the constitutional laws.

It took several months for the six laws summarized so far to be agreed upon, which allowed the lawyers in Congress to raise all manner of legal points, but the basic principles inherent in them provoked little dispute. In sharp contrast, there was considerable controversy over the second law, which was by far the most novel and reflected the growing division between the executive and the Congress. Sánchez de Tagle had accepted the division of powers, but he and his civilian colleagues were well aware of the potential for conflict among the three branches of government. They were also acutely conscious of the fact that, since independence, there had been more than one occasion on which executive–legislative rivalries had resulted in the enforced closure of Congress by the executive. Iturbide had used his military strength to close the first Congress and, somewhat ironically, Sánchez de Tagle and his colleagues owed their present status as representatives to the fact that Santa Anna, again using military force, had closed the previous Congress in May 1834. Furthermore, it was the ever-present shadow of Santa Anna which in the autumn of 1835 most concerned Sánchez de Tagle, Alamán and other centralist republicans. At that time, Santa Anna was at the height of his popularity, especially with the army, and he had made it clear to the legislators in his meetings with them in June of that year that he did not look kindly on the sort of constitutional reforms they were contemplating. The rumours of his dictatorial aims continued to circulate, and there was little doubt that he had the military support to stage a coup and dismiss the Congress as he had done previously and, indeed, would do again. It was the dangers of dictatorship which most concerned the civilian politicians, and as the inspirers if not authors of the constitution, Sánchez de Tagle and Alamán wanted to find a constitutional means of reducing those dangers, which, of course, they knew could never be eliminated. Sánchez de Tagle was deeply immersed in the works of Constant, and according to Noriega, it was there that he found the idea of a fourth power to serve as a neutral or moderating force against the possible excesses of the other three.[25]

It was on 4 December 1835 that the congressional committee, chaired by Sánchez de Tagle, introduced its proposal.[26] Experience, the committee said, had demonstrated the impossibility of achieving the right balance between the executive, legislative and judicial powers. Since independence, all three had been guilty of excesses or neglect, and it was vital to find some form of restriction or safeguard to ensure that they kept to the limits of their respective powers. The legislature was only to pass laws, but in the past it had abused its authority by ordering such things as prison sentences and exiles, which were matters pertaining to the judiciary. Legally owned property was supposed to be inviolate, but that principle had often been abused at the national and state levels. As for the executive, though it could not pass laws, it had resorted to issuing regulations with

25 Noriega Cantú, *Ideas políticas*, p. 127.
26 'Proyecto de la segunda ley constitucional presentado al congreso general en la sesión de 4 de diciembre de 1835 por la comisión respectiva, sobre organización de un supremo poder conservador', in *Diario del Gobierno*, 9 December 1835.

the force of law. It had imposed taxes, and on several occasions it had taken or tried to take emergency powers in order to ignore constitutional restrictions. Since independence the judiciary had never asserted its proper authority. The fact was that the three powers had never been independent. The theory of the division of powers was one thing but reality was another: 'The putative plan of our government has been as far removed from what was actually practised as the east from the west'. Thus, the committee proposed a fourth power, to be known as the Supremo Poder Conservador (Supreme Conservative Power), which would operate purely by the force of moral persuasion, never initiating but always being obeyed as the real 'social oracle' of the nation.

When the details of this proposal were released, there was at once heated and acrimonious debate. Discussion began in Congress on 9 December, and in his private diary, Carlos Bustamante clearly reveals that he and his colleagues knew that what Sánchez de Tagle had done was to lay down a challenge to Santa Anna and the supporters of dictatorship:

Wednesday, 9 December 1835. (Good day). Tomorrow, I am going to speak in favour of the proposal and I hope to show its necessity and convenience in the present circumstances, which are so difficult that they have given us the choice of either falling into the hands of a dictator, or choosing a king, or entrusting our salvation into the hands of five Mexicans.[27]

The debate continued on 14 December, and Tornel, representing the views of the executive and presumably Santa Anna, spoke vigorously against the proposal. On the next day, Sánchez de Tagle made a long and impassioned speech in favour, and on 16 December, amid what seems to have been intense lobbying behind the scenes by both sides, the vote was taken. The proposal was approved by a single vote out of 73 cast.[28] Carlos Bustamante wrote with evident relief, 'By a single vote, that was the chance on which the true freedom of the nation depended. What a disgrace. . . . My pen trembles when I describe what happened.'[29]

Santa Anna, Tornel and their allies among the clergy in Congress such as Barajas and Arrillaga lost the battle on the general proposal, but over the next four months, during which time Santa Anna was in Texas, they tried again to sabotage the project as each article was considered. Again, Tornel intervened in the debates, engaging in intrigue in the corridors within and outside of the national palace. Nevertheless, his efforts were in vain because a majority of the civilian deputies accepted Sánchez de

27 C. M. Bustamante, 'Manuscrito inédito en la Biblioteca Pública del Estado, Zacatecas', vol. 27, p. 356, cited in Noriega Cantú, *Ideas políticas*, pp. 136–7.
28 *Discurso del Sr. D. Francisco Manuel Sánchez de Tagle en la sesión del 15 de diciembre (1835) sobre creación de un poder conservador* (Mexico, 1835). Noriega Cantú, *Ideas políticas*, pp. 137–43, gives a detailed analysis of the speech.
29 Cited in Noriega Cantú, *Ideas políticas*, p. 143.

Tagle's premise that some form of independent control over the executive was required. The force of his argument was apparent in reality as well as in theory because it was just when the final votes were being taken in April 1836 that the sensational news of Santa Anna's victory at the Alamo was filling the pages of the daily press and his supporters were making no secret of their wish, if not intention, to proclaim him a dictator.

Thus, the second constitutional law was passed in April 1836. It provided for the creation of the Supreme Conservative Power (henceforth referred to as SPC) to reside in Mexico City and to consist of five members with one renewed every two years. They were to be elected in a three-stage process beginning with the departmental juntas. These would make nominations to the Chamber of Deputies, which would elect a short list to be passed to the Senate for the final choice. Those elected received a salary of 6,000 pesos per annum and were entitled to be addressed as Excelencia. The main qualifications for election were citizenship, a minimum age of 40, a minimum income of 3,000 pesos per annum and past service at ministerial level, the Supreme Court or Congress. The attributes were considerable. The SPC could declare any law unconstitutional and void if petitioned to do so by any of the three branches of government. It could nullify any act of the executive if asked to do so by the Supreme Court or Congress, and any decision of the Supreme Court at the request of either of the other two powers. At the instigation of Congress, it could declare the moral or physical incapacity of the president to hold office, and it could suspend both the Supreme Court and the Congress when it judged it to be in the public interest or at the request of the executive. If any of the three powers was dissolved as a result of rebellion, the SPC could restore it, and if asked, the SPC could decide what the will of the nation was in the event of extraordinary circumstances. Members could not be held responsible for their decisions except before 'God and public opinion'.

The central republic now had its constitutional base, and the faith of *hombres de bien* in the power of the written word seemed restored. Alamán was certainly satisfied with his work and that of his fellow centralists. Writing to Santa Anna in February 1837, he expressed his pleasure with the new charter, which 'in general is good and all of it is much better than the one which preceded it'.[30] In fact, Alamán's self-satisfaction was misplaced, because even by the time the Siete Leyes were published on 29 December 1836, amid much official celebration and patriotic songs in the theatres, they were already under attack. The opposition press naturally condemned the loss of states' sovereignty and the wholesale centralization of power in Mexico City. No feature was more ridiculed

---

30 Alamán to Santa Anna, 23 February 1837, *Obras: Documentos diversos*, vol. 4, pp. 152–6.

than the SPC, which the editor of *El Cosmopolita* suggested should be confined at once to a museum of politics. Lacking any means to assert its authority other than moral persuasion, this moderating power, in the words of Arrangoiz, 'was ridiculed from the day it started'.[31] For later historians also, the new constitution was scarcely worthy of comment: a juridical monstrosity, according to Reyes Heroles, and of no interest whatsoever for the history of Mexico's constitutional law, according to Emilio Rabasa.[32]

Despite the surge of criticism at the time and since, however, for Alamán and the 'conservative oligarchy', to use Justo Sierra's phrase, the Siete Leyes were a triumph.[33] The 'enemies of order', Alamán wrote, had finally been defeated and would never again threaten the social order because 'the system which has been established for elections to congress, the departmental juntas and governorships, places authority in the hands of respectable people and assures the stability of public order on the basis of individual property'.[34] 'Respectable people', in other words, *hombres de bien,* were now in full control. Henceforth the right to vote was restricted to those with an annual income of at least 100 pesos and candidature for any elected office required the minimum-income qualifications set out in the constitution. It is worth summarizing the extent to which the so-called popular representative system was restricted to the property-owning and professional classes:

	Minimum annual income (pesos)
Citizen with the right to vote	100
Local councillor	500
Deputy prefect	500
Prefect	1,000
Member of a departmental junta	1,500
Deputy	1,500
Governor	2,000
Senator	2,500
Member of the SPC	3,000
President	4,000

The effects of these income qualifications were varied. A minimum subsistence income has been calculated to be around 70 pesos per annum, and in the urban areas most employed workers earned in excess of 100 pesos. Municipal workers and unskilled peons, for example, received

31 Arrangoiz, *México desde 1808 hasta 1867*, pp. 372–3.
32 Reyes Heroles, *El liberalismo mexicano*, vol. 2, p. 226; E. Rabasa, *El juicio constitucional* (Mexico, 1955), p. 231, cited in Noriega Cantú, *Ideas políticas*, p. 175.
33 Sierra, *Evolución política*, p. 216.
34 L. Alamán to Santa Anna, 23 February 1837, in *Obras: Documentos diversos*, vol. 4, pp. 152–6.

between 120 and 150 a year while skilled artisans like carpenters, tailors and printers earned 150 to 200 a year. A few tradesmen were disenfranchised by the earnings rule – for example, shoemakers, weavers and blacksmiths – but by and large the 100 peso minimum probably did not significantly reduce the electorate in the cities.[35] In contrast, as Wenceslao Alpuche, a deputy for Yucatán, pointed out, the effects in rural constituencies like his own were dramatic. Most of his constituents, he said, lived at a minimum subsistence level, outside the cash-based economy of the city dwellers. They built their own houses, grew their own food and made their own clothes: 'They do not pay for their housing nor do they buy their food, go to the bullfights, need a cook, cleaner or tailor; indeed, nothing which costs them money'. They were honourable, industrious people, and he resented the charge made by Gómez Anaya in Congress that anyone with less than 40 pesos a month must be a vagabond.[36] The situation in the northern haciendas seems to have been similar, and as Cross found in his study of one estate in Zacatecas, monthly wages ranged between 3 and 7 pesos with an average of 4.34.[37]

It seems certain that most of the rural poor were disenfranchised under the new constitution, but again the practical effects in terms of votes cast were unlikely to be significant, since few took any part in the political process and certainly not in elections. The impact of the income qualification to stand for public office, however, was another matter, both in the cities and in the countryside. The myriad tradesmen and artisans whose life-style and earnings have been analysed by Shaw, Cross, di Tella and others were excluded even from local councils, and few except the most prosperous retailers and master craftsmen could earn the 1,500 pesos required to be a deputy in the national Congress or on the departmental juntas.

Finally, the exclusion of the unemployed and domestic servants, while not new – federal electoral laws had usually contained a similar clause – did have a major impact on the size of the electorate. It has been calculated, for example, that about 50 per cent of the capital's population was unemployed, and of those employed, about 30 percent were in domestic service. At least 80 percent of the city's population was thus immediately disenfranchised, and while the proportions were probably not as great in

35 Figures from Shaw, 'Poverty and Politics', chap. 2 and app. C. Di Tella gives wage rates for Querétaro in 1844 which would indicate that some groups of *menestrales*, like bricklayers and water carriers, earned 78 pesos a year while those in the tobacco industry made 122. None of the various categories of rural workers on the haciendas made as much as 100; T. S. di Tella, 'The Dangerous Classes in Early Nineteenth Century Mexico', *Journal of Latin American Studies*, 5 (1973), 79–105.
36 W. Alpuche to editors, 25 October 1836, *Diario del Gobierno*, 27 November 1836.
37 H. E. Cross, 'Living Standards in Rural Nineteenth Century Mexico: Zacatecas, 1820–1880', *Journal of Latin American Studies*, 10 (May 1978), 1–19.

the provincial cities, they would still have been significant. The various minimum age qualifications for candidates were also significant. They ranged from 25 years for a local councillor to 40 for a presidential candidate. These have to be considered in the context of the average life expectancy. According to one study of the capital's population, this was 27 years in the poorer parishes, excluding children who died at 3 years or under, but 40 years in the richer and better-serviced parishes. In short, only the affluent were likely on average to live long enough to reach an age where public office became a possibility.[38]

It was the property-owning and relatively affluent groups of landowners, financiers, entrepreneurs, large retailers, wholesalers, senior public officials and successful professionals – in short, the upper echelons of the middle class – who were guaranteed a monopoly of elected office, and that was what Alamán and his allies had long desired. For Alamán, universal suffrage and unrestricted access to political power in a nation such as Mexico was not only ludicrous but also highly dangerous. He wrote that suffrage had been given to a mass of people who voted for candidates without knowing why or even who they were. The representative process, as it had been, revealed no more than the 'metaphysical fiction of the popular will'.[39] The result, as the *Diario del Gobierno* warned, was as follows:

There is no evil comparable to a society without morality in which supposed freedom becomes licence and demagogy has its disastrous influence. Once the masses are roused, they destroy without reason, there is nothing that can restrain them and, ultimately, the most horrific anarchy becomes the norm.[40]

Alamán, Sánchez de Tagle, Lope de Vergara and the other conservatives knew that the significance of their constitution lay in its social bias rather than the political and administrative changes from federalism. They realized that given the topography, poor communications and immense diversity of Mexican regions, the centralization of power in Mexico City was as much an ideological gesture as a political reality because, outside the central regions, the government lacked the means to enforce its will. Other than relying on their patriotism and respect for law, there was no way that regional caudillos like Juan Alvarez could be forced into line, and with the national military effort concentrated on Texas, there was little prospect of successful military action against recalcitrant regional interests, even within departments near the capital. Hence, while they certainly retained their belief in the necessity of a written constitution,

38 Gayón Córdova, *Condiciones de vida*, pp. 11–40.
39 L. Alamán, 'Examen imparcial de la administración del general vice-presidente don Anastasio Bustamante', in *Obras: Documentos diversos*, vol. 3, pp. 268–9.
40 *Diario del Gobierno*, 10 May 1836.

they were pragmatists convinced that the best, if not only, way to ensure its acceptance throughout the republic was to appeal to the class solidarity of the proprietors, to urge *hombres de bien* in every town and region to look to their own interests and to those of their social peers. By ensuring that political power and access to it were vested entirely in their class, they hoped to establish a common bond and mutual defence which would transcend regional boundaries and local interests.

The centralists had to take into account one other factor. The political system they had devised might well gain the support of *hombres de bien* across the country, but there was still one force and one man whom recent experience had amply demonstrated could not be relied upon to respect any constitution. We do not know what Santa Anna – he says nothing in his memoirs – or the other generals in their military commands thought about the final text of the Siete Leyes. Their *fuero*, albeit subject to some criticism in Congress, was still intact and they retained their authority, both military and political, in their respective regions, at least until such time as the central government decided to renew the departmental governors. On the other hand, senior congressmen had repulsed Santa Anna's autocratic pretensions, and there was no doubt that the creation of the SPC with its substantial powers over the executive was intended at least in part to block any future attempt at legal dictatorship. For the army and for Santa Anna personally, therefore, the new constitution was tantamount to a challenge. Future action by rebellious military officers would be a direct attack on the *hombres de bien* and on the political system which guaranteed their social and economic domination. It may be, of course, that Alamán hoped that the concept of middle-class solidarity would also attract the loyalty of the officer corps, many of whose senior members came from the same sort of background as he did and presumably had similar social prejudices and attitudes toward the masses. The generals were thus, on the one hand, isolated and told to keep out of civilian affairs and, on the other, offered the opportunity to join in support of the new middle-class-dominated society. It was the failure of Santa Anna to participate in this alliance which was to cause many of the difficulties of the central republic, and it is noticeable that within a few years the future rebel and dictator-president, General Paredes, was still trying to persuade Santa Anna that the only way to safeguard the interests of both the army and the *hombres de bien* was to create a pact between the army and the 'productive and well-off classes'.[41]

For the time being, Santa Anna perhaps did not figure too prominently in the minds of either the civilian politicians or the senior army officers,

41 Several letters of Paredes y Arrillaga to Santa Anna and Tornel, April–May 1842, in García, *Documentos inéditos*, vol. 56, pp. 20–8.

because as the constitution was being written and sanctioned, he was in captivity in the United States, busily negotiating to save his own skin. The government, of which he was still technically the president, had publicly disowned him, and as rumours of the secret deals over Texas he was alleged to be offering surfaced, he was accused of treachery and of betraying his *patria*. Humiliated and in disgrace, he was, it seemed, no longer a force to be reckoned with, and he himself, after publishing a long defence, announced his retirement when he finally returned to Manga de Clavo in February 1837. How seriously his departure from public life was taken, however, is perhaps indicated by the fact that, as soon as he returned, Alamán still felt it prudent to write to brief him on developments during his absence.

Nevertheless, it is obvious that Santa Anna was not at the forefront of political affairs. This left the way open for the centralists to conclude the final stages of consolidating their new regime. These involved preparing for the election of a new president, a new national Congress and juntas in the departments. Two preparatory laws were issued. The first concerned the territorial division of the republic into departments. All the previous states were designated as departments, except that Coahuila and Texas were separated and Alta and Baja California joined as one. The former territory of Colima was added to Michoacán and that of Tlaxcala to Mexico. The second law was published on 30 November 1836 to regulate the forthcoming congressional elections.[42] The procedures were briefly as follows. Local authorities were required to divide their districts into sections of one thousand to two thousand residents, identify those eligible to vote, give each voter a ballot and publish the list of eligible voters. Each ballot was to carry the name and address of the voter and indicate whether he could read and write, and could be given only to those with an income of at least 100 pesos per annum. Voters also had to be more than 21 years of age if single and 18 if married. Domestic servants, those with criminal charges pending, public Treasury debtors, vagrants, unemployed and, finally, monks were ineligible. On election day, at the primary stage, voting booths were to be open from 9 a.m. to 2 p.m., and each voter was required to write, or have written, the name of his chosen candidate on the reverse of the ballot. The candidate receiving the most votes in each section would be declared the winner, or *compromisario,* and participate in the secondary or district elections. These consisted of all the *compromisarios,* who assembled a week later to choose one district elector per ten thousand inhabitants. The district electors then met for the third and final stage in the capital town of the department to choose the deputies

---

42 Dublán and Lozano, *Legislación mexicana,* vol. 3, pp. 215–22, 258.

by secret ballot. The qualifications to be a deputy were those specified in the constitution.

With the regulations in place, three weeks later on 24 December, the decree ordering the elections to be held was issued.[43] The primaries were to be on 5 February followed by the district stage and then the final election on 14 and 15 March. The departmental juntas were to be installed on 26 March and at once proceed to elect the senators and the president of the republic from the short lists to be drawn up by the executive, Congress and Supreme Court on various days in January. Finally, the new Congress was to begin its sessions on 1 June.

Everything was thus in place by the beginning of 1837 for the election campaign. The elections were to give the opposition what seemed a final opportunity to hinder, if not sabotage, the centralist bandwagon. The federalists and liberals had not been inactive during the two-year transition. On the public political front, notably in Congress, Couto, Neri del Barrio, Ramírez, Gordoa and their few sympathizers had tried to sustain the federal cause but eventually had given up in despair. Some town councils and other groups, among them the young Benito Juárez, in Oaxaca, Jalapa and elsewhere had petitioned Congress, and there had been a more or less continuous series of *pronunciamientos* in favour of the federal system.[44] Apart from the major rebellions in Texas and Zacatecas, most of these revolts had caused the government little concern and they had been suppressed without difficulty by loyal local commanders. Alvarez had rebelled at Texca in April 1835 but was quickly subdued by General Bravo, although the rebellion did spread into Oaxaca and Puebla and later Michoacán, where the leader was Gordiano Guzmán.[45] In November, José Antonio Mejía, leading about two hundred volunteers from New Orleans, briefly occupied the port of Tampico, and there were other revolts throughout 1836 at Huajapam (Oaxaca), Zacatecas, Alta California, Chiapas and Papantla. Some of these incidents, although they eventually adopted the federalist banner, had their roots in local grievances. Mariano Olarte at Papantla, for example, who had been in revolt since late 1835, had several demands concerning land and fees paid to the local clergy, but when he eventually issued his plan in December 1836, it contained no fewer than twenty-six articles ranging from the restoration of federalism to the abolition of all clerical charges for such services as baptism and marriage. Curiously, he also demanded the restoration of tithes, which he envisaged would be used to pay local clergy.[46]

43 Ibid., pp. 226–7.
44 For the text of the various *pronunciamientos*, see *Planes en la nación mexicana*, book 3.
45 J. Ortiz Escamilla, 'El pronunciamiento federalista de Gordiano Guzmán, 1837–1842', *Historia mexicana*, 38 (1988), 241–82.
46 The text of his plan is in *Planes en la nación mexicana*, book 3, p. 97.

The military actions on behalf of federalism, therefore, did not produce any immediate political result, but they served the purpose of maintaining an atmosphere of uncertainty and general instability, distracting the attention of the centralist authorities and absorbing precious resources. As Alamán commented in December 1835, 'There is no stability in the present order of things, and at every step it is necessary to send an army to suppress some revolt or other'.[47] In the capital, the federalist and liberal press maintained a barrage of criticism of the government, its actions and the proposed constitutional changes.[48] Individual ministers were subjected to prolonged campaigns of personal vilification, none more so than Tornel. He was accused of financial corruption when he purchased a house for a reported 30,000 pesos, money he was alleged to have acquired from supply contracts for the Texas campaign. His private carriage was said to have knocked down two blind people, but he had fixed things so that his driver was not charged with any offence.[49] Above all, he was accused of nepotism in the distribution of government jobs.[50] Among those who did receive his patronage were Sr. Dufoo, brother of the Minister of Hacienda, who was given a Treasury post at Oaxaca, and none other than Sánchez de Tagle, who was made director of the national pawn-shop, or Monte de Piedad.[51]

Against the background of the defeat in Texas, the economic recession, the copper money crisis, all the new taxes and the continuous military rebellions, the opposition had no difficulty in demonstrating its view that centralism did not and would not work. The editor of *El Cosmopolita* summed up the situation as he saw it:

The military are starving, redundant public employees, pensioners and widows of those defenders of the nation who perished on the battle-field, find no help nor do they expect any relief from their misery; public employees go in vain to the palace for their salaries; commerce is completely paralysed; the government has no credit; agriculture is ruined

47 L. Alamán to Duque de Terranova, 13 December 1835, in *Obras: Documentos diversos*, vol. 4, p. 315.
48 The main opposition papers in Mexico City in 1835–6 were *El Cosmopolita, la Oposición, El Anteojo* and *La Luz*. On the centralist side were *Diario del Gobierno, El Voto Nacional, La Lima de Vulcano, El Mosquito Mexicano, El Nacional* and *El Sol*. The government, and particularly Tornel, tried to silence the opposition press and with some success. *La Oposición* was forced to close in 1835, and in a notorious case at the time, the publisher, Francisco Torres, was jailed for publishing a hostile attack on Santa Anna. Tornel was again responsible and was accused before Congress of arbitrary actions, a charge he refuted.
49 *El Cosmopolita*, 2 November 1836.
50 Tornel was required to appear before a congressional committee to answer charges that he had made appointments illegally; ibid., 16 July 1836.
51 Tornel also ensured that past services were rewarded. Juan Wenceslao Barquera, a senator in the previous Congress, claimed his unpaid salary. Even though the government had stopped all back pay because of the financial crisis, Tornel told Barquera that he would be paid 'considerando los servicios que prestó en el año de 1834'; Tornel to Barquera, 20 April 1836, García Collection, Barquera; Documentos, 11B.

by the loss of its work-force; property owners and artisans tremble at the thought of the taxes that are being considered; citizenship brings no guarantees and the people are terrified of those military levies which were unknown in the federal regime. All that is the result of the prosperity which we were promised by those who wanted to change the form of government adopted in 1824.[52]

This political opposition in Congress, the *pronunciamientos* in the regions and the propaganda in the press appear at first sight to be uncoordinated. In fact, there is some evidence that all were the result to a certain extent of planning and organization. One man who was certainly involved was the former vice-president, Gómez Farías, whose personal archive contains many letters to and from him urging rebellion. After he had left the capital in the spring of 1835, he had travelled north, and after various diversions he finally settled in New Orleans. While there he kept in touch with developments, writing and receiving both reports from his supporters and the latest newspapers, and there is no doubt that Mejía's futile Tampico expedition was plotted and financed in New Orleans. Gómez Farías went so far as to tell Mejía that he personally, as the legal vice-president, authorized the revolt and guaranteed that the nation would repay its costs, if it was successful.[53] He then wrote to federalist generals like Esteban Moctezuma asking them to join the revolt.[54] There is also alleged evidence that Gómez Farías and thirty-six friends in New Orleans formed a secret society, or Junta Anfictiónica, whose plan of action included not just the restoration of the federation but also support for the Texas rebels. This plan was published in *El Mosquito Mexicano* on 6 December 1835, and although some conservative historians like Cuevas have accepted it as genuine and used it to condemn Gómez Farías as a traitor, most believe that the version in the newspaper was apocryphal.[55]

Nevertheless, even though the New Orleans plan may have been a fiction, there is some corroborating evidence that the federalists had begun to reorganize in a secret society. Carlos Bustamante attributed all the revolts and opposition attacks to the Grand Lodge of the *yorkinos* in the capital, and one of Gómez Farías's correspondents wrote in March 1836 of plans and secret alliances between *escoceses* and *yorkinos*.[56] This may well have been a reference to a development which José María Lafragua confided

52 *El Cosmopolita*, 8 June 1836.
53 V. Gómez Farías to Antonio Mejía, 28 October 1835, García Collection, Gómez Farías Papers, nos. 366, 370.
54 Ibid., no. 370.
55 The text is also in *Planes en la nación mexicana*, book 3, pp. 75–6. Fuentes Mares alleges that the Mejía expedition was financed by Texans; J. Fuentes Mares, *Santa Anna: Aurora y ocaso de un comediante* (Mexico, 1967), pp. 107–9. For a thorough discussion of the so-called Pact of New Orleans, see C. A. Hutchinson, 'Valentín Gómez Farías and the "Secret Pact" of New Orleans', *Hispanic American Historical Review*, 36 (1956), 471–89.
56 Bustamante, *Cuadro histórico*, vol. 4, p. 354; Gómez Farías Papers, no. 343.

to his personal memoirs. Lafragua was at this time a young lawyer living and working in Puebla. He was a federalist but was considered, he said, to be a moderate by the radicals, or *exaltados* as they were becoming known. He had not been especially active in public affairs, but he records that early in 1835 'a masonic society of yorkists-federalists was organized in Mexico City. It was also called *anficciones* because this had a higher grade'.[57] A branch of the new society was quickly set up in Puebla, and both he and his young friend and future president, Ignacio Comonfort, joined. Lafragua acted as secretary and began writing articles on politics in the press. The society, he adds, was very well organized and its national leader was General Manuel Gómez Pedraza.[58]

A former president and for a time prominent in the *escocés* rite, Gómez Pedraza was an *hombre de bien* in every sense. Born in Querétaro in 1789 to a prominent family, his early career paralleled that of many of his contemporaries in that he fought for the Spaniards in the war of independence and then supported Iturbide, particularly during his brief imperial interlude. Like so many others, he successfully managed the ideological switch to federalism and occupied several high offices during the Victoria presidency, including the governorship of Puebla and as Minister of War. In the presidential election of 1828, he was the candidate of the moderate *escocés* party, and although he won the election, rebellion by Santa Anna and the defeated *yorkinos* meant that he was unable to take the presidential chair and he retreated to exile in France. When Santa Anna overthrew Anastasio Bustamante at the end of 1832, he was recalled to serve the final few months of the presidency to which he had been elected in 1828.

Gómez Pedraza is one of the many prominent personalities of the Age of Santa Anna who has yet to find a biographer, but popular opinion at the time depicted him as a man of affluence, arrogance and intellectual ability, yet somewhat eccentric and absent-minded. Guillermo Prieto, who knew him well, tells the story that he forgot his own wedding day and a search had to be made to find him for the ceremony.[59] One of the social elite of the capital, he held his own *tertulia,* which other noted liberals like Mariano Riva Palacio attended, and after his flirtation with Iturbide monarchism, he gradually established a reputation as a moderate liberal or, as Mora would have him, a 'progressive'.

Gómez Pedraza emerged as the leader of the moderate liberal group which wanted to amend the 1824 constitution while preserving the federation, and his name was soon being floated as a presidential candidate.

57 Colección Lafragua (Biblioteca Nacional, Mexico City), no. 398.
58 *El Cosmopolita,* 15 June 1836, also refers to a new third party being formed by former *escoceses* and *yorkinos.*
59 Prieto, *Memorias,* vol. 2, p. 85.

The presidential elections were due in January 1837, but for several months beforehand, names were being mentioned. In August 1836 the U.S. diplomat Powathen Ellis reported that Gómez Pedraza was being talked of as a candidate, along with Bravo, Victoria, Tornel and Alamán. In his estimation, it was likely that a general, probably Bravo, would be chosen, although Alamán had a good chance if he would agree to stand, which was unlikely.[60] Similar speculation continued in the press and then, much to the anger of the liberals, one name began to be mentioned more and more. This was Anastasio Bustamante, whose appearance as a potential candidate came as a considerable surprise. He had been in exile in Europe since 1833 and, as far as is known, had neither exercised any influence nor had had any say in the course of events since that time. It is unlikely that his views on the centralist constitution could have been known, and there were even suspicions that he tended to favour federalism. On the other hand, there were several factors in his favour. During his earlier period in power, from 1830 to 1832, the administration he led had a number of positive achievements. It had resolved by way of a compromise the difficult problem of relations with Rome, and independent Mexico's first bishops had been consecrated. Other measures favourable to the clergy, notably the canons and prebendaries in the cathedrals, had been introduced. Bustamante derived the political benefits of being considered proclerical and thus had the support of the Church. Similarly, some progress had been made on economic and fiscal affairs, and controls had been imposed on what was considered the sensationalist and scurrilous press. Bustamante was also a general and presumed to share the view of the army's status and privileges as sacrosanct. Finally, he was an *hombre de bien,* and his earlier government was now seen as representing and defending the values of middle-class property owners against the threat of proletarian anarchism epitomized by Gómez Farías and the sansculottes.

In short, Bustamante was in several ways an ideal candidate to represent the interests of the Church, the army and the *hombres de bien.* We do not know the identity of the power broker behind the scenes who presumably contacted him before his return from abroad. While we know that the liberals and federalists had clubs and secret societies, there is no evidence of similar organizations in the ranks of the conservatives and centralists, and yet the emergence of Bustamante has all the signs of having been prearranged. Information was soon leaked to the press. In September, *El Cosmopolita* reported talk of the 'Church party' summoning him to take the presidency, and Couto wrote to Mora in November telling him that although Alamán's name was being mentioned, it was likely that Bus-

60 P. Ellis to Pres. A. Jackson, 26 August 1836, Justin Smith Papers, file 22.

tamante would win, if he returned in time.[61] When he finally arrived at Veracruz on 2 December on a French ship out of Le Havre, he was welcomed as a returning hero. Local authorities, diplomats and the mercantile establishment all turned out to greet him, and special performances in his honour were staged in the theatre. Similar celebrations took place when he moved to the capital, which he entered on 20 December to take up residence in the house of his friend, the textile manufacturer and speculator General Barrera.

The first stage in the election was procedural. According to the fourth constitutional law, there were to be three short lists, one each from the executive, Senate and Supreme Court, which were to be presented to the deputies, who would select three names to be sent to the departmental juntas. Since the Senate did not now exist as a separate body, a transitional article had allowed for a committee of nineteen members of Congress to be selected to fulfil the role of the Senate. The nineteen were duly elected, and on 24 January each of the three bodies met to select its short list. These were as follows:

Executive:	Bustamante, Bravo, Alamán
Committee:	Bustamante, Bravo, Alamán
Supreme Court:	Bustamante, Gómez Pedraza, Manuel Rincón

Bustamante thus appeared on all three lists, Bravo and Alamán on two, Gómez Pedraza and Rincón on one. These lists were passed to the full Congress, which voted on them the next day, 25 January. Three separate votes were held, with the winning candidate each time being placed on the final short list.[62] Amid what must have been very complex tactical voting, the results were as follows:

First vote	Second vote	Third vote
Bustamante, 56	Bravo, 50	Alamán, 43
Gómez Pedraza, 6	Gómez Pedraza, 12	Gómez Pedraza, 16
Bravo, 3	Alamán, 2	Rincón, 5
		Santa Anna, 2
		Pacheco Leal, 1

On the short list for the departmental juntas were Bustamante, Bravo and Alamán, but it is not clear whether the latter two were serious contenders. Bravo had a number of points in his favour, including a distinguished record on the side of the insurgency in the war of inde-

---

61 *El Cosmopolita*, 21 September 1836; B. Couto to J. M. L. Mora, 17 November 1836, García Collection, Mora Papers, 127(2), file 26.
62 The election results were published throughout the press from January to April 1837.

pendence. He had also been vice-president under Victoria, but in 1827 he had led an unsuccessful revolt against him, and as a result of that failure, he was exiled for several years. A well-known centralist and one time Grand Master of the Scottish Rite, he had chosen on his return from exile to go back to his estates and power base in the south at Chilpancingo, and although one of the regional chieftains who was in effect independent of central government, he had not been especially prominent in national affairs. Moreover, he had recently refused a command in Texas to which he had been appointed, and according to Carlos Bustamante, that had spoiled his chances of election because he was technically a deserter.[63] As for Alamán, although certainly very influential behind the scenes, he had refused 'all participation in the administration of public affairs', and he had declined to take up the seat in Congress to which he had been elected in 1835; he had also refused an appointment as ambassador to France 'because of my family's opposition'.[64] Also, of course, he was a civilian, and it is not clear how the army would have viewed his election.

Bustamante seemed a clear favourite, but everything depended on the vote of the departmental juntas. These were elected in March and early April, and once installed proceeded to cast their votes for the presidency. The first results from Mexico and Puebla were announced in the press on 29 March, and as more came in over the next few days, it was obvious that Bustamante was winning a landslide victory. Only Sinaloa chose Bravo, and only Nuevo León preferred Alamán. The other eighteen departments which voted opted for Bustamante, and after Congress opened the sealed envelopes on 17 April, he was declared the next president of the republic.

Immediately after the presidential election, the departmental juntas elected the twenty-four new senators from the short lists drawn up by the three central powers in Mexico City. The Senate results were announced soon afterwards, and it is clear from the list of names that once again the Church and the army were to be well represented, each having four representatives, or one-sixth of the total. It is also noticeable that ten of the senators were re-elected from the incumbent Congress.

The elections of the president and the Senate were by and large held behind closed doors, and it is difficult to penetrate the intrigue and electioneering which it may be presumed were certainly carried out.[65] We do not know what promises or deals were made in the departments or indeed how the conservative and centralist leaders in the capital were

63 Bustamante, *Cuadro histórico*, vol. 4, p. 428.
64 P. Ellis to Pres. A. Jackson, 26 August 1836, Justin Smith Papers, file 22; Valadés, *Alamán*, p. 362.
65 *El Mosquito Mexicano*, 10 January 1837, refers to the 'intrigas, confabulaciones y maniobras de ciertos aspirantes, marcados de muy bribones'.

able to make their preferences known, given the difficulty and slow pace of travel and communications, especially to the peripheral departments. In contrast, the elections for the Chamber of Deputies were based on a popular vote, albeit restricted to those citizens who could meet the 100 peso income qualification. Election day at the primary stage was set for 5 February. The press and other sources indicate that the elections in the capital were carried out in the usual haphazard and irregular manner. The liberals were said to have gained control of some of the polling stations,[66] and one resident in the capital recorded in his diary that 'most of the people hurried around the streets without being able to find their polling station; in several sections, no voting took place because there were no officials; in others the ballots were destroyed'.[67] Nevertheless, eighty *compromisarios,* or primary electors, were chosen for the sections into which the capital had been divided – one section returned nobody – and a week later they met to choose fourteen secondary electors, who in turn elected the nine deputies to represent the Mexico department. The successful candidates provided a typical cross section of *hombres de bien* represented in Congress, with one army officer, one public employee, two clergy, four lawyers and one professor of mining.[68]

Similar elections took place in each of the departments, and by early April all the results had been published. Although we lack detailed biographical data for most of the deputies, all of whom had to have an income of at least 1,500 pesos and were therefore obviously from the 'well-off classes', the composition of the new chamber was broadly similar to that of the Senate. There were at least ten clergy, including three from Oaxaca, where the Church seems to have dominated the elections, with a majority of the secondary electors being canons or parish priests. There was the usual strong contingent of lawyers and landowners, as well as four army officers, and as in the Senate a large proportion, or about one-third, of those who took up their seats were re-elected from the incumbent Congress.

These several elections held in the first three months of 1837 were in one sense the culmination of the transition from the federal system to a centralized republic and, in another, they were the first test of the new system of government. Both Alamán and Sánchez de Tagle had good reason to be satisfied with their efforts. Alamán had not won the presidency, but he retained a position in the centre of power when he was chosen to be vice-president of the Council of Government, and Sánchez de Tagle was re-elected to the Chamber of Deputies for his home de-

66 Ibid., 25 February 1837.
67 Anon., 'Diario militar y político, 1836–1837', García Collection, 441, 3 February 1837 entry.
68 List of names with occupations in *El Cosmopolita,* 15 March 1837.

partment of Michoacán. The Church and the army were again well represented in Congress, and there was no doubt, at least according to the government paper, that honourable *hombres de bien* had been elected to both the national Congress and the departmental juntas. Everything was thus in place for the conservatives and centralists to try to achieve the ordered progress they had promised, to solve the social problems of crime and immorality, to improve industry, commerce and agriculture and, above all, to ensure that the hated sansculottes never again threatened social dissolution. Much depended on the president-elect, who was to govern for the next eight years. As the British diplomat Richard Pakenham put it, 'I look forward to the return of General Bustamante to power as a last remaining chance for the salvation of this country'.[69]

69 R. Pakenham to Ld. Palmerston, 3 April 1837, P.R.O., F.O.50, 106, fols. 107–9.

6

Anastasio Bustamante and the centralist republic, 1837–1839

Anastasio Bustamante's presidency and the centralist constitution lasted four years and five months. Both were replaced in October 1841 by Santa Anna, who, after manoeuvring himself to the head of a successful revolt, forced Bustamante to resign and replaced the constitution with a new set of *bases* more in tune with his priorities. In comparative terms, Bustamante's survival for four years, or half the term to which he had been elected, was something of an achievement, equalled only by Guadalupe Victoria's term in office for the first forty years after independence. But in absolute terms, the experiment of a centralized republican form of government controlled by *hombres de bien* was an abject failure and did nothing to resolve the country's political, economic or social problems. The promises of the conservative manifesto so carefully expounded in 1835 were not fulfilled, and all the hopes that Alamán, Carlos Bustamante, Sánchez de Tagle and their colleagues had of ordered progress were frustrated. Why did the new regime, seemingly so solidly based on the essential interests of the 'well-off classes', fail? Why did Bustamante, who had been welcomed with such fervour in 1837, fail to impose himself or the new constitution? Why did many of the *hombres de bien* become disillusioned with their own creation? Why, despite the clear resistance to a military dictatorship from 1834 to 1836, did the safeguards against it built into the constitution, especially with the fourth moderating power, not succeed? How did Santa Anna finally manage to achieve his autocratic ambitions? It is with these and related issues that this and the next chapter are concerned.

It is appropriate to begin the search for the causes of the failure of centralism by considering first the performance of the president himself. It is also apt to start by asking who Anastasio Bustamante was, because he is one more major figure of the Age of Santa Anna who has yet to attract serious biographical study. The outline of his career, it must be said, is fairly well established. Born of Spanish parents at Jiquilpan (Michoacán) in 1780, he received his early education at the Guadalajara seminary.[1] Then he went to Mexico City to study medicine, where one of his fellow students and friends was Gómez Farías. Although he did not graduate as a doctor, he practised medicine for a time at San Luis Potosí until he chose to begin a military career. When the war of independence began, he promptly joined a Spanish army unit with the rank of lieutenant. He took part in a number of actions against the insurgents, but when Iturbide announced the Plan of Iguala, he switched sides and was made a divisional commander. Enjoying the confidence of Iturbide, to whom he remained devoted throughout his life, he was given senior military commands at the time of the empire and was promoted to field-marshall. When the empire ended and the federal republic was created, he retained his army rank and status but seems to have taken little part in politics until 1829, when he was made vice-president to Vicente Guerrero, who took office as president in April of that year. Seven months later, in December, while at Jalapa in command of a reserve army commissioned to repel a Spanish invasion, Bustamante rebelled against Guerrero. The latter was forced to flee the capital, which Bustamante entered in triumph on 31 December. For the next three years, still officially as vice-president, he led the administration in which Alamán and the conservatives tried to impose their view of an ordered society run by and largely in the interests of *hombres de bien*. Then in 1832 Santa Anna began his first serious bid for the presidency, and although Bustamante resisted the rebels for much longer than had been expected, he was eventually forced to resign. A few months later, with the radical liberal regime of his one-time school friend Gómez Farías in power, he found himself included among those who were sentenced to six years' exile under the terms of the infamous *ley del caso* of June 1833. He soon departed for Europe, to return, as we have indicated, at the end of 1836 to prepare for election as president of the central republic.

The foregoing brief, factual sketch of Bustamente's career reveals a conventional pattern for a successful Mexican general of the time. At the age of 57, rather older than many of his rivals, he had finally achieved the presidency, apparently largely on his reputation for prudent fiscal conservatism and proclericalism, which he had established in 1830–2. Nevertheless, beneath the superficial veneer of his public persona, there seem to have been aspects of his personality which made him an unlikely choice for the always difficult job of president and which were ultimately to lead to his downfall. Unlike several of his contemporaries – Gómez Farías, Paredes, Lafragua et al. – he left no personal archive, and we must rely on the descriptions of those who knew him and recorded their impres-

1 These biographical details are in *Diccionario Porrúa: Historia, biografía y geografía de México* (3rd ed., Mexico, 1970), pp. 303–4.

sions. The best personal portrait we have is undoubtedly that given by Guillermo Prieto, who for a time was in daily contact and much favoured by him.[2] Prieto tells us that he was a man of medium build, plump but lithe, round faced with small eyes, broad forehead and rather pursed lips and with a tendency to strut about splay-footed or 'with the toes pointing outwards'. His personal manservant was a tall, taciturn Negro called López who kept him regularly provided with the soft-boiled eggs of which he was especially fond. He was a man who enjoyed the polite conversation of good society, liked telling and hearing jokes and greatly admired men of action and firm decision. Completely honest in money matters, he lacked self-confidence, except, it seems, with the opposite sex, for he was reputed to have left illegitimate children both where he had been stationed as a soldier and in Paris, where he had spent part of his exile. As for his political views, again according to Prieto, he simply did not have any, always professing ignorance of political theory or convictions. He despised the insurgents he had encountered as a young man and always retained an admiration for the 'wise Spanish system'. On matters of religion, he was never fanatical but he did have a great respect for senior clergy and tended to follow their advice. Finally, among his intimate friends with whom he preferred to dine and socialize were Colonels Durán, Stávoli and Arista and the textile manufacturer Manuel Barrera, in whose splendid mansion, Prieto recalls, the best parties in the city were held.

Most of these personality features noted by Prieto are confirmed by other opinions – none more so than Bustamante's indecisiveness. Although welcomed by Pakenham and others as the best man for the job in early 1837, within just a few months, critical voices began to be raised at his and his government's inertia. The opposition press naturally attacked him at every opportunity, but one of the most virulent of his critics soon became Carlos Bustamante, who had previously been one of his staunch admirers. Objecting to many of his decisions but above all to what appeared to be his apathy in the face of mounting problems on every front, Bustamante published anonymous pamphlets attacking him and even went so far as to try to persuade Congress to declare him 'morally incapable' of continuing in office. Although admitting that he was well-intentioned and honourable, he concluded that his administration was a disaster, which was bringing disrespect and contempt for the country.[3]

Carlos Bustamante was by no means alone in accusing his namesake of apathy, incompetence and bad judgement. Writing to Lord Palmerston in 1841, Pakenham said, 'The President, General Bustamante, appears to labour under a sort of infatuation and to be altogether blind to the

2 Prieto, *Memorias*, vol. 2, pp. 27–9.
3 Carlos Bustamante, *Gabinete mexicano*, vol. 1, pp. 38–51, 65–6, 169–70.

difficulties and embarrassments of every direction that face him'.[4] He had never been noted for his intelligence, he added, but now 'age and plethora have, for some time past, reduced him to a state of mental disability'. Pakenham had good reason to dislike Bustamante, for he had managed to get few favours from him for British merchants and had not become a member of his intimate circle of advisers. In addition to General Barrera, in whose house he lived when he first assumed the presidency and whose carriage he borrowed for inauguration day, Bustamante seems to have preferred the company of a few military aides and, above all, of clergymen. Prieto had mentioned that he tended to follow priests' advice on policy matters, and in 1838 another British diplomat reported that he was controlled by a camarilla of priests and 'persons devoted to the priesthood'.[5] The editor of *El Cosmopolita* ridiculed the influence of this camarilla and urged Bustamante to assert himself, warning, 'Sr. Bustamante sees nothing; he sleeps on the crater of a volcano'.[6]

Prieto had also noted Bustamante's lack of political convictions, and it was his ambiguity on political issues of the day which was to be one of the root causes of the conflict in the central republic. As far as is known, Bustamante never proclaimed himself publicly either a centralist or a federalist, and the political factions never quite knew where he stood. For the centralists, of course, this was tantamount to betrayal, and within months of his inauguration, there were suspicions that he was in fact a closet federalist. According to Carlos Bustamante, he had not even bothered to read the new constitution,[7] and when he was often seen in the company of Gómez Pedraza and appointed known federalists to strategic military commands, the suspicions grew even stronger. As far as some of the federalists were concerned, his vacillation gave cause for renewed hope, and they believed that by increasing the propaganda pressure on him as well as maintaining a continuous series of *pronunciamientos,* it was only a matter of time before he could be pushed into giving them his support. On more than one occasion, he seemed to be on the brink of doing so, but at the last minute he always stepped back and either changed his mind or could not bring himself to take the final decision. This prevarication and indecision brought some federalists to the conclusion that he could not be trusted and that he was manipulating them for his own unexplained ends. Lafragua wrote in 1838 that his conduct displayed 'a consummate treachery, ignorance and the most obvious ineptitude'.[8] Similarly, Gómez Farías warned his allies that Bustamante was a hypocrite

4 R. Pakenham to Ld. Palmerston, 10 June 1841, P.R.O., F.O. 50, 145, fols. 179–81.
5 C. Ashburnham to Ld. Palmerston, 10 December 1838, ibid., 116, fols. 27–32.
6 *El Cosmopolita*, 5 December 1838.
7 Bustamante, *Gabinete mexicano*, vol. 1, p. 42.
8 Colección Lafragua, no. 398.

and could never be trusted. He was, he remarked, the Ferdinand VII of Mexico.[9]

The picture we have of Bustamante, therefore, is of an honest, unassuming, rather indecisive, simple man of no firm opinions on politics or religion who tended to be dominated by those around him, especially the clergy – in short, as Carlos Bustamante puts it, a tortoise rather than a tiger.[10] If this portrait is reasonably accurate, it is clearly odd that such a man was chosen to preside over the implementation of the centralist system and to try to control the whirlwind of Mexican political life. One explanation is offered by Carlos Bustamante, who admitted that his early admiration for the new president was based on the success of his first administration, which he came to realize was due not to Bustamante himself but rather to his ministers at the time, most prominent of whom was Alamán.[11] It is also possible that the conservative and centralist politicians, and especially the clergy, wanted someone whom they knew, or at least thought, they could control and that, having been liberated from the mercurial Santa Anna, a less flamboyant personality like Bustamante who was acceptable to the army fitted the bill. On the other hand, this interpretation of Bustamante may be an injustice to him, for the fact is that he did survive in office for a comparatively long period, which, according to Lafragua, was his overriding aim.[12] His vagueness with regard to the merits or otherwise of federalism or centralism may well have been contrived, because it allowed him to imply to all the feuding factions that he was sympathetic to their views. Equally, one of the main themes of political propaganda by all sides was the need to conciliate the rival groups and dispense with party interests for the sake of national unity. In other words, Bustamante's intention may have been to emulate his predecessor, Guadalupe Victoria, who during his presidency from 1824 to 1829 had pursued a deliberate policy of what was then known as 'amalgamation' in an attempt to persuade groups and individuals to sacrifice their particular interests on behalf of the common good.

Whatever Bustamante's hopes and aims were – and because of the lack of research on his career we can do little more than speculate on them – there is no doubt that he failed to impose his personality or to produce any coherent or definable policy to meet the pressing needs of the country. Again, it must be acknowledged that he had little opportunity to do so because the pressure of events was so immediate and intense that he had no room for reflection and little for manoeuvre. Nevertheless, when he

9 Gómez Farías to Manuel Gonzlez Cosío, 28 July 1838, Gómez Farías Papers, no. 505.
10 Bustamante, *Gabinete mexicano*, vol. 1, pp. 169–72. Calderón de la Barca describes him as 'an honest man and a brave soldier'; *Life in Mexico*, p. 345.
11 Bustamante, *Gabinete mexicano*, vol. 1, pp. 1–2.
12 Ms. of article for *Leonidas*, 26 December 1838, in Colección Lafragua, no. 398.

took the presidential oath on 19 April 1837, there was a mood of some optimism, which permitted a brief flurry of activity. A new cabinet was immediately announced. The Minister of Relations post went to Luis Gonzaga Cuevas, known to be a close friend and ally of Alamán. The Minister of the Interior was Manuel de la Peña y Peña, a lawyer with long experience in public office and a man said to be very devout. The new Minister of War was General José Mariano Michelena, the oldest appointment at the age of 55 and someone, again, who had been in and out of high office for many years. Finally, the key post at the Treasury went to Joaquín Lebrija, also a man of experience which included a spell in the same department in 1834. With his cabinet in post, Bustamante proceeded to name the new departmental governors, and there was a reshuffling of military commands.[13] Early in May, the selection of those who were to form the SPC was completed, and when the names were announced, it was evident that the conservatives were in firm control. The five members were Justo Corro, Rafael Mangino, José Ignacio Espinosa, General Melchor Múzquiz and Sánchez de Tagle.

Several measures were also quickly introduced or promised in an attempt to gain public support. New editors were appointed for the *Diario del Gobierno,* and on 27 April Bustamante urged all citizens to respect and uphold the law as he intended to do, promising that nobody would be persecuted for political opinions.[14] Public employees who had not been paid for months were promised that they would soon receive at least part of their salaries, and more changes were made to centralize control of tax offices and collections in the departments.[15] Then, on 3 May, as proof of the new era according to the government press, the text of a peace treaty signed with Spain was released and predictions of a boom in trade with renewed prosperity soon appeared. New regulations on pension rights, the administration of justice and the election of town councils were also published. In response to pressure from the cotton bloc, an additional levy was imposed on cotton imports, and all national textile manufactures were exempted from tax, as was cotton harvested within the republic.

These and various other measures were all published within a few weeks of Bustamante's taking office, and when the new Congress was formally opened on 1 June, the president set out, albeit in very general terms, his programme for the future.[16] Reforms would be made, he assured his audience and the public at large, in the legal system, the press, customs service and fiscal system. Law and order, and especially its policing, would be strengthened, education would be promoted at all levels, the army

13 *Diario del Gobierno,* 29 July, 14 August 1837.
14 Ibid., 1 May 1837.
15 Ibid., 9–10 May 1837.
16 The text of Bustamante's speech is in *México: Mensajes políticos,* pp. 38–40.

and navy would be improved. In foreign affairs, good relations were being established with the Papacy, which had finally recognized independence, and his government intended to renegotiate the foreign debt.

In many respects, Bustamante appeared to make an energetic start, but beneath the public façade of optimism and promise, almost from the day he took office, the problems he inherited from the preceding regime began to resurface. The most urgent was the revenue situation, because although procedural and administrative changes in tax collections were made, these did not bring any immediate improvement in the government's finances. The position had become so desperate – the Treasury was almost completely empty – that Bustamante and his ministers had to rely on regular hand-outs of a few thousand pesos from friendly financiers and at one point were reduced to appealing for charitable donations to be able to pay at least something to the capital's always restless garrison. Not surprisingly, Bustamante turned to his clerical friends for help, and the metropolitan chapter responded with a gift of 10,000 pesos, which was soon followed by another 80,000 from the religious orders.[17] Such sums were useful for meeting daily needs, but with the Treasury running a monthly deficit of at least 450,000 pesos, it was obvious that a larger-scale solution had to be found. The difficulty was that the millions needed could be raised only in the financial market-place of the now notorious *agiotistas,* and Bustamante had promised that no further ruinous loan contracts by which the government mortgaged future customs and tax revenues would be signed. But the moneylenders naturally would not lend without security or profit, and when the cabinet examined what assets could be used as collateral, it found that the national chest was virtually empty. There was nothing of significance left to pledge. There was one possible solution, however, a road which was so politically sensitive and dangerous that hitherto none except a radical had dared to venture down it. The solution was to find assets of sufficient value and scale, and only one institution met the bill: the Church with its enormous holdings of real estate and capital, not to mention the value of gold and silver ornaments within the churches. Faced with no alternative, Bustamante brought the question of Church wealth back on the political agenda.

Private soundings were made with the senior clergy of the metropolitan diocese, to whom it was suggested that the Church might act as guarantor of a loan of up to 10,000,000 pesos by committing its real estate and revenues as security. The clergy were sympathetic, taking the point made by government negotiators that if the administration fell, it could well

17 *El Cosmopolita,* 1 April, 7 August 1837; *Dictamen de la comisión y acuerdo del Illmo. Cabildo metropolitano de México sobre hipotecar los bienes eclesiásticos para el empréstito que solicita el supremo gobierno* (Mexico, 1837).

be replaced by another extremist regime like that of Gómez Farías, which had threatened to nationalize all Church wealth. A committee of three canons examined the proposal, and on 8 June 1837 they produced a twenty-seven-page report.[18] In this, they accepted the government's case of need and also stated, incidentally, that they found no reason in canon law to forbid such use of clerical goods, a point the liberals were to note with much interest. They did not feel, however, that the Church could risk as much as 10,000,000 pesos, and instead agreed that it would act as guarantor for the sum of 750,000, mortgaging its assets to that amount.

When news of this deal was made public, it at once caused much public debate and controversy. In simple terms, it meant that the government could now borrow up to 750,000 pesos from financiers, and if that money was not repaid, they could take possession of the clerical assets which guaranteed payment. The assets which were to be used were houses, belonging mostly to the religious orders. Those houses were rented not to clergy for the most part but to ordinary citizens, most of whom were *hombres de bien* or of the middle class. They now faced the certain prospect, given the record of any government's repaying of loans, of their landlord, which had always been a benevolent ecclesiastical institution, being replaced by a private speculator whose sole objective was profit. Needless to say, protests began to appear in the press and elsewhere. These were not based on theological arguments about the sacrosanct nature of Church property, which was usually the case when the issue was raised because the clergy themselves had justified the loan. Instead, they emphasized the individual personal consequences for tenants: 'Before very long, the tenants of half Mexico will be thrown onto the streets by the new owners on the pretext of repairing the houses'.[19]

Such predictions were not entirely fanciful if Carlos Bustamante is to be believed. He vehemently opposed any sale of Church assets, arguing the ultramontanist case that they were sacred and inalienable. For him, it could not be right that the dowry of a nun – usually about 4,000 pesos – should end up in the pocket of a financial speculator. He gave examples of convents which were obliged to surrender properties and claimed that honourable men were thrown onto the streets because they could not afford to pay the inflated rents demanded by their new landlords.[20] Gregorio Mier y Terán was at least one of the financiers who benefited from the new availability of ecclesiastical property. He eventually acquired from the Carmelite Order an hacienda and various properties in the capital valued at 241,754 pesos.[21]

18 *Dictamen sobre bienes eclesiásticos.*
19 *El Imparcial,* 3 November 1837.
20 Bustamante, *Gabinete mexicano,* vol. 1, pp. 17–18.
21 Cardoso, *Formación y desarrollo de la burguesía,* p. 145.

Some convent administrators saw which way the political winds were blowing, and realizing that such visible, tangible assets as real estate were easy targets, they began to sell property, reinvesting the proceeds in private loans and mortgages. They knew that since the time of the consolidation laws of 1804, invested capital had always been more secure because its confiscation involved forcing private citizens to redeem loans. The provincial of the Carmelites had written in 1834 that in certain times it was better to own property, but it was now more advisable to convert real estate holdings into investment capital.[22] The same order, and others, continued the policy in 1837 and 1838 and provoked criticism in the liberal press for doing so.[23] The government became aware of what was happening and the obvious threat to its use of Church assets as collateral. Bustamante was obliged to introduce the same measure the liberals of 1833 had enacted by which the regular orders throughout the republic were forbidden to sell any of their goods without permission of the government.[24]

The concern the senior clergy must have felt at this renewed interest in the Church's wealth was certainly justified. Despite their strong presence or support in Congress, the Council of Government and the SPC, four of whose members were said to represent the clerical interest, the continued poverty of the Treasury perhaps inevitably led to more and more demands. With the 1837 agreed mortgage as a precedent, it was not long before more radical proposals were being aired in Congress. On 13 June 1838, for example, Deputy José Mariano Troncoso (Chiapas) proposed that, in view of the financial crisis, all monastic wealth in the republic be nationalized, with the needs of the regulars being taken care of in future by the State. His idea attracted some support in Congress but was rejected at the committee stage.[25]

Such ideas were manifestly not what the clergy had expected to hear from a government headed by the pious Bustamante, and they contributed to the clergy's growing disillusion with both him and the centralist system. Moreover, their wealth was not the only issue to give grounds for concern. There were also increasing signs that the anticlericalism of earlier years was once again filling the pages of the liberal press. There were occasional voices, for example, demanding freedom of religious belief. In Mexico, as one put it, 'we have to be saints whether we like it or not', and several incidents stimulated much hostile comment.[26] One concerned the bishop of Yucatán, José María Guerra, who was attacked

22 Costeloe, *Church Wealth in Mexico*, pp. 123–4.
23 *El Cosmopolita*, 6 June, 21 July, 11 August 1838.
24 Dublán and Lozano, *Legislación mexicana*, vol. 3, pp. 538–9.
25 *El Cosmopolita*, 16 June 1838.
26 *El Momo*, 22 August 1838.

for setting up a diocesan censorship committee which he said would not just confiscate prohibited books but would also keep a check on who went to mass and who did not, warning the latter that they would be punished if they continued to neglect their religious duties.[27] The editor of *El Cosmopolita* warned the clergy, 'We believe that people need religion; but we also believe that ministers of the faith must be confined to the limits of their authority'.[28] Bishop Vázquez was described as a man 'despised for his devotion to the colonial regime',[29] and José María Alpuche e Infante, the radical and fanatically antiestablishment priest, insisted that 'every society can survive very well without bishops or canons'.[30] Other clergy were condemned for using their position to persuade their parishioners not to oppose government policies and for their influence at election time.[31]

With these and several other incidents, the Church found itself once more at the forefront of the political stage, and its manifest sympathy for and practical support of the centralist regime again made it a target of liberal reformers.[32] As far as the government was concerned, it intended to use the Church whenever it could, and it was to turn again and again to it for financial help. Further loans of 350,000 pesos at 5 per cent interest and 200,000 at zero interest were obtained, but even the use of Church wealth as collateral had little effect on the ever-mounting public debt, and Bustamante again had to resort to the speculators and to taxation.[33] In what Tenenbaum describes as 'a period of good will, high profits and euphoria for the moneylenders', he announced a series of loans, the largest of which was for 6,000,000 pesos to be raised by the Banco de Amortización.[34] Seventy-five per cent of the money was to be spent on the Texas campaign and 25 per cent on urgent needs.[35] A few state-owned assets were transferred to the Bank to strengthen its equity, including the possessions of ex-cloistered religious orders, some of the customs revenues and that part of the clerical mortgage agreement which had not yet been realized. Usually by the mechanism of the Bank, several other smaller loans were floated and an attempt was made to renegotiate Mexican debts to British bondholders in the hope that a new foreign loan

27 *El Cosmopolita*, 15 August 1838.
28 Ibid., 12 April 1837.
29 Ibid., 11 September 1837, 9 May, 11 July 1838.
30 Ibid., 27 September 1837. J. M. Alpuche e Infante, *Exposición o sea satisfacción que el que suscribe, hace al Supremo Gobierno de la república contra el despotismo del alto clero yucateco y metropolitano* (Mexico, 1837).
31 *El Cosmopolita*, 22 September 1838.
32 See, e.g., ibid., 8 and 11 August 1838.
33 Manuel Posada to Pérez de Lebrija, 11 January 1839, ibid., 20 February 1839.
34 Tenenbaum, *Politics of Penury*, p. 61.
35 Dublán and Lozano, *Legislación mexicana*, vol. 3, p. 459.

could be arranged. Many private deals were also made with individual financiers who were able to demand and get very favourable terms with quick profits of up to 376 per cent or more on the cash they advanced.[36] In January 1839, the Church was again called upon to help, and it agreed to provide a loan of 500,000 pesos with an initial 200,000 payable by means of 50,000 in cash and bills of 10,000 each over a period of months.[37]

These short-term deals, particularly with the *agiotistas,* enabled the government to avoid total bankruptcy, but as more and more of its regular revenues were mortgaged in advance, the real fiscal situation remained desperate. The Minister of Hacienda reported to Congress in July 1837 that the budget was running at an annual deficit of almost 18 million pesos, with the expenses of the army alone far exceeding the total antic-ipated revenues. A few weeks later, in trying to persuade the legislators to agree to a loan of 8 million pesos, he told them the government had simply run out of cash. He proposed, therefore, in addition to the loan, a 4 per cent increase in the sales tax, 1 per cent more on alcohol and increases on a range of other products. He also recommended salary cuts for all those paid out of the public purse.[38]

Despite all of these measures, there was no overall improvement during the fiscal year, and when the Minister again reported in July 1838, the picture was just as gloomy. Customs receipts had plummeted, as these comparative figures show:[39]

1834–5	8,920,408 pesos
1835–6	5,835,068
1836–7	4,377,579
1837–8	2,838,940

The decrease was due, the Minister explained, to several factors, including the copper money crisis and the shortage of silver. Most other normal revenues had also declined, and with dividends on the foreign debt of more than 49 million pesos amounting to almost 2.5 million pesos plus a huge but unknown internal debt, the deficit remained at almost 16 million pesos.[40]

Faced with this situation, Bustamante appealed to his supporters for help, but with little response. All of the departmental authorities were urged to encourage people to lend money to the Banco de Amortización

---

36 Details in Tenenbaum, *Politics of Penury,* pp. 61–2.
37 *El Cosmopolita,* 2 February 1839; Dublán and Lozano, *Legislación mexicana,* vol. 3, pp. 600–1; *Colección de los documentos más interesantes relativos al préstamo de medio millón de pesos ofrecido por el venerable clero secular y regular de este arzobispado* (Mexico, 1939).
38 *Diario del Gobierno,* 16 October 1837.
39 *Memoria de Hacienda* (1839).
40 *Diario del Gobierno,* 9 September to 10 October 1838; *Memoria de Hacienda* (1838).

to enable it to raise the 6 million peso loan, but the reply of the governor of Nuevo León was typical. He reported that he had circulated all the districts in his jurisdiction, but with one exception they had said they had no funds. The one exception was the villa de Santiago, which had raised 38 pesos 4 reales, which he was sending.[41] Appeals to the public at large produced next to nothing, and patriotic juntas were formed all over the country to raise funds, with the wives of both Santa Anna and Tornel playing a prominent role, but again with only minimum success. Bustamante summoned the leaders of the business community in the capital, and although they promised 30,000 pesos, it is unlikely that it was actually paid.[42]

There was only one option left, and that was to try to raise taxes. The fact that Bustamante and his ministers chose to do so is to some extent surprising because the several taxes on property and commerce already enacted had produced a disappointing yield, and in several departments – for example, New Mexico, the Californias, Sinaloa and Chiapas – despite the centralized tax system, nothing had been collected. Furthermore, those taxes had caused great resentment, or even hatred as the Minister of Hacienda noted, among the middle class, and it was clear that new impositions were likely to be similarly received and ineffective. Nevertheless, Bustamante had no other option and several new taxes were announced, two of which were exceptionally large and significant. The first came in a decree of 8 June 1838.[43] This authorized the government to raise an emergency tax of up to 4 million pesos to be levied throughout the republic on urban and rural property, commerce, professions and trades, wages and salaries, invested capital and luxury goods. In a series of accompanying decrees, the detailed assessment of each category was published. Property owners in the capital had to pay 2 pesos per thousand of the current value of every piece of urban property, less any interest-bearing mortgage. In the departmental capitals, the rate was 1½ pesos and elsewhere 1 peso. Rural property was assessed at 3 pesos per thousand of value and business premises on a scale ranging from 300 pesos for large, wholesale enterprises to less than 10 pesos for small cafés, public bathhouses, stables, slaughterhouses and diverse other retail businesses. The main theatre in the capital was to pay 20 pesos per performance, and the cock-fight establishment 14 pesos. In the professions category, non-salaried or self-employed lawyers were to pay 300 pesos, doctors and surgeons 200, brokers 100, architects and business agents 50 and teachers ranging from 25 to 8 pesos. Manufacturing premises varied from 300

41 *Diario del Gobierno*, 30 May 1838.
42 *El Cosmopolita*, 20 October 1838.
43 Dublán and Lozano, *Legislación mexicana*, vol. 3, pp. 512–13.

pesos for clothes producers, 200 for flour mills, 100 for tailors and silver-smiths, 50 for paper factories, 30 for breweries and anywhere between 1 and 40 pesos for a whole range of small-scale enterprises. All invested capital of at least 500 pesos was to pay 4 per cent of the annual interest, although it is noticeable that among the exceptions were sums invested as ecclesiastical benefices. Salaries, wages, pensions and all other regular daily, weekly, monthly or annual incomes were assessed at a rate of from 12½ per cent on 12,000 pesos to ½ per cent on 50 pesos per annum. Finally, a special charge was placed on luxury goods, from 20 pesos on four-seater carriages to 10 on pleasure boats, again with various amounts on other items, including 2 pesos on horses.

This was the most comprehensive piece of tax legislation introduced since independence, and although there were some exempted categories, it was designed to affect most of the working population.[44] Yet the likelihood of its being successfully implemented was remote. Just a few days before the details were released, a congressional Treasury committee had advised against direct taxation, arguing that the tradition of indirect taxation was so well established that it offered the only hope of increasing revenues.[45]

Not surprisingly, given the complexity of the new tax – it ran to twenty-two pages with several hundred clauses – and the inevitable time lag in trying to collect it, the yield again proved disappointing and did little or nothing to help the revenue problem. A few months later, on 10 December 1838, an even more radical and unpopular tax was announced which confirmed the government's desperation.[46] This imposed a monthly poll tax (*capitación*) on heads of families. Each individual was to be assessed at between 1 and 100 pesos per month according to income, and all corporations, both secular and ecclesiastic, were to pay between 30 and 500 pesos. The minimum income level for liability, however, was set at 12 reales a day, which meant that most of the working class and poor were exempt and the main burden of payment would again fall on the *hombres de bien*. Special collectors of the tax were to be appointed in every district, and they were to be paid for their efforts between 1 and 2 per cent of the amount they collected.

Neither the loans from the Church and the *agiotistas*, the sale of assets, nor these two major taxes and several other minor ones provided any sustained relief for the Treasury. From the viewpoint of the *hombres de bien*, the situation was rapidly deteriorating and the demands made on

---

44 One of the effects of the taxes on property was that private landlords increased rents; *El Mosquito Mexicano*, 29 December 1837.

45 'Dictamen de la comisión segunda de hacienda de la cámara de diputados', 5 June 1838, in *Diario del Gobierno*, 15 June 1838.

46 Dublán and Lozano, *Legislación mexicana*, vol. 3, pp. 568–9.

their individual purses were becoming more onerous by the day. There seemed to be no hope of improvement, and an air of pessimism and fear began to prevail. As one observer wrote in his diary:

Everywhere there are the ingredients of an explosion against the present situation; there is no class which is content; even those same writers and journalists who previously praised the government today attack all its actions and measures; poverty is rapidly and daily increasing; judges administer justice as they fancy; the roads are plagued with thieves; everything portends a general upheaval.[47]

The centralized republican form of government had manifestly failed to improve the national, departmental or municipal finances, and although there were further concessions to the cotton bloc as well as the trade treaty with Spain, there was no sign of anything like an economic recovery. If the *hombres de bien* were disillusioned with the lack of progress on the economic and fiscal fronts, they were soon equally sceptical that there would be any improvement in the other areas promised in the centralist manifesto. This was particularly the case in the always prominent issue of law and order and more general social policy. Although there is no statistical evidence of crime rates, public opinion as expressed in the daily and periodical press depicted a continuing rise in lawlessness and crime of every sort. *El Cosmopolita* maintained that law and order had collapsed completely, predicting at least one murder a day in the capital, rising to two if action was not taken.[48] Even the government's own *Diario* waged a campaign for better policing of the capital. The city, it said, was filthy, streets were filled with potholes in which people and horses risked breaking their legs, sewage overflowed in the streets whenever it rained and there were thieves and vagabonds at every corner. The system of *celadores,* or nightwatchmen, who were supposed to patrol the streets had become farcical. Their blue and white uniforms might be resplendent, but they were totally ineffective as policemen. They rarely received their pay and were easily and usually bribed by the gangs of thieves who operated with impunity.[49] The official response to such complaints was to blame the judicial process for failing to punish criminals when they were occasionally caught. The president of the high court refused to accept the blame, pointing out that most of those who were sentenced to the penitentiaries escaped and were then welcomed into the army by commanding officers.[50] The authorities chose to establish yet another type of municipal policeman for the capital, to be known as day or night watchmen (*vigilantes diurnos o nocturnos*).[51]

47 'Diario militar y político', 6 October 1837 entry, García Collection, no. 441.
48 *El Cosmopolita*, 18 August 1837.
49 *Diario del Gobierno*, 4 and 21 July 1838.
50 Ibid., 28 July 1838.
51 Dublán and Lozano, *Legislación mexicana*, vol. 3, pp. 470–8.

Although the presence of these new policemen on the streets added one more colourful dimension to the environment, as one paper remarked, neither they nor the press campaigns resulted in any notable improvement in law and order. There was also no progress in halting what the conservatives had long argued was a serious decline in social, moral and religious values. It seemed that the younger generation in particular would not accept the traditional or accepted standards of behaviour or morality, an attitude attributed to a declining respect for the Church and for the Roman Catholic faith. That decline in turn was said to be caused by a flood of obscene and impious literature which was circulating freely throughout the country and also by a shortage of properly trained teachers. Bustamante did set up an enquiry into school provision in every department, but most of the returns indicated that while some improvements were being made – there were forty publicly funded schools with 3,525 pupils in Zacatecas, for example – no area had the money needed to fund enough schools.[52] From Puebla, it was reported that 'it is not easy now to find theologians who know how to refute with ease and clarity the points used to challenge religion in the cafés and theatres.'[53] Prostitution, drunkenness, adultery and sacrilegious acts were said to be rampant in every town and city. Bishop Vázquez, who never minced his words, condemned the spread of 'impiety and irreligion', 'obscene books', and the 'illicit pleasures of the flesh'. There was, he said, a growing lack of respect for the churches, where many now went only to insult God in his own house.[54]

Part of the problem in the bishop's view was people's abuse of the frequent public and religious holidays on which no work was permitted and when the incidence of crime of all types apparently rose dramatically. The *días festivos* became a topic of public debate, and while the clergy condemned their abuse, others denounced the number as excessive. According to one estimate, work was permitted on only 198 days per year, to the obvious detriment of the economy.[55] The government agreed with both points of view and negotiations were begun with the Papacy to reduce them.

The 'black scene' of social change, to use Bishop Vázquez's phrase, at this time remains to be investigated, but there is no doubt that the change to a centralized republic brought no improvement, and the issues of law and order, education, morality and respect for religion continued to be

---

52 'Estado de la educación pública en el departamento de Zacatecas', *Diario del Gobierno*, 17 May 1838.
53 'Informe que da la comisión de visita de colegios al Exmo. Sr. gobernador de este departamento de Puebla', Puebla, 30 June 1838, in ibid., 18 August 1838.
54 'Carta pastoral', 16 December 1838, in ibid., 26 December 1838.
55 *El Imparcial*, 13 June 1837.

of primary concern to *hombres de bien*. Taken in conjunction with the economic and fiscal crisis, it was soon evident that the Bustamante government was in danger of being overwhelmed by the situation, and it was hardly surprising, though unusual, when the entire cabinet chose to resign just six months after taking office, saying publicly that the problems of the nation were beyond their abilities to resolve.[56] New ministers were appointed but with little effect, and although the conservative press continued to exhort property owners to defend their own interests and to warn of social dissolution if the anarchists were allowed to triumph, everything still seemed to deteriorate. There was one group, of course, which welcomed every sign of weakness and every difficulty the government faced. Almost from the moment of Bustamante's inauguration, the federalists and liberals had made it clear that they would not give up their campaign against centralism and rule by what they described as the 'leaders of the oligarchy'.[57]

There had been *pronunciamientos* on behalf of federalism throughout 1835 and 1836, and these continued at a more intensive rate, as did the propaganda campaign against Bustamante and his supporters waged by an expanding liberal press. Rebellions broke out in most departments, and while, as always, some were minor acts of dissident officers or local interest groups seeking to redress particular grievances, they did cause serious disruption at the local level, preventing any consolidation of the centralist regime. Officials were deposed to be replaced by federalists; legislation or the effects of it, especially on taxation, were suspended; and in some instances, for example, at the ports, the rebel leaders negotiated with ships' captains to allow them to bring ashore prohibited imports in exchange for substantial cash payments. Haciendas were ransacked and money, cattle, food and horses taken by marauding bands of rebels, and loyal government troops were authorized by Bustamante himself to requisition whatever they needed, promising to pay for it later.[58] In the towns and villages, those with money were subjected to confiscation of property and forced loans by whichever side was in the vicinity.

Many of these so-called rebellions were carried out on a very minor scale, involving little or no military action. To give just one example, Colonel Nieves Huerta, leading seventy men, took over the town of Zacapú (Michoacán), and reinstalled the previous local authorities, but according to one report there was no violence: 'All was carried out with complete order and with even the sale of brandy prohibited on that day'.[59] In contrast, however, events in New Mexico were notably more violent, at

56 Ibid., 17 October 1837.
57 *El Momo*, 8 August 1838.
58 A. Bustamante to Fernando Franco, 16 May 1838, Gómez Farías Papers, no. 478.
59 *El Cosmopolita*, 25 April 1838.

least according to the description given in Congress. There, several members of the departmental junta and other officials were killed, as was the local military commander, whose decapitated head was put on public display by the rebels.[60]

In addition to hundreds of these small-scale actions across the republic, there were simultaneously more organized and co-ordinated revolts. The first was centred on San Luis Potosí, but it had ramifications and support in neighbouring departments and attempts were made to spread it even further. Led by Lieutenant-Colonel Ramón García Ugarte, it began a few days before Bustamante's inauguration in April when on the 14th of that month, with the slogan 'Federation or Death', Ugarte issued his demands that the federation be restored.[61] Leading the men from the local garrison, he quickly took control of the town, arresting the authorities as well as prominent citizens, from whom he extracted a substantial ransom in cash, money which according to Alamán he used to suborn more recruits to his cause. Soon supported by General Esteban Moctezuma, 'a man of some influence around there and with a reputation in the army', it looked for a time as if the revolt would spread, but most potential supporters held off to see how things developed.[62] This allowed other military commanders loyal to the government to assemble their forces, and in due course the revolt was suppressed by Paredes in an action which resulted in the death of Moctezuma and eighty rebels.[63] Following the usual procedure, the surviving rebels were granted an amnesty, with their officers being exiled to Matamoros, where as Vázquez notes, 'there was promptly formed a centre of federal unrest in a port which was such a nerve centre of national life'.[64]

The government's success against Ugarte did nothing to stop the federalist revolts, and within a few months there was another serious situation in the north at Sonora, where the commander general, José Urrea, demanded that a popularly elected convention be summoned to restore and reform the 1824 charter. Urrea had only recently been appointed to the post by his friend Bustamante, and suspicions were soon voiced that the president himself had decided to throw in his lot with the federalists. What truth there was in this rumour is not known, but Urrea took control of the department, reorganized it on federalist lines and told the newly

60 Bustamante, *Gabinete mexicano*, vol. 1, pp. 33–7.

61 *El Cosmopolita*, 26 April 1837.

62 L. Alamán to Duque de Terranova, 30 April, 27 June 1837, in *Obras: Documentos diversos*, vol. 4, pp. 377–81. According to the *Diario* (11 May 1837), 200,000 pesos was seized from private citizens. Sierra says that 'el objeto real era apoderarse de fondos y favorecer negocios'; *Evolución política*, p. 218. Zamacois has more details of this revolt; N. de Zamacois, *Historia de México* (Barcelona, 1880), vol. 12, pp. 110–13.

63 C. Ashburnham to Ld. Palmerston, 2 June 1837, P.R.O., F.O. 50, 106, fols. 238–42.

64 *Planes en la nación mexicana*, book 2, p. 29.

elected state legislature in April 1838 that the state had regained its independence.[65] Elsewhere, Gordiano Guzmán rebelled in Michoacán, as did Mariano Olarte in Veracruz, and in dozens of other towns the federation was proclaimed. Almost all of these revolts were suppressed after a time, only for the central government to learn of a new round, and in the summer and autumn of 1838 there were rebels in Morelia, Tuxtla, Aguascalientes, and Tampico, where Urrea, having escaped from Sonora, reappeared to lead the federalist cause. Again, most of these were defeated, but not in Tampico, where government forces were repulsed in their attempts to dislodge the rebels. The result was that Urrea, with ample financial resources from the port and from confiscations, was able to consolidate his position, and the more he did so, the more backing he attracted from other places.

The federalist cause was not confined to military action. The many *pronunciamientos* were accompanied by an intense press campaign in which Bustamante, his ministers and their actions were daily attacked. All the problems of law and order, the economic stagnation, the revolts – in sum, the general instability and malaise of the country – were now blamed on the centralist form of government and the Siete Leyes. On every front, it was argued, the situation was materially worse than it had been under federalism; the only solution was to restore the 1824 charter and summon a convention to reform it. In the words of one federalist, 'The federation lasted eleven years and in the midst of the revolutionary whirlwind, the country never suffered even the smallest part of the ills which the new code has produced in eleven months'.[66]

The daily articles and editorials in the press were supported by dozens, if not hundreds, of petitions from around the country, pleading with Bustamante or the Congress to initiate the change, and just as centralism had been justified as the popular will expressed through similar petitions in 1835, the federalists maintained that the new popular will had to be respected. There was no noticeable regional bias to these petitions, coming as they did from Zacatecas and Durango in the north to Puebla and Oaxaca in the south and countless other places in between. Yet there are signs that, once again, the opposition reflected some kind of co-ordination and central organization. In his study of Gordiano Guzmán's revolt in Michoacán, Olveda mentions the arrival of Manuel Palafox, 'sent by the command centre of the federalist campaign set up in Mexico City', and Carlos Bustamante again claims that the *yorkino* Grand Lodge in the capital

65 *El Cosmopolita*, 21 April 1838.
66 *Exposición dirigida de la capital del departamento de Puebla al Exmo. Sr, Presidente general Don Anastasio Bustamante, pidiendo el restablecimiento del sistema federal* (Mexico, 1837). Lafragua was one of the signatories, and there is a copy of the document in his archive, no. 398.

was directing everything.[67] Rebel leaders in different areas certainly kept in touch, and one man who was definitely involved was Gómez Farías. Although still in exile in New Orleans, he stayed in close contact with federalist politicians and friends, who continued to send him newspapers and money.[68] He was also in contact with rebel leaders, most notably with Urrea, and his correspondents kept him in touch with the propaganda battle in the capital, one writing on 19 October 1837 that 'we have worked nonstop to form public opinion in our favour'.[69]

Then Gómez Farías returned to Mexico, arriving at Veracruz on 11 February 1838. He was given a warm public welcome with banquets in his honour, and when he entered the capital about a week later, a large crowd and, it was said, some fifty carriages waited to receive him.[70] In private, many people also sent their good wishes, and although some of these letters were from sycophants and job seekers of one sort or another, others were from prominent politicians, for example, Manuel González Cosío at Zacatecas.[71] It is clear that despite his prolonged absence in exile, Gómez Farías remained the political leader of the radical liberals and federalists. Mateo Ramírez wrote from Guadalajara in July urging him to lead the movement because 'your power in the hearts of these federalists is irresistible'.[72] It is also evident that he had no intention of relaxing the campaign against both Bustamante and the centralists. In April he had written to Ignacio Zuñiga to say that he had decided to play his full part in the struggle and that he now saw the political scene, as 'the struggle of today is that of freedom against slavery, light against darkness, civilization against barbarity'.[73] On the same day, he wrote to Urrea to thank him for a decree of the Sonora state legislature which had made him an honorary citizen and offered him a gift of lands in the state.[74]

Throughout the months after his return, therefore, Gómez Farías took part in the federalist campaign, using his reputation and influence wherever possible.[75] With a notoriously unreliable postal system and with

67 J. Olveda, *Gordiano Guzmán: Un cacique del siglo XIX* (Mexico, 1980), p. 161; Bustamante, *Gabinete mexicano*, vol. 1, p. 42. There are copies of dozens of the profederalist petitions in the Gómez Farías Papers; see, e.g., no. 554.
68 V. Gómez Farías to F. N. del Barrio y A. Garay, 27 June 1837, Gómez Farías Papers, no. 411.
69 Juan to Gómez Farías, 19 October 1837, ibid., no. 420.
70 *El Cosmopolita*, 21 February 1838.
71 Gómez Farías Papers, no. 436.
72 Ibid., no. 497.
73 Ibid., no. 463.
74 Ibid., no. 465.
75 For example, Manuel del Río wrote from Salvatierra on 13 September 1838 to tell Gómez Farías that he had been chosen as a district elector and to ask his advice on whom to vote for as deputies; ibid., no. 530. Similarly, José Pareja wrote from Guadalajara on 27 October to tell Gómez Farías that Mariano Ramírez, who had been elected a deputy, was a good liberal and would be cooperative; ibid., no. 546.

confidential letters often entrusted to messengers who could be easily
bribed, it was not difficult for the government to discover what was going
on. As the *Diario* put it, 'All over Mexico it is known' that the federalist
conspirators were active in the capital.[76] Bustamante, as always, hesitated
but eventually, on 7 September, orders were issued for the arrest of all
the leading federalists then in the capital. The following were detained:
Joaquín Cardoso, Francisco Modesto Olaguíbel, Ignacio Basadre, Juan
Zelaeta, D. N. Envides, José María Alpuche e Infante and Gómez Farías.
Some were held in military barracks, Alpuche in the former Inquisition
building and Gómez Farías in a cell of the Santo Domingo monastery.
Even after his confinement, however, in the more or less open prison
system of that time, Gómez Farías was able to lead the federalists until
the Minister of War, noting the constant stream of visitors to his cell,
ordered on 9 October that henceforth only his barber, lawyer, family and
those with legitimate reasons be admitted to see him.[77]

The removal of Gómez Farías and the other leaders did not stop opposition to the government. This was because after the defeat of the radicals
of 1833–4, which Santa Anna had achieved with the support of the so-
called moderates, the liberal ranks had split into two groups: the radicals
known as *puros* or *exaltados,* and the moderates, or *hombres de progreso.* With
the exile of the radical leaders, most notably Gómez Farías, the way was
left open for the moderates to gain control. The man who emerged as
their leader was Gómez Pedraza, whose supporters were known as *ped-
racistas.* While both groups shared common ground on many issues and
both were federalists, they differed on a number of matters – for example,
the degree of autonomy to be allowed the states, control or reform of the
Church and its wealth, universal or restricted franchise, unrestricted or
restricted press freedom. In essence, the radicals wanted the programme
of immediate fundamental changes to the Church, army and education
which they had tried to implement in 1833–4, whereas the moderates,
though not disagreeing with changes in those areas, wanted them to be
made at a more controlled, progressive pace.

This division in the liberal federalist ranks was largely obscured during
the absence of Gómez Farías, but with his return to the centre of the
political stage, the rivalry between the two groups, especially the hostility
between the two leaders, intensified. According to Lafragua's memoir,
there was a move in the masonic society to have Gómez Farías replace
Gómez Pedraza as leader, but although backed by powerful figures like
Crescencio Rejón, the attempt failed and 'from then onwards the liberal

76 *Diario del Gobierno,* 7 September 1838. In a letter to Gómez Farías of 12 July 1838, Juan N.
   Cumplido described the postal service as 'el primer banco del espionaje para los señores del día';
   J. Olveda, ed., *Cartas a Gómez Farías* (Mexico, 1990), pp. 54–5.
77 Gómez Farías Papers, no. 541.

party was divided'.[78] Thus, although Gómez Pedraza had failed to be elected to the presidency in the 1837 elections, he had remained at the forefront of the opposition, and his strategy when faced with the fait accompli of centralism seems to have been to maintain his image as an *hombre de bien* and moderate while gradually increasing pressure on Bustamante. His main demand was for a convention to revise the constitutional basis of the republic with a view to restoring a more controlled form of federalism, and although we have no details, rumours that he had put a specific programme to Bustamante, and that he was likely to accept it, were frequent in the summer months of 1838. Gómez Farías was warned by his allies that his rival could not be trusted.[79]

All the evidence suggests that Bustamante either did indeed hover on the verge of switching his allegiance to the moderate federalists or at least led them to believe that he was going to do so. There were persistent allegations that Alamán, Sánchez de Tagle and other centralists had become disillusioned with him and that, as early as November 1837, they were beginning to consider a replacement.[80] Carlos Bustamante continued his attacks, and hostile pamphlets such as *Tumba del Sr. Bustamante* began to appear on the streets. Rumours of a promonarchist conspiracy circulated, and relations between the executive and the Congress began to break down when Bustamante's requests for emergency powers were rejected. It was said that Bustamante himself believed that the SPC intended to remove him from office on the grounds of ineptitude, and the criticism of him in the press became ever more pungent.[81] With popular discontent spreading and in an atmosphere of intense speculation that something dramatic was about to happen, Bustamante decided early in December 1838 to take what for him was a bold and dangerous step. Three cabinet ministers resigned, including Paredes, who had been at the Ministry of War for only a week, and Pedro Echeverría, who had been at Hacienda for only a month. To the consternation of the centralists and the delight of the federalists, Bustamante offered posts to Gómez Pedraza and to Juan Rodríguez Puebla, also a known federalist. They accepted the posts formally on 13 December on the express condition, according to Rodríguez Puebla and others, that a new Congress would be assembled to reintroduce and reform the 1824 constitution.[82]

Later that same day, 13 December, the two ministers presented an

78 Colección Lafragua, no. 398.
79 Gómez Farías Papers, nos. 499, 513–14, 532.
80 J. A. Mejía to V. Gómez Farías, 28 November 1837, ibid., no. 423. Mejía, who was in Havana at the time, also says that some of Bustamante's recent appointments 'me hacen dudar de la reforma de Bustamante en sus ideas'.
81 Bustamante, *Gabinete mexicano*, vol. 1, p. 42.
82 J. Rodríguez Puebla, *Tres días de ministerio* (Mexico, 17 December 1838).

initiative to the Council of Government which, they said, had been drawn up that morning with the president. They proposed an immediate convention of one deputy per department, a new Congress to reform the constitution and the granting of emergency powers to Bustamante. Introducing their demands, Gómez Pedraza spoke of the critical situation facing the country, the public discontent and the danger of anarchism if radical measures were not taken. The councillors, including Alamán and Bishop Morales, listened and then a heated exchange of views took place. Some told Gómez Pedraza that his ideas would be unconstitutional, to which he replied that there was no point in preserving a constitution which had brought chaos. Others predicted even greater factional division if they agreed, and some suggested that the way to satisfy the federalist pressure was not to reintroduce the federal charter but to give departmental governors and juntas much wider powers. After a meeting which lasted four and a half hours, from 7 p.m. to 11:30 p.m., a vote was taken and the nine councillors present unanimously rejected the initiative.[83]

The next day, 14 December, with mass demonstrations in the streets and shouts of 'Constitution without strings and pure federation', the Congress held an emergency session to discuss what had happened.[84] After talks with Bustamante, who assured the deputies that they were free to decide what they wanted, Congress resolved to send a small delegation to Gómez Pedraza and Rodríguez Puebla. Another lengthy meeting took place, but the congressmen, including Couto and Espinosa de los Monteros, refused to agree to the demands.[85] Meanwhile, on the streets of the city a growing number of demonstrators appeared and there was some violence, including an assault on Alamán's house and looting of shops.[86] One group of demonstrators went to where Gómez Farías and Alpuche were imprisoned and released them. In an atmosphere of expectation that federalism would be restored at almost any moment, they escorted Gómez Farías to his house, apparently stealing his watch on the way.[87]

Eventually, Congress resolved that the whole issue should be decided by the SPC, which was asked to declare what the popular will was. Though voicing some technical objections over the manner in which the request was drawn up, it agreed to consider the matter. After some deliberation, it produced a surprising, controversial and tentative suggestion to the effect that if, given the current state of public disorder, the government

83 Act of the Council of Government session of 13 December 1838, published in *La Lima de Vulcano*, 22 December 1838.
84 Bocanegra, *Memorias*, vol. 2, pp. 760–1.
85 For one version of the meeting, see 'Verdadera noticia de los tres días de Ministerio', in *El Mexicano*, 22 February, 14–28 March 1839.
86 C. Ashburnham to Ld. Palmerston, 31 December 1838, P.R.O., F.O. 50, 116, fols. 158–63.
87 Reported in *El Mexicano*, 21 March 1839.

should fall, none other than Santa Anna should be given wide powers to restore the constitution and the government. Gómez Pedraza and Rodríguez Puebla persisted with their demands, now including one for the seizure of Church wealth, for another twenty-four hours but, as Carlos Bustamante notes, not a single general came out in their support.[88] They realized that their attempted political coup had failed, and after just three days in office, they decided to resign on 15 December.

Throughout what became known as the 'Three-Day Ministry', Bustamante seems to have performed a particularly difficult balancing act on his own very precarious rope, but his real part in the episode is difficult to fathom. There seems little doubt – none in the minds of Gómez Pedraza and Rodríguez Puebla – that he did agree to support a change to federalism. Two weeks after the event, the British diplomat Charles Ashburnham reported to London that 'the conditions on which these men entered office were in fact the re-establishment of the Federal system', and in the days and weeks which followed, others, notably Rodríguez Puebla, made the same assertion.[89] For the federalists at large, Bustamante's conduct was a betrayal, and Lafragua, still in Puebla, wrote on 14 December of his total lack of good faith and his 'consummate treachery'.[90]

Assuming the federalists' beliefs to be true, why did Bustamante promise them his support and why did he then fail to make good his promise? Certainly immense pressure was put on him throughout the summer and autumn of 1838 by Gómez Pedraza and the moderates, and this in conjunction with the known plots of Gómez Farías and the radicals together with the federalist revolts throughout the country may have led him to conclude that the moment was right to defuse the pressure and save his own career by switching sides. Such an explanation is definitely plausible, especially because some two years later he was to do almost exactly the same thing in a last desperate ploy to stay in power. On the other hand, as he must have taken into account, the centralists dominated the corridors of power in the Council of Government, the SPC and the Congress, and there is no doubt that his close advisers among the clergy, much as they resented the recent demands on the Church's wealth, greatly feared the return of the federalists, who might well eventually include the hated Gómez Farías. Furthermore, although most of the senior army officers in the regions remained silent, except for ritual declarations of support for the government, there is no evidence that they woulld permit a return to federalism. In short, Bustamante's conduct remains rather enigmatic but

88 Bustamante, *Gabinete mexicano*, vol. 1, pp. 146–50.
89 C. Ashburnham to Ld. Palmerston, 31 December 1838, P.R.O., F.O. 50, 116, fols. 158–63.
90 Colección Lafragua, no. 398.

there is one other possible explanation. As indicated earlier, one of the main features of his personality in the eyes of his contemporaries was vacillation and a chronic inability to act decisively. The sequence of events in December suggest that he did give in to the pressure of Gómez Pedraza and others only to have second thoughts, change his mind or find himself unable to take the final step. In the words of *El Cosmopolita*, 'He hesitated, he stammered, he repented'.[91]

Whatever the explanation for his behaviour, the events of December 1838 were to mark the beginning of Bustamante's fall from power and of the abandonment of the Siete Leyes because they produced a most unexpected development, namely, the return of Santa Anna to the political arena. The background to his reappearance involved a final major problem for Bustamante and the centralists which was a significant contributory factor in all the difficulties they had to confront. As if the economic, social, political and internal military crises were not enough, they also had to contend with foreign aggression in the form of a war with France. The origin and course of the dispute need only brief description. Many French citizens, together with those of other nations and, of course, Mexicans, had suffered loss and damage to their property and businesses during the revolts and other disturbances since independence. Some merchants had suffered losses in the Parián riot of 1828 and in similar occurrences in Puebla, Veracruz and elsewhere. Claims for compensation had been made by both French and British diplomats, but no agreement had been reached, and the matter was not given much priority by the Mexican government. Then early in March 1838, a French squadron arrived off the coast of Veracruz, and Baron Deffaudis, the senior French diplomat, issued an ultimatum to the Mexican government in which, among other things, he demanded 600,000 pesos in partial settlement of claims, including one from a pastry chef at Veracruz who claimed 60,000 pesos. He also demanded exemption of French citizens from any forced loans. On the evening of 20 March, the cabinet reported to Congress that it had received this ultimatum and also that it was to be completely rejected.[92] The French responded by breaking off diplomatic relations and blockading the port of Veracruz.[93]

The blockade was only partially effective because Bustamante opened other ports to international trade, but it did have a serious effect on the

91 *El Cosmopolita*, 19 December 1838. The government's own explanation was that Bustamante was trying to achieve 'la fusión de los partidos' in the interests of national unity; *Circular que el Supremo Gobierno ha dirigido a los gobernadores de los departamentos sobre los acontecimientos de estos días* (signed J. de Iturbide, Mexico, 17 December 1838).
92 *Diario del Gobierno*, 27 March 1838.
93 Details in Barker, *The French Experience in Mexico*, pp. 60–70.

government's cash flow and added to the already mounting deficit. Bustamante was also able to use the situation to justify expanding the army and increasing taxes to pay for it. The government's propaganda machine went into high gear in an attempt to condemn the federalist rebels as traitors, particularly when it became known that there had been contact between some rebel leaders and the French commanders. Although the government knew that the French were in no position to invade, the public was led to believe that a full-scale war of national survival was imminent. When it was learned that the French king's third son, the 20-year-old Prince de Joinville, was with the fleet, word spread rapidly that a European monarchy was to be founded.[94] Talks were held between the two sides in November without success and later that month, on the 27th, the French began to bombard Veracruz. News of the commencement of hostilities reached the capital within a few hours, and in an atmosphere of panic, Bustamante announced in an address to the nation that 'war is declared'. He called on the people to prepare to fight, and a blanket military conscription of all adult males capable of bearing arms was decreed. There were to be no exceptions: 'Nobody who has property, a business or an honourable way of life will be exempted from enlistment in these units'.[95] Many of the capital's most prominent citizens volunteered, and the press published long lists of names, one of which was headed by Neri del Barrio, Escandón, Loperena and Garay.

Reinforcements had been sent to Veracruz in anticipation of hostilities, but the French bombardment had a rapid effect, and within days the Mexican commanders of the old fortress of San Juan de Ulúa and of Veracruz decided to surrender. News of this reached the capital on 30 November and an estimated two thousand people went to the central square.[96] The government's response to the news was to order the expulsion of all French citizens and to command the officers at Veracruz who had agreed to the treaty with the French to answer charges of dereliction of duty. They were relieved of their posts, and Santa Anna, who had already gone to Veracruz from his country estate, was appointed to the command with Guadalupe Victoria as his deputy.

Since his return from Texas in disgrace in February 1837, Santa Anna had remained in relative obscurity, spending his time as a gentleman farmer tending to his domestic and business interests on his spacious country estate. He had published a long defence of his conduct in the United States and occasionally sent letters to the press in Mexico City to

94 Ibid., pp. 70–6.
95 Decree of 1 December in *Diario del Gobierno*, 1 December 1838.
96 *El Cosmopolita*, 8 December 1838.

deny the fairly frequent rumours that he was involved in revolts or conspiracies to establish a dictatorship.[97] He was never entirely isolated, however, and he kept up his correspondence with friends such as Alamán who reported the latest developments. When the French bombardment of Veracruz began, he hastened to the port, where he conferred with the local commanders, General Gaona and General Rincón, and after inspecting the fortifications at San Juan de Ulúa, they agreed it should be surrendered and the city itself declared a neutral zone. The government refused to accept these terms, dismissed Gaona and Rincón and appointed Santa Anna. He had returned to Manga de Clavo, but on receiving his new orders returned to Veracruz, where he arrived at 11 a.m. on 4 December. He informed the French commander, Admiral Baudin, that the neutral-city proposal had been rejected and then held a council of war with his own officers. Later that same night, General Arista arrived with reinforcements, and he and Santa Anna discussed the situation until about one o'clock in the morning of the 5th, when they both went to bed.[98]

The events of that day, 5 December, were to be the most dramatic in Santa Anna's long career, and his compatriots were never allowed to forget them as long as he remained a power in the land. Exactly what happened is unknown, and whether Santa Anna was a hero, coward, lucky or unlucky remains unclear. In brief, the French decided on an early-morning attack and sent three raiding parties into the city around dawn. Two of these were to seize two forts and the third, led by the Prince de Joinville, was to capture Santa Anna, at the time asleep in bed. The noise involved in forcing open the city gates awoke him, and grabbing his clothes, he rushed down the stairs. The French soldiers who were entering the house did not recognize him and let him through, but Arista was captured and Santa Anna's aide was badly wounded in the ensuing melee. Santa Anna escaped to the outskirts of the city, where he managed to assemble a few other escapees and promptly went back to pursue the departing French. They had placed a cannon at one end of a street to cover their withdrawal, and as Santa Anna galloped up the street – or as some would have it retreated when he saw the cannon – the grapeshot was fired. Santa Anna's horse was killed under him, and he was hit in the left hand and leg. Several of his men were killed or wounded.

The wound to Santa Anna's leg was obviously severe, because three

97 See, e.g., his letter of 7 July 1837 from Manga de Clavo published in *El Investigador Mexicano*, 15 July 1837.
98 These and the following details of the events of 5 December 1838 are mostly from Callcott, *Santa Anna*, pp. 156–60. There are several other accounts; see, e.g., that by Santa Anna's aide-de-camp, Manuel María Giménez, himself badly wounded in the skirmish; García, *Documentos inéditos*, vol. 59, pp. 308–13. See also the summaries given in Díaz y Díaz, *Caudillos y caciques*, p. 147, n. 51.

physicians who were quickly found to examine him concluded that the leg must be amputated, an operation they decided to perform the next day, 6 December. Whatever his physical condition, Santa Anna's mental capacities do not seem to have been impaired, because in the hours before the operation, which he perhaps genuinely believed were to be his last, he was able to compose a report to Bustamante and on a broader level to all his compatriots which, in terms of sentimentality, hyperbole and self-glorification was to surpass anything he wrote before or after. A glorious victory had been gained, he proclaimed, with more than one hundred of the enemy dead and many more wounded compared with the loss of twenty-five Mexican heroes, dead and wounded. This triumph would stop future foreign aggression, but 'probably this will be the final victory I offer my country'. He wanted, he said, to be buried in the sand dunes of Veracruz, and he asked that no retribution be taken against innocent French residents of his country. Finally, he pleaded with Mexicans to forget his past errors and to remember him only as a 'Good Mexican'.[99]

In Callcott's words, Santa Anna 'was thoroughly enjoying this orgy of emotion and his own glorious death-bed scene', and on the next day in what was apparently a badly executed operation, his left leg was amputated.[100] Both he and the amputated limb were carried back to Manga de Clavo for what was to be an astonishingly rapid convalescence and recovery. Within less than two weeks, he was again busily dictating letters, writing, for example, to General Luis Cortazar to thank him for his good wishes and to assure him that he was now out of danger.[101]

When word of these extraordinary events, and Santa Anna's version of them, reached the capital, reactions were no doubt mixed. Some, but not all, must have regretted the likely passing of the hero of Tampico, while at first (though the illusion was soon dispelled) all must have welcomed the claim that the French had suffered a major defeat. Within less than a week, after Bustamante sent two doctors and their assistants to examine him, which they did on 11 December, it was known that Santa Anna would survive.[102] Presumably apprised of the prognosis, the SPC reached its decision on 14 December, amid the Three-Day Ministry crisis, that Santa Anna should be given power to restore order if the government fell. A week later, Santa Anna wrote to the newly appointed Minister of War – once again Tornel – to accept his appointment as commander of the army to resist the French.[103]

---

99 Santa Anna's report was published on 8 December 1838 in the *Diario del Gobierno*.
100 Callcott, *Santa Anna*, p. 160.
101 Letter published in *Diario del Gobierno*, 28 December 1838.
102 The doctors were Pedro Escobedo and Manuel Andrade. Santa Anna's resident physician was Dr. Mendizabal; *Diario del Gobierno*, 19 December 1838.
103 Ibid., 27 December 1838.

What Anastasio Bustamante thought about Santa Anna's entirely un-expected resurrection to the status of national hero can only be imagined, but it was one more factor which must have given him pause for thought. Beset by difficulties on every front with no solutions in sight and certainly aware that he was increasingly considered a liability by those who had put him into office, it seems that the pressure was too great to bear. He began to look for an escape route, for something which would allow him to retain his dignity and, possibly, restore if not enhance his political reputation. He had already asked Congress for permission to lead the army in person, and then it was learned that the federalist rebellion in the north was spreading. More and more towns were issuing *pronuncia-mientos,* and on 16 December, at Santa Ana de Tamaulipas, Urrea pub-lished a set of demands which attracted the adherence of many other rebel groups.[104] This provided the opportunity that Bustamante was seeking, and again he asked to be allowed to lead an army to fight the rebels. This time his request was granted, and following the lead given by the SPC, Congress resolved that despite his medical condition, the interim presi-dency should be offered to Santa Anna.[105] Once more Bustamante had self-doubts and began to query the prudence of his decision, but although he equivocated and delayed his departure for weeks, there was nothing he could do. Santa Anna, or 'the cripple' as he was now scornfully referred to by his enemies, prepared once again to rule Mexico.

104 *El Restaurador Mexicano,* 2 January 1839.
105 *Diario del Gobierno,* 21 January 1839. According to the constitution, Bustamante's interim replacement should have been José Morán, president of the Council of State. He pleaded illness, conveniently leaving the way open for Santa Anna.

7

Santa Anna versus Bustamante: the end of the Siete Leyes, 1839–1841

Some of the more obvious reasons for the failure of the centralized republican system are now apparent. At no time since the take-over by the centralists in the summer of 1835 had there been any semblance of progress or even stability in the political, social or economic life of the country. Although so far unsuccessful in their ultimate objective of regaining power, the federalist campaigns, both military and political, had served to sustain the general instability and ensured that the new constitution, or Siete Leyes, had no chance of being consolidated. Faced with the relentless pressure from countless *pronunciamientos* in the regions, added to the Texas disaster and the French blockade, the national government had been forced to give priority to increased expenditure on the military. Additional funds had had to be sought by way of either loans or taxation from the clergy and the *hombres de bien* in whose interests the regime and the system of government were supposed to have been created. With the exception of the textile industry, where some expansion was taking place, economic activity remained depressed, and with government revenues still in serious deficit, soldiers, public employees, widows, pensioners and all those dependent on the public purse suffered accordingly. No visible improvement had been made in any of the areas of reform which had been promised in the conservative manifesto. The administration of justice remained corrupt and chaotic; the taxation system was still bedevilled by inefficiency and bureaucratic excess; few Mexicans had access to any form of education; respect for the Church, its ministers and the faith was in decline; crime and law and order in general were of growing concern; and finally, nothing had been done to stop the spread of what the traditionalists believed were perverse, dangerous social and moral values. In short, all seemed to point to the imminent political and economic collapse of the country and, above all, to the dreaded 'social dissolution' in which the accepted norms of social behaviour and the relationship of one class to another would disintegrate into anarchy. Once again the spectre of the French revolutionary 'Terror' was conjured up with its 'immense upheaval

in ideas, both in logic and in morality, which is even more important'.[1]
Hombres de bien were warned that their apathy was opening the door to
demagogues, and the 'industrial, agricultural and mercantile classes' were
urged to help defend their own interests.[2]

These factors, allied to the overall failure to meet expectations, weakened the conservatives' faith in centralism, but they were not the direct
cause of its collapse. That was to come from events and developments in
the years 1839 and 1840, when the coalition of *hombres de bien*, the Church
and the army finally disintegrated. That coalition, which had been formed
in 1834, had brought together various groups and individuals from across
the political spectrum who felt that their own or the nation's best interests
were threatened by radicalism. The authors of the Siete Leyes had then
constructed a political framework designed to protect those interests and
to ensure through the reformed electoral system that only the upper levels
of the middle-class *hombres de bien* in every region could achieve and exercise
power. Their hope was that by emphasizing continually through propaganda in the daily press the common social and economic interests as well
as the moral and cultural values of the *hombres de bien* regardless of where
they lived in the republic, it would be possible to suppress or at least
restrain regional diversities and rivalries. In other words, it was accepted
that the political opinions and economic interests of the miner in Zacatecas, the landowner in the Bajío, the textile manufacturer in Puebla, the
tobacco farmer in Veracruz and the army officer or clergyman anywhere
were different and perhaps incompatible. But as those individuals were
reminded so often, they shared a need to protect their status, life-style
and values against extremists who, attempting to mobilize the support
of the masses, threatened the abolition of privileges, the redistribution
of wealth and property and even the sacred religious faith of their forebears.
They well understood the implications when they read in the liberal press
that 'Mexico offers the scandalous spectacle of a few affluent people who
have more than enough side by side with a hungry mass who have
nothing'.[3]

The centralist republic thus depended on a political structure which
was based firmly on a coalition of middle-class interests. The coalition
had been subjected to intense pressures throughout 1835-8 because a
significant number of *hombres de bien* who had welcomed the defeat of the
radicals in 1834 refused to accept the political ideology of centralism
while accepting its socioeconomic position. They believed that their own
and the national interest would be best served by a reformed federal system.

1 *Diario del Gobierno*, 2 May 1839.
2 Ibid., 7 and 11 April 1839. To encourage property owners to participate, two so-called commercial
  battalions of militia were formed; see ibid., 20 April 1839.
3 *El Cosmopolita*, 22 May 1841.

The direct attacks by dissident or profederalist groups as well as by the radicals represented by Gómez Farías, attacks which, of course, were both political and military, had so far weakened but not destroyed the coalition. That was to be brought about by further demands made on the pockets of the *hombres de bien* by taxation, loans and all the other effects of the fiscal crisis; the continuing problems of law and order and education; the changing socioreligious values; and, above all, the manifest inability of the central government to control the situation. Not surprisingly, the disillusionment of a large number of *hombres de bien* of all categories and shades of opinion turned to despair, and they began to lose their faith not only in centralism but also in any form of republican and representative government. Remembering what seemed more and more like a golden age of peace and prosperity in the late eighteenth century, the minds of some began to turn to the merits of monarchy as the best, and proven, form of government for Mexico, and for others the solution came to lie in the strong, authoritarian rule of dictatorship.

This process of disintegration of the coalition was not immediately evident when Bustamante announced that he was to vacate the presidency to lead the army against the federalist rebels in the north. On the contrary, the news that Santa Anna, despite his medical condition, was to resume office brought hope that things might improve, and when the wounded hero arrived in the capital on 17 February 1839, borne on a litter and surrounded by crowds of admirers and curious, there was much public rejoicing. Rockets, parades, military bands and poetic eulogies abounded.[4]

Santa Anna's interim presidency, however, was to last only for a few weeks, and on 10 July the hero of Veracruz, as he was now known, retired once again to Manga de Clavo. Brief though it was, Santa Anna's tenure of executive power nevertheless resulted in several incidents which contributed to and accelerated the fall of Bustamante and the end of the Siete Leyes. The first occurred on 31 March when, following talks with General Luis Cortazar, whose base was Guanajuato, Santa Anna issued a personal manifesto in which he deplored the destruction of the 'social order' and 'public morality'. The incessant revolts and unrest had, he said, 'perverted the character of a people no less gentle than generous' and 'loosened the ties which hold society together'. It was now essential to restore order to society and he accepted that reform of political institutions was required. What he favoured was a 'moderate and just freedom which excludes both licence and detestable arbitrariness'.[5]

This was not the first time that Santa Anna had tried to place himself

---

4 Published in *El Mexicano*, 22 February 1839. Of course, the anti–Santa Anna press was not so complimentary. *El Restaurador Mexicano* (13 February 1839), for example, referred to 'la venida del Anti-cristo'.
5 Santa Anna's manifesto was published in *Diario del Gobierno*, 31 March 1839.

in the middle ground of the political spectrum, and his words had major implications for both centralists and federalists. To the former, it seemed that he was withdrawing his support with his call for political reform, while to the latter, and particularly the Gómez Pedraza group, it appeared that he was accepting their long-argued case that the centralist constitution and institutions needed at least serious surgery.[6] As always, however, Santa Anna was imprecise except in his condemnation of the radicals, and neither group was certain of his meaning or intentions. Nevertheless, there was no doubt that he now favoured reform of the Siete Leyes, an opinion he reconfirmed in his farewell message on 10 July, repeating that 'fundamental parts of the constitutional laws require reform'.[7]

A week later, Santa Anna raised another issue in which he also seemed to be trying to attract the support of the moderates. This concerned the daily and periodical press. For some weeks, the *Diario del Gobierno* had been waging a highly critical campaign against the so-called opposition press. Liberal and federalist writers were described as 'extreme and fanatical', 'perverted and vicious', 'scum of the parties', and men who ignored all the boundaries of common decency.[8] Control of the excesses of the press was essential, the editor argued.[9] The opposition papers answered like with like, castigating the government, ministers, their policies and actions and openly calling for revolution to overthrow the oligarchs who were ruling the nation purely for their own selfish benefit.

On 8 April Santa Anna acted, provoking an outcry at what was interpreted as an attack on the freedom of the press guaranteed by the constitution. He issued a strongly worded circular condemning what he saw as abuse of freedom of the press and, rather unusually, naming the guilty or accused papers, all of which, of course, were liberal federalist. *El Cosmopolita*, *El Restaurador* and *El Voto Nacional*, he said, were responsible for promoting discord, revolution and anarchy, and their incessant attacks had brought disrespect for the government and the rule of law. It was time for that 'race of delinquents' to be stopped, and he called on authorities in the capital and throughout the department of Mexico to arrest and jail those responsible for subversive publications of any type. Those arrested should be sent to the fortress prisons of San Juan de Ulúa or Acapulco, and military commanders would give any support needed.[10] A few days later in Congress, Deputies Berruecos and Méndez de Torres proposed amendments to the existing legislation. Every publisher, they

---

6 Yañéz suggests that it was at this point that the centralists broke with Santa Anna; A. Yañéz, *Santa Anna: Espectro de una sociedad* (Mexico, 1982), p. 140.
7 Published in *Diario del Gobierno*, 10 July 1839.
8 Ibid., 10 March 1839.
9 Ibid., 17 February 1839.
10 Dublán and Lozano, *Legislación Mexicana*, vol. 3, pp. 616–17.

suggested, should pay a deposit of 1,000 pesos, which would be used to meet fines that might be imposed in future. Any editor of a subversive publication should be sentenced to two years' imprisonment, and those who sold or distributed such writings should be sentenced to hard labour on public works.[11]

The editors and publishers of *El Cosmopolita, El Restaurador* and *El Voto Nacional* knew from what had happened to their predecessors in 1834 that such threats could not be ignored, and they together with much of the rest of the opposition press in the capital decided to stop publication for the time being. Since independence, however, freedom of the press had become a sacred cow for *hombres de progreso* and was seen by them to be an essential feature of an independent, civilized society. Protests were soon forthcoming against Santa Anna's action, and with the opposition cowed into silence in the capital, these came from the departments. The departmental junta of Zacatecas, for example, petitioned Congress to withdraw the circular, and similar requests were soon received from elsewhere.[12] Eventually, after petitions were also made to the Supreme Court, the matter was referred to the SPC to rule whether the circular contravened the guarantees of freedom of the press given in the constitution.

A third aspect of Santa Anna's brief sojourn in the presidential office concerned the federalist revolts. Although some of these had been defeated, others were breaking out around the country, most notably for the future, in Yucatán. At Tampico, Urrea, now joined by José Antonio Mejía, continued to resist, and Bustamante had set out for the north to lead the army against them. His progress, however, was very slow, and Urrea and Mejía were able to escape and move south, eventually arriving on the outskirts of Puebla, where they were joined by federalist sympathizers and prepared to attack the city. It was an opportunity for glory which Santa Anna could not resist. He announced that he would leave for Puebla to command the government forces, and on 30 April, again carried on a litter, he left the capital. Three days later, the opposing forces met at Acajete, and the federalists were heavily defeated, losing, it was reported, six hundred men. Santa Anna, having stayed behind to organize the reserves, missed the battle, but Mejía was captured and promptly executed. Urrea managed to escape and make his way back to Tampico, where shortly afterwards he also was defeated, not by Bustamante, who had still not arrived, but by General Mariano Arista.[13]

11 'Dictamen de la comisión respectiva sobre arreglo de la libertad de imprenta', 15 April 1839, in *Diario del Gobierno,* 28 April 1839.
12 For the Zacatecas petition, see *El Cosmopolita,* 7 September 1839.
13 For further details on the battle of Acajete and other federalist revolts, see Zamacois, *Historia de México,* vol. 12, pp. 174–87. The execution of Mejía added another strand to the Santa Anna

Both presidents, Bustamante and Santa Anna, thus missed the chance to lead their forces to victory, but the manner in which their respective participation was reported illustrates the difference between them. Bustamante's slow progress north was ridiculed in the press and there were suggestions that either he was reluctant to fight – his supporters said he wanted to avoid bloodshed – or his profederalist inclinations inhibited him from doing so. Bustamante, in short, derived no praise or advantage, and his image as an indecisive, incompetent bungler seemed to be strengthened. In sharp contrast, Santa Anna played up the events at Puebla for all they were worth. His allies in the press seized on the victory to renew their eulogies of him and his military prowess. When he returned to Mexico City on 8 May, accompanied by Tornel and Valencia, who had commanded the forces at Acajete, he was given a hero's welcome with a triumphal procession through the streets amid a 'huge and extraordinary crowd'.[14] Special medals were struck to commemorate his victory of 5 December against the French and presented to him by Bishop Angel Morales in a spectacular ceremony. He was the hero of Tampico, Veracruz and now Acajete. Not a word was now said about Texas.[15]

Although his medical condition was still causing him problems, Santa Anna's political health was thus fully restored, especially his reputation with the army. It is noticeable that from the day he took office on 20 March, a stream of promilitary decrees followed as he made sure his fellow officers knew where his priorities lay. On 21 March, Tornel, again Minister of War, repeated earlier orders to all departmental authorities that commander generals were to be consulted about any expenditure; 'not a single peso should be distributed without their knowledge' and army pay was always to be given priority.[16] Long lists of promotions were announced, especially for those who had fought the French, and on 20 March Congress approved a peace treaty with France in which Mexico agreed to pay 600,000 pesos in settlement of French claims. Soon to be denounced as a humiliating retreat, the negotiations had been held before Santa Anna took over and Bustamante was held responsible while the hero of Veracruz took the military glory.[17]

There is no doubt that Santa Anna used his interim presidency very astutely to restore and enhance his reputation, above all with the army. He had done in a few weeks what Bustamante had failed to do in two

---

legend. Mejía was allowed three hours to prepare for the execution. When asked how long he would have given Santa Anna, he replied, three minutes; see Callcott, *Santa Anna*, p. 163.

14 *Diario del Gobierno*, 8 and 9 May 1839.

15 Ibid., 9 June 1839; Malo, *Diario*, vol. 1, p. 168.

16 Circular published in *El Cosmopolita*, 28 August 1839.

17 *El Cosmopolita* (21 August 1839) noted that the salary bill of the Ministry of War had tripled in ten years from 18,174 pesos in 1827 to 76,158 in 1837. For hundreds of promotions, see the list in ibid., 14 August 1839.

years. He had silenced the radical press, publicly but obtusely backed constitutional reform and defeated the main federalist revolt. Not surprisingly, there were again whispers of dictatorship,[18] but on this occasion, it seems that Santa Anna's health was a genuine reason for his decision to withdraw from the arena. He left for the country on 11 July to recuperate and bide his time.[19]

With Bustamante still not back from the north, General Bravo was sworn in to act as president on 10 July. Nine days later, Bustamante did arrive to resume his powers but almost immediately had to confront the first symptoms of the breakdown of the coalition which had put him into power. The disintegration of that coalition occurred on several levels over the next two years, beginning with the national institutions created by the Siete Leyes and the relationship between the four powers – executive, legislative, judicial and the SPC. The last had been created mainly by Sánchez de Tagle, still one of its members – the other four were Carlos Bustamante, Manuel de la Peña y Peña, Cirilo Gómez y Anaya and Tornel – to act as a moderating force on the other three and particularly to resolve contentious issues, deciding what the national will was. Certainly to the surprise and anger of the political factions, including the centralists, it had already displayed an unexpected degree of resilience and independence. In what Carlos Bustamante described as its 'first useful act' in November 1838, it had rejected a decision of the Minister of War on a relatively minor matter and the Minister promptly resigned in protest.[20] Then, again to the surprise of many, it had come up with the idea that Santa Anna should take over the government if it fell or was forced from power. When Bustamante returned, he inherited two issues Santa Anna had originated which had already or were soon to be referred to the fourth power for final resolution. The first concerned the attack on freedom of the press, which had been welcomed by government supporters. For the SPC, however, political considerations were not a relevant factor, and when the 8 April circular was referred to it at the behest of the Supreme Court, it declared the measure unconstitutional and thus null and void. Most of the opposition newspapers quickly recommenced publication. Two days earlier, on 31 July 1839, the SPC had also pronounced that the executive had acted illegally and without proper authority in negotiating a loan in London for £130,000.[21] The loan contract was declared null and void.

---

18 See 'Discurso sobre los inconvenientes de la dictadura en las naciones modernas', in *El Independiente*, 30 October 1839. Such articles were always a sign that there were rumours of dictatorship.
19 *El Mexicano*, 11 July 1839.
20 For a good summary of the SPC and its decisions, see Noriega Cantú, *Ideas políticas*, pp. 149–67.
21 For details of this loan and the dispute it provoked, see *Diario del Gobierno*, 31 July 1839.

These decisions by the SPC indicated the potential for disunity and conflict, and it was only a matter of weeks before open and public warfare existed in the corridors of power. The next divisive issue was another inheritance from Santa Anna. His backing for constitutional reform had already encountered resistance in the Council of Government. In its initial response to the executive's proposal, it had rejected the case for substantive changes to the constitution, arguing that there were no 'fundamental defects' in it. An irate exchange of letters ensued, with the Minister of the Interior insisting that 'there is no doubt that opinion and experience condemn as defective the constitutional laws of 1836'.[22] After this public display of disunity, a compromise formula was reached and approved by Congress for referral to the SPC to decide if it was the public will that the Siete Leyes be amended.

After weeks of deliberation, the SPC produced a compromise verdict which satisfied nobody, angering both centralists and federalists. Its judgement was that even though the six-year limit before changes could be made had not yet expired, circumstances dictated that reforms could now be considered. Such reforms, however, could not alter in any way the basic principles of the constitution, in particular, religion, freedom of the press and the form of government. In other words, the politicians could tinker with the constitution but not change it in any substantive way. Centralists complained that the decision was unconstitutional, while federalists denounced it as a sell-out to the conservative lobby. In Congress, nine federalist deputies presented a report condemning the decision and demanding that there be no restriction on the nature or extent of the reforms.[23] The editor of *El Cosmopolita* launched a bitter attack on the fourth power and the constitution, that 'political Lazarus; a monster of abnormalities'.[24]

The divisions in the government were now clear for all to see and they were again highlighted by a public slanging match between Tornel and the SPC. Tornel had stopped attending the latter's meetings or had been deliberately excluded from them when he became Minister of War in December 1838. He lost his ministerial job soon after Santa Anna's departure in July 1839, and then in a blatant attempt to discredit them, he published a pamphlet in which he claimed that in the previous December when he himself had been a member of it, his colleagues on the SPC had unanimously voted to offer an unrestricted dictatorship to Santa

22 For the correspondence and reports on this controversy, see ibid., 11, 13, 15 and 21 July 1839.
23 For the text of the representation by the nine deputies, dated 13 November 1839, see *El Cosmopolita*, 16 November 1839. A second lengthy report from the same nine, dated 26 November 1839, is in ibid., 4 December 1839. The same deputies also accused Carlos Bustamante of lying and demanded his impeachment; see ibid., 8 January 1840.
24 *El Cosmopolita*, 20 November 1839.

Anna.[25] Immediately, his former colleagues publicly branded Tornel a liar, accusing him of 'a constitutional infringement and a scandalous transgression of all the principles and rules of morality and decency which every public official, every citizen and any ordinary man should follow'.[26] Tornel was not the man to take such abuse without response, and in a second publication to defend himself, he revealed something of the nature of the conflict that was now rampant in government circles:

In this capital of the republic, there is still an old political sect which learned the science of government in the school of the viceroys and of those demigods known as *oidores*. This fraternity, as invisible as it is certain in its calculations, is the same one which through varied although comparable ways has preserved a decisive and constant influence on the affairs of state.[27]

This war of words with Tornel lasted for weeks and no doubt provided entertaining reading for the federalists. They did not have long to wait for even more evidence of a complete break between the four branches of government. This time the issue was a law of 13 March 1840 in which, in a futile attempt to stem the rising tide of violence and crime on the streets and highways, Bustamante ordered that henceforth thieves were to be placed under military jurisdiction to be tried and sentenced by court-martial. The Supreme Court promptly objected and asked the SPC to rule the decree unconstitutional. Sánchez de Tagle was a lone voice in defence of the measure, and when he was outvoted by the other four members, he resigned. The SPC decision, announced on 13 May, that the decree was null and void carried therefore only four signatures. On the grounds that any decision required the unanimous vote of all five members, the executive refused to accept the ruling and asked Congress to declare its agreement that a unanimous vote was essential. Congress did agree and declared the SPC's decision void.[28] Undaunted, the SPC in turn declared the congressional decision void. For his part, Bustamante ignored the latter and ordered the military to obey the law. Then the Supreme Court instructed all judges to ignore it.[29]

Chaos reigned supreme in the government, with all sides publicly attacking one another. The SPC, which had also refused to grant emergency powers to Bustamante in August, bitterly condemned the executive for disobeying its rulings and deliberately seeking to bring its members into disrepute. The 'fight among the powers', it said, was scandalous.[30]

25 Tornel's statement is in ibid., 18 December 1839.
26 For the SPC's statement on Tornel, see ibid., 8 February 1840.
27 Tornel's second statement is in ibid., 4 March 1840.
28 The decree declaring that five signatures were required is dated 11 July 1840; Dublán and Lozano, *Legislación mexicana*, vol. 3, p. 723.
29 Details in Noriega Cantú, *Ideas políticas*, pp. 156–8.
30 SPC statement dated 19 October 1840, in *El Cosmopolita*, 18 November 1840.

In reply, Bustamante and the Congress openly called for reform, if not abolition, of the neutral or moderating power as an intolerable restriction on effective government.[31]

This breakdown of relations among the four branches of government was certainly one major factor in the disillusion of *hombres de bien* with the centralist constitution. Still at the national level, they also witnessed a growing hostility in the departments and regions to the centralized control exercised, at least in theory, from Mexico City. Excluding for the time being the continuing federalist revolts, complaints began to pour in from all directions. From the far north, there were daily reports of atrocities committed in Indian raids and the departmental governors and juntas, especially of Chihuahua, appealed with mounting concern and anger for military and financial aid.[32] As the marauding Indians continued on the rampage from Tamaulipas to Sonora and as far south as San Luis Potosí, frustration increased as it became obvious that the central government was unwilling or powerless to help. In the far south, widespread discontent over a range of issues brought Yucatán to rebellion and the eventual declaration of its independence. Always a marginal state, to use Justo Sierra's phrase, effectively separated from the central cone by topography, nonexistent communications and diverse economic interests, Yucatán had rather surprisingly accepted the centralization of power in the capital.[33] But since the Siete Leyes, Bustamante's government had adopted a number of measures which adversely affected the region. Listing the reasons for the insurrection, Sebastián Peón, a federalist deputy in Congress for the department, blamed the taxes on foreign imports, the poll tax and recent military conscriptions in which *yucatecos* were forced from their homes and workplaces to be taken to fight, perhaps as far away as Texas.[34]

Apart from declaring as pirates any ships used by the rebel authorities and inviting foreign vessels to attack them, Bustamante could and did do nothing to stop the Yucatán separation, and it was to be several more years before the situation was resolved. Added to the government's manifest failure to do anything to reconquer Texas, despite all the pledges and extra taxation for that purpose, it was further evidence of the inherent weakness of the centralized regime. In some respects, the tensions between the government and these frontier areas in the north and south were due

---

31 Bustamante used his address to Congress on 1 January 1841 to make his attack on the SPC; for the text, see *México: Mensajes políticos*, pp. 53–4.

32 'Dictamen de la junta de Chihuahua', 30 June 1840, in *El Cosmopolita*, 5 August 1840; 'Representación de la Excelentísima junta departamental de Chihuahua al Excmo. Sr. presidente de la república pidiéndole auxilios y medidas contra la guerra de los bárbaros', 1 March 1841, in ibid., 17 March 1841.

33 Sierra, *Evolución política*, p. 228.

34 Congressional session of 9 April 1840 in *El Cosmopolita*, 15 April 1840.

to special regional factors which did not apply to other departments, but soon most of the latter had their own grievances. Guanajuato, for example, protested against a proposal to close regional mints, pointing out that its miners could not afford to transport their silver to the capital and adding that the only people who would benefit were the notorious *agiotistas*.[35] Mexico, supported by Tamaulipas, protested against the taxes on urban and rural property.[36] Puebla campaigned for more restrictions on foreign cotton imports, and Michoacán went so far as to send a delegation to Mexico City to appeal for financial aid to enable it at least to pay its local garrison. The Morelia gazette accused the government of abandoning the departments, concluding, 'To date, there is not a single favourable fact to merit a gesture of respect towards the prevailing institutions or an act of gratitude to those persons who are filling the first ranking positions in the nation'.[37]

In addition to these particular grievances in the departments, there was more and more concern and comment over the disparity of wealth in the capital and that in the regions. A Veracruz paper attacked the domination of Mexico City and the luxurious life-style of the so-called *notables* which the rest of the population in the country had to pay for by means of increased taxation and forced loans. Members of the political clique in the capital, especially the *agiotistas,* were enriching themselves, but it warned, 'the scandalous luxury displayed by prominent people, the gold braid which encircles the president, that grandeur which likens our capital to the first cities of Europe, all prove the decadence of the republic and its approaching ruin'.[38] The same theme of the disparity of wealth between the centre and the departments was expressed in the liberal press. It was, the editor of *El Cosmopolita* wrote, 'wicked, alarming and worthy of the utmost contempt'.[39] When Oaxaca was hit by a drought which caused a poor harvest and increased maize and bean prices, and then by a serious outbreak of smallpox, even the *Diario del Gobierno* felt obliged to urge the 'rich', and the clergy, to use their wealth to alleviate the suffering.[40]

It is clear that discontent was spreading in the departments, and rule by governors and commanders appointed by central government did nothing to inhibit it. Indeed, it is probable that local elite families, like the Peóns in Yucatán, resented their loss of dominance and control over their immediate environment as much as they resented the demands made on

35 Representation of departmental junta, 3 July 1840 in ibid., 15 July 1840.
36 Ibid., 16 November 1839.
37 Reprinted articles from *Gaceta de Michoacán* in ibid., 17 March 1841.
38 *El Monitor,* Veracruz, 6 April 1840, reprinted in ibid., 18 April 1840.
39 Ibid., 12 June 1840, 7 July 1841.
40 *Diario del Gobierno,* 22 April, 12 June, 24 July 1839.

their purses.[41] They had to contend with civil and military officials imposed on them from the centre, and although we cannot be certain until much further research is done into local and regional clans, it seems likely that their influence was much reduced. At the same time, they had to tolerate the federalists, who continued to campaign and organize rebellions in several departments. It was not long before Yucatán, where Gómez Farías went to help, reintroduced the former federal system and its authorities. Again the insurrection spread to Chiapas, Tabasco and other places, and although mostly suppressed or kept under control by loyal army units, such events sustained the level of instability and demonstrated the government's inability to maintain public order. Meanwhile, the propaganda war in the press by both sides became ever more virulent and abusive, which again illustrated Bustamante's failure to achieve his promised 'fusion of the parties'. In some respects, the progovernment press campaign against the federalists and the horror stories they printed were also counterproductive because they seemed to demonstrate the chasm that now existed. The federalists, many of whom were, of course, *hombres de bien,* readily accepted in the highest social levels, were described as vandals, rapists, assassins, thieves and 'apostles of anarchy'. Gordiano Guzmán was reported to have published a proclamation inviting anyone to join in the sacking of Zamora, which was then ransacked and looted by three thousand vandals.[42] It was said that federalists always seized a rich man and held an auction for parts of his body. The victim was invited to top the highest bid for each limb; if he did, and only if he did, was he released.[43] Such horror stories, spurious or not, discredited the federalists, but they also emphasized the total collapse of law and order. For the time being, the sophisticated and cosmopolitan residents of the capital who read such reports were certainly shocked, but they were not personally affected, for the conflict and alleged atrocities took place far away in what they considered the less civilized rural areas. Then, in July 1840, what every *hombre de bien* had feared since independence occurred. A coup was attempted which brought violence, looting, anarchy and the indiscriminate destruction of life and property onto the streets of the capital. For twelve days the city became, in Carlos Bustamante's words, a 'theatre of terror'.[44]

The coup, which began on 15 July, was perhaps the major factor in the disintegration of the centralist republican coalition, not because of its

41 For information on the Peón family in the next generation, see A. Wells, 'Family Elites in a Boom or Bust Economy: The Molinas and Peóns of Porfirian Yucatán', *Hispanic American Historical Review,* 62 (2), 1982, 224–53.
42 *El Mexicano,* 2 and 23 May, 1 June 1839.
43 Ibid., 22 February 1839.
44 Bustamante, *Gabinete mexicano,* vol. 2, p. 78.

military effects, for it failed to achieve its political aims, but because of the psychological impact it had on the *hombres de bien*. I have examined the course of events in detail elsewhere, and hence only a skeleton account is given here.[45] The rebel leaders were Urrea and Gómez Farías. Urrea had been brought to the capital following his capture after the fall of Tampico, and Gómez Farías was also in the city. At dawn on 15 July, a dissident infantry battalion freed Urrea from jail in the old Inquisition building, and he led them through the streets to the national palace. They successfully entered the palace and quickly cornered Bustamante in his bedroom. Rebel officers then went to Gómez Farías' home and invited him to join them. He returned with them to the palace.

News of the coup and arrest of Bustamante spread like wildfire through the city, and the rebels, joined by a large number of volunteers, began to make defensive preparations, occupying the towers of the cathedral, the roofs of the *ayuntamiento* and other nearby buildings leading to the central square and placing cannon at strategic points. Meanwhile, cabinet ministers and other officials were informed of what had happened, but most government supporters, deciding that prudence was a better course than valour, chose to disappear from sight for the time being. Some army officers, however, summoned by the Minister of War, Juan Nepomuceno Almonte, did assemble at the city's main arsenal, the Ciudadela, or Citadel, and General Valencia, who had refused an invitation to join the rebels, took command of the units which remained loyal. Having fortified the Citadel, he moved his headquarters to the monastery of San Agustín (until recently the Biblioteca Nacional).

The battle-lines were thus drawn and the theatre of conflict was to be the most densely populated area of the city. Within a 500-yard radius of the central square, about 17 per cent of the population, or some 28,000 people, lived. It was the ceremonial, political and administrative hub of the country, and it encompassed many of the private residences of the city's most prominent families as well as much of the commercial establishment. Further densely populated suburbs beyond the inner ring were also in range of the cannon and within a 1,000-yard radius of the centre, two-thirds of the population, or some 130,000 people, were to be found.[46]

At 2 p.m., the first gunfire echoed through the city. There is no more vivid description of the effect it had than that of Sra. Calderón de la Barca, who watched from her window:

The firing has begun! People come running up the street. The Indians are hurrying back to their villages in double-quick trot. . . . The cannon are roaring now. All along the street people are standing on the balconies, looking anxiously in the direction of the

45 Costeloe, 'A *Pronunciamiento* in Nineteenth Century Mexico', pp. 245–63.
46 Shaw, 'Poverty and Politics in Mexico City', pp. 47–8.

palace, or collected in groups before the doors, and the azoteas, which are out of the line of fire, are covered with men. They are ringing the tocsin – things seem to be getting serious.[47]

Thus, the July *pronunciamiento* started, and for the next twelve days both sides proceeded to bombard each other, destroying buildings, including parts of the national palace, houses, businesses and lives of innocent civilians who were caught in the cross-fire. People began to flee the city whenever and in any way they could, and normal life came to an abrupt halt as shops closed and food and water supplies became almost unobtainable. Gangs of thieves roamed the streets, and looters ransacked houses and shops indiscriminately. In sum, anarchy reigned supreme.

The political objectives of the July coup were the restoration of federalism, but for various reasons, including the failure of promised support to materialize, they were not achieved. Bustamante, who was released or escaped from the palace on 16 July, displayed unexpected resilience and refused to accept any of the rebel demands. Just as important, as the violence and bloodshed on the streets mounted daily – the U.S. ambassador estimated the dead and wounded at five hundred to seven hundred – federalist supporters among the *hombres de bien* recoiled in horror at the scenes they witnessed.[48] Gómez Pedraza, Rincón, Lafragua and Herrera were among many who refused all invitations from Gómez Farías to join him at the palace, and when it became known that Santa Anna was en route from Veracruz, the rebels gave up and surrendered at 6:30 a.m. on 27 July.[49]

For *hombres de bien* like Carlos Bustamante, whose own home was hit by stray bullets, the revolt of July 1840 was one never to be forgotten. There is no doubt that Bustamante and others were deeply shocked by the level of violence, the destruction of property and the random killing

47 Calderón de la Barca, *Life in Mexico*, p. 226. Sra. Calderón's account of the revolt is one of several by contemporary witnesses. See, e.g., Bustamante, *Gabinete mexicano*, vol. 2, pp. 78–81; Malo, *Diario*, vol. 1, pp. 180–4. Sra. Calderón's husband, who was the Spanish ambassador at the time, also offered a detailed and vivid description in the reports he sent back to Spain; see those of 23 and 28 July 1840 in *Relaciones diplomáticas hispano-mexicanas*, vol. 1, pp. 124–30.

48 P. Ellis to J. Forsyth, 28 July 1840, García Collection, Justin Smith Papers, pp. 175–7. Malo gives the following official casualty figures: rebels, 172 dead and 184 wounded; government, 51 dead and 137 wounded (*Diario*, vol. 1, p. 184). A day-by-day account of dead and wounded is given by Bustamante, *Gabinete mexicano*, vol. 2, pp. 79–80. His estimate is 886 dead and wounded. Pakenham reported about 400 dead and many civilian casualties; R. Pakenham to Ld. Palmerston, 29 July 1840, P.R.O., F.O. 50, 136, fols. 171–80.

49 What in effect was the rebel archive compiled during the revolt is in the Gómez Farías Papers, nos. 711–887. The rebels were granted a full amnesty, interpreted by many as another sign of Bustamante's weakness. Each rebel was given a document certifying that he was included in the amnesty. The one given to Gómez Farías has the following interesting physical description: 'edad = 57 años; estado = casado; estatura = alta; pelo = entrecano; ojos = pardos; nariz = regular; barba = id.; oficio = comerciante; casa = calle de Cocheras no. 6; señas particulares = /'; García Collection, Gómez Farías Papers, no. 740.

of innocent civilians. The sight of rotting corpses on the streets being torn apart by packs of dogs was deeply offensive to them, and it seemed that the long-feared social dissolution had finally happened.[50] Even for those who were sympathetic politically to the aims of the rebels, such scenes of anarchy were too much to swallow. If this was the price of federalism, it was too much to pay. Gómez Farías found himself almost totally isolated, and the radical cause which he represented and led lost, at least for the time being, whatever support it had among all moderates. By the same token, however, the July revolt confirmed that the current political system and the constitution on which it was based could not protect the interests of the property-owning classes. *Hombres de bien* of all political persuasions began to consider alternatives.

With the political system so discredited and the weakness of the Bustamante government so manifest, many other groups now began to display their disaffection with the regime. Most of these were precisely from the 'well-off classes' which Alamán and his fellow conservatives had hoped to attract, and their grievances reflected their concern that centralism would never deliver the stable conditions in which their entrepreneurial and commercial interests would prosper.[51] The national fiscal situation remained on the brink of total collapse, and despite the failure of the taxes and loans of 1837 and 1838, Bustamante and successive Ministers of Hacienda continued to find no alternative to more of the same. New loans were imposed, and the clergy, although strengthened by the appointment of the first archbishop of independent Mexico, Manuel Posada y Garduño, were again alarmed at the pressure on them to contribute and even more so by talk of religious tolerance. New taxes were also devised, including another 3 mill on urban and rural property and, even more controversial, a 'personal tax' of between 1 real and 2 pesos a month decreed on 8 March 1841. The revenue from this tax was to be put towards the budget deficit and other pressing needs of the Treasury. It was imposed on all males over the age of 18 who either had assets or were capable of work.[52] Protests were soon forthcoming. *El Cosmopolita,* which reported that shopkeepers and tradesmen increased their prices to the obvious detriment of the poor as well as everyone else, complained that 'the middle class and the poor bear the burden of the tax; the law was not aimed at the class in power'.[53] From Celaya, the town council warned of rising discontent with the burden

50 The mutilation of corpses by dogs is mentioned in *El Cosmopolita,* 29 July 1840, and by Bustamante, *Gabinete mexicano,* vol. 2, p. 74.

51 See, e.g., E. de Antuñano, 'Exposición respetuosa que el que suscribe dirige a las augustas cámaras de la nación', in *Diario del Gobierno,* 4 July 1839. Antuñano begins, 'No habrá paz en México mientras no haya industria ilustrada y honesta generalizada, y en progresión'.

52 Dublán and Lozano, *Legislación mexicana,* vol. 3, pp. 7–10, 11–21.

53 *El Cosmopolita,* 3 July 1841.

of taxation. For thirty years, the councillors wrote, the people had awaited the benefits promised by independence, but their hopes were now dispelled. The new tax smacked of the old Spanish tribute, and the poor now believed that the federal system had demanded less of them than the central republic.[54]

It was not only the middle- and lower-level income groups who were discontented with the government's fiscal policy. Taxes on trade were also increased, especially on imported goods, and again with an inevitable effect on prices. The *derecho de consumo*, or levy on foreign imports sold in the interior, was increased from 5 to 15 per cent in 1839, which together with other levies raised the taxes on imported goods to 49.5 per cent.[55] British, French and other foreign merchants again besieged their embassies to demand repeal of the law. Various changes were also introduced to refund existing debts, and new contracts, together with charges on the shrinking customs revenues, were negotiated with the financial community, including another attempt to amortize copper currency. While some of the financiers involved made a 'beautiful profit' on these complex dealings, popular opinion against the *agiotistas* increased and Bustamante was accused of selling out to the speculators.[56]

The government also managed to alienate many industrial and agricultural interests, mostly in the regions, which greatly resented the apparent domination of the *agiotistas* in the capital. Desperate to fulfil the pledge to reconquer Texas or at least to be seen to be trying to do so and thus restore some of the government's credibility, the Minister of War, Almonte, authorized General Arista to allow the importation of a large quantity of foreign yarn through the port of Tampico on the pretext that the import dues would be put towards the Texas campaign and towards giving at least some soldiers some pay.[57] This decision was in direct contravention of the existing ban on foreign textile imports, and both Mexican cotton planters and manufacturers vehemently protested. Already hit by bad harvests and drought, unable to compete with contraband textiles still flooding their markets, they warned that this latest blow would be the last straw for the country's domestic textile industry, which in recent years had seen some notable expansion. Much of the cotton-producing areas were in the department of Veracruz, and significantly the

54 'Representación que el muy ilustre ayuntamiento de la ciudad de Celaya dirige a su gobierno y junta departamental, pidiendo que se inicie a las cámaras la revocación de la ley de 8 de marzo del presente año que estableció una contribución personal', 28 May 1841, in ibid., 19 June 1841.
55 'Memorandum on the Heavy Additional Internal Duty Levied on Foreign Manufactures', 9 March 1841, P.R.O., F.O. 50, 150, fol. 24. An international commission decided in 1841 that Mexico was liable for 2 million dollars to meet U.S. claims.
56 Tenenbaum, *Politics of Penury*, pp. 64–6.
57 For details of the Arista affair, see Potash, *Banco de Avío*, pp. 132–4.

cotton lobby there chose to appeal for support to their most influential local resident, Santa Anna. He obliged and in February 1841 sent a strongly worded representation to Bustamante, urging him to stop the imports.[58] The cotton manufacturers had other powerful connections which they used to the full. Alamán, for example, together with leading figures in the industrial sphere with whom he had only recently formed a Sociedad para el Fomento de la Industria Nacional, joined the protests and submitted a highly critical memorandum predicting disaster for the domestic industry.[59] Former president Corro also joined in the clamour, as did Juan Alvarez from his base in the south.

The Arista affair, as it became known, was a serious political blunder by the government, and it dragged on for weeks as Bustamante tried to salvage something from what in Alamán's words was seen to be a 'ministerial anarchy'.[60] The Senate instituted proceedings against Almonte, and although he was later absolved by the deputies, the SPC intervened to declare that his action had been a violation of the constitution. Still Bustamante hesitated to act, and the foreign merchants who had entered into contracts for the imports threatened that if they were forced to break them, they would demand compensation. Alamán warned Bustamante that 'our country will descend into chaos and anarchy will establish itself on the remnants of the government'.[61] Eventually, an unsatisfactory compromise was reached, after the political damage was done, whereby the government decided to stop the imports and to compensate the contractors. *El Cosmopolita* summed up the affair: 'Great and extremely grave are the charges which can and should be made against the legislators who are held to be children of the monster of 1836; but none is so degrading as that of the yarns; in that, everything has been humiliated'.[62]

If the cotton bloc and the merchants, both foreign and Mexican, were disenchanted with the government, so too were those involved in the tobacco industry. Control of it had been vested in the Banco de Amortización in January 1837, but in response to pressure from Alamán and others, a private monopoly was awarded in a public auction to a company based in Mexico City whose shareholders included several prominent entrepreneurs and financiers. The tobacco producers who had been outbid at the auction were incensed.[63] They tried every legal means as far as the Supreme Court to get the decision revoked, and they too looked to their

58 'Exposición dirigida al Escmo. Sr. presidente de la república por el Escmo. Sr. D. Antonio López de Santa Anna', 6 February 1841, in *El Cosmopolita*, 13 February 1841.
59 'Exposición dirigida al congreso de la nación por los fabricantes y cultivadores de algodón', in ibid., 13 February 1841.
60 Alamán, *Obras: Documentos diversos*, vol. 2, p. 506.
61 Ibid., 488.
62 *El Cosmopolita*, 24 February, 10 March 1841.
63 Details on the tobacco industry are from Walker, 'Business as Usual', pp. 675–705.

powerful allies, notably Tornel, who was from the tobacco-producing area of Orizaba, to put their case to the government.[64] The new company, by trying to implement changes in managerial and working practices, infuriated its many employees, and five thousand tobacco workers in the capital rioted in the summer of 1839. In the provinces, the local authorities protested against their loss of revenue from the tobacco trade and at the growing centralization of economic power in the capital, and by April 1841 fifteen departments had petitioned for the abolition of the private monopoly. The company at first resisted these pressures, and the partners made sure they retained Bustamante's favour by making several large loans to the Treasury. But they soon found that the tobacco contract was not the profitable venture they had anticipated. By December 1840, they were to renegotiate with the government, and using all their contacts in the corridors of power, they were offered highly favourable new terms in April 1840. Another storm of protest followed, and Bustamante was obliged to abandon the agreement. The entrepreneurs were left with a contract on which they were losing a large amount of money, and they, like so many other groups, began to look for a change of government.

The cotton and tobacco interests, with their powerful allies, both foreign and Mexican merchants, were thus alienated from the regime, and they were joined by many other groups from the property-owning class. When the government awarded effective control of the gunpowder supply industry to Cayetano Rubio and others, local authorities, miners and landowners from Guanajuato and Zacatecas protested.[65] In 1837, in an attempt to stimulate trade and reduce smuggling, a system of ports of deposit was decreed, but only Veracruz and San Blas were designated in the new category, which soon brought complaints from less privileged regions.[66] In the capital, where the price of imported goods rose following the increase in the consumption tax, wholesalers and retailers demanded that the additional levy be removed.[67] Finally, there were the *empleados,* thousands of men who had obtained prized posts in the civil bureaucracy and who prided themselves on having achieved the status of *hombre de bien.* Their main complaint was nonpayment of salaries both in the capital and in the departments; for example, in Oaxaca in August 1839 it was

---

64 Tornel's representation to the Chamber of Deputies, written by him as the *apoderado* of the tobacco farmers of Orizava and Jalapa, dated 12 February 1841, is in *El Cosmopolita,* 17 February 1841. He followed this with one to the Senate: 'Manifestación presentada a la cámara de senadores por el general José María Tornel, apoderado de las diputaciones de cosecheros de tabaco de las ciudades de Jalapa y Orizava', in ibid., 21 April 1841.

65 Representation in ibid., 6 May 1840.

66 'Representación que los comerciantes y propietarios principales de esta ciudad de Santa Ana de Tamaulipas elevan al Sr. Presidente de la república, en solicitud del remedio de los males que se manifiestan', 4 August 1840, in ibid., 16 September 1840.

67 Representation in ibid., 29 December 1839.

reported that public officials were owed twenty-six months' pay, and six months later the debt to them was put at 222,117 pesos.[68] The frequent changes in ministers and regulations did little to help their morale, nor did several decrees critical of their performance. For example, departmental heads were accused of morosity and employing deliberate delaying tactics in carrying out orders. Public employees were accused of malingering and taking advantage of the willingness of doctors to provide medical certificates. In future, it was ordered, if an alleged illness was such that an employee could still go out into the street, only half his salary would be paid. Then, in a decree of 13 May 1839, the government confirmed that the *empleados,* or at least many of them, were active participants in the party political strife. What it called the frequent and scandalous defection of many was a major cause of the continuous insurrections. Henceforth, every employee would have to take an oath of loyalty to the government, and nobody would be appointed without evidence of aptitude, good moral and political conduct and 'loyalty to the fundamental laws'.[69]

By the summer of 1841, the centralist government had demonstrably lost the support of the conservative and middle-class constituency which had created it. Relations among the four powers at the national level had broken down, the departments were either in rebellion or wholly disillusioned with centralism, the campaign for constitutional reform was gaining strength and, above all, the entrepreneurial, financial, industrial, commercial, agricultural and professional interest groups all had serious grievances. There remained only one pillar of the regime to defect before the final disintegration of the *hombre de bien* coalition. The army, always in its own estimation the ultimate arbiter of the national will, had not done badly under the centralized republic. In terms of resources, promotions and extension of its powers to the civilian sphere, its role had been strengthened. Santa Anna, and particularly Tornel while Minister of War, had also introduced a whole range of reforms from new uniforms to a complete restructuring of military commands. Committees of senior officers were formed to examine every aspect of recruitment, discipline and training, and although it was largely a theoretical exercise, the government was authorized to increase the size of the army to 60,000 from the presumed existing number of 32,442. An urban militia was formed, and Tornel claimed in his annual report that within any one month, up to 50,000 men could be called to service.[70] Retired military personnel

68 *El Regenerador,* Oaxaca, 26 August 1839, reprinted in *Diario del Gobierno,* 4 September 1839; *El Cosmopolita,* 29 January 1840.
69 Decrees in Dublán and Lozano, *Legislación mexicana,* vol. 3, pp. 621–3.
70 'Memoria de la secretaría de estado y del despacho de la guerra y marina, leída por el Escmo,

were promised priority when posts in the bureaucracy were being filled, and they were guaranteed their army pay levels if their new job paid less.[71] With these and many other measures, support for the army was demonstrated to remain a national priority as Santa Anna and Bustamante emphasized in their speeches. Tornel was always ready to criticize the quality of the military and never reluctant to voice his criticisms, but his basic philosophy was the same as that expressed in a newspaper of which he was said to be the sponsor and editor: 'We will not stop repeating that a more or less large army is a necessity and while institutions remain weak, physical power takes the place of moral power'.[72]

There can be no doubt that the status of the army remained supreme, but at the same time there were many signs that it was no longer sacrosanct. The defeat in Texas, the loss of the fortress of San Juan de Ulúa and the port of Veracruz to the French in 1838, the failure to be seen to be able to stop the federalist rebellions or to prevent Indian raids in the north were all factors in the growing public resentment at the inordinate proportion of national revenues always allocated to the military budget. According to the editor of *El Mosquito Mexicano* (17 July 1840), the army was a sad reflection of what it had once been, now revealing the 'vulgarity, ignorance, vice and crime which distinguish very many military men in these times'. The soldiers themselves, mostly unwilling conscripts, fearful of being sent to Texas or even worse to Yucatán, often failed to receive their pay and officers complained constantly of the lack of even the most basic equipment. The retired, although promised privileged treatment, soon found, like other pensioners, that the Treasury was in no position to meet its obligations to them and they had to appeal for help.[73]

Tornel was fully conscious of the army's deteriorating image, and in his enthusiasm for reform, he introduced a new system of recruitment in January 1839. Designed to replace the hated *leva*, or forced conscription, recruitment was in future to be by annual lottery (*sorteo*) held on the first Sunday of October. Each departmental governor would announce in September the number of men needed, and with certain exceptions, all bachelors and widowers without children between the ages of 18 and 40 were eligible, subject to health and size requirements (70 Mexican inches in bare feet). Those fortunate enough to be chosen as defenders of the nation, to use the words of the law, had to serve a term of six years but

Sr. general D. José María Tornel, en la cámara de diputados el día 7 de enero de 1839 y en la de senadores el 8 del mismo', in *Diario del Gobierno*, 6 May 1839.
71 Santa Anna circular in *El Mexicano*, 5 August 1839.
72 *El Independiente*, 2 November 1839.
73 'Exposición que dirigen al congreso general los apoderados de los militares retirados, manifestándole la triste situación a que se hallan éstos reducidos', 5 March 1840, in *El Cosmopolita*, 1 April 1840.

anyone of those chosen could be exempted provided that he supplied someone to take his place.[74]

This new or more refined process of military conscription – there had been lotteries in earlier years – stimulated a wave of public protest when implementation began in the autumn of 1839. *El Mosquito Mexicano* described the resentment and protests, calling the reform 'pernicious and impractical',[75] and *El Cosmopolita* used the unpopularity of the measure to step up a campaign for a reduction in the size of the army and its privileges. Letters hostile to the military were published in its columns, and incidents of what were said to be typical examples of military despotism were regularly included. Soldiers from the barracks in the capital, for example, were said to roam the streets and take by force and without payment straw and barley (*paja y cebada*) from Indian carriers.[76] José Francisco Fagoaga took a complaint to the Supreme Court which was given wide publicity. He alleged that the tenant of one of his haciendas in Michoacán had been forced by the military commander to supply horses, maize and straw plus 35 pesos a month for the local troops. Open threats had been used, and even though such demands were made under the guise of a forced loan, they were, Fagoaga argued, illegal and unconstitutional.[77]

In February 1841, the government tried to raise army morale, or buy officer support, by asking Congress to appoint four new divisional generals. The current quota was fourteen, and of those only one was on active service, the rest holding full-time political office or so old and infirm as to be useless. Liberals in Congress took the opportunity to reinforce the antimilitary campaign being waged in their newspapers. The theoretical complement of the army was sixty thousand but in reality, as the Minister had to concede, there were only seventeen thousand men under arms. Why then, Deputy Ahumada asked, with ninety-three generals and more than eighty colonels already for a force of only seventeen thousand, was it necessary to appoint even more? Other deputies – Chico, Liceaga and Ramírez de San Miguel – also attacked the proposal as a wasteful use of scant resources.[78] The bitter tone of their criticism was to be duly noted by the army's supporters.

Excepting the die-hard centralist republicans, and there were few of them left, *hombres de bien* of all origins and persuasions were forced by the ever more obvious political crisis to reconsider their position. There is no doubt that after just four years of the Siete Leyes, there was a fast-emerging

74 Decree of 26 January 1839, Dublán and Lozano, *Legislación mexicana*, vol. 3, pp. 582–9.
75 *El Mosquito Mexicano*, 12 November 1839.
76 *El Cosmopolita*, 18 April 1840.
77 Ibid., 11 April 1840.
78 The congressional session of 4 February 1841 in which the state of the army was discussed is in ibid., 10 March 1841.

consensus that a better method of governing the country had to be found, more capable of protecting their economic interests and more in tune with the social values they espoused. The first significant, tangible sign of their stark disillusion with the political system and the reappraisal of the situation that was under way had come in the immediate aftermath of the July 1840 revolt in the capital. More representations had come from the departments asking for constitutional reform, and the subject was again being debated in Congress, the main point of contention being whether the incumbent assembly should do the work or whether a new convention should be summoned specifically for the purpose. Then, on Sunday, 18 October 1840, a pamphlet was published in which it was argued that the solution to the nation's problems lay not in amending the republican system but in re-establishing a monarchy under a European prince.[79] Rumours of promonarchist plots had surfaced regularly for many years, and there is no doubt that the idea was discussed behind closed doors, usually within the foreign diplomatic community. Nothing had ever come of such talk, and the suggestion was always dismissed with contempt by all sections of the press. On this occasion, however, reflecting the crisis of political faith among *hombres de bien* in the weeks after the July revolt, the reaction was markedly different. This was partly because the author of the pamphlet was José María Gutiérrez Estrada, a former minister, one of the architects of the take-over by *hombres de bien* but still in Mora's judgement an *hombre de progreso*. Gutiérrez Estrada, from a wealthy Yucatecan family, was an integral and respected member of the social elite. Married to a daughter of Count José María Justo Gómez de la Cortina, head of one of the country's most prominent families, well educated and widely travelled, he was reputed to be a man of honesty, principle and patriotism.[80] When such a man with all his evident social and political connections stood up to advocate a monarchy, he was, in Sra. Calderón de la Barca's words, 'to cause a greater sensation in Mexico than the discovery of the gunpowder plot in England'.[81]

Gutiérrez Estrada had returned to Mexico in 1840 after four years of travelling abroad, and on his arrival at Campeche he was first confronted with the rebellion in his native department. After spending some time there, he journeyed to the capital to take up his seat in the Senate, and he quickly concluded that a virtual state of anarchy already existed, telling his friend Mora in a letter of 4 July, 'We will go from bad to worse every

79 J. M. Gutiérrez Estrada, *Carta dirigida al Escmo. Sr. Presidente de la república sobre la necesidad de buscar en una convención el posible remedio de los males que aquejan a la república y opiniones del autor acerca del mismo asunto* (Mexico, 1840).
80 F. J. Sanders, 'Proposals for Monarchy in Mexico, 1823–1860', Ph.D. diss., University of Arizona, 1967, pp. 123–36.
81 Calderón de la Barca, *Life in Mexico*, p. 271.

day'.[82] He also advised Mora that there was much talk of a dictatorship, and that the only reason it had not yet happened was the disagreement among the factions over the three leading contenders – Bustamante, Valencia and Santa Anna. Eleven days later, the 15 July revolt with all its carnage on the streets began and Gutiérrez Estrada's own elderly father-in-law was one of those wounded by stray gunfire.

The scenes which Gutiérrez Estrada witnessed during those eleven days of anarchy seemed to have confirmed in his mind that republicanism was inappropriate for Mexico. He may well have discussed the matter with his friends and relatives, but he cannot have expected the outcry which his monarchist solution provoked. Couto told Mora in a letter of 25 October, 'You cannot imagine the hornet's nest that this has aroused'.[83] Within days of the appearance of the pamphlet, a wave of hostile criticism appeared in both the liberal and conservative press. Protests poured in from around the country, and powerful figures like Valencia and Guadalupe Victoria wrote to the government to express their anger.[84] Santa Anna, who curiously enough seems to have had a preview of the pamphlet, presumably sent to him by the author, wrote in a private letter on 11 October – that is, a week before it was released – that his reaction was one of 'utmost contempt'.[85] Bustamante himself issued a proclamation in which he described it as subversive and seditious. The ever-energetic Tornel quickly composed and published a long condemnation, accusing Gutiérrez Estrada of an 'attack of madness' and suggesting that he be put in a lunatic asylum.[86] In Congress there were moves to have him charged before a grand jury, and the Supreme Court was soon involved. Then the owner of the press which had printed the work, Ignacio Cumplido, was arrested and the government ordered that all copies be collected.

Gutiérrez Estrada did get some support in two papers, one being *La Hespería,* which was the mouthpiece of the Spanish community, and the other *El Correo de los Dos Mundos,* which was edited by a Frenchman and generally served the French residents. This proved of no help, for accusations were soon being made of promonarchist plots in the embassies, and Tornel, among others, broadened the issue to an attack on all Spaniards and what they had done to Mexico.[87] For his part, Gutiérrez Estrada

82 García, *Documentos inéditos,* vol. 60, 'Papeles inéditos del Doctor Mora', pp. 539–40.
83 B. Couto to J. M. L. Mora, 25 October 1840, García Collection, Mora Papers, 127 (3).
84 Sanders, 'Proposals for Monarchy', p. 136; G. Victoria to Minister of War, 22 October 1840, in *El Cosmopolita,* 14 November 1840.
85 Santa Anna to Manuel María Jiménez, 11 October 1840, García Collection, Correspondencia autógrafa de Santa Anna a M. M. Jiménez.
86 'J. M. Tornel a D. José María Gutiérrrez o sea algunas observaciones al folleto en que ha procurado la destrucción de la república y el llamamiento al trono mexicano de un príncipe extranjero', 30 October 1840, in *El Cosmopolita,* 31 October 1840.
87 See Tornel's article in ibid., 9 December 1840.

defended himself as best he could, but with mounting calls for his arrest and imprisonment, he went into hiding and soon to exile abroad.

The monarchist option was clearly rejected by all sectors of the Mexican community, and it is difficult to gauge what if any support it had. The *hombres de bien* were obliged to look for an alternative. As with monarchy, for years there had been talk of dictatorship or some form of military autocracy as being the only way to control the factional rivalry and chronic political turmoil, but on each occasion, either circumstances prevented it, or the civilian politicians, both liberal and conservative, successfully resisted. The Siete Leyes, especially the SPC, had been designed to prevent dictatorship at a time when there was still faith in the republican and representative system, but after the experience of eleven years of federalism and five of centralism, military despotism became all the more attractive. Couto had told Mora of the rumours of a dictatorship just before the 15 July revolt and mentioned that three candidates were being talked about – Bustamante, Valencia and Santa Anna.

Santa Anna had been at his country estate throughout the turmoil of 1840 and the early months of 1841. He watched and analysed the various developments, noting the revolts and other signs of popular discontent in Yucatán, Chiapas, Jalisco, San Luis Potosí and elsewhere, and of course he was well aware of what had happened in the 15 July revolt. A stream of visitors went to see him, and he received the various delegations of cotton planters, tobacco farmers and others who pleaded for his support. Then another visitor arrived. This was an English gentleman by the name of Morphy, probably Francisco.[88] He had been commissioned by the 'general body of merchants' in the capital to ask Santa Anna to use his influence to persuade Bustamante to remove the additional duties on foreign merchandize. What exactly passed between Morphy and Santa Anna is not known, but Morphy returned to Mexico City furnished with letters from the general to Bustamante and members of Congress in which he urged them to abolish the levies. They did not do so and later, early in July 1841 and following a meeting of merchants in the capital, Morphy again travelled to Manga de Clavo.[89] From there, he moved to Guadalajara.

The situation in Guadalajara was a local and regional reflection of the national scene. In January 1841, the departmental junta had petitioned Congress to enact constitutional reform, and in April the town council

---

88 These details regarding Morphy are taken from a report which Pakenham sent to the Foreign Office, dated 9 October 1841, P.R.O., F.O. 50, 147, fols. 58–63.

89 According to Carlos Bustamante, the merchants were said to have met in La Lonja, their exchange and club in the capital, where they plotted the revolt; *Gabinete mexicano*, vol. 2, p. 131. Tenenbaum states that in due course the tobacco merchants provided Santa Anna with a hundred troops and that Manuel Escandón and Lorenzo Carrera, both prominent entrepreneurs, discussed financial arrangements with him; *Politics of Penury*, p. 66.

had urged the junta to demand the abolition of the levy on foreign goods.[90] The new tax, the council maintained, had destroyed commerce, which in turn had seriously jeopardized municipal revenues. In 1839, the council's share of the *derecho de consumo* had yielded 15,079 pesos. In 1840, when the higher rate was applied, 11,209 had been received but, in the first three months of 1841, a mere 854. Taking the department as a whole, taxes had produced 680,000 pesos in 1831 but only 322,173 in 1840. Changes must be made as a matter of urgency. The merchant community in Guadalajara shared the council's worries. Like the tobacco and cotton lobbies, however, they turned to Santa Anna directly, asking him to secure the abolition of the increased *derecho de consumo*.[91]

It may well have been the receipt of this request from the merchants of Guadalajara which persuaded Santa Anna to send Mr. Morphy to the city as his envoy. Again what Morphy did there is unknown, but it seems to have been no coincidence that early in August a sequence of events took place which were assumed at the time and subsequently to have been prearranged. On the evening of 3 August, the governor of the department, Antonio Escobedo, received a note from the regional commander general, Paredes, asking for an urgent meeting. At the meeting, Paredes reported that the entire garrison in the city had been incited by local merchants to rebel against the levy on the *derecho de consumo* and that he, their commander, could and would do nothing to stop them. After another meeting the next day, Escobedo agreed to issue a decree reducing the tax on imports and also suspending that on personal incomes, which, he said, was causing much popular discontent. On 6 August, he reported these events to Mexico City, expressing the hope that his tax reductions had calmed the situation but adding a warning that the atmosphere remained tense.[92]

Throughout the next two days, 7 and 8 August, Guadalajara was alive with rumour and activity. Soldiers began to arrive in the city, including 800 infantry, 200 cavalry and 100 artillerymen. The merchant community donated 950 uniforms to them, and the local Treasury made an interim payment to the officers.[93] Preparations were made to start a newspaper, and agents set out with messages to other military commanders in the

90 'Representación que el muy ilustre ayuntamiento de la ciudad de Guadalajara ha elevado a la Escma. junta departmental para que se sirva iniciar la derogación de la ley del 15 por 100', 26 April 1841, in *El Cosmopolita*, 19 May 1841.
91 'Representación dirigida por el comercio de Guadalajara al Escmo. Sr. general D. Antonio López de Santa Anna, suplicándole interponga sus respetos para con el soberano congreso nacional a fin de que derogue la ley del 26 de noviembre de 1839', 20 April 1841, in *El Cosmopolita*, 19 May 1841.
92 A. Escobedo to Minister of Interior, 6 August 1841, ibid., 21 August 1841.
93 Ibid., 14 and 18 August 1841. *El Cosmopolita* compiled a day-by-day account of the events in Guadalajara. See also Bustamante, *Gabinete mexicano*, vol. 2, pp. 131–2.

region. Then, on the 8th, the officers gave a banquet in the garrison and all ranks were ordered to assemble at 11 a.m. outside Paredes' house. He duly appeared and addressed the assembled soldiery. He told them of his intention to lead them in revolt with the following main objectives: a new national congress to reform the constitution; a new interim president to be appointed by the SPC; Bustamante to be declared incapable of exercising power. He invited all present to lend their signatures to his plan; only three officers refused.[94] During the next few days, he replaced the municipal and departmental authorities with his own supporters. Finally, leaving two militia companies, recruited and paid for by local merchants, and with 30,000 pesos also from the merchants, he left the city leading 700 men in the direction of Lagos.

During these events, one rumour had been persistent: that Paredes' real objective was to establish a military dictatorship. He apparently revealed this to Escobedo, who in turn told his friends, and the rumour was soon rampant in the city. The name on everybody's lips, however, was not that of General Paredes but of Santa Anna. Paredes had written two letters to him on 6 August, two days before the public *pronunciamiento*.[95] He explained the reasons for his actions, the unrest caused by the taxation laws, and invited Santa Anna to support the cause. He did not mention dictatorship or that he favoured Santa Anna for the job. On 15 August, Santa Anna wrote from Manga de Clavo to the Minister of War merely to say that he had learned of the disturbances at Guadalajara and that all was peace and quiet in his area of command.[96] The next day, the local newspaper at Veracruz, *El Censor,* which was often used by Santa Anna to test the waters, published an editorial welcoming the revolt and predicting that it would attract national support.[97]

It is not clear what Bustamante and his cabinet made of these events, although some precautionary steps were taken. Paredes was relieved of his command, various generals presumed loyal were summoned to the capital and others ordered to take the field against Paredes, if necessary. Congress was told formally of the news on 12 August, and the Senate noted it with regret, asking to be kept informed.[98] Publicly, the incident at Guadalajara was dismissed as a barrack room revolt of no significance, but the indications are that Bustamante knew that much more was at stake. In private talks with leading congressmen, he was said to have asked for emergency powers and for additional resources. Also, almost

94 *El Cosmopolita,* 18 August 1841. Bustamante gives the text of the Paredes plan; *Gabinete mexicano,* vol. 2, p. 133.
95 Both letters were published in *El Cosmopolita,* 25 August 1841.
96 Santa Anna to J. N. Almonte, 15 August 1841, in ibid., 21 August 1841.
97 The editorial from *El Censor* was reported in ibid., 21 August 1841.
98 Archivo del Senado, Actas secretas, July–December 1841.

certainly known to the government, Paredes' sympathizers in the capital were in a state of excitement and unusual activity, sending messages around the country asking for support.[99] The British minister reporting on 14 August, was in no doubt that what had happened at Guadalajara had 'all the appearances of a general movement throughout the country'.[100] Bustamante was also, of course, well aware of the long-standing rumours concerning the dictatorial ambitions of Santa Anna, and while his innocuous letter of the 15th may have offered him some slight comfort, it is unlikely to have convinced him of Santa Anna's loyalty. As far as Pakenham was concerned, all was clear. Regarding the new president demanded by Paredes, he wrote, 'This individual, it is scarcely to be doubted, will be General Santa Anna, who, there is reason to believe, is at the bottom of all that is going on'.[101]

The next stage did in fact take place in the department of Veracruz and bears all the hallmarks of Santa Anna's talent for conspiracy. On 24 August, he composed a long letter to Almonte in which he disassociated himself entirely from everything the government stood for and had done. He denounced the 1836 constitution, attacked the laws on taxation and claimed the government had lost all authority. It had brought the nation to a state of ruin, unable to defend itself, and to the verge of social dissolution. Paredes, he insisted, was an honourable man with honourable intentions and the government must find a peaceful solution to its differences with him. For his part, he, Santa Anna, would help as a mediator, if the government so desired.[102]

Twenty-four hours after the dispatch of this letter, a crowd of people at Veracruz assembled and demanded an emergency meeting of the town council, which took place at midnight on 25 August. The council voted to abolish several taxes, including those on foreign imports and the personal tax, and to abolish the tobacco monopoly in the department. The authorities in Jalapa, Orizaba and Córdoba adopted similar resolutions, and all asked Santa Anna to back their demands. The next day, 27 August, with the popular mandate in his pocket, Santa Anna, having ordered the customs house to send no more money to the capital, left in his carriage for Perote, where about 1,500 men were assembling.[103] Shortly after arriving there, he wrote another hostile letter to Almonte.

99 Unsigned letter from Mexico City, 14 August 1841 in García Collection, Paredes y Arrillaga Papers, 14C'1.
100 R. Pakenham to Ld. Palmerston, 14 August 1841, P.R.O., F.O. 50, 146, fol. 82.
101 Ibid.
102 Santa Anna to J. N. Almonte, 24 August 1841, in *El Cosmopolita*, 1 September 1841. Santa Anna's offer of mediation was described by Prieto as 'la mediación de un lobo entre dos mastines que riñen'; Prieto, *Memorias*, vol. 2, p. 40.
103 These details of events at Veracruz are from *El Cosmopolita*, 1 September 1841; Bustamante,

Reporting these events at Veracruz, the British vice-consul in the port noted that 'this is only the first act of a great Drama which has been long and silently preparing: namely, a return to a monarchical form of government'.[104] The next act took place while Bustamante and his colleagues were analysing Santa Anna's behaviour, and if that had come as no real surprise to them, they were certainly stunned by what occurred on their own doorstep soon after noon on 31 August.[105] At about 3:30 p.m. on that day, the street vendors in the central plaza began to cry 'revolution', the shops at once raised their shutters and word spread quickly through the cafés and taverns that General Valencia had occupied the Citadel and declared his support for the Guadalajara revolt. Valencia had indeed pronounced and almost before Bustamante could have realized what was happening, he and his soldiers – probably about a thousand – had fortified the Citadel and occupied nearby buildings, including the Acordada jail, from which political prisoners were released. At 5 p.m., having recovered from the shock he must have felt at the desertion of Valencia, who was considered his most loyal ally because of his defence of the regime in the 15 July revolt, Bustamante led a column of men from the national palace towards the Citadel. This lay just beyond the south-western fringe of the built-up area in the centre of the city, and Bustamante marched as far as the Alameda park, where he decided to stop. Later that same evening, as cadets from the Military College marched in formation to join Valencia, other soldiers loyal to the government occupied the most prominent buildings around the national palace. Meanwhile, Valencia published his proclamation. His aims, he said, were to obey the will of the people as expressed at Guadalajara. The people did not want a tyrant and would never support one. Three days later, he issued his plan: a popular junta to choose an interim president, a new congress to produce a new constitution and complete independence of the judiciary.[106]

As the military took up their positions and decided which side to support, Congress met in emergency session on the morning of 1 Sep-

Gabinete mexicano, vol. 2, pp. 135–6; M. Rivera Cambas, *Historia antigua y moderna de Jalapa y de las revoluciones del estado de Veracruz* (Mexico, 1959), vol. 8, pp. 102–11.
104 F. Gifford to Ld. Palmerston, 2 September 1841, P.R.O., F.O. 50, 148, fols. 136–7.
105 The details given here of what happened in the capital during September and early October are based on accounts by several contemporary witnesses. Most, if not all, the newspapers ceased publication once fighting started on the streets of the city, but the editors of *El Cosmopolita*, which closed down on 4 September, kept a day-by-day, at times hour-by-hour, diary, which they later published from 6 October to 10 November 1841. Other, often vivid, eye-witness accounts are in Bustamante, *Gabinete mexicano*, vol. 2; Calderón de la Barca, *Life in Mexico*; Malo, *Diario*, vol. 1; Bocanegra, *Memorias*, vol. 2; Prieto, *Memorias*, vol. 2; see also the dispatches from the Spanish embassy in *Relaciones diplomáticas, hispano-mexicanas*, vol. 1.
106 'Exposición que dirigió el Escmo. Sr. general en gefe de las tropas pronunciadas por el plan regenerador de la república al Escelentísimo Sr. D. Anastasio Bustamante', 31 August 1841, in *El Cosmopolita*, 4 September 1841. Valencia's plan is in *Boletín Oficial*, 6 September 1841.

tember. Having heard reports from Almonte, the deputies passed several hours in irate debate, attended for part of the time by councillors of state Alamán and Manuel Eduardo Gorostiza. Eventually, having refused to grant Bustamante emergency powers, the congressmen reached a compromise to the effect that the SPC should declare what was the will of the nation in the present crisis. The SPC met the following day and interpreted the national will as being against any form of despotism. At the same time, the executive was authorized to take whatever steps were needed to restore order. Bustamante at once took advantage of his now virtually unrestricted powers. The city was declared in a state of siege, freedom of the press on political subjects was suspended, taxes on foodstuffs brought into the city were lifted and the now notorious *derecho de consumo* was abolished. Changes to the law imposing the *contribución personal* were also announced, with the minimum income before liability being raised to 500 pesos a year, effectively excluding most of the poor from payment.

These various measures indicate that Bustamante had every intention of resisting the revolt, and the next few days were spent in the preparation of more military defences, including the digging of trenches across the streets leading to the palace. Much time and effort were also devoted by both sides to disseminating propaganda. Valencia had taken the precaution of acquiring a printing press, and presumably printers, who produced a regular *Boletín de la Ciudadela*. In response, the government suspended publication of its official daily paper, the *Diario,* and replaced it with a daily *Boletín Oficial*.[107] This proceeded to attack every statement put out by the rebels and to publish Bustamante's proclamations, in which he repeatedly stressed that the rebel aim was military dictatorship and unrestrained tyranny. Both sides claimed military superiority, and more and more soldiers did arrive in the city, some to join the rebels and others the government. The constant movement of soldiers about the streets was accompanied by intermittent skirmishes, and Valencia soon began to fire his cannons in the direction of the palace, causing substantial damage to buildings as well as to the civilian population.

The people of the capital, of course, well remembered the devastation caused by the 15 July revolt slightly more than twelve months earlier. The respective rebel—loyalist strongholds were now reversed, but once again the noncombatant population was caught in the middle. Anticipating what was to come and ignoring Bustamante's decrees to the con-

---

107 There were forty issues of the *Boletín Oficial* and rather less of the *Boletín de la Ciudadela,* which was issued at two- to three-day intervals; for what is probably a complete run of both, see García Collection, Gz.G927.04.M681.v5. Each publication contains the proclamations, letters, propaganda, etc. of both sides. Prieto says he wrote the *Boletín Oficial;* Prieto, *Memorias,* vol. 2, pp. 40–1.

trary, shops and businesses closed, churches no longer rang their bells and those who could began to flee the city. The city council appealed to both sides, and a delegation of councillors went to the Citadel, where Valencia promised them he would not fire unless attacked. Despite this promise, heavy firing soon recommenced, buildings were damaged, civilians, including two nuns, were killed or injured and bands of thieves again began to roam the streets taking advantage of the collapse of law and order.[108]

By 10 September, a kind of uneasy military stalemate had been reached, with both sides firing occasionally at each other across the rooftops. Then over the next four days, several developments occurred which considerably weakened Bustamante's position. First, it was learned that Luis Cortazar, commander of Guanajuato, together with its garrison, had come out in support of Paredes and that the authorities of Guanajuato, after talks with Paredes, had also agreed to back his demands. Juan Alvarez from the south also declared against Bustamante, and similar defections by senior military officers at Querétaro, Tampico and elsewhere were soon public knowledge.[109] Santa Anna, having delayed a week, probably to assess the situation, abandoned publicly any pretence of neutrality or mediation and on 9 September issued his Plan of Perote. His main demands were now as follows: Bustamante should cease to be president; the plan published by Valencia on 4 September should be approved; all Mexicans should join in a 'conciliatory embrace'.[110]

Faced with what was now a national movement against him spreading in the north, south, east and west, Bustamante decided to offer what was to be the first of several political compromises, including an offer to share power with Santa Anna and Bravo.[111] None of these offers were accepted, however, and by the middle of September, Bustamante's position had become untenable. Almost daily, garrisons around the country joined the rebels and Bravo, from his base in Chilpancingo, refused to bring his men to the capital, pointedly not condemning the rebellion in his proclamation. Bustamante decided to seek formal permission to lead the army and to hand over the presidency temporarily to Bravo in his capacity as president of the Council of Government. Bravo, as indicated, refused,

---

108 Many instances of damage to property and person are noted by all observers. Among the more bizarre is one mentioned by Malo, *Diario*, vol. 1, p. 201: one Don Alvaro Muñoz had lost a leg as a result of a wound suffered in the July 1840 revolt and was again hit by a stray bullet, this time, in his wooden leg.

109 J. Alvarez to Minister of War, 10 September 1841, in *El Cosmopolita*, 20 October 1841. Alvarez also wrote to Valencia telling him he would leave Acapulco and come to the capital, if needed; ibid., 16 October 1841.

110 For the full text of the Plan of Perote, see *Boletín Oficial*, 17 September 1841. Almonte had written to Santa Anna on 4 September reprimanding him and reminding him of his duty as an army officer; letter in *El Cosmopolita*, 6 October 1841.

111 Archivo del senado, Actas secretas, 13 September 1841.

and when the Congress offered the job to José Antonio Romero, he also declined. Eventually, a replacement was found in Javier Echeverría, former Minister of Hacienda, who after resisting for several days agreed to become acting president on 23 September. Meanwhile, within the city the civilian exodus became a flood. Such was the demand that even the rich found that money could not buy temporary lodgings in the surrounding towns and villages. Heavy thunderstorms, earthquake tremors, rumours of typhus, shortages of food and water, daily fighting on the streets, the fearsome sound of cannon fire, bands of marauding thieves all added to the atmosphere of panic.

The arrival of five hundred loyal troops from Puebla caused more problems for Bustamante because he was unable to find lodgings for them, and more private residences had to be requisitioned. Then, perhaps in view of the anarchy on the streets, the loss of life and damage to property, or possibly for the more practical reason that he had no fodder left to feed his horses, Bustamante led his troops out of the city to the village of Guadalupe.[112] With Paredes nearing the capital and Santa Anna approaching from Puebla, he decided to try to negotiate. He went to the hacienda de la Lechería where Paredes was camped with his bedraggled column of 'rather drunken' infantry.[113] Almonte went to meet Santa Anna, who arrived at Tacubaya at noon on 26 September, where he was joined shortly afterwards by Valencia, Cortazar and Paredes. The initial round of talks produced no agreement on the main issues, but an armistice was agreed upon at later sessions held at the hacienda de los Morales. Then on 28 September, following what seem to have been irate discussions between the rebel generals, or 'three allied sovereigns' as Sra. Calderón put it, Santa Anna sent Almonte the text of what, he said, were their agreed demands. This new plan, the so-called Bases de Tacubaya, contained thirteen articles which, in sum, demanded the following: all powers, except the judicial, created under the 1836 constitution, would cease at once; a junta composed of two deputies per department and chosen by Santa Anna would elect a provisional president to take office immediately with unrestricted authority to rule the country; a Congress would be summoned to produce a new constitution.[114]

The news of Santa Anna's intentions and the confirmation that he was to take autocratic powers produced yet another unexpected and bizarre reaction in the capital. Bustamante first resigned the presidency, issuing his resignation statement on 29 September. Then he led his men back into the city, and rumours immediately began to circulate

112 The shortage of fodder is suggested by Bustamante, *Gabinete mexicano*, vol. 2, pp. 210–11.
113 Calderón de la Barca, *Life in Mexico*, p. 426.
114 For the full text of the Bases de Tacubaya and details of the negotiations and correspondence, see *El Cosmopolita*, 23 October 1841.

that he was going to pronounce himself in favour of the restoration of federalism. Almonte spent much of that day arranging this extraordinary development, and no doubt much to the amusement of Gómez Farías, who for years had been condemned for trying to mobilize the populace, agents were sent into the streets to persuade people to join and weapons and ammunition were distributed. The next day, crowds began to assemble outside the palace and Bustamante appeared at 10 a.m. Amid the ringing of church bells, salvoes and cries of 'Long live the federation', the populace proclaimed a federation. Almonte summoned leading federalists to a 6 p.m. meeting, but because only eight turned up, the meeting had to be postponed. It took place the following day, 1 October, in the Colegio del Seminario, where some two hundred people drew up a more formal declaration in which they rejected the Bases de Tacubaya and demanded the immediate restoration of the 1824 federal constitution.[115] Other plans circulated around the streets, and irate citizens issued statements that their signatures on them had been forged. Acting president Echeverría retired in despair to his private residence. In the words of Sra. Calderón, 'Everything is in a state of perfect anarchy and confusion'.[116]

Further talks were held between the contending parties but no progress was made. On 2, 3 and 4 October, there was renewed heavy firing in the city, with rebel shells landing in the palace and many casualties. Santa Anna withdrew from Tacubaya and arranged his forces on the outskirts at Piedad de la Viga, where there were further bloody skirmishes with Bustamante's supporters, in full view of crowds of civilians who left the city on foot and in carriages to watch the action.[117] Then Bustamante, realizing the futility of his too sudden conversion to federalism, which had attracted no significant support, returned to the city, reviewed his troops and withdrew all his units to Guadalupe, leaving only a hundred men to guard the palace under the command of Juan Orbegoso. Rebel soldiers promptly surrounded the building, and at 5:30 p.m. on 5 October, they were allowed to enter by Orbegoso, who surrendered it to them. Half an hour later, Valencia led his men from the Citadel down to the palace. With the centre of government secure, at 7:30 p.m. Santa Anna offered Bustamante another chance to surrender, pointing out the vast superiority of his nine thousand men over the government's rapidly

115 The text of the Plan del Seminario is in *Boletín Oficial*, 2 October 1841. One of the few remaining generals loyal to Bustamante, Valentín Canalizo, issued his own profederal plan, declaring that he and his men would fight to the death to support it; see *El Cosmopolita*, 6 November 1841.
116 Calderón de la Barca, *Life in Mexico*, p. 430.
117 Bustamante, *Gabinete mexicano*, vol. 2, p. 208. For the view of one of Santa Anna's officers who took part in the fighting, see 'Memorias del coronel Manuel María Giménez', in García, *Documentos inéditos*, vol. 59, pp. 315–16.

dwindling army. For several more hours, Bustamante deliberated, and finally at 4 a.m. on 6 October, he replied and agreed to talk. Later that day, representatives of both sides met at Presa de la Estanzuela and at 9:30 in the evening, Bustamante's delegates accepted in effect the Bases de Tacubaya.[118] The Bustamante presidency and the centralist republican regime of the Siete Leyes were finally over.

The irony of his fate cannot have escaped Bustamante as he prepared once again to go into exile. His administration, at least in the early years, had especially favoured the merchant-financier community, some members of which had made large fortunes from the government's myriad financial dealings, and Bustamante had found himself as a result pilloried in the press for being in the pocket of the speculators. Now it was the same merchant community which had turned against him and arranged with the army for his removal from office. Indeed, for most Mexican observers of the time, the whole sequence of events from August to October was the direct responsibility of foreign merchants. For the most part, we do not know the identity of those at Guadalajara, Veracruz and the capital who conspired with and financed the generals.[119] Nor do we know what messages Morphy conveyed from the 'general body of merchants' in the capital to Santa Anna or Paredes, and it is unclear to what extent, if any, there was a prearranged triangular plot between Santa Anna, Paredes and Valencia. The only identifiable character is Morphy, and there remains some confusion regarding his identity and role. According to most sources, he was Francisco Morphy, senior partner in the Spanish firm of Morphy & Morzán, but as indicated earlier, Pakenham states that he was an English gentleman. In fact, Morphy was Spanish born but a naturalized Englishman.[120] When news of his various journeys to Santa Anna and Paredes became known in the capital, there were loud demands in Congress in early September for his arrest as a conspirator. Morphy sought refuge in Pakenham's house, where he remained for several weeks. It would seem unlikely that the British minister would have been unaware of the purpose of his travels. But Pakenham was too diplomatic to give details in his report to the Foreign Office, saying that he had not questioned Morphy about his activities.

Bustamante may have also reflected on the old adage that history repeats itself, for this was the second time he had been forced from

118 *El Cosmopolita,* 10 November 1841. For the correspondence between Santa Anna and Bustamante, see the issue of 9 October 1841.

119 Bustamante says their identities were well known but he does not reveal them; *Gabinete mexicano,* vol. 2, p. 175. Paredes later submitted accounts of his expenditures and stated that he had received 20,000 pesos from one Ignacio Ramírez of Guadalajara; see documents published in *El Cosmopolita,* 8 and 22 January 1842.

120 This is stated by the Spanish ambassador, P. P. de Oliver, in a dispatch dated 26 October 1841, in *Relaciones diplomáticas hispano-mexicanas,* vol. 1, p. 279.

office by Santa Anna. From 1830 to 1832, he had led the first attempt to centralize the political structure of the nation and to consolidate the control of *hombres de bien* and the largely conservative values he and they espoused. His administration had been judged a success in several spheres, but all its achievements were to no avail when Santa Anna chose to take on the mantle of standard bearer of liberal federalism. At that time, in 1832, Bustamante had resisted the military and political pressure for several months, but in the end the desertion of the army had made his defeat inevitable. Now in 1841, although for very different reasons and ends, a similar process had taken place. Santa Anna once again had raised the banner of revolt, and one by one the senior army officers on whom the regime's survival ultimately depended deserted it. But at least Bustamante had redeemed something of his personal reputation in the summer and autumn of 1841. There is no doubt that he had entirely lost the confidence of all the middle-class groups who had originally supported him because of his policies, but he was also seen, rightly or wrongly, as a weak, irresolute, slothful, incompetent bungler who simply had neither the intellectual ability nor physical stamina for the demanding job of president. Yet such judgements by Pakenham, Carlos Bustamante, Gómez Farías and many other of his contemporaries do not seem to fit well with his conduct in 1841. The charges of apathy and inertia in particular do not correspond to his frantic political and military activity during the revolt as he wrote speech after speech, conferred with advisers, cajoled Congress and the SPC, made daily military manoeuvres and engaged in battle, going, it is said, for days on end without sleep. Despite the overwhelming odds against him, he steadfastly refused to give up, and it is quite possible that he did so only because he ran out of money to pay his men, who promptly deserted to the richer rebel cause.[121]

However one judges Bustamante's life and role in Mexican history, and it is one of many which merit much more research, the events of August to October 1841 marked the end of his long career in government, and he soon departed for his second period of exile in Europe. He returned in 1844, and although he was elected to Congress as a kind of senior statesman figure and also carried out several military commissions, he never again achieved national prominence. He retired to San Miguel Allende, where in 1853 he died at the age of 73. Somewhat ironically, it was in the year of his death that the man who had twice driven him

---

121 Bustamante mentions the lack of money and adds that, in the final days, most of the soldiers the president had left were drunk; *Gabinete mexicano*, vol. 2, p. 211.

from office finally achieved the full dictatorial powers he had coveted for so long. For the time being, in 1841, under the terms of the Bases de Tacubaya, Santa Anna did not yet have his formal dictatorship but he had, in Pakenham's words, 'almost absolute power'.[122]

122 R. Pakenham to Ld. Palmerston, 9 October 1841, P.R.O., F.O. 50, 147, fols. 97–107.

8

'La dictadura disfrazada con el hermoso nombre de regeneración política'

Unfortunately, we do not know what transpired inside the walls of the archbishop's palace at Tacubaya when Santa Anna, Paredes, Valencia, Cortazar and Tornel met around the table to construct the future political organization of the country. Whatever the mood or nature of the discussions, and Sra. Calderón implies that they were by no means amicable, Santa Anna emerged the victor.[1] How he managed to impose his will, what deals were struck and promises made have still to be explained because the others present, notably Paredes and Valencia, were by no means lacking in personal ambition, as subsequent events were to demonstrate. The rumours of impending military autocracy had been current throughout the revolt against Bustamante, but Santa Anna was not the only potential candidate for the dictatorship. The others most often mentioned were precisely Paredes and Valencia, and it seems unlikely that they had agreed in advance that Santa Anna should emerge as the main beneficiary of their combined efforts. Escobedo had claimed in Guadalajara that Paredes had revealed his aim of dictatorship, and government propaganda had emphasized that this was the real objective. In contrast, Paredes, in discussions with Cortazar and the Guanajuato authorities early in September, apparently assured them that he was not seeking to establish a dictatorship, and it was on that basis that they joined the rebels. Later meetings, again called by Paredes, were held with representatives from the departments of Jalisco, Guanajuato, Zacatecas, San Luis Potosí, Querétaro and Aguascalientes. When they learned of the Bases de Tacubaya, and especially of the choice of Santa Anna as president, they protested and demanded that executive power be given to a person chosen in effect by themselves, implying that they would choose Paredes.[2]

If Paredes was persuaded to give up his personal ambitions and return to Guadalajara with only a promotion to divisional general to show for

---

1 The chapter title is a quotation from a representation to Congress, 5 April 1845, in *El Estandarte nacional*, Puebla, 5 April 1845, Colección Lafragua, 398. Sra. Calderón's impression of the talks is from Calderón de la Barca, *Life in Mexico*, p. 427.
2 *El Cosmopolita*, 4 September, 13 October 1841.

his efforts because, according to Bancroft, he concluded that Santa Anna would make the best president, it remains unclear why Valencia also gave way.[3] Aged 46, he had followed the conventional career pattern of a successful army officer. Born in Mexico City, he had been in the royalist army during the war of independence, until he joined Iturbide in February 1821. Then he participated in various military campaigns, including those in Texas and against the French in 1838, and as he rose through the ranks his name became more and more prominent, especially after his victory over the federalists at Acajete in 1839. By 1840, according to Gutiérrez Estrada, he had become a very popular figure in the army, carefully expanding his circle of supporters, and after his defence of Bustamante in the 15 July revolt, there were strong rumours, reported by the Spanish ambassador in August, that the advocates of dictatorship were looking to him as their candidate.[4] Every observer, however, both foreign and Mexican, invariably commented on aspects of his personality which alienated the *hombres de bien*. The U.S. diplomat Waddy Thompson referred to his lack of education and good manners, 'which very strongly mark the parvenu', and the Spanish ambassador noted his womanizing, excessive drinking and gambling.[5] Sra. Calderón, in a private letter, described him as a 'vulgar, ambitious upstart'.[6] At the same time, nobody was in any doubt regarding his ambition, and it seems improbable that he should have willingly renounced his personal aspirations in favour of Santa Anna. Yet he did so and was content for the time being to accept the material rewards Santa Anna liberally showered on him in the months following the Tacubaya negotiations. He was given various profitable sinecures in the patronage of Santa Anna, allowed to acquire extensive properties and quickly became a wealthy man, provoking much adverse press comment on his new-found and ostentatious opulence.

Santa Anna, therefore, took the spoils of victory, but although he may have been able to buy the acquiescence of his military rivals, his own resurrection still begs a number of questions, particularly concerning the willingness of both merchants and moderate politicians like Gómez Pedraza once again to entrust executive power to his notoriously fickle hands. It is as well to remember that Santa Anna was far from being the macho caudillo of the Juan Manuel Rosas of Argentina type, who was receiving much publicity and praise in the Mexican press at this time. By October

3 Bancroft, *History of Mexico*, vol. 5, p. 229.

4 J. M. Gutiérrez Estrada to J. M. L. Mora, 4 July 1840, in García, *Documentos inéditos*, vol. 60, pp. 539–40; A. Calderón de la Barca to Secretary of State, 23 July, 28 August 1840, in *Relaciones diplomáticas hispano-mexicanas*, vol. 1, pp. 124–8, 144–6.

5 Thompson, *Recollections of Mexico*, p. 87; *Relaciones diplomáticas hispano-mexicanas*, vol. 1, pp. 144–6.

6 F. Calderón de la Barca to W. H. Prescott, 19 September 1841, in R. Wolcott, ed., *The Correspondence of W. H. Prescott, 1833–1847* (Boston, 1925), pp. 249–50.

1841, he was 47, lame with his wooden leg, in bad health and, according to those who met him in person, more a quiet, dignified philosopher than a dynamic military personality. Physically, in terms of height and build, he was not an imposing presence and certainly not in the mould of a Porfirio Díaz. Carlos Bustamante noted that age had given him a 'grave and angry look', but Sra. Calderón, after her first meeting in December 1839, described him as a 'gentlemanly, good-looking, quietly dressed, rather melancholy looking person, with one leg, apparently something of an invalid'.[7] Almost two years later, in November 1841, she met him again at the opera and her first impressions were confirmed: 'We met the great man *en face* and he stopped and gave us a cordial recognition. Two years have made little change in him in appearance. He retains the same interesting, resigned and rather melancholy expression; the same quiet voice and grave but agreeable manner; and surrounded by pompous officers, he alone looked quiet, gentlemanly and high bred'.[8]

Santa Anna's quiet and melancholy appearance, however, contrasted sharply with other well-known features of his personality. Sra. Calderón wrote privately that he was an 'energetic robber'.[9] Everybody knew of his avarice and venality, and the tales of his corrupt financial dealings and 'his colossal fortune' were legendary, according to the Spanish ambassador.[10] By the early 1840s, he was in modern terms a multimillionaire, owning according to his own account 483,000 acres in the department of Veracruz, which brought in an income of more than 28,000 pesos a year from livestock breeding and rents from his many tenant farmers. He also owned houses in the capital, and his wealth was such that he was able to give each of his daughters a dowry of 50,000 pesos.[11] Nobody doubted that such vast assets had been gained through anything other than corrupt means, through private deals with the *agiotistas* and entrepreneurs, through payoffs and bribes from grateful contractors as well as through straight pillaging of the Treasury. Of course, evidence of such corruption is now virtually impossible to obtain, although the British diplomat P. Doyle does reveal some instances in his reports to the Foreign Office. In one case involving a British mining company, he reports that Santa Anna was willing to bend the law in return for 25,000 pesos and, after haggling, was willing to come down to 20,000. In another concerning tax exemptions for an annual trade fair, he explained, 'This fair

7 C. M. Bustamante, *Apuntes para la historia del gobierno del general don Antonio López de Santa Anna* (Mexico, 1986), p. 80; Calderón de la Barca, *Life in Mexico*, p. 32.
8 Calderón de la Barca, *Life in Mexico*, pp. 443–4.
9 F. Calderón de la Barca to W. H. Prescott, in Wolcott, *Correspondence of W. H. Prescott*, pp. 249–50.
10 P. P. Oliver to Secretary of State, 20 September 1841, in *Relaciones diplomáticas hispano-mexicanas*, vol. 1, p. 263. Oliver succeeded Calderón de la Barca as ambassador in 1841.
11 Callcott, *Santa Anna*, pp. 217–18.

has been established principally with a view of benefiting the property of the President, General Santa Anna'.[12]

Such personal corruption does not seem to have been viewed with anything other than sanctimonious distaste by his contemporaries, probably because Santa Anna in this respect was little different, except perhaps in scale and opportunity, from many other successful generals and politicians. Nor do his notorious duplicity and lack of principle seem to have lost him any support. Pakenham, who knew him well, wrote in 1837 just after Santa Anna had returned from the United States and had declared his loyalty to the government and the Siete Leyes, 'I have witnessed too many acts of duplicity and bad faith on the part of General Santa Anna to place much confidence in them'.[13] After his desertion of the federalist cause in 1834, he was naturally despised by Gómez Farías and the radicals, but no political party or group of any persuasion was under any illusion that he could be trusted. In ideological terms, he represented nothing except the vague generalities of independence and liberty, which he invariably used in his public proclamations. On none of the political issues of the day – federalism or centralism, liberalism or conservatism, free trade or protectionism, ecclesiastical patronage and so on – or on other matters of economic or social policy had he ever expressed or taken a consistent position. In short, nobody knew what, if any, his political beliefs were, and by 1841 most recognized that he was an unprincipled, corrupt and untrustworthy opportunist, always willing to accumulate cash and glory to his own account.[14]

Yet, paradoxically, they not only permitted but actively encouraged him to take power time and again. Why they did so is difficult to explain, but there are some indications from the time of the Bases de Tacubaya. Notwithstanding his reprehensible qualities, and perhaps partly because of them, he was undoubtedly the most famous man in the country, a fact which every foreign visitor immediately realized. Sra. Calderón wrote that 'his name has a prestige, whether for good or evil, that no other possesses', and her husband told his colleagues in Spain that he was the 'most popular leader in the country'.[15] His successor in the Spanish embassy agreed, describing him as 'undoubtedly the most influential character in the republic', and the U.S. traveller Albert Gilliam noted that his name 'filled the inhabitants with awe and reverence'.[16] The origins of that reputation

12 P. Doyle to Ld. Aberdeen, 25 May 1843, P.R.O., F.O. 162, fols. 86–90 and 163, fol. 52.
13 R. Pakenham to Ld. Palmerston, 4 March 1837, ibid., 106, fols. 53–6.
14 Bancroft, *History of Mexico*, vol. 5, p. 261.
15 Calderón de la Barca, *Life in Mexico*, p. 345; A. Calderón de la Barca to Secretary of State, 22 January 1840, in *Relaciones diplomáticas hispano-mexicanas*, vol. 1, p. 28.
16 P. P. Oliver to Secretary of State, 26 August 1841, in ibid., 251–4; Gilliam, *Travels in Mexico*, p. 248.

lay in aspects of both his career and his personality. By 1841 he had been on the national scene for twenty years and had been involved in every event of any significance from the downfall of Iturbide to the removal of Bustamante. Throughout those years, whatever the alleged reason for his participation or intervention, he had always contrived to depict himself as a genuine patriot concerned only with the good of his country. However hypocritical or mendacious his accounts of his own conduct were – for example, in the United States – few of the newspapers were willing to expose him openly, especially as he acquired the reputation of being a great survivor and someone always likely to recover from setbacks. Those who supported him, apart from his immediate coterie, constantly eulogized his alleged achievements, even adopting his name in the newspaper *El Santanista Oaxaqueño*. Massive publicity was always given to his military victories, few and far between though they actually were, and the easily remembered labels of hero of Tampico, Veracruz and Acajete served to keep him in the public mind as a warrior of Napoleonic stature. Similarly, his addiction to his fighting cocks and to the national passion for gambling, his many conquests of the opposite sex, his love of flamboyant display from military parades to Te Deums, his regal demeanour on public occasions always surrounded by brilliantly dressed and obsequious courtiers – all added up to a public image of larger-than-life proportions far removed from the melancholy invalid portrayed by those who saw him close to hand.

It was this image, a blend of his personal virtues and vices, which gave him the prestige he enjoyed in the popular mind as a man of exceptional power, influence and authority. Most Mexicans, of course, never met or saw him in person, and they could only derive their impressions from the press and word-of-mouth accounts of his exploits. Nevertheless, for the army, where his prestige was also unequalled despite his humiliation in Texas, there were more direct causes of gratitude and admiration. Throughout his career, Santa Anna never failed to heap praise on the military profession and to back that up at every opportunity with medals, promotions, monetary rewards and protection of privileges. Although he was resented, if not feared, by rival senior officers whose own careers since independence had been eclipsed by his, his popularity with junior officers and those in the lower ranks was undeniable and his ability to recruit support for any cause he chose to champion, especially in the Veracruz region, was always feared by every government.

Thus, Santa Anna was able to create very successfully a cult of his own personality and a larger-than-life image among the people at large and the army in particular, but it still remains to be explained why perceptive, intelligent men like Alamán, Tornel, Gómez Pedraza and so many others who well knew what lay behind the public façade were willing to support him. Certainly by 1841 part of the answer lies in another feature of his personality which again was noted by all who knew him. Even after his debilitating injury and the loss of his leg, he remained a man of great energy and decisiveness. Pakenham observed that 'General Santa Anna's activity and energy of character always impart a degree of vigour to the Government unknown under other circumstances'.[17] Pascual Oliver spoke of 'the energy of his character and his decisiveness, qualities very rare among his countrymen', and even his arch-enemy, Gómez Farías, admitted him to be 'active and bold by nature', adding, it must be said, that he was also 'evil and immoral'.[18] It was this personal dynamism and ability to get things done, so sharply in contrast to Bustamante's inertia, which seem to have persuaded politicians of most parties, if not to welcome, at least to accept Santa Anna's assumption of power in 1841. Even the editors of *El Cosmopolita* accepted that the Tacubaya accord was necessary and were willing to place their hopes in him.

There were two other explanations for the support he received from the social, political and financial elite. One was again suggested by Gómez Farías in a letter to Mora some three years later in 1844. Those who put Santa Anna in power in 1841, he recalled, believed that by flattering him, by playing on his vanity, they would be able to control him and thus use him to protect and advance their own interests.[19] That was to be a mistake which had already been made in the past and which would again be made, notably by Alamán, years later in 1853. Oliver suggested another possibility. Thoroughly disillusioned with the political anarchy and total lack of progress in every field since independence, *hombres de bien* in general had come to accept that some form of autocracy might provide the stability they desired. They were prepared to overlook Santa Anna's known corruption and lack of principles because they believed that he was the one man who had the public prestige and, above all, popularity with the army to enforce public order. In Oliver's words, he offered them 'sensible doctrines such as assuring his country a compact and strong government which would get the nation organized . . . and put it in a respectable state of defence'.[20]

In other words, Santa Anna, in return for autocratic power, offered the promise of stability and order and, especially, a halt to the changing values which threatened 'social dissolution'. But these were generalities

17 R. Pakenham to Ld. Aberdeen, 24 February 1843, P.R.O., F.O. 50, 161, fols. 76–9.
18 P. P. Oliver to Secretary of State, 20 September 1841, *Relaciones diplomáticas hispano-mexicanas*, vol. 1, p. 263; draft of letter by V. Gómez Farías in García Collection, Gómez Farías Papers, 966.
19 V. Gómez Farías to J. M. L. Mora, 23 April 1844, in García, *Documentos inéditos*, vol. 60, pp. 545–7.
20 P. P. Oliver to Secretary of State, 20 September 1841, *Relaciones diplomáticas hispano-mexicanas*, vol. 1, p. 263.

which he always promised and usually failed to deliver, and there had to be more concrete commitments. Here we touch upon an aspect of Santa Anna's career for which his many biographers have not done him justice. He was, more than anything else, a supreme manipulator, negotiator and fixer of deals behind the scenes. His many visitors to Manga de Clavo in the spring and summer of 1841 went to get something from him, and his co-operation was no doubt conditional. Once again, details cannot be known, for such bargains were not committed to paper, but decisions reached after Santa Anna took office allow reasonable deductions to be made. These suggest that promises or arrangements were made with several interested parties and were honoured by him.

The most obvious payoff was to the military. As already noted, Paredes received the rank of divisional general and Valencia was given more direct monetary rewards. Generals Cortazar and Julián Juvera were promoted to brigadier-general, and dozens of other officers received promotions. As Santa Anna's aide-de-camp recalled in his memoirs, 'Almost everybody in the army was promoted'.[21] Then, in a series of laws issued from October to December 1841, new cavalry and infantry regiments were formed in the departments of Veracruz, Michoacán, Mexico, Jalisco, Oaxaca, Puebla and Querétaro. To fill the ranks of these and vacancies in existing units, a widespread forced levy was imposed, with people including *hombres de bien* dragged from their homes. According to Carlos Bustamante, hundreds of these conscripts, followed by their destitute women and children, were forced to march to the capital, where they were housed in several of the larger monasteries and where some were to die of hunger.[22] New commander generals with both military and political authority were appointed in several departments, and as always, renewed instructions regarding uniforms were soon emanating from the presidential office.

The merchant community also had its rewards. Morphy, for example, quickly accumulated substantial wealth from various concessions and deals. One was made with the tobacco contractors, who included Cayetano Rubio, Neri del Barrio and Escandón. They had been trying without success to get out of the contract they had signed in 1839 on which they were losing large amounts of money and they looked to Santa Anna for help. He kept his bargain, and with Morphy acting as intermediary, in return for a percentage, a decree of 12 November cancelled the contract with the entrepreneurs.[23] The government agreed to purchase the company's entire inventory valued at almost 4 million pesos, and to pay this,

21 'Memorias del Coronel Manuel María Giménez', in García, *Documentos inéditos*, vol. 59, p. 316.
22 Bustamante, *Apuntes*, pp. 7–8.
23 This deal was agreed to at a meeting on 8 November attended by, among others, Santa Anna, Gómez Pedraza, Tornel, Escandón, Rubio, Neri del Barrio and Morphy; see *El Cosmopolita*, 27 November 1841.

various revenues, including some of the customs, were assigned and given for the time being at least a protected status. A new Dirección General de Tabaco was set up to run the industry; it quickly replaced existing management with political appointees and also revoked licences for kiosks (*estanquillos*), which were reallocated to those felt more suitable by the government. It was not just the tobacco contractors who benefited from Santa Anna's favour. On 20 December, the planters had their reward when the import of all classes of foreign tobacco was banned, and the planters' corporate bodies were later given new rights and privileges.[24]

The cotton lobby also benefited from Santa Anna's largesse when on 21 October he ordered that rather than being sold in public auction, as had been the practice in the past, all contraband raw cotton, yarns and *mantas* were to be burned as soon as they were seized.[25] For merchants, especially foreign importers, and everybody in the wholesale and retail trade, he repealed the additional *derecho de consumo* which had been the pretext for Paredes' revolt in Guadalajara and which had caused widespread protest, not least because of the increased prices of imported goods.[26] Foreign merchants and residents also welcomed another of his early reforms. Under existing legislation, they were prohibited from buying real estate, a bone of contention in the embassies for many years. Following consultation and various reports on the matter, the ban was duly lifted.[27] Finally, as if to indicate Santa Anna's determination to improve the economy, the government ordered the formation throughout the country of 'committees for the development [of industry], and of commerce and tribunals responsible for the administration of justice in mercantile affairs'. These new bodies, designed to promote industry and commerce, were given considerable powers.[28]

Hence, Santa Anna rewarded those who had supported and probably financed his overthrow of Bustamante, and he fulfilled his pledges. Nevertheless, there were some individuals and groups who did not immediately derive any advantage from the change of regime. While some favoured financiers certainly had their reward, there were others among the *agiotistas* who were stunned to learn that within twenty-four hours of taking office, Santa Anna ordered a suspension of payments on all government debts, including the various funds which had been created to repay loans by mortgaging the customs and other revenues. Although he resumed pay-

24 Details in Walker, "Business as Usual", pp. 699–702.
25 Dublán and Lozano, *Legislación mexicana*, vol. 4, p. 40; Potash, *Banco de Avío*, p. 135.
26 Ibid., p. 39.
27 The decree was not published until 11 March 1842, but it was promised to the Spanish ambassador in October 1841; see P. P. Oliver to Secretary of State, 26 October 1841, in *Relaciones diplomáticas hispano-mexicanas*, vol. 1, pp. 271–4. Bustamante says this was one of the things agreed upon with Morphy at Manga de Clavo before Santa Anna rebelled against Bustamante; *Apuntes*, p. 36.
28 Dublán and Lozano, *Legislación mexicana*, vol. 4, pp. 56–8.

ments at half-rates three days later, for the next several months creditors were to besiege the government with their claims.[29] Another group of merchants who found him less than co-operative were those who had been involved in the Arista affair and who had contracted to import a large quantity of yarn. The Bustamante government had agreed to compensate them, but the details had not been worked out and no payment made. In January 1842, the contractors tried to negotiate a compromise, offering to reduce the quantity, but Santa Anna, after taking advice from the Junta de Industria, rejected their proposals.[30]

The clergy also quickly found that they were not among Santa Anna's favoured few. The Church's attitude to the fall of Bustamante is not entirely clear, although it is unlikely that it welcomed the departure of a president who was at least willing to surround himself with priests. Santa Anna was to some degree an unknown risk or at best a mixed blessing. He had championed or used the clerical cause in 1834 and protected its privileges, but he had always expected a substantial financial return for his protection. Now there were rumours that he intended a major attack on Church wealth as a means of solving the fiscal crisis, and when on 13 October he renewed the prohibition on the sale of Church assets without government approval, the alarm bells began to sound. A few days later, the Minister of Justice instructed all the diocesan authorities to provide up-to-date accounts of the tithe revenue, and the message seemed to be clear.[31] Then, against a background of more talk in the press of the need for freedom of thought and religious tolerance, the clergy's worst fears were realized. On 31 December, Sabás Sánchez Hidalgo introduced a proposal in the advisory council of departmental representatives, which Santa Anna had set up after the abrupt termination of the previous Congress.[32] His proposal, the most radical since the Gómez Farías administration of 1833–4, envisaged the complete nationalization of all Church-owned assets, including invested capital. Henceforth, the Church and its ministers would be maintained by the State, and all ecclesiastical taxes and fees for services would be abolished. All surplus revenues after the needs of the ministry had been met would be used to pay interest on and amortize the public debt. The publication of these proposals and the ensuing debate over Church wealth in the press, allied to the rumours of Santa Anna's intentions, must have caused panic in the episcopal palaces and chapter houses around the country. The government issued a denial of any hostile intentions towards Church wealth, but it can be no coin-

29 Tenenbaum, *Politics of Penury*, p. 66; *El Cosmopolita*, 19 February 1842.
30 Potash, *Banco de Avío*, p. 136.
31 Minister of Justice circular, 23 October 1841, in *El Cosmopolita*, 30 October 1841.
32 For the text of Sánchez Hidalgo's proposals, see *El Crepúsculo* (Puebla), 11 January 1842. For the debate on religious tolerance, see *El Mosquito Mexicano*, January–February 1842.

cidence that within days of the proposal being put, and rejected by the council, Santa Anna informed the archbishop that he wanted to use clerical assets as collateral for a substantial loan of up to 1,000,000 pesos.[33] At the same time and acting on his orders, the commander general of Puebla instructed the bishop of that diocese to hand over the silver belonging to the Jesuit Order which was stored in the cathedral.[34] Confronted with these threats, the clergy promptly entered into negotiations with the government, which produced an agreement for a loan of 200,000 pesos, half from the secular and half from the regular clergy.

Demonstrating the energy and decisiveness on which his reputation depended, Santa Anna also turned his attention to a long-standing problem which was causing renewed difficulties. This concerned copper money, much of it counterfeit, which had again flooded the market-place with the collapse of law and order during the revolt against Bustamante. Uncontrolled devaluation of the coins followed, and there were fears of serious social unrest in the capital, where basic food prices were spiralling and bread had become almost unobtainable because millers refused to sell their flour for anything but silver. Pakenham reported, 'It has in some instances been necessary to make use of actual force to compel the holders of corn and other articles of first necessity to bring their commodities to market'.[35] In Puebla, the situation seems to have been even more critical. Peons on the haciendas refused to work unless they were paid in silver, and soup kitchens had to be hurriedly set up by local philanthropists to aid the increasing number of destitute. One Puebla paper urged the wealthy to help out of Christian charity but also 'because of the well-founded fear that hungry people may commit dreadful assaults, especially on food retailers'.[36] Riots outside food shops, which had to be guarded by soldiers, began to occur in the capital, Puebla and elsewhere, and women workers in the capital's cigar factory protested so violently against their wages being paid in copper that troops had to be brought in to restore order.[37]

Santa Anna's response to this rising popular discontent was first to decree that counterfeiters would be court-martialled, and property owners found to have counterfeiting equipment would be fined up to 4,000 pesos or three years of imprisonment. Then he set up a committee including financiers like Cayetano Rubio and Francisco Iturbe, as well as the ubiquitous Morphy, to advise on ways of amortizing copper money. Eventually,

33 *El Cosmopolita*, 12, 29 January 1842.
34 Bustamante, *Apuntes*, pp. 38–9.
35 R. Pakenham to Ld. Aberdeen, 11 December 1841, P.R.O., F.O. 50, 147; 'Representación hecha al Escmo. Sr. Presidente por los ciudadanos (comerciantes en el ramo de panadería) que suscriben', 4 November 1841, in *El Siglo XIX*, 8 November 1841.
36 *El Crepúsculo*, 15 January 1842.
37 *El Cosmopolita*, 5, 9, 16 and 19 February 1842; Bustamante, *Apuntes*, p. 46.

on 24 November it was announced that a new copper coin 'in eighths of a real' was to replace the existing currency, which would remain legal tender for a maximum of thirty days within the department of Mexico and sixty days elsewhere. Everybody was urged to hand in the old coins, which it was promised would be exchanged for the new within six months. The thirty-/sixty-day deadline was apparently made after assurances from the superintendent of the mint in the capital, Bernardo González Angulo, that he could mint and start issuing the new coins as early as 29 November. The day after that date, the Minister of Hacienda apologized for the nonappearance of the money and sacked the superintendent. The new coins would appear, he assured the public, as soon as possible. Meanwhile, Santa Anna ordered that the city's garrison be paid in silver.[38]

The thirty-day deadline after which the old coins in circulation, genuine or counterfeit, were to be worthless brought panic to the city, causing further rapid devaluation and price increases. *El Cosmopolita* reported, 'Poverty is increasing in this capital; the price of everything is going up; money has lost half its value and everywhere you hear complaints and quarrels over payments'.[39] The government realized its mistake, and the Minister of Hacienda announced that the deadlines would apply only from the date on which the new coins were available. Simultaneously, and presumably to reassure the public that the new currency could be funded, the Banco de Amortización was abolished and all its assets, mostly paper credits, were assigned to the amortization of copper money and to meet its other liabilities. The public remained unconvinced and for the next week there was chaos; no retailer or anyone else would accept the old coins, and everybody tried to exchange them for silver at any rate they could get. On 18 December, the new coins began to be released, which meant that the deadline for the old was definitely in January. The crisis mounted, spreading to Puebla, Oaxaca, Veracruz, Michoacán and elsewhere. Pulque sellers, who had to pay the taxes on their product in silver, were reported to be pouring pulque onto the streets because they had no silver, and the prices of meat, maize, chocolate, bread and other basics again rose. Within a week, even the new coins were being forged, and two counterfeiters were arrested in the capital. Eventually the situation stabilized as more of the new coins were produced, and after initial discounting, it was reported on 12 January 1842 that the new issue was rising in value. In the departments where the sixty-day deadline applied, the panic lasted a few more weeks and there also, as the new coins became more available, relative calm returned.[40]

38 Dublán and Lozano, *Legislación mexicana*, vol. 4, pp. 58–9; *El Cosmopolita*, 24 November, 4 December 1841.
39 Ibid., 8 December 1841.
40 *El Cosmopolita*, December 1841 through February 1842.

If Santa Anna had promised that he would do something about the copper currency problem, he seems to have succeeded, albeit at considerable cost to the poor. He also kept one final bargain, at least in part, which was even more significant and unexpected. The *bases* agreed at Tacubaya had given him 'almost absolute power', as Pakenham noted, but his exercise of that power was to be temporary. The fourth *base* committed him to arrange for a new Congress to meet within six months of being summoned. Its exclusive function was to reconstitute the nation 'as it sees fit'. In other words, there were to be no restrictions regarding the future form of government. By clear implication since the centralist constitution had been abandoned in the first *base* and monarchism strongly rejected in 1840, either a formal military dictatorship or a return to some kind of federal structure seemed most likely. The latter, of course, had been the principal demand for several years of the moderate liberal federal group led by Gómez Pedraza, and it quickly became apparent that Santa Anna appeared to be giving them his support. One early sign of this came when the membership of the Junta de Representantes was announced.[41] This body had been stipulated in the second *base* and was to comprise two deputies per department chosen by Santa Anna. His choices reflected his priorities in that there were eleven members of the previous Congress, thirteen army officers and at least three clergymen, but most significantly, the members included Gómez Pedraza, Rodríguez Puebla and a rising newcomer in the federalist ranks, Mariano Otero. Their first task was to choose a provisional president. Santa Anna was chosen with 39 votes out of 44. Then he was able to announce his cabinet, which he did on 10 and 11 October. It included the ever-present Tornel at the Ministry of War and also Gómez Pedraza as Minister of Internal and Foreign Affairs. Furthermore, although he refused it, the key post of Minister of Hacienda was offered to Francisco García, radical federalist and former governor of Zacatecas, whom Santa Anna himself had attacked in 1835 because of his defence of states' autonomy.

How far these appointments were prearranged at Tacubaya is impossible to say, but according to the Spanish ambassador, they were part of the deal (*transacción*) which Gómez Pedraza negotiated with Santa Anna on behalf of the federalists.[42] Another sign of the new confidence of the federalists was the appearance of a new daily, *El Siglo XIX*, which quickly became the most influential and long-lived paper in the country, lasting until 1896. It was founded by Ignacio Cumplido, and its editors and

41 For details of the Junta de Representantes, see L. Moreno Valle, 'La Junta de Representantes o congreso de los departamentos (1841–1842)', *Estudios de historia moderna y contemporánea de México* (Mexico, 1972), vol. 4, pp. 105–5.
42 P. P. Oliver to Secretary of State, 26 October 1841, in *Relaciones diplomáticas hispano-mexicanas*, vol. 1, pp. 271–4.

contributors included Gómez Pedraza, Otero, Lafragua, Juan Bautista Morales and most other leading federalists. From the first issues, they put the case against a centralized form of government, arguing that the centralists had failed to keep any of the promises made in their manifesto of 1835: 'Where is the development of industry and agriculture? Where are the great commercial enterprises? Where is the excellent education? Where is the new dawn (*ilustración*)?' They also took care to reassure *hombres de bien* in general by distancing themselves from radical federalism. Federalism had been rejected by many moderates because of a mistaken association with popular radicalism, but 'the federation was confused with sanscullotism; both expressions became synonymous and hence every federalist was labelled a sansculotte'.[43]

This unexpected resurgence of the moderate liberal federalists under the patronage of Santa Anna, however, soon ran into difficulties. Gómez Pedraza resigned his cabinet post within a few weeks, and he did so because of another quite untypical ideological position adopted by Santa Anna. The issue was the regulations for the new Congress, which he was obliged to publish within two months, that is, early in December. First he asked the Junta de Representantes to advise him. The Junta began its deliberations and found itself bombarded with suggestions from provincial and local authorities around the country. The department of Jalisco, for example, was specific on the qualifications it wanted for the franchise. It argued that only those who could read and write should be allowed to vote in the primaries. Voters and candidates should possess 'capital or business', and those whose salary derived from the public purse should be excluded from any participation. The main qualifications for congressmen, apart from literacy and income, were that they be 'heads of families' (*padres de familia*) and residents in the department. Finally, the Congress should not be held in Mexico City but in the provinces, preferably in Guanajuato.[44]

These ideas of restricting the franchise and choice of candidates to the literate, affluent heads of families and of transferring the Congress away from the capital received strong support from other areas and from some sections of the press. Veracruz, San Luis Potosí, Aguascalientes and Querétaro also wanted property or income and literacy qualifications for voters and candidates, and all supported the idea of the representatives being restricted to heads of families. Other ideas began to emerge from these various submissions and from press editorials. In all previous elections,

43 *El Siglo XIX*, 27, 30 October 1841.
44 'Junta departamental de Jalisco', 11 November 1841, in *El Cosmopolita*, 4 December 1841. I have examined the 1842 congressional elections in an article from which several of the following paragraphs are taken; see 'Generals versus Politicians: Santa Anna and the 1842 Congressional Elections in Mexico', *Bulletin of Latin American Research*, 8 (1989), 257–74.

the number of deputies from each department had been determined by its population, with the more populated states in the central region thereby having far more congressmen than the less inhabited areas on the periphery. In line with the reaction against centralism and the growing resentment of the political and economic domination of Mexico City and its hinterland, most departments now included as their main reform equality of representation. Their demand was for four deputies from each of the twenty-four departments regardless of size or population.[45]

As these representations were being received, a committee appointed by the Junta de Representantes considered its report. It is clear from its recommendations that it accepted some of the points made by the departments, particularly the idea that population should no longer determine the number of representatives. It also recommended that all males over the age of 18, except criminals, domestic servants, unemployed and other such groups should have the vote. Primary electors should be over 25 if unmarried, 21 if married and resident in the municipality. Deputies should be at least 30 years of age, secular and born or resident in the department for at least five years.[46]

While all this was being debated in the press, the departments and the Junta, it seems that there was also a furious argument going on behind closed doors in the cabinet. Gómez Pedraza favoured, and may well have been the original inspiration for, several of the reforms being suggested in the public arena. In particular, he wanted the equal number of deputies per department regardless of population. Apparently, he felt that the liberal values he espoused would be threatened if the larger departments were allowed to keep their predominance, because they tended to send to Congress men who were the 'most Levitical and reactionary'. Also, he wanted the clergy explicitly banned from election, whereas others argued that if the *padre de familia* idea was adopted, that would be a more politic way of achieving the same end.[47]

Santa Anna refused to agree to Gómez Pedraza's demands, and so he resigned from the government on 17 November. Three weeks later, on 10 December, Santa Anna published his decision on the electoral regulations in which he confirmed his rejection of all the significant innovations put forward by Gómez Pedraza, the departments and his own advisory junta. The basis of representation was to be, as in the past, the size of

45 For the representations of several departments, see *El Cosmopolita*, 8 December 1841; *El Siglo XIX*, 26 November 1841.
46 For a summary of the report which was printed in *El Cosmopolita*, 8 December 1841, and *El Siglo XIX*, 6 December 1841, see C. Noriega Elío, *El Constituyente de 1842* (Mexico, 1986), pp. 64–5.
47 P. P. Oliver to Secretary of State, 6 December 1841, *Relaciones diplomáticas hispano-mexicanas*, vol. 1, pp. 290–2.

population, with one deputy for each seventy thousand inhabitants. All male citizens over the age of 18, subject to the usual exceptions of criminals and so on, had the right to vote. One primary elector per five hundred inhabitants was to be chosen, and the district assemblies were to elect one district representative per twenty primary electors. Qualifications for a deputy were full citizenship, an age of at least 25 years and an income of at least 1,500 pesos from employment or capital. All things being equal, those who were married, widowed or heads of family were to be preferred.[48]

Santa Anna thus clearly rejected all the demands of the provinces and elsewhere to restrict the franchise. There was to be no literacy test, no property or income qualification for voters, and he had resisted the considerable pressure to grant equality of representation for all departments. Also, he insisted that the Congress be held in Mexico City and not, as proposed by several departments, in Guanajuato, Querétaro or elsewhere. In fact, Santa Anna's decree surprised most observers, who had expected at least some restrictions on the popular vote. Carlos Bustamante described it as 'quite liberal'.[49] *El Siglo XIX* declared that 'the regulations for the convocation are eminently liberal', and Pakenham agreed: 'The Election, in its first stage, is to be as general and popular as possible and with certain qualifications, persons of every class are declared eligible to the assembly'.[50]

Santa Anna had given all the parties, but especially the liberal federalists, their opportunity, and the politicians had three months for the campaign before election day on 6 March 1842. The public campaign, conducted largely through the press, was unusually muted, with only occasional editorials urging the electorate to act responsibly by electing men known for their integrity rather than their party affiliation. The profederalist press carried lengthy essays on the merits of federalism and articles condemning the centralist experiment, which had brought the nation to the point of economic collapse, but no group or faction presented any kind of manifesto or political programme. The emphasis was on people rather than ideas, with the electorate constantly warned that the only way to ensure future prosperity was to choose good men, or 'liberals who are not extremists, patriots who are not fanatics'.[51]

Though the public campaign was muted, there is no doubt that behind

---

48 Dublán and Lozano, *Legislación mexicana*, vol. 4, pp. 67–74.
49 Bustamante, *Apuntes*, p. 26.
50 *El Siglo XIX*, 13 December 1841; R. Pakenham to Ld. Aberdeen, 11 December 1841, P.R.O., F.O. 50, 147. The *Diario del Gobierno*, 18 December 1841, has articles from several departments welcoming the new regulations.
51 *El Siglo XIX*, 25 February 1842.

the scenes there was much intrigue and manoeuvring.[52] In the all-important department of Mexico, for example, leading political figures co-ordinated by federalist Mariano Riva Palacio used their network of contacts throughout the region. On 31 January, General Bravo wrote to Riva Palacio to express his agreement that the future deputies must be 'honourable men who are genuine liberals'. He would, he continued, do all he could to achieve the result they wanted: 'I will do all in my power to ensure that the electors from these towns reach agreement with you'.[53]

Santa Anna's supporters campaigned under the so-called Banner of General Valencia, while those of the liberal federalist group were known under the 'Banner of the People'.[54] According to Carlos Bustamante, there was 'a lot of heat generated by both parties', and at first it was not clear which side was in the ascendancy.[55] By the secondary stage, however, held on 20 March, it became clear that the federalists were winning, and their leading candidates were elected to represent the capital in the final electoral college.[56] In the districts outside the capital, the federalists were equally active in their campaigning and co-ordination of candidates. On 22 March, General Alvarez wrote to Riva Palacio to tell him that in the south of the department all had gone according to plan and that those chosen as electors would see him when they arrived in the capital 'to reach agreement'.[57] Santa Anna, realizing that his opponents had a majority in the electoral college, tried to disrupt its proceedings by challenging the eligibility of some of the electors, but his intervention was too late.[58]

When the final results were declared, the liberal federalists were victorious, and the planning co-ordinated by Riva Palacio was successful. Almost all of their candidates were elected, including Gómez Pedraza, Morales, Olaguíbel, Gordoa, Herrera and Rodríguez Puebla. Of the twenty deputies chosen, only two – Bravo and Melchor Múzquiz – were considered by *El Mosquito Mexicano* not to belong to the 'people's party'. As for the rest, they were 'revolutionary representatives, intolerant federalists who will tolerate no other view but their own . . . representatives who are very stupid, depraved, penniless, cheats, traitors to their native land'.[59] The same types, the paper reported, had been elected in the other

52 Cuevas alleges without supporting evidence that masonic lodges provided the organizational framework for the liberal campaign; *Historia de la nación mexicana*, p. 628.

53 Details of this correspondence, which is in the Riva Palacio archive at the University of Texas, is given in Noriega Elío, *El Constituyente de 1842*, p. 69.

54 For further details on the election campaign, see my 'Generals versus Politicians'.

55 Bustamante, *Apuntes*, p. 48.

56 Full details of the secondary elections are in *El Cosmopolita*, 22 March 1842.

57 Correspondence in the Riva Palacio archive detailed in Noriega Elío, *El Constituyente de 1842*, p. 69.

58 For a detailed report on the proceedings of the electoral college, see *El Cosmopolita*, 13 April 1842.

59 *El Mosquito Mexicano*, 15 April 1842.

departments and the elections in Morelia and Zacatecas, for example, 'have been useless'. For the profederalist press, of course, the results were a cause of jubilation. *El Siglo XIX* praised the whole electoral process as worthy of a truly democratic, representative system which 'has been carried out with order, decency, a dignity and a patriotism which leaves nothing to be desired'.[60]

There was one important exception in the regions. At Guadalajara, the electoral college had been dominated by radicals, and the credentials committee had found reasons to exclude a number of electors, with the result that those who opposed the exclusions refused to attend. Hence, when the voting took place, only twenty-two were present against thirty absentees. The governor and military commander was Paredes, and in a letter of 11 April to the Minister of Relations, he explained how he had intervened to defeat the radicals. On the grounds that a minority attendance invalidated the proceedings, he had told them that their actions were illegal and that new elections would have to be held. After some hours of defiance, most of the twenty-two electors dispersed, although four remained in the council house until past midnight.

The Minister replied to this letter on 15 April, telling Paredes that the government fully approved of his conduct and intention to hold new elections.[61] Three days later, Tornel also wrote to express approval and hope that next time Paredes would ensure the right result. What had happened in Guadalajara, Tornel added, had come as no surprise, for they had known of the triumph 'of the disruptive 1833 faction' in Jalisco and everywhere else except Oaxaca and Querétaro. It was, he admitted, the government's own fault for being too tolerant and for neglecting the elections, and the leaders of the 1828 and 1833 factions had taken good advantage. They were now threatening all manner of vengeance, and they had named General Herrera as their future president. They wanted the Congress held in Maravatío (Michoacán), they were going to separate military from political commands in all departments, re-establish the civic militia and 'destroy the regular army'.[62]

In both tone and content, Tornel's letter reveals the bitter reaction which Santa Anna and his allies felt at their defeat in the elections, and faced with the certainty of a hostile Congress dominated by federalists and liberals, they spent the next few weeks deciding what, if any, action to take. Correspondence and envoys now circulated among Santa Anna, Paredes and Valencia, and although the evidence is circumstantial, there

60 *El Siglo XIX*, 11 April 1842.
61 These letters and supporting documents were published in *El Cosmopolita*, 20 April 1842.
62 J. M. Tornel to M. Paredes y Arrillaga, 18 April 1842, García Collection, Paredes y Arrillaga Papers, 140/28. Some of the letters referred to in following paragraphs have been published in García, *Documentos inéditos*, vol. 56.

are strong indications that they considered the possibility of a complete military take-over. As he had done in preparing the revolt against Bustamante, Santa Anna decided to send his trusted envoy, Morphy, to confer with Paredes at Guadalajara. Paredes had already been in touch with Valencia, and on 22 April he wrote again: 'I anxiously await Mr. Morphy to learn what the President and you think about the great issue you mention and to see how I can help to achieve the great task'.[63] Morphy arrived, and the day after his interview with him, Paredes wrote to Santa Anna. The problem the government faced, he argued, was that not having built any political constituency because of the decision not to be affiliated with any faction, it was left exposed to attack from all sides. The solution was for Santa Anna to use his prestige to attract the affluent groups in society, offering them the guarantees they sought. It had obviously been a mistake to allow the proletariat into Congress with no distinction between working classes and property owners. It was rather like holding a council of war in which generals, officers and men all had a vote – obviously the men would win. What should now be done was to attract the 'well-off classes, who in politics are what the Generals are in war'. He did not think, however, that the remedy for the situation lay in a popularly inspired military movement to invest Santa Anna with his present unrestricted powers for an indefinite period. That would be too dangerous and would provoke countless revolts. What was needed was a pact between the army and the productive, affluent people in society, property owners, merchants, clergy, all the wealthy who had most to lose from the threat of demagogy posed by the extremists who had won the elections.[64]

During the first three weeks of May, Paredes wrote more letters on the same lines to Santa Anna and Tornel, urging them to resist the 'frightful and pernicious proletariat' and to seek the support of the rich in a new party. Santa Anna, as diligent as ever with his correspondence, replied with several letters in which he appeared to reveal his final decision on the election results. He had decided, he wrote on 30 April, that although the results had produced widespread alarm, they must be accepted for the time being. Neither the army nor himself should be seen to be breaking the promises made at Tacubaya, and therefore the Congress would open on the designated day. If it acted responsibly, all would be well. If not, the nation would decide what action to take, and neither the government nor the army would be held responsible for any misconduct by the deputies. A week later Santa Anna reaffirmed his decision, urging Paredes not to lose heart. If Congress did not do what we wanted, he assured him, his ideas would be adopted, but for the time being it was government

63 M. Paredes y Arrillaga to G. Valencia, 22 April 1842, Paredes y Arrillaga Papers, 140/31.
64 Correspondence in ibid., 140/33, 38.

policy to allow Congress to meet. 'I have', he concluded, 'received your brother, given him 200 pesos, and ordered that a good job be found for him'.[65]

It seemed that Santa Anna had decided by the end of April that the most prudent course of action was to allow the Congress to meet and see what it produced. His soundings regarding a full military take-over had not brought the backing he wanted, but the rumours persisted and led to an angry dispute with Paredes. On 21 May, Santa Anna wrote again to Guadalajara.[66] Given the victory of the 1833 extremist faction in the elections, he said, he had wanted to consult his friends. Hence, he had sent Mr. Morphy to Guadalajara, but to his surprise and displeasure rumours at once spread in that city that Morphy had gone to propose a military dictatorship and that Paredes had rejected the prospect out of hand. It was being said, Santa Anna added, that 'the rumour is being attributed to you'. He insisted that Paredes should end it immediately.

In his reply to this letter, Paredes denied that he had started any rumour or had told anyone of the visit of Morphy and the 'secret he confided in me'.[67] What this secret was is not known, but the dictatorship issue surfaced again in the capital towards the end of April. An anonymous pamphlet entitled *Plan proyectado sobre dictadura* called for Santa Anna to be made dictator for life, and according to *El Cosmopolita*, the proposal was a subject of public debate for several days. Santa Anna denied that he was behind the pamphlet and announced on 28 April that the author had been discovered. It was one Antonio Landero, whom, Santa Anna admitted, he knew well. His action in issuing the pamphlet, however, was no more than the act of a madman.[68]

Despite this denial, it remains probable that Santa Anna was indeed using the well-tried method of the anonymous pamphlet to test the public's and the army's reaction to his becoming a fully fledged dictator. Added to the mysterious travellings of Morphy and his 'secret' and Paredes' rejection of a military take-over, the evidence certainly suggests that dictatorship was on Santa Anna's mind in response to the results of the elections and the prospect of a hostile Congress. Once again, his ambitions were frustrated.[69] Despite his autocratic powers and the fact that army officers mostly appointed by him controlled political and military authority in the departments, the civilian political opposition seems to have been too strong. Crucially, he had failed to control the elections, and

65 Ibid., 140/39, 42.
66 Ibid., 140/46.
67 Ibid., 140/47.
68 *El Cosmopolita*, 30 April, 4 May 1842.
69 According to Bustamante, a major factor in Santa Anna's decision not to attempt a full military take-over was that his wife was seriously ill at the time; *Apuntes*, pp. 52–3.

though he had tried to do so, the operation had been bungled. Paredes told Tornel in a letter of 11 April that he had intervened in the elections because 'I had received a clear and categorical recommendation from the President to use my influence to make sure that the 1833 group did not get control'.[70] Presumably, other military commanders/governors around the country received similar recommendations from Santa Anna, but to no avail. If Santa Anna expected the departmental authorities to control the elections, it must be assumed that he would do the same within the department of Mexico and certainly in the capital. Yet, as Tornel admitted, they had neglected to be vigilant and their attempts to intervene were clumsy and too late.[71]

Santa Anna had lost the propaganda battle, and despite his considerable influence over the press and his patronage of jobs and financial rewards, the liberal federalist group had outmanoeuvred him. Whatever deals he had made with them at Tacubaya, he had quickly lost their support and also that of the other interest groups he had at first favoured. After the settlement of obligations arising from Tacubaya, he seems to have made no effort to retain or attract the support of any group. The army as a whole still kept his attention – more units were created, uniforms designed and a large number of recruits conscripted – but the harmony among the top generals was soon strained. There was the angry exchange of letters with Paredes and his apparent refusal to go along with a complete military take-over. Valencia and Paredes also were soon involved in a public slanging match over the expenses they had incurred in staging their revolts against Bustamante.[72] Alvarez and Bravo combined to petition the government for the creation of a new department of Acapulco by separating several districts from the southern area of the Mexico department. Santa Anna equivocated on the request, but both Riva Palacio and Gómez Pedraza wrote to Alvarez reprimanding him for promoting such a contentious proposal in the first weeks of the new administration.[73]

For their part, the lower classes and the poor in general were already alienated by economic distress exacerbated by the copper money fiasco, and the decision to hold a military draft just as the electoral registers

70 Paredes y Arrillaga Papers, 140/1.
71 The day after the election results came in, 11 April, on an obvious pretext Santa Anna ordered the arrest of the leading federalist, José Joaquín de Herrera, who was one of those elected a deputy. Herrera was taken to the Perote prison but soon released; *El Cosmopolita*, 16 April 1842; T. E. Cotner, *The Military and Political Career of José Joaquín de Herrera, 1792–1854* (New York, 1969), pp. 99–101.
72 'Manifiesto del ciudadano Gabriel Valencia ... sobre su conducta en la última revolución' (1 October 1841), in *El Cosmopolita*, 18 December 1841; 'Exposición que el general D. Mariano Paredes y Arrillaga hace a sus conciudadanos en manifestación de su conducta política, militar y económica en la presente revolución', in ibid., 23 October 1841.
73 Details in Noriega Elío, *El Constituyente de 1842*, pp. 53–5.

were being compiled had hardly added to the government's popularity. The clergy continued to be deeply concerned at Santa Anna's casual attitude towards Church wealth, and they were obliged to tolerate more confiscations of their assets. In February 1842 the so-called Pious Fund of the Californias, originally established to maintain the missions, was brought under State rather than episcopal control – Valencia was made the director – and predictably, a few months later, all of its assets were confiscated and sold. Several other former ecclesiastical buildings were sold, and one former Church-owned hacienda was given to Valencia in a simulated sale in which no money changed hands.[74]

If the priests watched Santa Anna's behaviour with growing anxiety, the merchant community also quickly found that he could not be trusted. After the initial pay-offs had been made in the form of concessions and legislation favourable to their interests, Santa Anna concluded that, with an empty Treasury, revenue-raising measures had to be given priority. Payments to those who held credits against the customs revenues, except those to the British debt and the former tobacco company, were suspended on 19 February. Even the cotton bloc was soon disillusioned with its erstwhile protector. On 8 April, a new general tariff was published, and while this reduced the ad valorem levy on imports from 30 to 25 per cent in the hope of stimulating trade, it also reduced some of the restrictions on certain types of foreign textiles. Manufacturers protested, and they were already angry at a tax which had recently been put on each spindle in their cotton mills. As domestic cotton production failed to meet the demand and prices stayed high, some manufacturers began to campaign for a relaxation of the protectionist policy and the entry of imported supplies. Those in Puebla, however, disagreed, as did the plantation owners, and the former united front of manufacturers and growers collapsed.[75]

There were other discontented industrial and agricultural groups, like the sugar plantation owners, whose brandy was taxed to pay for new prisons, but their protests were minor compared with the outcry which greeted the publication of a series of decrees in the first week of April. Precisely at the time of the elections and, indeed, in some instances only hours before the final electoral colleges convened, Santa Anna chose to announce a whole range of new taxes. New ones were imposed on every form of industrial and commercial business and on all incomes above 300 pesos per annum. A special tax on luxury goods was introduced, and on 7 April a poll tax with almost no exceptions was ordered for all adult males between the ages of 18 and 60. Given the adverse reaction and

74 Cuevas, *Historia de la nación mexicana*, p. 127.
75 Potash, *Banco de Avío*, pp. 135–6.

opprobrium which similar taxes, especially the detested head tax, had brought on Bustamante, it is surprising that Santa Anna chose to go down the same road exactly when every member of every electoral college throughout the country was about to cast his vote.

If such measures antagonized the poor and the *hombres de bien*, who had to pay proportionately more in the graduated charges, Santa Anna's total disregard of the election and failure to make any attempt to attract the vote seemed to confirm something which was giving even greater cause for concern. He gave the impression that he considered himself above the world of politics and electioneering, as someone who had no need of popular support, certainly not from civilian politicians. As the hero who had saved *hombres de bien* from social dissolution, he was entitled to their gratitude and obedience. Always inordinately fond of pomp and ceremony, his demeanour and public appearances were increasingly regal, and there were suspicions that his personal ambitions were now not confined to dictatorship but extended to imperial status. Oliver noted the trend at a banquet given by Santa Anna on New Year's Day 1842, remarking that the regal splendour of the occasion 'fuels the suspicion which gains ground daily that this leader aspires to a crown'.[76]

Santa Anna, therefore, was not concerned with electioneering, which he probably considered against his 'elevated character'. He apparently left such details to Tornel and his small clique of military officers and advisers on the assumption that by using the well-tried techniques of ballot rigging, bribery and intimidation, they would be able to achieve the desired result. But Tornel, as he himself admitted, neglected the elections and allowed all those who opposed Santa Anna and his regal pretensions to operate freely. Through neglect or simple incompetence, as evidenced by the belated intervention in the electoral college in the capital, and through the alienation of most groups which had welcomed him to power, Santa Anna suffered a resounding defeat in the elections. He once again found himself isolated politically, as Paredes pointed out, and faced with the prospect of a very hostile Congress which would certainly not look kindly on his personal ambitions or even his continuation in the presidential chair.

As always with Santa Anna, however, given his incomparable talent for Machiavellian intrigue, we must allow for another possible explanation. Realizing in the summer of 1841 that the pressure for a new Congress to reform the constitution was too great to resist and that elections would have to be held, he may well have concluded that in order to maintain the façade of his belief in representative government, he might as well

76 P. P. Oliver to Secretary of State, 3 January 1842, *Relaciones diplomáticas hispano-mexicanas*, vol. 2, pp. 8–9.

permit a reasonably unrestrained franchise. After all, as he reassured
Paredes, if the new Congress did not do as he wanted, it could always
be closed. In other words, he chose to keep his options open. The elections
would be held and his supporters under the 'Banner of General Valencia'
might get control. If they did not, the liberal federalists would be so
extreme in their proposals that a backlash would enable him to justify
executive action against them. His case for lifelong autocratic rule by
himself would be all the stronger and those groups most threatened by
the radicals, including the clergy, might well come round to seeing him
as their only hope for salvation. In effect, there would be a rerun of the
events of 1833–4, after which, it will be recalled, his ascent to absolute
power was interrupted only by the unfortunate intervention of Samuel
Houston.[77]

By the time the new Congress assembled in the capital to open on 10
June, it was already public knowledge that its deliberations were not to
be, in the words used at Tacubaya, 'as it sees fit'. Santa Anna had made
his attitude known in several ways. Intimidation tactics were used against
several prominent liberal federalists. For example, Juan Bautista Morales,
one of the editors of *El Siglo XIX* and elected to Congress, was arrested
and accused of treason because of his articles critical of government policy
on Texas.[78] Manuel Crescencio Rejón, a federalist leader and expert in
constitutional law, was persuaded by Santa Anna to remove himself on a
diplomatic mission to South America. Such pressure on individuals naturally alarmed the delegates as they prepared to travel to the capital, and
some decided not to attend. Santa Anna kept up the pressure by ordering
on 24 May that all the delegates take an oath of loyalty to the Bases de
Tacubaya before taking their seats. Lafragua told his friend Comonfort in
a letter four days later that refusal to obey the order might give Santa
Anna a pretext to keep the Congress from opening, and when the matter
was discussed in the preparatory sessions, that fear persuaded all except
one – Olaguíbel – to comply.[79] Santa Anna also insisted that his cabinet
ministers be allowed to attend and speak in all the sessions and again,
after some resistance, the deputies agreed. Finally, on 10 June, in his
opening address, he made his opposition to federalism crystal clear: 'I
declare, as an absolute certainty, that the multiplication of independent
and sovereign states is the inevitable precursor of our ruin'.[80]

77 As early as 17 February, Pakenham reported rumours about Santa Anna's intentions. They included
    the seizure of Church wealth, his seizure of power to become a king or fully fledged dictator and
    his closure of Congress; P.R.O., F.O. 50/153.
78 Details in *El Cosmopolita*, 9 July 1842.
79 J. M. Lafragua to I. Comonfort, 28 May 1842, Centro de Estudios Históricos (Fundación Cultural
    de Condumex, Mexico City); henceforth referred to as Condumex, Lafragua correspondence,
    p. 38.
80 The text of Santa Anna's speech is in *El Mosquito Mexicano*, 14 June 1842.

With this unequivocal warning still ringing in their ears, the deputies began their deliberations on the following day, 11 June. The total number elected was 175, although many were not present, and within a week Lafragua reported that they were only 55 in attendance.[81] Their social and occupational backgrounds have been studied in some detail by Noriega, who found that they were comparatively young, most being between the ages of 23 and 40. The largest occupational group were lawyers, followed by military officers and lower clergy, and they were mostly born in the provinces rather than in the capital. Some, about one-third, had experience in public office, but 84 per cent were participating for the first time in a representative assembly.[82] In terms of political beliefs, most of course were liberal federalists but there existed important divisions in their ranks. Basically, there were two groups, known as *puros* and *moderados*. The *puros,* who included Melchor Ocampo, Ezequiel Montes, Olaguíbel, Morales and Rodríguez Puebla, were heirs to the Gómez Farías programme of radical reform, and they wanted their ideas with regard to the army, Church, press, education and form of government safeguarded and expressed within a loose, federal system of autonomous states. The second group, or *moderados,* was led by Gómez Pedraza and included Lafragua, Riva Palacio, Otero, Espinosa de los Monteros and Octaviano Muñoz Ledo.[83] They, as their label implied, were more moderate, wanting a federal structure and liberal reforms but under greater centralized control. Finally, there was a small group of conservatives led by José Fernando Ramírez, Malo and Couto, who resigned his seat very quickly. The divisions in the Congress, therefore, were a direct continuation and reflection of the developments which had occurred since 1834, particularly the split in the liberal ranks, which Lafragua recalled first took place in 1835.

The debates over the following months and the complex tactical manoeuvring and intrigue have been analysed in depth by several scholars, and limitations of space prevent repetition here.[84] The key committee, obviously that charged with preparing the draft constitution, consisted of Antonio Díaz Guzmán, Joaquín Ladrón de Guevara, Pedro Ramírez, José F. Ramírez, Espinosa de los Monteros, Otero and Muñoz Ledo. The committee members began working immediately, and on 26 August two reports were presented to the full Congress.[85] The first was signed by four members of the committee, or a majority, namely, Díaz Guzmán, Ladrón de Guevara and the two Ramírez. The second was a minority report by

81 J. M. Lafragua to I. Comonfort, 18 June 1842, Condumex, Lafragua correspondence, p. 39.
82 Noriega Elío, *El Constituyente de 1842*, pp. 84–5.
83 Tena Ramírez, *Leyes fundamentales de México*, p. 304.
84 The best analysis of the debates is in Noriega Elío, *El Constituyente de 1842*.
85 For the full text of the constitutional projects, see Tena Ramírez, *Leyes fundamentales de México*, pp. 307–402.

the remaining three. The main difference between the two groups for the time being rested on one word. Both advocated a popular, representative, republican form of government with a division of powers, division into departments and the usual individual guarantees of property, freedom and personal security. The minority, however, insisted that the word *federal* be added to the form of government.

Debate on both projects occupied the next few weeks, with the result that the majority report was rejected and returned to the committee by a vote of 36 in favour to 41 against, which indicated that the federalists had a majority in the Congress. The minority group then decided in a complicated tactical manoeuvre arranged behind closed doors largely by Lafragua to withdraw their own project for the time being.[86] Everything thus was referred back to the committee.

As these debates were in progress and as they made it certain that the Congress would adopt the federal system as well as incorporate radical reforms, what the deputies always knew was probable was announced: on the grounds of ill-health, Santa Anna was to vacate the presidency and withdraw to Manga de Clavo. His replacement as provisional president was to be Bravo. From bitter experience, everybody knew what Santa Anna's decision portended. During the months from June to October while the Congress was sitting, he had continued to govern the country, issuing a series of decrees which Callcott aptly describes as a 'queer mixture of financial juggling and constructive activity'.[87] The Church suffered further losses. The ban on the sale of its assets without government approval was repeated, with its provisions extended to the redemption of invested capital, and the so-called amortization tax on newly acquired assets was raised to 15 per cent. In economic policy, the usual inconsistency prevailed. Chihuahua and Oaxaca benefited from Santa Anna's decision to establish mints in their areas, but in contrast he handed control of the Zacatecas mint to a British company with a contract described as 'scandalous'. In brief, the company was given the mint for fourteen years at an annual rent of 2,000 pesos, but the anticipated profits were in excess of 100,000 pesos per annum. Of course, there was a sweetener of a 100,000 peso downpayment, which Santa Anna promised would go towards the Texas and Yucatán campaigns.[88] The Zacatecan junta, judiciary, council, Junta de Fomento, clergy and congressional representatives all protested, denouncing the contract as a sell-out to Mexico City interests at the expense of the department.[89] Zacatecas was not the only department at

---

86 Lafragua explained the tactics adopted in a private memoir, largely reproduced in Noriega Elío, *El Constituyente de 1842*, pp. 94–6.
87 Callcott, *Santa Anna*, pp. 217–18.
88 Amador, *Bosquejo histórico de Zacatecas*, vol. 2, p. 463.
89 The various protests are in *El Siglo XIX*, 1 October 1842.

odds with Santa Anna. The far northern provinces continued to be devastated by Indian raids and Michoacán loudly objected to the closure of its port of Manzanillo. Military expeditions were sent to Texas and Yucatán, but no progress was made in bringing those areas back into the union.

Some positive, although not necessarily beneficial, measures were also enacted. Contracts for the construction of railways in several places were awarded, and the terms of the debt to British bondholders were renegotiated. The colonial monopoly system for the production of playing cards, saltpetre and sulphur was re-established, and the Banco de Avío was abolished to be replaced or superseded by a new industrial guild. In the sphere of social amenities, Santa Anna was especially energetic. A programme of repaving the entire central area of the capital was announced; it was to be paid for in part by a tax on carriage wheels and on householders who had external drains outside their properties. New regulations for the theatres, which it was said had become veritable dens of iniquity, were drawn up. In addition, there was a full revision of postal charges. Finally, in education a new Dirección General de Instrucción Primaria was formed. With a head office in the capital and branch offices in the departments, its brief was to introduce the Lancasterian system of instruction in primary schools throughout the country.

With these and numerous other measures, Santa Anna justified his reputation for being energetic, but there was no perceptible coherence in either his economic or his social policy. Moreover, of greater concern to *hombres de bien,* his regal demeanour was ever more exaggerated. For example, on 11 September expensive and elaborate celebrations were held to mark the anniversary of his victory over the Spaniards at Tampico in 1829. Four thousand troops paraded before him as he stood on the balcony of the national place, after which he waited in state in a newly refurbished reception room to receive the congratulations of the civil and ecclesiastical authorities. In the evening, he hosted a sumptuous banquet at which 'the table was set with abundance and exquisitely decorated'.[90] Once again, suspicions of his monarchist ambitions began to fill the columns of the press and the reports of the diplomatic community.[91]

When Santa Anna announced that he was to leave for Veracruz, it was generally understood that he was doing so, first, to dissociate himself from the Congress and, second, to prepare for its dissolution. The deputies knew that their days were numbered and that it was not a matter of if, but when, they would be told to pack their bags and leave. Nevertheless,

90 *El Cosmopolita,* 14 September 1842.
91 Oliver again reported the suspicion that 'Santa Anna tenga intenciones de coronarse si es que no lo arreda el ejemplo de Iturbide'; P. P. Oliver to Secretary of State, 22 December 1842, *Relaciones diplomáticas hispano-mexicanas,* vol. 2, pp. 181–4.

having chosen to challenge Santa Anna already and having refused to allow themselves to be intimidated, they continued their sessions and their debates on the third and final draft of the constitution, which their committee had presented on 14 November. Though it must have confirmed Santa Anna's worst fears, the draft was quickly approved by a vote of 36 for to 28 against. The radicals had by and large prevailed. Without federalism being specified, the recommended form of government was to be federal in all but name, with the departments given considerable autonomy, their own constitutions, assemblies, judiciary and control over revenues. At the national level the division of powers was to continue, but with the executive authority more curtailed than in the past. In particular, Congress would determine the size of the army and set recruitment levels, and several clauses suggested that future priority in military affairs would be given to militia forces rather than to the regular army. Departments were to have their own national guard, which would not have the *fuero militar*. The Church was another long-standing target of the reformers; one of the first articles to be approved, with only eleven votes against, in effect permitted some religious tolerance for the first time in Mexico's history. Roman Catholicism was to remain the official religion of the State and the only one to be practised in public, but the private observance of others would be permitted. Private education was likewise to be virtually unrestricted, with no obligation to teach Roman Catholic doctrine, and there were to be no restrictions on the press except when it dealt with religious dogma.

The debate and exposition of these principles, however, were conducted in an air of total unreality because the deputies knew that their constitution had no chance of being accepted by Santa Anna or by the army. Tornel, who had personally presented the government's opposition in several of the debates, had already prepared military commanders around the country for what was to come. In a circular to them on 19 November, he said, 'The constitutional project was a code for anarchy; under the cloak of progress, it would have accelerated the destruction of society and would have led to the triumph of the cruel and intolerant demagogy of 1828 and 1833.'[92]

It took just two weeks to close the Congress, and the procedure conformed to the usual pattern. On 11 December, in the small town of Huejotzingo near Puebla, the mayor, councillors and some twenty residents assembled in the muncipal offices and compiled, or probably copied, a set of demands. These were, in brief, that the people did not and would not accept the proposed constitution; the provisional president should close the Congress; a junta of notables should be summoned to reconstitute

92 Quoted in Arrangoiz, *México desde 1808 hasta 1867*, p. 379.

the nation.[93] It took two days for this plan to reach and be circulated in the capital, and as *El Siglo XIX* put it in a special supplement on 13 December, it signified the 'battle cry' against the Congress, adding that 'even the least well-informed knows that this plan did not originate with the rebels; it was not possible for a handful of insignificant people to decide to take such a radical step; some other impulse is driving them'. Over the next few days, news arrived of support for the *pronunciamiento* by garrisons all around the country, from San Luis Potosí, where the plan was dated 9 December, Jalisco, Zacatecas, Michoacán, Querétaro and dozens of other places. The whole process had clearly been organized and co-ordinated centrally, probably by Tornel, acting on Santa Anna's behalf. Carlos Bustamante recalled that agents had been dispatched from the capital two weeks before to organize things in the provinces, where illiterate mayors of villages were signing statements filled with concepts about which they knew nothing.[94]

As the plans arrived, acting president Bravo passed them to the Congress, which promptly returned them as irrelevant to its business. Then, at 4 a.m. on 19 December the capital's garrison, led once again by Valencia – it was his third revolt for or against the government in three years – occupied the corridors leading to the congressional debating chamber. After a few hours of futile defiance, the deputies, accepting the inevitable, drew up a final statement in which they defended their conduct and retired to their homes. The 'red congress', as Arrangoiz called it, was over.[95]

Radical though it was in many respects, the 1842 Congress had tried to find a compromise between the ideas of the extreme liberals represented by Gómez Farías and those of what *El Cosmopolita* described as 'a few sophists and partisans of the colonial regime'.[96] They had not openly declared federalism; they had not proposed full religious tolerance; they had not abolished military or clerical *fueros;* they had not touched Church wealth; they had allowed freedom of the press but not on religious dogma; they had allowed an unrestricted franchise for the popular vote but kept income qualifications for congressional candidates. Hence, they had sought what was described at the time as a 'middle way' (*justo medio*), to reconcile what they envisaged as the basis of a modern, progressive, secular society with the demands of those who wanted to retain what they in turn saw as the essential religious and social values inherited from their colonial past. Above all, they had tried to articulate and represent the interests of the middle-class *hombres de bien* from whose ranks they themselves were

93 For the text of this and dozens of other *pronunciamientos*, see *Planes en la nación mexicana*, book 4, pp. 126–217.
94 Bustamante, *Apuntes*, pp. 90–8.
95 Arrangoiz, *México desde 1808 hasta 1867*, p. 379.
96 *El Cosmopolita*, 26 November 1842.

drawn. In the words of Otero, who had provided much of the intellectual inspiration in the debates, their aim was to 'concentrate power in the middle class to avoid the evils of the upper and lower classes'.[97] But it was not a coalition or alliance of bishops, landowners, financiers or merchants, nor of the lower classes of peasants and urban poor, which had rejected the Congress. Santa Anna had made no perceptible attempt to create or attract a political constituency of the 'well-off classes' as Paredes had advised. On the contrary, he had antagonized most of the influential interests, and in Oliver's view, he had evidently decided in favour of outright military absolutism. Hence, he kept his promise to Paredes and presumably to other military officers to use the army to close the Congress if it did not conform to his or their wishes. Faced from the beginning with the certainty that this would happen, the mostly civilian Congress had valiantly tried to uphold the principle of representative government, but perhaps we may leave the final to word to Pakenham's sound sense of British understatement: 'The prudence of the majority of the late constituent assembly in insisting on carrying out a form of constitution so unpalatable to the military supremacy of the day may well be questioned'.[98]

97 M. Otero to G. Ignacio Vergara, 4 June 1842, cited in Noriega Elío, *El Constituyente de 1842*, p. 150. Otero's influential essay *Ensayo sobre el verdadero estado de la cuestión social y política que se agita en la República mexicana* was published in June 1842. For a critical study of Otero's ideas, see J. Reyes Heroles, *Estudio preliminar a las obras de Mariano Otero* (Mexico, 1967).

98 R. Pakenham, P.R.O., F.O. 50/155.

9

Santa Anna and the Bases Orgánicas

In his long and spectacular career in Mexican politics, Santa Anna experienced many peaks and many troughs. Probably the most humiliating of the latter occurred in the first week of December 1844, when his carefully and long constructed personality cult came literally crashing to the ground. The remains of his amputated leg were disinterred from the tomb in which he had had them reverently buried. An angry and hostile mob dragged them through the streets of Mexico City for the amusement and ridicule of the populace. A recently built theatre bearing his name was forcibly entered and his statue smashed to pieces. Pictures and portraits were torn down. He was stripped of the office of president, the Congress voted to arraign him and his ministers and a sequence of events began which led to his ignominious defeat and exile.

Santa Anna's dramatic fall from grace was partly the result of his conduct in power during the two years following his closure of the 1842 Congress. In Bancroft's words, his government had been characterized by 'despotic, dishonest and extravagant measures . . . , seizure and illegal sale of national or corporation property . . . , outrageous contracts, suspended salaries and payments . . . , embezzlement of funds'.[1] With this kind of behaviour, added to his extraordinary disregard of social conventions with his marriage, by proxy, to a 15-year-old girl just six weeks after the death of his respected wife of nineteen years, he had completely alienated all the powerful socioeconomic groups in the country and had lost the support of senior army officers on whom his survival ultimately depended. Yet Santa Anna's personal excesses, his corruption and deviousness were certainly no surprise in the light of his earlier career, and they were not in themselves the cause of his fall. He was driven from office more by the consequences of paradoxes inherent in his own political actions and decisions.

As we have noted several times before, in the opinion of almost all of his contemporaries and all of the foreign diplomats who met and observed

1 Bancroft, *History of Mexico,* vol. 5, p. 281.

him at close quarters, Santa Anna aspired to be the dictator of Mexico. Since his overthrow of Bustamante in 1832, the rumours to that effect had been constant, and there is much circumstantial evidence that he repeatedly sounded out opinion and prepared the ground for his accession to lifelong autocratic power. His popularity with the army suggests that he had the means to realize his ambition. Yet, paradoxically, despite the opportunities in 1834, 1841 and again in December 1842, he made no obvious or known attempt to establish a permanent military dictatorship. Instead, he always expressed his belief in the republican and representative form of government, and after each seizure of power and dismissal of Congress, he permitted the election of a new Congress and the drafting of a new constitution. In 1834, after removing the Gómez Farías administration, he had permitted elections for the 1835 Congress, which turned out to be dominated by centralist republicans who told him plainly that they would oppose any move on his part towards dictatorship. In 1841, after removing Bustamante and the incumbent Congress, he had allowed, against all advice, a reasonably unrestricted franchise, which produced a Congress diametrically opposed to his autocratic ambitions. For the third time, he used the army to close the Congress. Now, in December 1842, perhaps having learned from his mistake in allowing elections, he had personally appointed a new assembly. But his instructions to it were to produce a new constitution, and when that duly appeared, with his approval, it stipulated another elected, representative form of government. The cycle, in other words, was repeated. A new Congress was elected under the terms of his own constitution, and that Congress promptly opposed everything he wanted to do. Predictably, he decided to use the army once more to close it, but here the cycle deviated from the norm. For the first time since independence, an elected Congress successfully resisted a military challenge to its authority. It was able to do so because Santa Anna had alienated *hombres de bien* of every political persuasion and had antagonized powerful military rivals.

Hence, we have the enigma of Santa Anna's dictatorial ambitions being in conflict with his acceptance of constitutional and representative government. One explanation seems to be that on each occasion he concluded that his military support was never quite sufficient in itself to secure what he wanted and that he therefore needed the backing of at least some of those civilian groups which controlled the social and economic life of the country. Paredes had urged him to forge an alliance with the 'well-off classes', but it was at this political level that Santa Anna always failed. His third opportunity to create this kind of coalition came in December 1842. In the decree of 19 December, issued by his substitute Bravo, which terminated the 1842 Congress, it was announced that a Junta de Notables was to be summoned to deliberate on the future constitutional form of government. The membership of this junta, which it may be said with certainty was handpicked by Santa Anna, was published four days later.[2] It was composed of eighty men who were presumably selected because in their political beliefs, as well as in their economic and social standing, they represented groups whose support Santa Anna believed he could rely on. For the most part, therefore, they were individuals from the upper levels of the propertied classes, the Church and the army. A detailed analysis by Noriega shows the following characteristics.[3] Seventy-eight per cent were over the age of 40, which was in sharp contrast with the young radicals of the 1842 Congress, more than half of whom were younger than 40. In terms of occupation, 36 per cent were lawyers, 18 per cent military officers, 13 per cent clergy and 12 per cent public officials. Within each category, however, again in notable contrast to the previous Congress, almost all the army officers and clergy were from the senior ranks. There was no officer, for example, below the rank of colonel – three-quarters were generals – and 91 per cent of the clergy were canons or bishops. Furthermore, Santa Anna made little attempt to provide any significant regional representation. More than 30 per cent gave the capital as their place of origin, and another 15 per cent were from the Department of Mexico. Finally, almost all had experience in government at the national or state level, in Congress or in other public office.

Clearly, just as the 1842 Congress had been dominated by and tried to represent the middle-class *hombres de bien,* the Junta de Notables was intended by Santa Anna to reflect the upper levels of the elite or, as Noriega puts it, those who controlled the 'key posts of government' (*puestos directivos*). Almost all of the members were consequently well-known and prominent figures in politics, the Church and the army. Valencia, Paredes and Canalizo were among the generals, while Archbishop Posada y Garduño and Bishop Portugal of Michoacán headed the list of ecclesiastics. Among the conservatives were Joaquín Haro y Tamariz and the still active Basilio Arrillaga. But while the Congress was dominated by military, conservative and clerical interests, perhaps surprisingly, the liberal federalists were also represented in the persons of General Alvarez, Bernardo Couto, Andrés Quintana Roo, Ignacio Alas, Manuel Dublán, José Joaquín Pesado and Juan Rodríguez Puebla.[4] Santa Anna's motives in including such obvious opponents may have been to encourage some kind of reconciliation between the contending parties, and their presence again reflects the fact that social standing often superseded political rivalries. Nevertheless, for some of the liberals, to serve on such a body in the

---

2 Decree of 23 December 1842, Dublán and Lozano, *Legislación Mexicana*, vol. 4, pp. 354–6.
3 Noriega Elío, *El Constituyente de 1842*, pp. 124–31.
4 Reyes Heroles gives the political allegiances of the leading members; *El liberalismo mexicano*, vol. 2, p. 316, n. 38.

circumstances was too great a betrayal of their cause, and several, including Couto, Pesado and Rodríguez Puebla, refused the appointment. Similarly, for unknown reasons, some of the conservatives also declined to attend.[5] Thirty-seven were present at the first preparatory session and more soon took their seats, and having elected Valencia as their president, they began their deliberations on 6 January 1843.[6] Their instructions were to formulate the Bases Orgánicas, safeguarding independence, religion and again, notably, the popular, representative, republican form of government. At first, it was not clear whether such *bases* were to be the principles on which a future Congress would base a constitution or whether they were to be the constitution. After some debate, the notables sought clarification from the executive and were told that their *bases* should comprise a 'complete reorganization of the republic so that afterwards there should be no need for another constitutional law'.[7]

It was to take the next five months, until June 1843, for the Junta de Notables to complete its work. During that interlude, it became apparent that Santa Anna had resolved to change his previous policy of leniency towards those who opposed him. Although he did not return in person to the capital until 5 March, he maintained his usual vigilance, and with Tornel restored to the Ministry of War, he was able to direct affairs from his country estate. The first to suffer from his determination to assert his authority was the press. On 14 January 1843, the earlier decree of 8 April 1839 was reimposed. This, it may be recalled, had threatened dire penalties against editors and printers in the Mexico department and had frightened the main papers of that time into closure, in particular, *El Cosmopolita, El Restaurador* and *El Voto Nacional*. Two days later, the decree was declared to be in force across the entire country. It had the same effect as before. The editors of *El Siglo XIX* announced on 15 January that they could not continue to publish under the new law and suspended publication as a protest. Two weeks later, they recommenced publication, but with a warning to their readers that there were many matters they would be unable to discuss. During the absence of this main opposition paper, the publication of a new paper was announced with the declared intention of filling the gap. This was named *El Estandarte Nacional* but within a short time, the government applied pressure to its printer and it too ceased publication.[8] Finally, the long-lived and very influential *El Cosmopolita* came to an end. Since 1835 it had been one of the most serious and balanced in

5 In total, eleven refused the appointment; for the list of names and their replacements, see *Aguila Mexicana*, 10 January 1843.
6 Bustamante, *Apuntes*, pp. 108–10.
7 Reyes Heroles, *El liberalismo mexicano*, vol. 2, pp. 316–17.
8 *Aguila Mexicana*, 25 January 1843; *El Cosmopolita*, 31 May 1843.

its examination of the political controversies of the day. It survived until 8 July, when the final editorial was headed 'ONE LESS'. *El Siglo XIX* lamented its loss with these words: 'In modern nations, the pages of the newspapers contain the annals of the people. By reading their pages, you can follow day by day the history of the struggle which the republic endured in that time of such great historical interest'.[9]

While Bravo was carrying out this closure of the opposition press, Santa Anna remained in the country, but as ever, he kept up his correspondence, particularly with Paredes. As a result, a sequence of events was to follow which years later Santa Anna would blame for his own downfall and disgrace in the autumn of 1844. Before explaining these, it is necessary to say something of Paredes' career and personality. Born in Mexico City in 1797 – three years after Santa Anna – he had followed the conventional pattern of fighting for the Spanish cause during the war of independence and then joining Iturbide's Plan of Iguala in March 1821. Promotion had come slowly, and he had risen only to the rank of battalion commander – Santa Anna was a lieutenant-colonel by 1821 and shortly afterwards a general. Like Santa Anna, he rebelled against Iturbide but his rewards for backing the winning side were insignificant, and he was given only minor military postings for the next few years. Favoured by the procentralist regime of Anastasio Bustamante, however, he was promoted to colonel in 1831 and the following year, at the age of 35, to general. In 1835 he took part in Santa Anna's attack on Zacatecas, and after successfully subduing various other federalist revolts and serving for a few days as the nominal Minister of War in 1838, he was confirmed in his appointment as commander general of the department of Jalisco.

He had thus risen to a senior position in the army, and as the chief military authority of an important region, he now had the opportunity to consolidate both his personal standing and his political ideology. Apparently not a very striking figure personally – 'small in stature, Roman nose and small eyes, straight hair, proud and pretentious', according to one contemporary – he acquired the reputation of being arrogant and unusually cantankerous, which, it was said, had made him unpopular with his fellow officers and the cause of his slow rate of promotion.[10] He had married into a wealthy Guadalajara family that was related to several noble houses in both Spain and Mexico, and he and his circle became the leaders of Guadalajara society. His wife was described as a dominant personality, exercising a strong influence on him, especially in matters of

9 *El Siglo XIX,* 15 July 1843.
10 The physical description of Paredes is in Prieto, *Memorias,* vol. 2, pp. 121–2. There is a portrait in M. Rivera Cambas, *Los gobernantes de México,* (Mexico, 1964), vol. 5, p. 125, which, although stylized, confirms Prieto's description.

religion, in which she was a devout Roman Catholic and an intolerant enemy of the anticlerical liberals.[11]

As a landowner, financially and socially secure, Paredes held political views that reflected the milieu in which he lived. He was both an ardent centralist and a fervent conservative who admired the stability and class-based society of the colonial era.[12] Intensely proud of his career in the army, he despised the proletariat, and he believed that a liberal democracy and federal structure were ill-suited to his country in its current state of development. As he had tried to persuade Tornel and Santa Anna in 1842, he felt that Mexico could and should be governed only by an alliance of the army and the rich, affluent classes, including the clergy, whose education, ownership of property and integrity enabled them to maintain the political stability without which no progress in any field could be made. His home in Guadalajara became a centre for those of like mind, and he discussed his ideas with friends as he tried to formulate his own political philosophy and programme. For example, in September 1843, one of his regular correspondents in Guadalajara gave him this advice:

I have said to you before that what the French call 'le juste milieu', which is the equivalent of fusing the three Estates to a central point, does not exist here. In this country there are only two estates: first, the clergy, military, proprietors and merchants; second, our impoverished artisans, whom we call *chaquetilla* and day-labourers. To try to reconcile the interests of both at the same time is impossible. The first Estate, therefore, must be united. Otherwise our position will deteriorate. It should not be forgotten that the government commands and that he who gives orders should make himself obeyed by using the force of Power if, as here, there is no force of principles; nor will there be any until the government succeeds in forming what we call morality'.[13]

Clearly a political reactionary and strongly proclerical, Paredes was well respected by the social elite of clergymen, merchants and property owners who dominated Jalisco and its capital city of Guadalajara.[14] His close connections with the local merchant community were a major factor in his decision in the summer of 1841 to join the conspiracy against the Bustamante government. But after Santa Anna took the spoils of victory at Tacubaya, he once again seems to have received little reward for his efforts, and as already noted, there were soon signs of his dissatisfaction with having to return empty-handed to Guadalajara. First, there was his public dispute with Valencia over their respective expenditures during

---

11 Prieto, *Memorias*, vol. 2, pp. 121–2.
12 Arrangoiz states that in 1832 Paredes told him that he believed that only a monarchy could save Mexico from anarchy and the United States; *México desde 1808 hasta 1867*, p. 389.
13 F. Martínez Negrete to M. Paredes y Arrillaga, 12 September 1843, García Collection, Paredes y Arrillaga Papers, 140/358.
14 According to U.S. diplomat Waddy Thompson, who was in Mexico at this time, Paredes was 'greatly beloved and respected' in Guadalajara; *Recollections of Mexico*, p. 85.

the revolt, and then after the liberal victory in the 1842 elections, there was his angry exchange of letters with Santa Anna over the rumours of dictatorship.

Despite the obvious cooling of his relationship with Santa Anna, Paredes did support closure of the Congress, issuing a protest in the name of the Guadalajara garrison and public officials against the liberal deputies.[15] This was dated 14 December 1842, or five days before the army in the capital moved against the Congress, and it seems to have been sufficient to reassure Santa Anna of his loyalty, because when on 23 December the membership of the Junta de Notables was announced, Paredes was included. We do not know if he had prior notice of his appointment, which he accepted even though by doing so he was required not only to vacate his posts as commander general and governor of Jalisco but also to leave his large family to travel to and live in Mexico City. His decision to leave his power base in Jalisco for what was a relatively unimportant post in the new assembly certainly astonished his friends in Guadalajara, who promptly began to plead with him to return.[16] Although he did not trust Santa Anna, it seems that ambition had persuaded him to accept an enticing offer which was not publicly known at the time. Writing some time later, Santa Anna reminded Paredes that he had asked him to come to the capital to act as interim president during his own absences in the country.[17] Despite the mutual mistrust and the strained relations between them over the previous few months, Paredes decided to take the risk and accept the offer.

Ostensibly, therefore, he travelled to the capital to take up his post on the Junta de Notables, but shortly after his arrival, Tornel announced that he was being appointed to command an expeditionary army destined for Yucatán. This development was perplexing in several respects. Although Santa Anna was in Veracruz, it was inconceivable that he did not know and approve of the appointment. Yet, as already noted, he said he had asked Paredes to the capital to serve as acting president. Paredes must have presumed or suspected some duplicity on Santa Anna's part because the posting to Yucatán was in effect tantamount to political ostracism and a dangerous move for any ambitious army officer to make. This was, of course, also obvious to Tornel, and it can have come as no surprise when Paredes refused to accept, pleading ill-health.[18] Then, on 20 Feb-

15 'Representación que la guarnición y varios empleados del departamento de Jalisco dirigen al supremo gobierno provisional', 14 December 1842, in *El Cosmopolita*, 24 December 1842. Paredes also issued his own proclamation defending the closure of Congress; ibid., 7 January 1843.

16 See, e.g., F. Martínez Negrete to M. Paredes y Arrillaga, 27 January 1843, in García, *Documentos inéditos*, vol. 56, p. 33. Martínez Negrete refers to the 'gran sensación' in Guadalajara caused by Paredes' decision to go to Mexico City.

17 Santa Anna to M. Paredes y Arrillaga, 23 May 1844, in ibid., pp. 69–70.

18 *El Cosmopolita*, 18 February 1843. Apparently, Paredes was suffering from a urinary infection;

ruary, Santa Anna wrote him to say, with his accustomed air of innocence, that he had recently learned of the posting and had heard that very day that he was suffering from an 'accident to your health'. He hoped he would soon recover.[19]

In the same letter, Santa Anna told Paredes that he had decided to return to the capital to resume control of the government and a week later, on 5 March, between 5:30 p.m. and 6 p.m., he entered the city amid the pomp and ceremony which always accompanied his entrance.[20] He settled down to work at once, and the first thing he began to do was to make changes in the cabinet and other important posts. Some of these changes were announced on the next day, 6 March, and in particular both the governor and commander general of the department of Mexico were relieved of their posts. The person appointed to both posts was Paredes. His formal letter of appointment was released on 7 March. The exact time that he received it is not known, but it was followed in the next few hours by an extraordinary series of events which were to lead to his public humiliation and, according to Santa Anna, to the real cause of the revolt against himself in November 1844.[21]

I have examined what happened in the next few hours in an article and much of the detail is omitted here.[22] In brief, Paredes, having received his good news, decided to celebrate and, in the company of at least one aide, went to have a few drinks. By about 10:30 p.m. on 7 March, he was drunk.[23] Having unsuccessfully tried to force his way into Santa Anna's private apartments in the national palace, he went to a nearby barracks, where he engaged in a noisy and angry confrontation with the commanding officer, General José Mariano Salas, who reported that Paredes was not in control of his senses or, to use his words, was 'deprived of his moral powers by liquor'.[24]

see J. M. Jarero to M. Paredes y Arrillaga, 24 February 1843, in García, *Documentos inéditos*, vol. 56, pp. 39–40.

19 Ibid., p. 39.
20 *El Cosmopolita*, 8 March 1843.
21 Decrees in *El Siglo XIX*, 8 and 10 March 1843. J. M. Bocanegra to M. Paredes y Arrillaga, 7 March 1843, in García, *Documentos inéditos*, vol. 56, p. 45. In his memoirs, written long after the events, Santa Anna wrote that Paredes had rebelled against him in November 1844 because of what happened on 7–8 March 1843: 'Paredes pretendía vengarse. Fue depuesto de los mandos político y militar del Distrito de la capital por excesos de embriaguez ante tropa formada y guardaba rencor'; 'Mi historia militar y política', in García, *Documentos inéditos*, vol. 59, p. 26.
22 Michael P. Costeloe, 'Los generales Santa Anna y Paredes y Arrillaga en México, 1841–1843: Rivales por el poder o una copa más', *Historia Mexicana*, 39 (1989), 417–40.
23 In one of her private letters, Sra. Calderón said that 'Paredes is *always* drunk'; F. Calderón de la Barca to W. H. Prescott, 19 September 1841, in Wolcott, ed., *The Correspondence of W. H. Prescott*, pp. 249–50.
24 This account of Paredes' movements and behaviour is based on the *sumaria*, or evidence, collected by military investigators at the time. The full text of the *sumaria*, including statements by Salas

Following this altercation with Salas, Paredes went home. The next day at 12 noon, he took formal possession of his post as governor in front of the city's authorities. Less than three hours later, government orders were issued which dismissed him from both his posts and placed him under arrest in his own residence.[25] The news spread quickly through the city and naturally caused a sensation. As one paper put it, 'All the public in the capital await the outcome of this grave and unexpected event'.[26] What had in fact happened was that on the morning after the altercation with Salas, the latter had gone to Santa Anna and made a formal complaint against Paredes, accusing him of personal abuse and using insulting language against the president. Santa Anna accepted Salas' account, ordered Paredes' arrest and dismissal and a full military enquiry into the incident.

Over the next few weeks, Paredes was both privately and publicly humiliated by Santa Anna. The reports of the military enquiry were published in the daily press for all to see, and on 5 April Tornel, writing for Santa Anna and using quite unequivocal language, sent him what was a clear rebuke and criticism of his honour as a soldier and his patriotism. He had, said Tornel, refused to serve the nation on the field of battle in Yucatán and twice had rejected an invitation to serve on the Junta de Notables. In view of his attitude, the government had decided that he should leave the capital and report to barracks at Toluca.[27]

Paredes left the capital in disgrace, and it may be stated with certainty that he was a very angry and disillusioned man. He had lost everything he had worked for throughout his career, and now at the age of 46 he had been publicly disgraced by the man he had helped to power. His personal reputation as an upright pillar of the community, devout and principled, had gone and he was branded a drunkard. He had lost the governorship and military command of Jalisco, his seat on the Junta de Notables and his prestigious posts as governor and commander general of Mexico. Even more important to him as a career army officer, his honour as a soldier had been sullied, and to add insult to injury, he had been accused of cowardice. Although later in the year, there was some reconciliation, again in humiliating circumstances for him when Santa Anna made him a senator, there is no doubt that Paredes never forgave

and several witnesses, was published in *El Siglo XIX*, 5 April 1843, and *El Cosmopolita*, 12 April 1843.

25 J. M. Tornel to M. Paredes y Arrillaga, 8 March 1843, in *El Cosmopolita*, 15 March 1843. Tornel said the charge against him was 'una falta grave contra la dignidad del gobierno'.

26 *El Siglo XIX*, 9 March 1843.

27 J. M. Tornel to M. Paredes y Arrillaga, 5 April 1843, in ibid., 8 April 1843. Robertson suggests that Paredes had been the victim of a 'frame-up' by Santa Anna; F. D. Robertson, 'The Military and Political Career of Mariano Paredes y Arrillaga, 1797–1849', Ph.D. diss., University of Texas, 1955, p. 156.

his former ally. For months he was to lick his wounds in silence, awaiting his opportunity for revenge.

Paredes was by no means the only one to suffer Santa Anna's wrath. Apparently determined to assert his authority over his military rivals and the political opposition, Santa Anna also quickly came into conflict with Valencia. The conflict arose from another bizarre incident, this time involving the theatre. In February 1843 a very popular actress of the time, María Cañete, was appearing to packed houses at the Teatro de Nuevo México, and such was the demand for tickets that Valencia failed to get one. On two occasions, gangs of soldiers, thought to be acting on his behalf, disrupted the performance, and when the city council complained of this behaviour to the military commander, nothing was done. Instead, the governor, an ally of Valencia's, deprived the council of its control of public entertainment, and the councillors in turn suspended their activities, despite the threat of a 200 peso daily fine. The row rumbled on, but when Santa Anna returned, he took the councillors' side, restoring their powers and sacking the governor. More significantly, his action was a 'direct and thunderous blow against Valencia'.[28]

With his immediate rivals put in their place, Santa Anna turned his attention to the political opposition, especially the liberal federalist group. His pretext was, first, the rumour of an impending revolt which was supposed to have been revealed in a letter from Gómez Pedraza to Juan Alvarez and, second, a report of an assassination attempt being plotted against himself. In the event neither was found to have any substance, as Santa Anna probably knew, but he used them to intimidate the opposition. At 8 p.m. on Sunday, 30 April, he gave orders, which were immediately carried out in the capital, for the arrest of most of the liberal federalist leaders. Gómez Pedraza, Otero, Riva Palacio and Lafragua promptly found themselves imprisoned on charges of plotting a revolt. Dozens of others were arrested over the next few days, and an atmosphere of panic began to spread in the city as people speculated on what was taking place. *El Cosmopolita* noted that 'the public's alarm continues; the political horizon is no clearer; the veil of mystery seems to cover everything; there is talk of more imprisonments'.[29] Although Alvarez wrote from Acapulco on 9 May denying that he had had any recent contact with Gómez Pedraza and insisting that talk of a revolt in the south was false, military prosecutors were nevertheless appointed to investigate.[30] The *Diario del Gobierno* predicted a revolt at any moment, and when Bravo reported on 17

28 Details in Yañéz, *Santa Anna*, pp. 148–9.
29 *El Cosmopolita*, 6 May 1843.
30 The Alvarez letter is in ibid., 17 May 1843. There is a manuscript copy of the *sumaria*, or evidence collected, against Gómez Pedraza and the others in the García Collection, 449, entitled 'Prisión de los Sres. Pedraza, Riva Palacio, Lafragua y Otero'.

May that three thousand Indians led by *gente de razón* from the capital and Puebla were amassing to attack Chilapa and restore the federation, it seemed that the predictions were true.[31] In reply, the liberal press denied that any revolt was imminent and refused to accept that the incident at Chilapa was politically motivated, which, it turned out, it was not.[32] Meanwhile, Gómez Pedraza and his colleagues remained imprisoned in the monasteries, which were often used to house political detainees, and their wives tried in vain to secure their release.[33] Eventually, after forty-four days of confinement and much of that incommunicado, they were released under the terms of an amnesty which Santa Anna granted to mark his birthday (or saint's day) on 13 June.

The arrest of such prominent figures certainly frightened the opposition, and their persecution seems to have been the result of Santa Anna's increasing anxiety over public discontent with his government.[34] The cause of that discontent was concern not so much over the niceties of constitutional reform being debated by the Junta de Notables as over yet another direct assault on the pockets of *hombres de bien*. Within days of returning to power, Santa Anna had decreed a series of measures which both reduced salaries and raised taxes. He cancelled recent salary increases, increased taxes on various imports and exports, imposed the *alcabala,* or sales tax, on property sales and introduced a monthly tax payable in advance on all commercial establishments throughout the country. Then, having declared the campaigns in Texas and Yucatán to be national wars in defence of the country's territorial integrity, he raised import tariffs in general by 20 per cent on the pretext of finding funds for the armies in those dissident regions.

While the commercial community was reeling from this assault on their businesses, Santa Anna broadened his attack on the propertied classes. In the previous January, an agreement had been reached with the United States whereby Mexico promised to pay 2 million pesos in regular instalments towards its debts to U.S. citizens.[35] The first payment of 270,000 pesos was due on 30 April, and on the 19th of that month,

---

31 N. Bravo to J. M. Tornel, 17 May 1843, in *El Siglo XIX,* 27 May 1843.

32 For details on the Chilapa incident, which involved land, water, timber rights, etc., see Díaz y Díaz, *Caudillos y caciques,* pp. 171–4; J. M. Hart, 'The 1840s Southwestern Mexico Peasants' War: Conflict in a Transitional Society', in Katz, ed., *Riot, Rebellion, and Revolution,* pp. 249–68; Reina, *Las rebeliones campesinas,* pp. 85–116.

33 Gómez Pedraza's wife was Juliana Azcárate; Riva Palacio's, Dolores Guerrero; Otero's, Andrea Arce; *El Siglo XIX,* 5 July 1843.

34 Other pressures were applied to the liberal federalists. For example, tax collectors forcibly removed 200 pesos' worth of goods from Olaguíbel's home on the grounds that he owed 12 pesos in tax; see *El Siglo XIX,* 11 April 1843. Lafragua was again jailed briefly in September because the government objected to what he was going to say in a speech to mark independence; see ibid., 27 and 28 September 1843.

35 Details in Arrangoiz, *México desde 1808 hasta 1867,* p. 383.

Santa Anna summoned to the palace leading entrepreneurs and other wealthy people to ask them for help in making the payment.[36] Although 280 invitations were sent, only thirty individuals attended the meeting and a mere 7,000 to 14,000 pesos were promised.[37] Santa Anna had warned those present that if they did not cooperate, he would impose a forced loan, and he kept his word, announcing on the next day that a loan of 2.5 million pesos was to be levied on all departments. The department of Mexico's share was 588,000 pesos, of which 270,000 was to be collected in cash within ten days, or by 30 April. Those liable for payment included secular and regular clergy, clerical institutions of all kinds and all those people known to have substantial assets. The Mercantile Court, in consultation with representatives of the Church and other bodies, was instructed to draw up a list of payees, and this was published four days later on 24 April. It allocated amounts varying from 3,500 pesos to 25 pesos and nobody was exempted. All the main ecclesiastical corporations and senior clergy were listed, as were the city's merchants and other prominent residents. Even the military did not escape; Valencia was assessed at 850 pesos and Tornel 600 pesos, which compared with the 300 pesos demanded of Alamán.[38] Santa Anna himself was included, which prompted an irate letter on his behalf to the effect that as his assets were in the department of Veracruz, he should pay only whatever was assigned in that area. Howls of protest naturally followed the publication of the names of those who had to pay, and there were accusations of favouritism over the amounts charged, those with influence being charged at too low a rate. Some tried to refuse to pay, only to find soldiers at their door to confiscate their goods. One Mariano Cosío, for example, claimed he could not pay 1,000 pesos, and his new English-made carriage was confiscated to be sold in public auction.[39] Letters of complaint poured into the press, and *El Siglo XIX* observed that interest rates in the money market were rising as moneylenders took advantage of the desperate scramble for cash.[40] Foreign businessmen were also included, which brought complaints from the British, Spanish and French ambassadors.[41] Despite all the public outrage, however, the measure was remarkably successful, at least financially, and the first instalment of 270,000 pesos was handed over to the U.S. ambassador on 29 April.

In his at times desperate pursuit of revenue, Santa Anna had also

---

36 P. Doyle to Ld. Aberdeen, 24 April 1843, P.R.O., F.O. 161, fols. 276–9.
37 *El Siglo XIX*, 19 April 1843.
38 For the list of contributors to the forced loan and the text of the decree, see *El Cosmopolita*, 22 April, 6 May 1843.
39 Details in *El Siglo XIX*, 30 April 1843.
40 Ibid., 3 May 1843.
41 P. Doyle to Ld. Aberdeen, 25 May 1843, P.R.O., F.O. 161, fols. 70–5.

antagonized several specific groups, most notably the protectionists in the cotton industry. In response to demands from some manufacturers to improve the supply of cotton, he arranged a contract with Sres. Aguero González y Cía, which was authorized to import 60,000 quintales of yarn in return for a payment to the Treasury of 360,000 pesos.[42] Rumours that he was going to make such a deal had circulated for weeks beforehand, provoking appeals from the Puebla Junta de Industria and letters from Alamán urging him not to relax the import restrictions.[43]

Santa Anna's conduct of affairs in the first few weeks after his return perplexed the merchant community and the affluent classes in general. On the one hand, he was imposing more and more demands on their pockets. On the other, as he was doing this, the notables he had hand-picked as representatives of the social and economic elite were busily writing a new constitution which was supposed to safeguard their interests against the threats posed by political radicals and the proletariat. His message seemed to be that the army, personified by himself, would impose order and protect the status of the Church and all those other economically and socially privileged groups, but at a price, and that price was to be ever-rising cash contributions. There was no attempt on his part to negotiate any deal or pact as Paredes had advised. In short, if they wanted his protection, they were going to have to pay for it.

The Junta de Notables finished its work on 8 June when Valencia as president of the assembly delivered to Santa Anna the final text of what was entitled Las Bases Orgánicas.[44] Four days later on 12 June, he gave it his official sanction. Never one to miss the opportunity for a public spectacle when he was the centre of attention and even more so when the occasion happened to coincide with his birthday, he had ordered lavish celebrations to mark the new constitution. On his birthday, 13 June, a full programme of spectacular events was held with a Te Deum in the cathedral and a special performance at the theatre in the evening when in his presence songs composed for the occasion were sung in his honour. A military parade of six thousand men with musical accompaniment had entertained the populace in the morning, and Santa Anna had appeared on the palace balcony, throwing 500 pesos of specially minted silver coins to the crowd below. In the afternoon, he had made a triumphal visit in an open carriage with full escort to the Alameda Park, which had been specially decorated and where free sangría flowed from the fountains. The

---

42 Details in *El Cosmopolita*, 20 April 1843. One quintal = 100 pounds.
43 'Representación dirigida al E. Sr. presidente de la república por la junta de industria de Puebla, a fin de que se queme el algodón introducido clandestinamente', 21 February 1843, in ibid., 22 February 1843. A second representation from the same body, dated 23 February 1843, is in ibid., 8 March 1843. Alamán's letter of 25 February 1843 is also in ibid.
44 The full text is in Tena Ramírez, *Leyes fundamentales de México*, pp. 405–36.

only hitch had come when rain forced the postponement of the bull-fight and delayed the fireworks display.[45]

With the celebrations over and the full text available, the new charter began to be analysed. At first the reactions were muted. *El Siglo XIX*'s instant comment was that some parts were good and some were bad. A few days later, it was rather more critical, asking, 'Is there, or is there not, freedom of the press?' and querying the legitimacy of the Junta de Notables and therefore the constitution itself.[46] After this initial response, however, it quickly became evident that what the notables had produced was a much more refined and definite centralization of power than that incorporated in the Siete Leyes. In Rabasa's words, there was to be in future a 'constitutional despotism' with all power vested in the centre and exercised exclusively by the upper classes.[47]

Mexico was to be, or continue to be, a republic with the usual division of powers – the fourth-power concept was abandoned – ruled by a popularly elected representative government. The executive would be headed by a president elected by departmental assemblies for a five-year term. Congress would consist of an elected Chamber of Deputies and a Senate, two-thirds of the latter being chosen by the assemblies and one-third by the president, deputies and Supreme Court. The provinces or departments were to be governed by elected assemblies of between seven and eleven members and a governor appointed by the president from a list proposed to him by the assemblies. There was to be freedom of the press except on religious topics, and the military and ecclesiastical *fueros* were to continue. Finally, Roman Catholicism was to remain the exclusive religion of the State.

The basic principles and structure of government, therefore, remained much as before, but it was in the detail of presidential powers and the electoral process where significant changes were made. For example, in the Siete Leyes the president appointed the departmental governors from a short list supplied by the assemblies. He was empowered to reject the first list but had to choose from a second. Now, provided that Congress agreed, he could reject the lists indefinitely until a name which met with his approval was submitted. The Council of Government had previously been chosen by the president from a list proposed by the Senate. Now the president alone appointed the councillors. Also, in the first elections to be held under the new system, one-third of the Senate was to be directly appointed by the president. With these and other refinements, the powers of the executive were considerably strengthened. Noriega has expressed

45 For a description of the celebrations, see *El Siglo XIX*, 16 and 17 June 1843.
46 Ibid., 13, 20 and 27 June 1843.
47 Cited in Reyes Heroles, *El liberalismo mexicano*, vol. 2, pp. 317–18.

the change quite succinctly: 'In this charter, the central government is everything and the whole of the central government is in the hands of the executive'.[48]

In the legislative branch and electoral process, the concentration of power was even more evident. In the first place, qualifications for citizenship, which carried the right to vote, were changed. The income qualification, which had been 100 pesos in 1836 was now doubled to 200 pesos. Within seven years or by 1850, literacy would also be required. To be a secondary elector in the three-stage electoral process, which was retained, required a minimum income of 500 pesos, although the income qualification for a deputy was reduced from 1,500 pesos to 1,200 pesos. It was in the Senate that the most obvious change was made. Two-thirds, or forty-two, of the senators were to be chosen by the departments, but from very restricted socioeconomic groups. They were to find five from each of four 'classes', that is, landowners, miners, property owners/merchants and manufacturers. Those chosen had to own property worth at least 40,000 pesos. The other senators elected by the departments had to have held high office or rank, for example, as divisional generals, bishops, governors or former senators. Finally, the income qualification remained 2,500 pesos.

Thus, in Santa Anna's eyes constitutional rule was restored to Mexico and what he called his own 'conditional dictatorship' established by the Bases de Tacubaya was brought to an end.[49] The conservatives were no doubt relieved that their control of the political scene had finally been consolidated, and it must have been reassuring that their interests had been given such priority. The moderate liberal federalists, whose leaders were kept imprisoned until the constitution was sanctioned, had had little or no opportunity to voice their opposition, but as elections were to be held for a new Congress, they knew that once again the ballot box offered them their opportunity. For the radicals and especially Gómez Farías, there was 'no other course but revolution'.[50] Gómez Farías had left Yucatán to go to New Orleans, and from there on 11 May 1843 in a letter to Antonio Canales, he made his position clear. Santa Anna, he said, was a tyrant, and the new constitution was being designed to give him permanent power as a military autocrat. The only response was revolution: 'Let us have no more plans of the so-called *filosóficos* by a handful of stupid people; war is an evil but in our circumstances, it is a necessary evil. I

48 Noriega Elío, *El Constituyente de 1842*, p. 155.
49 Proclamation by Santa Anna, 12 June 1843, in *México a través de los informes presidenciales*, pp. 61–2.
50 Unsigned but by V. Gómez Farías to F. M. Olaguíbel, 28 July 1843, García Collection, Gómez Farías Papers, no. 923.

have come here with the purpose of provoking it in any way I can and I will work constantly to achieve it, as I worked in Yucatán'.[51]

Santa Anna remained in the capital for a further three months, until early October, when ill-health again obliged him to depart for Veracruz. He spent the summer months with his accustomed energy, sanctioning decrees on all manner of subjects, infuriating many affected groups and seeming to ignore the election campaign. One of the first and most controversial things to attract his attention was the so-called Parián in the south-western corner of the central square. Consisting of a large collection of stalls surrounded by wooden walls, it had once been the business centre of many import merchants and the best place in the city to buy the latest fashions. The centre of the serious riot of 1828, it had subsequently become dilapidated, and when Santa Anna announced that it was to be pulled down, some welcomed his decision.[52] Others, however, were incensed, especially those merchants who still traded there and the council which received the rents. They protested loudly but to no avail. Santa Anna had decided.[53] The Parián was duly demolished to be replaced by a monument to independence.

If Santa Anna's demolition of the Parián was controversial, some of his other measures were bizarre or inexplicable, at least in the British ambassador's estimation. Mexican industrialists and manufacturers had been pressing for the same kind of protection from foreign competition enjoyed, at least for most of the time, by the cotton manufacturers. On 14 August 1843, Santa Anna responded to this pressure by announcing a total ban on the import of 180 articles, in addition to those already banned in the general tariff.[54] These included all types of carriages, furniture, pianos, toys, coffee pots, spittoons, chamber pots, cigar cases, snuff boxes, dog collars and chains and diverse other finished products. Also included, however, were such items as anvils, saws and files. Since these things were not manufactured in the country, it was difficult to see what advantage was to be derived by local industry, and those businesses that needed them were naturally annoyed. Doyle reported to the Foreign Office that foreign businessmen were also angry, and he believed the whole thing was the work of Tornel either to help Santa Anna in the forthcoming elections or for the 'personal advantages which he has reaped from it'.[55] A few weeks later, the foreign community was even more incensed when Santa Anna ordered that foreigners could no longer engage in retail trading and had just six months to close their businesses. Finally, on 26 Septem-

51 Gómez Farías to Antonio Canales, 11 May 1843, ibid., no. 906.
52 *El Siglo XIX*, 30 June 1843.
53 Protests, etc., in ibid., 29 June to 15 July 1843.
54 Potash, *Banco de Avío*, pp. 139–40.
55 P. Doyle to Ld. Aberdeen, 29 August 1843, P.R.O., F.O. 50, 163, fols. 161–6.

ber, a new tariff was published. This incorporated the earlier list of banned articles, increased the ad valorem tax from 25 to 30 per cent and in general strengthened the protectionist policy which Santa Anna had opted to follow.[56]

It is possible as Doyle suggested that Santa Anna was making some attempt with these various measures to court popularity in view of the presidential election to be held on 1 November. The same thing may explain some of his decisions affecting the Church. Like so many others, the clergy must have been bemused by the apparent inconsistency of Santa Anna's attitude towards them. In the Bases Orgánicas their *fuero* had been protected and religious intolerance confirmed, but the claims to national patronage had not been abandoned and the same powers claimed by the State in previous constitutions had been retained. They had pressed the Junta de Notables for restrictions on freedom of the press to safeguard the faith, and they had demanded express written guarantees against freedom of religion.[57] While some of their demands were met, they were by no means satisfied that the new charter gave them sufficient protection, and when called upon to take the oath of loyalty to it, the bishop of Guadalajara and his twenty-one-strong cathedral chapter issued a protest. There were too many 'obscurities' on ecclesiastical affairs, they said, and they were taking the oath on the strict understanding that 'they were doing so without prejudice to the rules of the Roman Catholic religion, which the nation itself has sworn to profess and protect to the exclusion of any other'.[58]

In addition to harbouring these doubts about their status and security, the clergy also found, as they always did, that Santa Anna's government made heavy demands on their coffers. The biggest contributors to the forced loan were the convents and monasteries. In July the former Church-owned Colegio de Todos Santos buildings were sold by the government to one of Santa Anna's favoured financiers, Ignacio Loperena, for 55,000 pesos against a valuation of 99,000 pesos.[59] The Church was already forbidden to sell its property without prior government approval, and in August the same restriction was added to gold and silver ornaments and any precious objects within the churches. In contrast to these seemingly hostile measures, however, Santa Anna permitted some innovations which the clergy and their supporters had long wanted. For example, in the

---

56 Potash states that 'the philosophy of protectionism may be said to have reached its highest point since independence'; *Banco de Avío*, p. 141. *El Siglo XIX* (22 November 1843) welcomed the protectionist policy and there were reports of a 'buy Mexican campaign' to encourage local industry.

57 *Observaciones que sobre el proyecto de bases orgánicas hacen a la h. junta legislativa el obispo y cabildo de Guadalajara* (Mexico, 1843).

58 The protest is printed in *El Siglo XIX*, 17 July 1843.

59 Report in ibid., 27 July 1843.

hope that they might have some success in pacifying the Indian tribes in the north, he decided to allow the re-entry of the Jesuit Order, but only in the northern provinces. In September, again after pressure from the clerical lobby, he agreed to allow the entry of Spanish religious orders that had been expelled from Spain, and finally, early in October, the Sisters of Charity were permitted to set up their organization.[60]

Two other areas received much of Santa Anna's attention. The stated pretext for his persistent demands for more and more revenue from taxation was always the need to strengthen the army for the Texas and Yucatán campaigns. Recruitment of more men continued, but as far as Texas was concerned, although there was much diplomatic activity, there was no progress in Santa Anna's stated aim of reconquest. Yucatán also proved impossible to subdue. Military units were dispatched, and there had been several engagements between the contending forces but no real progress in ending the region's separation. Then in June 1843, after considerable diplomatic manoeuvring by both sides, a cease-fire was arranged, and Yucatán agreed to send envoys to the capital to negotiate with Santa Anna. The talks broke down at one point, but in December an agreement was reached by which Yucatán was granted almost total autonomy. In return for recognizing Santa Anna's government and the Bases Orgánicas, it was left to arrange its own internal affairs, appointing its own officers, dictating its own fiscal policy and retaining its tax revenues for its own use. The department was not to be asked to contribute men to the Mexican army, and the central government was not to impose taxes on it. With these and many other concessions, Santa Anna resolved the Yucatán problem but at the cost of what was seen at the time and later as a humiliating climb-down.[61]

Santa Anna left the capital on 5 October 1843. Apart from his alleged chronic ill-health, we do not know why he did so or what factors were in his always calculating mind. His timing probably had something to do with the fact that the congressional and departmental assembly elections had been concluded only a few days before. The Bases Orgánicas had stipulated that a new national Congress and assemblies were to be elected, and on 19 June Santa Anna had published new electoral regulations.[62] These conformed to the basic procedure set out in the constitution and set a timetable for the three-stage process of primary, district and electoral college. At each stage, the elections were to be held on designated Sundays, beginning with the primaries on the second Sunday in August. Four

60 Cuevas, Historia de la nación mexicana, pp. 630–1.
61 The text of the treaty with Yucatán is in Dublán and Lozano, Legislación mexicana, pp. 675–8. Arrangoiz described it as 'vergonzosísimo'; Méxeico desde 1808 hasta 1867, pp. 382–4.
62 The Junta de Representantes or Consejo de los Departamentos set up after Tacubaya continued to meet until the end of 1843.

weeks before that day, local authorities were required to appoint com-
missioners to compile the electoral register of those entitled to vote in
each district and to hand out voting slips to them. Alamán, for example,
was appointed commissioner for section 24 in the capital.[63]

With the procedure in place and the registers being compiled, the
campaign began. In public – that is, through the press – it was fairly
muted. *El Siglo XIX* published almost daily articles urging people to vote
for *hombres de bien,* and it was not until 12 August that it came out openly
in favour of federalists. Papers in Oaxaca, Puebla, Chihuahua, Michoacán
and elsewhere preached the same message, advising people to vote for the
person rather than the party.[64] The primaries were held on Sunday, 13
August, throughout the country, and in Mexico City 234 *compromisarios,*
or primary electors, were chosen 'amid a profound calm', according to *El
Siglo XIX*.[65] These included many well-known men from across the political spectrum, and it was not clear which if any group had predominated.
For example, they included Alamán, Díez de Bonilla, Generals Cervantes,
Filisola and Lombardini, as well as liberal federalists such as Gómez
Pedraza, Otero, Riva Palacio and Cumplido. There were indeed so many
old faces that the editor of *El Siglo XIX* commented that it would have
been preferable to see more new ones.[66]

Over the next few days, results came in from around the country. In
most places, it was reported that the elections had passed off without
incident and in an atmosphere of 'harmony and decency',[67] but by the
time the secondary elections were held on 4 September, there were persistent reports of party political negotiations and deals. In the capital,
those engaged in these talks seemed to have failed to reach agreement.
The liberals had their list of choices printed by the publisher García
Torres, whose premises were occupied at one point by the police in an
attempt to seize all copies of the list, but after protests were made they
were released. When voting began, there were two main groups, described
as centralists and liberals. Once the results were declared, it was immediately clear that the centralists had prevailed; of the fourteen district
electors chosen for the capital, only two were from the liberal list. The
same thing seems to have happened elsewhere in the thirteen districts
into which the whole department of Mexico was divided, and it was

---

63 Alamán's letter of appointment is in his *Obras: Documentos diversos,* vol. 4, pp. 138–9.

64 *El Mercurio Poblano,* 18 July 1843; *La Voz de Michoacán,* 2 July 1843. Articles from *El Regenerador
de Oaxaca, Revista de Chihuahua* and several other provincial papers were reprinted in *El Siglo
XIX,* 15 August 1843.

65 *El Siglo XIX,* 14 August 1843. There was supposed to be 1 elector per 500 residents but not
all sections returned their results.

66 Ibid., 16 August 1843.

67 For some exceptions to this, see the reports in ibid., 26 and 30 August, 3 September 1843.

noticeable that seven of those selected *curas* to represent them in the electoral college.[68]

The electoral college began to meet on Sunday, 24 September, that is, a week before the final election of the deputies. Again, according to *El Siglo XIX,* there was much intrigue and negotiation behind the scenes, with various complex tactical voting deals being struck, and when the final results were announced, it was again apparent that the liberal federalists had been defeated. Of the twenty deputies for the Mexico department, only Riva Palacio was a definite federalist and among the losers were Gómez Pedraza and Manuel Dublán. The results of the departmental assembly elections confirmed the same pattern, with Gómez Pedraza, Espinosa de los Monteros, Rodríguez Puebla and other liberals again defeated.

As the names of the successful candidates in the other departments came in, they seemed to confirm that Santa Anna or his acolytes had been able to produce the results they wanted. All of Michoacán's deputies, for example, were men of long experience in public office, including Ignacio Barrera, who had been on the Junta de Representantes.[69] Puebla also returned well-known conservatives such as Bishop Diego Aranda, General Ormaechea and Antonio Haro y Tamariz, and Veracruz elected Tornel's brother José Julián for his first experience in the national Congress. Nevertheless, the victory of the conservative group may not have been all that it seemed, at least as far as it implied support for Santa Anna. *El Siglo XIX* had referred several times to secret deals, but it never revealed – perhaps it did not know – what they were. Some indication, however, is revealed in Otero's archive. It contains several letters to him from friends in his home town of Guadalajara. Surprising as it may seem, these refer to a deal that had been struck between the clerical party and the moderate liberals whereby both groups had compromised and moderated their more extreme policies. On 13 October, Pedro Zubieta wrote to tell him how successful the arrangement had been. Looking at the list of those elected, he said, 'You will see the proof of the fusion of the parties known as clerical and liberal. The deal has been made with sincerity and good faith'.[70]

Santa Anna had reserved for himself the nomination of one-third, or twenty-one, members of the Senate, and all those he appointed were drawn from the senior ranks of the government, army and Church. They

---

68 The detailed results, lists of candidates and votes received were all published in ibid. from 4 September onwards.

69 Results and career records of Michoacán's deputies are given in *La Voz de Michoacán,* 5 October 1843.

70 P. Zubieta to M. Otero, 13 October 1843, Archivo de Mariano Otero, fols. 53–4. I have used a microfilm copy of Otero's archive provided by the University of Texas.

included three bishops and one canon, two former ministers, two Supreme Court judges and several senior army officers. One of the officers was Paredes, who seems to have decided in October to swallow his pride and appeal for Santa Anna's clemency. He wrote asking to be allowed to return to the capital on the grounds of his deteriorating health. In his reply, Santa Anna said he was grateful to receive the letter and that he had sent one of his aides to Toluca to enquire of Paredes' health and to offer his services. He was glad to learn that he was better, and he had given orders that same morning that he be permitted to return. He had also, he said, instructed that he be given 500 pesos. Finally, in a postscript in his own hand, he added that he had appointed him to the Senate.[71]

The remaining two-thirds of the Senate were elected by the departmental assemblies, with twenty representing the four classes of landowners, miners, merchants/propietors and manufacturers, each of whom had to have assets worth at least 40,000 pesos. There was rather more freedom in the choice of the remainder, and it was among them that the liberal federalists finally gained some successes, presumably reflecting their greater support in the departments rather than the centre. Among those elected were Couto, Camacho, Elorriaga, Morales, Rodríguez Puebla and Gómez Pedraza. The liberal federalists had finally managed to get their leaders in the Congress.

There was one final ballot to take place on 1 November, the election by the assemblies of the next president of the republic. For several weeks beforehand, *El Siglo XIX* ran its own campaign, suggesting three suitable candidates. They were Elorriaga, who had been the final president of the 1842 Congress; Juan Ignacio Godoy, a deputy several times in the 1820s and later on the Supreme Court; and Manuel Rincón, a general and former governor/commander general of Veracruz and Puebla. The editors were almost certainly aware that their campaign was futile, because everybody knew that Santa Anna's hat was in the ring. Oliver reported to Spain on 16 October that he would win by a landslide victory, and he was correct. When the votes were finally received, only two departments of the twenty-two which participated failed to vote for Santa Anna. Oliver himself was intrigued by the result. The departments, he wrote, had elected for five years a man whose faults were manifest and yet who was able to persuade everyone to bend to his will. He was able to do this, he suggested, because 'he knows how to make himself respected'. Moreover, the people, tired as they were of continuous revolts, were willing to forget his faults and accept a military government, which they now recognized was better than the alternative of no government or anarchy. This, he thought, was the

71 Santa Anna to M. Paredes y Arrillaga, 4 October 1843, in García, *Documentos inéditos,* vol. 56, p. 68.

secret of the paradox of a man so widely hated as Santa Anna gaining the votes of the distinguished men on the assemblies. Also, he added, the departmental governors, all creatures of Santa Anna and 'submissive to the word of the imperious and energetic General Tornel', had no doubt used their influence. How long Santa Anna would remain content with the title of president, he concluded, only time would tell.[72]

Thus, Santa Anna, for the second time in his career – the first was in 1833 – was elected by an overwhelming majority to the presidency. As on the first occasion, however, he was absent, enjoying life in the country on El Encero, another hacienda he had recently acquired, and as before, he chose not to return for the time being to the centre of things.[73] Instead, he left affairs of state in the hands of his loyal friend, General Valentín Canalizo. The latter's career was again typical of his generation. Born in 1794 at Monterrey, he had joined a Spanish infantry regiment in 1811 but changed sides to support Iturbide. In following years, he rose through the ranks and held several senior posts as commander general of Oaxaca and governor of the department of Mexico. Not known to have any strong political views, he made his only public declaration in the final days of the Bustamante administration in October 1841, when he swore to defend the federation which Bustamante had too belatedly decided to proclaim. Known for his friendship with Santa Anna, he was promoted by him to divisional general in 1841 and subsequently held various military posts.

Canalizo took office as substitute president on 4 October 1843, and he was to remain in post until June of the following year, when Santa Anna at last decided to return. Nobody was in any doubt that Canalizo was merely a puppet, closely supervised and controlled by his absentee master. In fact, before leaving, Santa Anna had taken precautions to ensure that his wishes would continue to be obeyed. First, he decreed that the future Congress had no power to repeal any of his legislation enacted since October 1841 or, in particular, to revoke any contracts he had signed. Second, he reserved for himself the right to appoint and dismiss ministers. Third, he ordered that decisions be made by a majority vote of the cabinet plus Canalizo, knowing of course that Tornel still dominated the cabinet. In other words, Canalizo's hands were tied from the start, and over the next few months regular letters arrived from Veracruz giving him instructions and telling him, for example, whom Santa Anna wanted as military commanders and governors in the departments.[74]

72 P. P. Oliver to Secretary of State, 16 October 1843, 25 November 1843, in *Relaciones diplomáticas hispano-mexicanas*, vol. 2, pp. 294–5, 307–8.

73 He continued to acquire properties through various, at times, dubious means; see Díaz y Díaz, *Caudillos y caciques*, p. 169.

74 Jones, *Santa Anna*, pp. 86–7. He gives details of the various letters from Santa Anna to Canalizo, which are in the García Collection.

According to the Bases Orgánicas and the election schedule, Santa Anna should have begun his five-year term on 1 February 1844. In late January, he let it be known that he did not intend to leave Veracruz. The reasons for this reluctance almost certainly lie in what for him was an unexpected spirit of independence and defiance displayed by the new Congress from the first day of its sessions. Even though he personally had appointed one-third of the Senate and many of the other senators and deputies were not known to be in the opposition ranks, it was immediately obvious that the Congress was not going to allow itself to be bullied by Santa Anna, Tornel or Canalizo. In the first place, many of the deputies failed to arrive for the opening sessions, which were inquorate, and Gilliam noted that 'this indisposition of the deputies was supposed by some to have been more the result of a mental than a bodily cause'.[75] Then, the president of the Chamber of Deputies criticized Canalizo's opening address, and three days later, Gómez Pedraza set even more sharply the tone of what was to come. He proposed to the Senate that the whole government lacked legitimacy on the grounds that Canalizo's powers had been curtailed by Santa Anna and cabinet ministers were not to be held responsible for their actions, 'which is monstrous in a representative system'. He had taken an oath of allegiance to the Bases Orgánicas, he said, not because he supported them but because acceptance of them was the only way to avoid the sword of Damocles hanging over the people. The dictatorship was over and it was essential to have constitutional rule, and yet it was the government itself which was in flagrant violation of it.[76]

Gómez Pedraza's powerful speech caused a sensation inside and outside of Congress, but although his proposals were given a second reading, they were voted down in the Senate by 35 votes to 2, those being of Gómez Pedraza himself and Juan Bautista Morales. In the meantime, some deputies took up the cause, and on 8 January they proposed that from the opening of the Congress the executive had ceased to have any legislative power. Despite an intervention by Tornel in the debate, their proposal received a second reading by a vote of 48 in favour to 4 against, and the committee to which it was referred came out in their support.[77] Both sides resorted to the press to put their case. The *Diario del Gobierno* attacked Gómez Pedraza, and the French-owned *Correo Francés* described his ideas as 'political imprudence and parliamentary recklessness'.[78] The deputies were also condemned in the progovernment press, but they kept their support in the Chamber, and on 27 January a motion was passed which declared that 'the authorizations to legislate given to the Executive by

75 Gilliam, *Travels in Mexico*, pp. 103–4.
76 The text of Gómez Pedraza's speech is in *El Siglo XIX*, 5 January 1844.
77 Ibid., 9, 11–14 and 17 January 1844.
78 Ibid., 21 January 1844.

the various legislative powers of the nation have ceased'.[79] This was, as Carlos Bustamante recorded, like 'an electric spark for Santa Anna, who wanted to legislate on everything'.[80]

Santa Anna obviously now knew that, as so many times in the past, he was going to have trouble with the Congress, and he chose not to come to the capital. This meant that an interim president had to be found by the Senate, and Santa Anna used all his influence to ensure that Canalizo was again elected. In this he was successful, but the vote was by no means unanimous, with General Melchor Múzquiz, who was not a serious candidate, attracting thirteen protest votes and Tornel and Rincón two each against Canalizo's twenty-four. Emboldened by their success and support, more congressmen were willing to oppose the government, and by March the British ambassador was able to report that 'in the chamber of deputies, the majority are in opposition to Santa Anna'.[81] This development in turn encouraged liberal federalists outside of Congress to begin to organize. In one of his memoirs, Lafragua recalls how he, Otero, Olaguíbel and Comonfort began to meet with some of the deputies to form an opposition group known as the 'invisibles' and how, within Congress, liberals and *escoceses* formed pacts with the aim of getting rid of Santa Anna altogether.[82]

Congress was not the only source of difficulties for Santa Anna. In September 1843 a major conflict had broken out in Sonora, and although this concerned local rivalries rather than national issues, it served to show that, like his predecessors, Santa Anna was unable to guarantee public order. His capitulation to Yucatán was widely condemned and gave considerable encouragement to federalists like Gómez Farías, who from New Orleans continued to write to his allies around the country urging them to organize revolts. In a letter to Olaguíbel, he vowed that he personally would wage war as long as he lived against the 'perfidious and evil Santa Anna'. His constitution had given power to the 'privileged classes', and the middle class, 'where are found men of probity, honour and knowledge, is going to be ignored and unable to aspire to posts'.[83]

For the middle ranks of *hombres de bien,* this loss of influence in the corridors of power was compounded by the continued demands on their pockets, which were again brought home to them in February when they were reminded that the fourth instalment of the forced loan was due to be paid. All the recent tax demands were still in force, and those in the public service still went without their salaries. The Mexico assembly pleaded for more revenues to be given to the departments because their

79 Bustamante, *Apuntes,* p. 249.
80 Ibid.
81 C. Bankhead to Ld. Aberdeen, 31 March 1844, P.R.O., F.O. 173, fols. 27–32.
82 Colección Lafragua, no. 398.
83 Gómez Farías Papers, no. 906.

own officials lacked even paper and ink and there was growing poverty in all social classes.[84] In the capital, however, there was a splendid new Gran Teatro de Santa Anna and a bronze statue of the hero of Tampico in the newly constructed Plaza de Volador with his right arm extended towards Texas and also towards the Treasury. There was the splendid mausoleum in the cemetery of Santa Paula where the remains of his leg had been buried and another newly erected statue of him in Puebla. But there was no improvement in the more mundane environment in which *hombres de bien* had to live. Crime was still a constant fear in daily life, and despite new regulations to clean up the streets of the capital, the city remained a dangerous and dirty place in which to live.[85]

Even Santa Anna's main pillar of support soon showed signs of discontent. He had already quarrelled with Paredes and Valencia, and in April 1844 his long-standing friendship with Tornel was disrupted. The cause of their break is not clear, but according to Carlos Bustamante, Santa Anna resented Tornel's increasing affluence and the public adulation he attracted on a visit to Puebla. 'He does not tolerate rivals', Bustamante remarked, and Santa Anna decided to put Tornel in his place, ordering Canalizo to dismiss him from his post as Minister of War.[86] For others of senior rank, there was also cause for concern. Santa Anna had ordered the formation of new units and the recruitment of an additional 15,440 men divided among all the departments, which, incidentally, was another cause of discontent in the provinces. But in Congress, two deputies presented a plan on 29 February for the complete reorganization of the army. Within a short time, word of a revolt began to spread, and it is significant that the origin of the rumor was said to have been a protest in Jalapa against the proposed reorganization.[87]

Santa Anna was in trouble, and he knew it. His well-tried tactic of withdrawing from the scene to see how things developed was not working, and discontent at all levels was rising. What he needed was an issue or pretext to deflect attention from the domestic situation and which would enable him to return to restore order and assert his authority. In 1829 the Spanish invasion had given him his opportunity; in 1835 Texas had done the same; in 1838 the French blockade had made him a hero and

---

84 'Iniciativa de ley que la Asamblea departamental de México dirige a la cámara de diputados, sobre recaudación de rentas nacionales y parte que de ellas debe darse a su Departamento', 30 January 1844, in *El Siglo XIX*, 5 February 1844.

85 Residents were ordered not to throw their household rubbish onto the streets and to clean the area outside their houses daily; regulations dated 13 February 1844 in ibid., 27–9 February 1844.

86 Bustamante, *Apuntes*, pp. 249–50.

87 Decree of 29 December 1843 in Dublán and Lozano, *Legislación mexicana*, vol. 4, p. 721. The number of recruits required varied according to department, ranging from 4,169 from Mexico to 140 from Aguascalientes.

rescued him from oblivion. Now, in yet another of the remarkable co-incidences which mark his career, an opportunity came his way just when he needed it. In May 1844 a messenger from the United States arrived on the doorstep of his country house, bringing confirmation of the news that the United States was going to annex Texas. He prepared at once to leave for Mexico City. He had his issue. It was again to be the reconquest of Texas, on which he would stake his career. If Congress refused to grant him the emergency powers he wanted, he had his simple but direct solution, succinctly expressed by the British diplomat Charles Bankhead: 'I believe these powers will be given but if Santa Anna finds any difficulty on the part of congress in granting them, he will send them about their business and assume any degree of authority he thinks fit'.[88] Thus, Santa Anna prepared to challenge Congress once again. This time, he would not win.

88 C. Bankhead to Ld. Aberdeen, 30 May 1844, P.R.O., F.O. 174, fols. 86–92.

10

'La revolución de tres horas'

The national Congress is one of the unsung heroes of the Age of Santa Anna. From the time of Iturbide onwards, successive generations of congressmen displayed considerable courage in their determination to sustain the independence of the legislative power, often in the face of open hostility from the military-dominated executives. Iturbide's response was to jail recalcitrant deputies and to use his military strength to close the Congress. During the Victoria and Guerrero presidencies, the Congress reasserted its authority, and neither executive was able to dominate or even restrain it to any significant degree. Bustamante, under the subtle tutelage of Alamán, was rather more successful, but even his carefully organized administration was obliged to resort to threats and intimidation against a resolute minority who steadfastly opposed his policies. Santa Anna was even less able to control the representatives, and it is probable that he failed to turn up for his first inauguration day in 1833 because he knew that he could not dictate to them and their majority of radical liberals. Like that of Iturbide before him, his solution was to use the army to lock the doors of the debating chamber, but even that was achieved only after defiant and prolonged resistance by the Congress. As we have seen in previous chapters of this study, Bustamante's second administration witnessed many disputes with Congress until Santa Anna again brought its sessions to an abrupt end with his Bases de Tacubaya. Then in 1842, for the third time, after failing either to influence or to frighten the congressmen, he resorted to force in order to stop their deliberations.

To a significant extent, not so far appreciated or acknowledged by historians of the period, it was this rivalry between the largely civilian legislative branch and the general-presidents who ruled the executive which generated much of the political tensions and turmoil of the time. Yet the conflict between the two powers is also surprising, especially after 1830, when successive regimes went to some lengths to ensure the election of what they hoped would be political sympathizers from among the upper echelons of the *hombres de bien*. They changed electoral laws and regulations several times, imposed income and other qualifications on the electorate and the elected and, in general, intervened with whatever threats, bribes or promises were possible or appropriate in the circumstances. At first sight, such tactics were usually successful, except, notably in the 1842 elections, and the 'right' men were chosen, always including clergymen, army officers, senior bureaucrats and others who appeared to represent the interests of the dominant social class. Nevertheless, and excepting those opposition politicians who slipped through the electoral net designed to keep them out, once elected, a substantial number in every Congress of those who it was presumed would be supporters of the incumbent regime quickly asserted their independence and refusal to be dictated to by the executive.

There is probably no better illustration of a Congress resisting a seemingly omnipotent military executive than the one in session during the year of 1844. As seen in the preceding chapter, it had been elected under the terms of the Bases Orgánicas, which Santa Anna's own handpicked Junta de Notables had devised, and the election results had indicated once again that the 'right' men had been chosen. They were almost all from the socioeconomic elite, and those senators with assets of at least 40,000 pesos were rich men by any standard of the time in either America or Europe. Santa Anna himself had been elected almost unanimously, and he must have assumed that those to whom he had delivered legislative power would not jeopardize their own dominance by undermining his position and authority. Yet they had done just that from the opening day of the sessions, and as in many previous assemblies, a significant number had made it clear that they intended to sustain the principle of the separation of powers.

When Santa Anna returned to the capital on 3 June, he already knew, therefore, that he could not count on the servile co-operation of the Congress. It is possible he calculated that the Texas issue would generate some kind of consensus and that the deputies and senators would not risk being branded as unpatriotic or even as traitors by opposing his personal crusade for reconquest. If that was his assumption, he made a grave miscalculation, because it quickly became evident that many Mexicans of all political persuasions did not share his belief or wish that it was either possible or desirable to mount a successful military campaign in the north. The problem of Texas had somewhat paradoxically been at both the centre and the margins of political life for the preceding eight years. Since Santa Anna's defeat by Sam Houston in 1836, every Mexican government had made reconquest a central plank of its manifesto, and many of the new taxes on property and incomes as well as the forced loans had been justified on the grounds of paying for a military campaign. Vast expenditure had been committed to the armed forces, and more men had been recruited, at least on paper, but in practice no progress had been made, and the few military engagements and border skirmishes that did occur from time to time had not resulted in any significant political or territorial gain. While always in the background, Texas had been overshadowed by myriad other issues of domestic conflict. By the early 1840s, it was increasingly obvious to many that Santa Anna's dream of reconquest, which may well have been shared initially by most of his compatriots, was not going to be realized.

The military impotence of Mexico was self-evident, and when the diplomatic community began to take an active interest, the possibilities of a peaceful solution seemed attractive. The British, and to a lesser extent the French, governments had both taken a keen if not anxious interest in the future status of Texas, and when the U.S. elections brought the annexationist James Polk to the presidential office, the British government in particular renewed its pressure on the Mexican authorities.[1] The British position was relatively straightforward. It wanted to stop the annexation of Texas by the United States, and it strongly advised the Mexican government that the only secure way of doing so was for Mexico to recognize Texan independence. If Mexico was willing to concede that recognition, Britain suggested that it would guarantee the territorial integrity of what was left of the republic, including California, which the Manifest Destiny thesis of the United States had long since predicted would also eventually be absorbed.

The foregoing summary, of course, is an oversimplification for the sake of brevity of the issue as it stood in May 1844. It does not include the very difficult problems concerning the exact borders of Texas and the nature of the protection which Britain might offer Mexico in the future. These matters were to preoccupy diplomats intensively in coming months, but for the time being, they were superfluous because for Santa Anna, either because of a genuine conviction that he could reconquer Texas or for reasons of personal political opportunism, there was nothing to talk about. He would reconquer Texas, and that was his message as he returned to the capital.

He remained in Mexico City for just three months, during which time he faced serious personal and political difficulties. His wife, Doña Inés García de Santa Anna, became critically ill in July and died at Puebla on 23 August. By all accounts, she was a well-respected and admired lady, regardless of her husband's reputation and career, and her death provided Santa Anna with what seemed at the time a sincere reason to leave the capital and return to the family home at El Encero, which he did early

---

1 There are several good studies of the Texas situation and U.S.–Mexican relations in general at this time; see, e.g., D. M. Pletcher, *The Diplomacy of Annexation: Texas, Oregon and the Mexican War* (Columbia, Mo., 1973); G. L. Rives, 'Mexican Diplomacy on the Eve of the War with the United States', *American Historical Review*, 18 (1912–13), 275–94.

in September. Within six weeks, however, invitations were being sent out to a ceremony in which the absent Santa Anna, represented by Juan de Dios Cañedo, was to marry a 15-year-old girl, María Dolores de Tosta. The religious ceremony, followed by a sumptuous banquet, was held in the capital on 3 October, soon after which the young bride was taken to El Encero. Santa Anna's apparent utter disregard for the social conventions of mourning was looked on with distaste, if not disgust, by the society of the capital. Carlos Bustamante, in language unusually subdued for him, noted, 'The people of Mexico did not look with approval on this marriage because it was so soon after the death of Sra. García'.[2]

On the political level, Santa Anna already knew that there were serious obstacles to be overcome before he could start any military campaign in Texas. The Ministry of War provided a budget estimate of more than 22 million pesos if all the armed forces were to be on active duty.[3] At the same time, the Minister of Finance in his annual report revealed a projected deficit on the national account for the year 1844 of almost 12 million pesos, with the military estimate of 22 million being almost double the expected net revenue for the year.[4] It was obvious to most observers that the country simply did not have the resources even to contemplate a war which it was accepted would inevitably involve the United States. Such details did not deter Santa Anna. Within a week of his arrival, he sent an initiative to Congress requesting two things: authority to recruit an additional 30,000 men for the army and 4 million pesos to be raised by Congress. A few days later, he ordered that with the sole exception of the head tax, all revenues collected in the departments were to be paid into the central Treasury, and then, presumably to reduce expenditure, he ordered a 25 per cent reduction in army rations for all ranks below commanding officers.

Santa Anna did not specify how Congress was supposed to raise this enormous sum, and all manner of rumors quickly began to spread. It was being said, *El Siglo XIX* reported, that either restrictions on the import of cotton were to be lifted or there was to be a large-scale mortgage of Church wealth. Furthermore, the paper began to raise the question whether the reconquest of Texas was worth the cost: 'The Texas war is one of those in which the gains do not compensate for the losses'. Even if the army were successful, it added, 'what would this victory be worth?'[5]

2 Bustamante, *Apuntes*, p. 301. For a description of the marriage ceremony, etc., see *El Siglo XIX*, 5 October 1844.
3 'Presupuesto del gasto que debe erogarse al año en los ramos de guerra y marina, siempre que estén sobre las armas todos los cuerpos de milicia activa, y así éstos como los permanentes con las fuerzas de su dotación', 30 June 1844, in *El Siglo XIX*, 5 July 1844.
4 'Memoria de Hacienda' (July 1844), in ibid., 15 November 1844.
5 Ibid., 16 June 1844. The pro–Santa Anna press, of course, saw the situation differently. According

These doubts expressed in *El Siglo XIX* were soon seen to reflect a similar reaction in Congress, and over the next few weeks as opposition grew, there was a growing public rift with the executive. Santa Anna's initiative was referred to a combined War and Treasury committee which produced a majority report on 19 June.[6] This rejected the request for 30,000 men, proposing instead that the departments be required to supply the 15,440 already ordered in the decree of 29 December 1843. These recruits should be found within two months, with all citizens from 18 to 50 years of age being eligible. The new units, however, were to remain in the departments until Congress decided otherwise. On the financial side, the committee recommended a doubling of all direct taxes except the head tax, but all additional revenues collected must be devoted exclusively to the war and the executive must provide detailed accounts. Two members of the committee – Cuervo and Parrodi – submitted minority reports in which they advocated that the full 30,000 men should be authorized and that a 4 million peso loan should be raised in the departments by mortgaging future tax revenues.[7] On 22 June, the deputies went into permanent session to discuss this report, and in what was a heated debate, the divisions in the Congress over the Texas issue were revealed. Rafael Espinosa, for example, urged compliance with Santa Anna's request because the reconquest of Texas was vital to national honour: 'We must wage war on Texas; this is demanded by national honour and public necessity. National honour demands a rational and just vengeance for the insults and offenses committed against it'.[8] Rosa, among others, disagreed. As far as they were concerned, the cost was too great for the nation to bear and public opinion was not in favour of. Carlos Bustamante voiced his fears that any money raised would end up in the pockets of the *agiotistas*, 'that class of people cursed by God and abhorred by the whole nation'. He did not oppose the number of men wanted, but he objected to the barbaric methods of recruitment used in the past: 'Up to now we have noted that conscripts have been found only by seizing them from the humble shacks of the poor in such a cruel way that I have seen a man led by a chain, looking more like a lizard than a man'.[9]

The deputies rejected the committee report by 43 votes to 23 and then decided to consider the Parrodi alternative, a decision which was reached by a vote of 35 to 34. Eventually, they approved the 30,000-man target

to *El Defensor de la Integridad Nacional* (19 October 1844), the situation was simple: 'O la guerra de Tejas, o la pérdida de la independencia de México. Este es el dilema que hoy tiene que resolverse'.

6 'Dictamen de las comisiones primera de hacienda y primera de guerra sobre los asuntos de Tejas, leído en sesión extraordinaria de la cámara de diputados la noche del presente mes', in *El Siglo XIX*, 24 June 1844.

7 The text of these minority reports is in ibid.

8 Ibid., 23 June 1844.

9 Bustamante's speech is reported in ibid., 30 June 1844.

but rejected the proposed forced loan, again in a very close vote of 37 to 35. Other deputies came forward with their own schemes, and everything was referred to another committee. It duly produced its own ideas for an emergency tax of 1.5 million pesos to be levied throughout the republic and a new tax on rents of urban properties to be paid by tenants.[10] These ideas were revised, and a more detailed schedule of taxes on rents was concocted. This now suggested a 14 per cent tax on rents payable by property owners and a graduated tax on tenants according to the amount of rent they paid.[11]

Again, these proposals provoked much controversy and opposition among the deputies, but they were approved with amendments for referral to the Senate. There they also met with opposition led by Gómez Pedraza and Morales, and the committee which examined them dismissed them as impractical and unfair, pointing out that a tax on rents would penalize urban residents much more than those in the countryside. Instead, they proposed a combination of taxes on the value of urban and rural property together with a tax on rents of more than 5 pesos a month.[12] Cabinet ministers had attended the committee's meetings to try to persuade the senators to adopt the deputies' scheme, but they resisted this pressure and approved their own ideas, which were referred back to the deputies. They once more spent several days on the matter, with more committee reports and suggested variations, until finally on 21 August, with the approval of both houses, a law was published.[13] The main articles were as follows: a 2 peso per mill levy on the value of rural property payable by hacendados, if they wished in products rather than cash; 3 pesos per mill on textile factories; 8 per cent on urban rents collected by individual and corporate owners; a graduated scale payable by tenants; the reimposition of the tax on luxury goods decreed on 7 April 1842; the same tax on industrial establishments decreed on 5 April 1842.

Throughout these debates in both the Chamber of Deputies and Senate, it was obvious from the very close voting that a significant group in both houses was determined to resist Santa Anna's demands. This was again illustrated on 24 July when the executive asked for authority to raise all tax levels as and when it deemed necessary. The deputies rejected the request on the grounds that the power to levy taxes corresponded exclusively to the legislative branch. Articles promptly began to appear in the

10 'Dictamen de la comisión especial que para los asuntos de Tejas y arbitrar recursos para el erario, nombró la cámara de diputados del congreso nacional', 30 June 1844, in ibid., 1 July 1844.
11 Text in ibid., 5 July 1844.
12 'Dictamen de la comisión primera de hacienda del senado sobre el acuerdo de la cámara de diputados relativo a proporcionar los cuatro millones de pesos que ha pedido el supremo gobierno', 22 July 1844, in ibid., 30 July 1844.
13 Dublán and Lozano, *Legislación mexicana*, vol. 4, pp. 760–4.

Diario del Gobierno attacking the congressmen and a pamphlet appeared on the streets entitled *Mientras tengamos congreso, no esperemos progreso.* Speculation rose that Santa Anna, who was believed to be behind the pamphlet, was preparing to dismiss the Congress, and there were reports of secret meetings of senior army officers at Tacubaya, where he was staying. Bankhead reported to London that the huge increase in the size of the army was 'as much to sustain General Santa Anna in power as they are destined for the invasion of Texas' and that the new units would probably be used to resolve any difficulties with Congress.[14] Morales used the columns of *El Siglo XIX* to protest the pressuring and intimidation of the congressmen, and he warned that, by all signs, Santa Anna was plotting to move against them. In retaliation, his article was denounced as subversive, all copies of the paper were ordered seized and the Minister of Justice started proceedings against him in the Senate.[15]

Outside the capital, where the split between Santa Anna and the Congress was public knowledge, there were many signs of discontent. The departments were faced with having to conscript 45,440 men, and some – for example, Mexico – quickly issued regulations for the draft which confirmed that all able-bodied males between the ages of 18 and 30 were to be liable, although, as usual, those with the means were allowed to provide a substitute. The conscription was rapidly applied, and on 31 July Bankhead reported that 'recruits (chained together) are arriving daily'.[16] Even less welcome to the population as a whole were a range of new taxes which several departments felt obliged to introduce to make up for the loss of those now paid to the national Treasury. Querétaro, for example, raised its local head tax and Veracruz imposed a surcharge of 4 reales on each quintal of cotton harvested in the department. In the Mexico department, special taxes were put on flour, brandies and pulque. None of these had much immediate effect on revenues, and in an unusually outspoken editorial, *El Siglo XIX* condemned what it called the criminal neglect of the departments, where poverty had reached crisis levels. Their internal administration was in chaos and their revenues had become the 'patrimony of the army'. With little or no money being collected, or else taken by the military commander for himself and the garrison, public employees everywhere remained unpaid and destitute.[17] In a letter to the press, written precisely, he said, to draw public attention to their plight,

14 C. Bankhead to Ld. Aberdeen, 29 June 1844, P.R.O., F.O. 50, 174, fols. 294–8.
15 The Morales editorial is in the issue of 11 August 1844. Following issues contain details of the charges against him.
16 C. Bankhead to Ld. Aberdeen, 31 July 1844, P.R.O., F.O., 50, 175, fols. 137–41.
17 *El Siglo XIX*, 30 July 1844. The progovernment press argued that the head tax provided enough revenue to meet the needs of the departments; see *El Defensor de la Integridad Nacional*, 24 August 1844.

one Francisco G. de Medina stated that 'I am surrounded by a young and very large family and neither they nor I have anything to eat because I have not been paid even half a real of my salary for the whole of August nor for the present month'.[18] Widows and pensioners who were lucky enough to receive a credit note for their benefits were selling them to speculators at up to 95 per cent discount in order to survive. To add to the pervasive air of poverty and hopelessness, hurricanes and ten days of heavy rainfall caused serious flooding and the loss of the harvest in several areas of central Mexico. At Iguala, more than two thousand Indians rebelled against the head tax and threatened to ransack Taxco.

Santa Anna ignored but was not oblivious to this rising tide of discontent, taking precautions against a possible assassination attempt on his life that was being rumoured 'from one moment to the next'.[19] He busied himself with signing contracts with his favoured speculators and entrepreneurs for equipment he would need on the Texas campaign. Cayetano Rubio, for example, was given a contract to supply thirty thousand uniforms and tents and another entrepreneur was asked to supply £40,000 worth of arms and ammunition, much of which was to be acquired in Britain. In reporting these deals, which were made 'at an enormous sacrifice to the country', Bankhead added that Santa Anna had 'without the slightest doubt, a large *personal* interest, so intense is his love of money' and that there was the 'most barefaced corruption in every branch of government'.[20] The problems with Congress over the demand for 4 million pesos also did not deter Santa Anna. On 30 July he met with his cabinet to draw up another executive initiative for an immediate congressional vote for a loan of 10 million pesos. By now, the Congress had had enough, and although it discussed the demand at length, with several more committee reports, it rejected it.

The final rejection of the demand for 10 million pesos came on 15 October. It was no surprise because there was no doubt that those who opposed Santa Anna now felt themselves strong enough to challenge him openly. Always an indication of a rise in the political temperature of the day, several new newspapers had appeared, some pro–Santa Anna but others openly, as they stated, of the opposition, and Bankhead correctly reported that 'the rumour gains ground that the congress are every day more averse to the warlike views of the government'.[21] Santa Anna had

18 *La Abeja*, 10 October 1844.
19 Unsigned to V. Gómez Farías, 31 August 1844, Gómez Farías Papers, no. 1010. Two Englishmen, Patrick Jordan and James White, were deported because of suspicions that they were 'engaged in a conspiracy to murder Santa Anna'; C. Bankhead to Ld. Aberdeen, 31 July 1844, P.R.O., F.O. 50, 175, fols. 87–9.
20 C. Bankhead to Ld. Aberdeen, 31 July, 29 August 1844, ibid., fols. 137–41, 207.
21 C. Bankhead to Ld. Aberdeen 24 September 1844, ibid, 176, fols. 111–14. The new papers

announced early in September that he was retiring to the country, officially in mourning for the loss of his wife, but his tactic of withdrawing from the scene when confronted by a hostile Congress had been used too many times before to have any credibility. Hence, it was generally believed that he had decided to force the dismissal of the legislators. They in turn still refused to be intimidated, and they again displayed their determination to act independently when it came to choosing an interim president. The choice rested with the Senate, and Santa Anna's preferred candidate was again Canalizo. In the first ballot, however, both he and General Rincón received 22 votes each, and two more ballots had to be held before Canalizo scraped home by a margin of just 2 votes – with 24 against 22 for Rincón – including 1 in his favour cast by his brother, who was a senator. Canalizo was not in the city at this time and the president of the Council of Government, José Joaquín de Herrera, took over until he could return and take the oath on 20 September.

Canalizo, therefore, was left to face the Congress, although as before, nobody was in any doubt that it was Santa Anna who was pulling the strings. Whether planned in advance or not we do not know, but early in October the opposition majority in Congress launched what seemed to be a concerted attack on the government. It began with an editorial in *El Siglo XIX* asking what was happening to all the money collected in recent months from the additional taxation. More and more was being demanded, and yet public employees were not being paid and now even soldiers were not getting their pay.[22] Other opposition papers both in the capital and in the departments took up the same theme. *La Abeja* estimated government revenues at 1.5 million pesos a month, and yet most of those dependent on the public purse were receiving nothing. Why was it, the editor asked, obviously making insinuations, that the military garrisons in and around Jalapa – that is, Santa Anna's home territory – were always paid, whereas those in Guadalajara were getting nothing?[23] *El Jaliciense*, published at Guadalajara, asked, 'What are they doing with the revenues?' The same paper calculated that Mexicans paid higher taxes than anyone in the world. In 1833 taxes had been 20 pesos per capita compared with 11½ in England, 7½ in Holland and 4 in Spain. Since then, the Mexican rate had increased to at least 30 pesos per head, 'something unheard of even in the most despotic government on earth'.[24]

In Congress, deputies began to ask the same questions and on 8 October they approved a motion put by Deputy Rosa that the executive branch

included *La Abeja* and *El Nacional*, both hostile to Santa Anna, and *El Lucero de Tacubaya* and *El Defensor de la Integridad Nacional*, both pro–Santa Anna.

22 *El Siglo XIX*, 5 October 1844.
23 *La Abeja*, 20 October 1844.
24 *El Jaliciense*, 29 October 1844, quoted in ibid., 6 November 1844.

provide details of all contracts signed for the Texas campaign. Bankhead commented that this was something 'his Excellency will find it very difficult to accomplish' because everyone knew that Santa Anna and a few favoured friends received an 'enormous douceur' on government contracts.[25] The Minister of Hacienda, Ignacio Trigueros, informed Congress that his department had not signed any contracts, but on 12 October his colleague at the Ministry of War, Isidro Reyes, replied that such matters were strictly confidential and that he would not reveal any details.[26] The deputies promptly set up a committee which advised them two days later that the executive must be obliged to provide the information requested.[27] When the cabinet refused, the deputies resolved to institute proceedings against General Reyes. Meanwhile, the opposition press opened a major campaign against all the ministers, calling for their resignation, and on 16 October Deputy Llaca made a widely reported speech in which he attacked everything the government had done since 1841. The promised regeneration, he said, had not happened. Instead, the *agiotistas* were more influential than ever, the civil and military lists were not paid and 'revenues are being scandalously wasted'. He demanded the sacking of the ministers and their replacement with honourable men.[28]

The first minister to capitulate under this pressure was Trigueros, who resigned and was replaced by a Santa Anna loyalist from Puebla, Antonio Haro y Tamariz.[29] He seems to have tried, presumably with Santa Anna's blessing, to defuse the criticism by cancelling some of the orders which had deprived the departments of their revenues.[30] The concessions did nothing to diminish the opposition campaign, and then the cabinet made what turned out to be a cardinal error, although presumably it was again acting on instructions from its absentee master. Santa Anna was formally appointed by the Minister of War to command an army that was to suppress a revolt in Jalisco. Within days, the Congress summoned all four ministers to answer charges being brought against them. The first of these was minor, involving alleged interference with the postal services. Haro y Tamariz admitted the charge, claiming that only letters from dissident regions had been intercepted. The second charge was more

25 C. Bankhead to Ld. Aberdeen, 24 September, 30 October 1844, P.R.O., F.O. 176, fols. 119, 152–4.
26 The letters from Trigueros and Reyes to the deputies are in *El Siglo XIX*, 13 October 1844.
27 'Dictamen de la comisión primera de hacienda, relativo a las contratas para el ejército de Tejas', 14 October 1844, in ibid., 18 October 1844.
28 The text of Llaca's speech is published in *La Abeja*, 19 October 1844. For other editorials attacking the cabinet, see ibid., 7 and 10 October; *El Mercurio Poblano*, 26 October 1844; *El Siglo XIX*, 29 October 1844.
29 For Haro y Tamariz's career, see J. Bazant, *Antonio Haro y Tamariz y sus aventuras políticas, 1811–1869* (Mexico, 1985).
30 *La Abeja*, 21 October, 1 November 1844.

serious. It stated that the power to appoint someone to command the army was vested exclusively in Congress and that therefore the Minister of War, who had signed the order appointing Santa Anna, had acted unconstitutionally. The ministers tried to defend themselves, but the deputies persisted and voted to arraign the Minister of War before a congressional Grand Jury.

The success and, to some extent, the timing of this campaign against Santa Anna and his government reflected the determination of opposition leaders like Gómez Pedraza and Lafragua to capitalize on the widespread despair among *hombres de bien* and on the popular resentment in the departments, especially against the hated head tax, which was provoking disorder in all directions.[31] It also involved, however, events which had taken place or at least been revealed in Guadalajara at the end of October. The government had ordered the Jalisco Treasury to provide several hundred thousand pesos to pay notes held by the *agiotistas* Cayetano Rubio, Manuel Escandón and José Ignacio Basadre.[32] That order, according to Carlos Bustamante, provoked the departmental authorities and assembly to draw up an initiative to be sent to the national Congress in which three demands were made: ministers were to be held responsible for their acts and Santa Anna's decree of 3 October relieving them of that responsibility was to be repealed; the decree of 21 August 1844 creating additional taxes was to be revoked; Congress was to reform the constitution and eliminate those articles harmful to the prosperity of the departments.

Following normal procedure in a *pronunciamiento*, the civilian assembly then asked the local commander general, Brigadier-General Pánfilo Galindo, and his garrison to support these demands. On 1 November, the garrison met and agreed to do so. The soldiers also voted to offer the leadership of the movement to a comrade who was at the time residing in Guadalajara. This was Paredes. The next day, he accepted the command and published a long manifesto, obviously prepared well in advance. This condemned every aspect of Santa Anna's government and demanded that every decision it had made between 10 October 1841 and 31 December 1843 be treated as conditional until reviewed and approved by Congress. Furthermore, until this revision was concluded, Santa Anna should cease to occupy the office of president.[33]

Hence, Paredes began to seek his revenge on Santa Anna for having humiliated him after the bizarre events on the night of 7 March 1843. Since his superficial reconciliation in October of that year, Paredes had

---

31 See *El Mercurio Poblano*, 26 October, 1844. The head tax provoked rebellions in the rural areas, especially in the south of the Mexico department; see Reina, *Las rebeliones campesinas*, pp. 107–16, 245–6.

32 Bustamante, *Apuntes*, p. 305.

33 Bustamante gives the full text of the various proclamations in ibid., 312–30.

bided his time patiently and largely in silence. He had accepted the seat in the Senate to which Santa Anna had appointed him, and he had occasionally attended the sessions in the early months of 1844. But he ceased all correspondence with his former comrade-in-arms for seven months. The silence was ominous, and Santa Anna must have known it. Then, to his evident surprise, Paredes chose to reopen contact between them; on 15 May 1844, he wrote to him, apparently in an attempt to defend his record as a soldier and his conduct since 1841. Santa Anna's reply was even more supercilious and barbed than usual. He was pleased, he said, that the silence between them had at long last been broken because it had grieved him not to receive a single word for so long, not even a word of congratulation on his election to the presidency. He knew that Paredes was still a friend and patriotic supporter of his government; he had not believed all the rumours he had heard to the contrary. Moreover, there had been no need for Paredes to justify his conduct because he never doubted his loyalty and that was why he had asked him to come to the capital to take over the presidency. It was unfortunate that events in March had frustrated his intentions, but he had had no choice but to do what he had done to safeguard the dignity of the presidency. He accepted that Paredes had intended no harm to the government or to himself and that all it amounted to was an 'indiscretion which caused you to say things which were interpreted in a way that was unfavourable to you'. He retained his affection for him, and he had the same regard for his abilities which had persuaded him since their co-operation at Zacatecas in 1835 to favour him with the insignia of a brigadier-general and to make him commander of Jalisco.[34]

The condescending tone and patronizing reprimands in this letter can have done nothing to persuade Paredes to forget the past, as Santa Anna urged him to do. A few weeks later, he broke his last ties with the regime by insisting on resigning his Senate seat, alleging ill-health.[35] Santa Anna, of course, realized that he had not been forgiven, and he knew that Paredes would be a focal point for the opposition against him. Hence, he tried one last ploy to remove him from the scene by ordering that he take over the governorship and military command of the distant department of Sonora. Within the military hierarchy, a posting to Sonora was a major demotion and the message was clear. It was, as one of Paredes' friends wrote to him, 'the final blow to your self-esteem and the peak of disdain for your services'.[36]

The order to go to Sonora, however, did give Paredes an excuse to

34 Santa Anna to M. Paredes y Arrillaga, 23 May 1844, in García, *Documentos inéditos*, vol. 56, pp. 69–70.
35 M. Paredes y Arrillaga to Senate, 23 July 1844, in ibid., p. 71.
36 J. V. Amador to M. Paredes y Arrillaga, 12 October 1844, in ibid., pp. 81–2.

leave Mexico City, and by early October he had returned to his family and friends in Guadalajara. Rumours immediately circulated that he was preparing a revolt, and Canalizo, Rejón and other ministers wrote private letters to say, as if to reassure themselves, that they did not doubt his loyalty.[37] Paredes wrote respectful letters to Santa Anna, and he was careful to distance himself from the liberal federalists, who were among many who assumed it was only a matter of time before he rebelled. In answer to letters from Otero, for example, he wrote as follows:

Do not think that I am trying to proclaim any political plan or even to provoke one; that is what the anarchists want so that they can achieve their aims of destroying the army and proclaiming their lamented federation. I am determined, very determined, and you can publish this letter if you like, to sustain at any cost the Bases Orgánicas and the present government. If my enemies say federation, I say Bases.[38]

Nevertheless, with his allies, if not agents, keeping him regularly supplied with reports on events and the public mood of hostility towards Santa Anna, Paredes began to sound out support among his fellow officers. Envoys were dispatched throughout the central and northern departments. Pedro Cortazar wrote from Celaya on 26 October that he would not move until Paredes had at least four thousand men, and from San Luis Potosí, Pedro Barasorda reported that following his talks with various generals, Romero at Morelia had pledged his support, General Amador would do what he could, García Conde had promised the backing of Chihuahua and Durango.[39] Bernardo Flores wrote from Lagos that 'I have seventy men but no rifles', asking that, if weapons could be sent, someone should also come to show his men how to use them.[40] Other arrangements were put in hand to acquire money and munitions, and on the day on which he issued his proclamation, Paredes gave orders to customs officials at S. Blas and Mazatlán to issue notes payable by the customs and offering discounts for cash.[41]

Once the *pronunciamiento* was declared, letters of support poured into Guadalajara, although Cortazar decided not to join what was rapidly becoming a bandwagon.[42] Some of the letters were conditional, saying

37 These letters are in the García Collection, Paredes y Arrillaga Papers, 141/40–5.
38 M. Paredes y Arrillaga to M. Otero, 4 September 1844, Otero Archive. Paredes' letters to Santa Anna were published in *El Lucero de Tacubaya*, 21 November 1844.
39 P. Cortazar to M. Paredes y Arrillaga, 26 October 1844, García Collection, Paredes y Arrillaga Papers, 141/82; P. Barasorda to M. Paredes y Arrillaga, 25 October 1844, ibid., 141/83. F. Franco, commander general of Zacatecas, also promised his support; 12 November 1844, ibid., 141/167.
40 B. Flores to M. Paredes y Arrillaga, 27 October 1844, ibid., 141/97.
41 Paredes y Arrillaga to J. M. Castaños, 2 November 1844, ibid., 141/107. The customs officer at Mazatlán replied that he would cooperate, and Paredes noted, 'Enterado, gracias y que sus buenos servicios serán atendidos'; ibid., 141/133.
42 Cortazar wrote on 3 November that he would do nothing to oppose him; ibid., 141/108.

that they would not give support if Paredes intended to restore the federation. He replied that that was not his intention or that of the departments which were backing him. In a letter to Angel Guzmán, he stated that his aims were to restore the situation which had prevailed at the time of the Tacubaya accord; to force Santa Anna to account for the 60 million pesos spent in the past two years; to end the activities of speculators; and, finally, to return to Congress its full constitutional liberties.[43]

With so much correspondence and so many agents travelling the highways, Canalizo and his ministers were well aware of what was going on, but they did try to withhold the news from Congress for several days.[44] Once the congressmen were formally told of the events in Guadalajara and in a deliberate act of defiance, they agreed to consider the Jalisco assembly initiative. Santa Anna also had his network of informers; he too must have known that the revolt had been well prepared and was gaining significant support. Thus, he chose to return to the capital, where he arrived on 19 November, ostensibly to prepare to lead an army against Paredes. He displayed his customary energy, and military units were dispatched to the north to wait for him at Querétaro.[45] His efforts to calm the political opposition were less successful. The newspapers warned him not to attempt to close the Congress, pointing out that by accepting a military command, he had given up his presidential immunities and that he could, if things went badly, be subjected to a court martial like any ordinary soldier.[46] He summoned a selected group of senators and deputies to Guadalupe where he was staying, and in a meeting which lasted from 9 a.m. to 4:30 p.m., he sought to reassure them that he had no hostile intentions towards the Congress.[47] Secret talks were also held with liberal leaders, who were approached by Haro y Tamariz to see if a deal could be arranged. They told him that nothing could be agreed upon unless the government was willing to restore the federation, and when this was put to Santa Anna, he accepted the condition, saying he would implement it after Paredes was defeated. But the liberals, according to Lafragua, who was one of the negotiators, assumed he was lying.[48]

Bankhead again seems to have assessed the public mood correctly when he wrote on 12 November that 'it is not to be denied, however, that the

43 M. Paredes y Arrillaga to A. Guzmán, 27 November 1844, ibid., 141/339.
44 There are dozens of letters in the Paredes archive relating to the revolt. See also Robertson, 'Paredes y Arrillaga'.
45 Santa Anna issued his usual proclamation defending his conduct; the text is in *El Siglo XIX*, 26 November 1844.
46 *La Abeja*, 20 November 1844.
47 The meeting took place on 20 November 1844; see *El Siglo XIX*, 22 November 1844. Santa Anna and his cabinet also met with Bankhead to discuss British proposals on Texas. Bankhead's report of the meeting, dated 29 November, is in P.R.O., F.O. 50, 177, fols. 76–83.
48 Lafragua memoir, Lafragua Collection, 398.

prestige heretofore attached to General Santa Anna's name has of late been much damaged for even with the apathy naturally belonging to this People, they now begin to express themselves loudly in opposition to the wholesale corruption that has distinguished General Santa Anna's administration and the fallacy of the late attempts, by prohibitions, to prop up an artificial home manufacture'.[49] Seemingly frustrated at every turn, Santa Anna left Guadalupe with his army on 22 November to take the road to Querétaro in the hope of rescuing his position with a spectacular military victory over Paredes. Rich merchant houses in the capital were said to have loaned him 800,000 pesos to see him on his way.[50]

The events of the next two weeks were extremely dramatic, even compared with the normal level of turmoil in Mexican political life. There were two scenes of action, Querétaro and Mexico City. Santa Anna travelled quickly, arriving in Querétaro on Sunday, 24 November. Unusually, and much to his displeasure, none of the local dignitaries were there to greet him. There were two reasons for this calculated snub. First, Querétaro had already declared its support for the Jalisco initiative which formed the basis of Paredes' *pronunciamiento*. Second, the city's authorities considered that as Santa Anna was now technically an army officer and no longer president, his status did not require all the usual public courtesies. The next day, Santa Anna summoned the governor and commander general and reprimanded them for not arresting those members of the departmental junta who had signed the initiative to Congress. Then he summoned the deputies and the council, and at noon he gave them twenty-four hours to retract what they had said and done. Emergency meetings of various bodies in the city were held, but no retraction was forthcoming. Santa Anna carried out his threat and began to arrest the public officials, ordering that they be taken immediately to Perote. After the intervention of local clergy, he rescinded that order but still demanded a retraction and apology. Again, neither was forthcoming.[51]

While these events were taking place at Querétaro, things were also developing rapidly in the capital. The deputies had resolved to proceed with charges against the cabinet for appointing Santa Anna to the military command, and then news arrived of his behaviour at Querétaro. The deputies at once insisted that the ministers make personal appearances before them, but when they appeared on 30 November, they refused to answer any questions, making only disparaging and insulting remarks to the assembled congressmen.[52] The reason for the ministers' confidence was that on the day before, 29 November, a draft decree had been drawn

49 C. Bankhead to Ld. Aberdeen, 12 November 1844, P.R.O., F.O. 50, 177, fols. 3–7.
50 *La Abeja*, 23 November 1844.
51 Details in Bustamante, *Apuntes*, p. 340.
52 *El Siglo XIX*, 1 December 1844.

up, almost certainly with Santa Anna's knowledge, which ordered three things: that Congress be suspended immediately; that Santa Anna continue as president and Canalizo as his substitute; that the government take whatever steps were necessary to restore order and conduct the war in Texas, without increasing taxes.

This decree closing Congress was not published immediately and remained secret because it was first taken to Santa Anna for his approval.[53] Hence, when the deputies reassembled on 1 December, they were ignorant of the threat which hung over them. Again, they demanded the presence of the cabinet, but only Haro y Tamariz put in an appearance and said nothing. Messages were sent to Canalizo, but his reply was that he and his ministers were too busy to attend. In reply, the deputies voted to remain in permanent session until they were given a satisfactory explanation of Santa Anna's conduct at Querétaro. By midday, several had left, and when they tried to return, they found their way blocked by armed guards, who said they were acting on government orders. When this was confirmed, it was clear to the remaining deputies what was happening, but refusing to be intimidated, they spent the next several hours composing a protest. In this, they stated that they would not accept any orders issued by Santa Anna because his military appointment was invalid; the ministers were to be arraigned for their conduct; Santa Anna's actions at Querétaro were unacceptable.[54] On the same evening of 1 December, the senators went to their own chamber, only to be refused entry. They went to the home of their president and discussed the situation. At 1 a.m. on 2 December, they too released a strongly worded protest, denouncing all the arbitrary acts of Santa Anna and the executive.[55]

Exactly what happened next is not entirely clear. It seems that late at night on 1 December, government officials went to the home of the president of the Chamber of Deputies, Luis Solana, to get the keys to the chamber. They did not succeed in their mission and the deputies were able to reassemble on 2 December, when they voted to approve the following motions: that Congress did not acknowledge that the executive had the power to close it; that the executive's actions were unconstitutional and illegal; that Congress would continue in session in a convenient location. Finally, it was proposed and agreed that the deputies would not leave the capital and would hold themselves ready to attend when called. Of the fifty-five members present, forty-five signed the statement.[56]

53 Probably by Baranda, who went to Querétaro on 30 November; ibid.
54 'Protesta de la representación nacional', 1 December 1844, in *Correspondencia entre el Supremo Gobierno y el General D. Antonio López de Santa Anna* (Mexico, 1845), p. 1.
55 The text of the Senate protest is in ibid., p. vii.
56 The sequence of events, congressional debates, decisions, etc. are based on press reports of the time.

At the same time that this session was in progress, Canalizo published the closure decree of 29 November, ordering also that authorities and employees who wished to continue in post must take an oath of obedience to the decree and warning press editors and publishers that anything subversive would be punished with a four-month jail sentence at Ulúa. The editors of *El Siglo XIX* decided to suspend publication but others refused to be intimidated. The Mexico departmental assembly and city council had already voted on 30 November to withdraw recognition of the government, a decision released on 3 December. Canalizo responded by sending soldiers to dissolve the council. Then, judges on the Supreme Court and the Military Court and both the archbishop and his chapter protested the closure of the Congress and refused to take an oath of obedience to the 29 November decree.[57] News also arrived that the governor and assembly of Puebla had voted to withdraw recognition.

During the next forty-eight hours, letters from Santa Anna were written and probably reached the city. He wrote separately to the newly appointed Minister of War, José Ignacio Basadre, and to Canalizo, applauding the 29 November decree and urging them to stand firm: 'Revolution is fought with revolution and now that we have placed ourselves in the middle of it, we must win or die'. The protests of the deputies and senators were, he added, 'quite ridiculous', and he advised Canalizo to arrest Gómez Pedraza, who he knew for certain was the 'brains behind the disturbances'. In another letter to Haro y Tamariz, he expressed his sympathy that his brother had signed the Puebla protest, adding that perhaps he had been forced to do so, and he advised that Canalizo should remove loyal troops to Tacubaya as soon as possible, keeping them from possible seduction by the opposition.[58]

This last advice, written by Santa Anna on 6 December, was too late. Shortly after noon on that day, Haro y Tamariz hurriedly wrote to him to tell him that, 'at this very moment', General Céspedes and about three hundred men with a 'despicable little cannon' had pronounced from the Citadel.[59] In fact, several army units had already decided to desert the government, and the man who was approached to lead them, or who was involved beforehand – it is not clear which – was José Joaquín de Herrera. By 2 p.m., he and a number of deputies, more of whom were arriving all the time, were in the San Francisco monastery. From there he sent Canalizo a note calling on him to restore constitutional order. Canalizo replied almost immediately, offering to hand over power provided that his own personal safety and that of his ministers and other officials in the

57 García Collection, Paredes y Arrillaga Papers, 141/382, 408.
58 Santa Anna's letters were published in *El Siglo XIX*, 11 and 12 December 1844.
59 Published in ibid. Haro also sent him 6,000 pesos and carte blanche to take what he needed from his haciendas; Bazant, *Haro y Tamariz*, p. 36.

palace were guaranteed.[60] Herrera gave that assurance, and about 3 p.m. the 'three-hour revolution' was over, without a shot being fired. When the news reached the deputies in the monastery – there were thirty-two present by this time – they discussed what the next step should be and Deputy Llaca proposed a symbolic march on foot back to their chamber. This was agreed to with acclamation, and the deputies marched out onto the streets now crowded with people, some to be carried on the shoulders of their enthusiastic supporters back to the palace, where they arrived at 4:30 p.m. to reopen the Congress.[61]

With the sight of the deputies en route to the palace and the news spreading rapidly around the city, the populace took to the streets. Both sides – government and opposition – had been trying in previous days to persuade leaders of the *barrios* to organize demonstrations. According to Carlos Bustamante, government ministers wanted them to pronounce in favour of a federation, and as Canalizo had used the same tactic in October 1841 in the final days of the Bustamante regime, it is quite feasible that, as a last resort, he tried the same manoeuvre.[62] It failed and the crowds opted to vent their anger on Santa Anna. His imposing bronze statue in the plaza del Volador was pulled to the ground and destroyed, other statues and portraits were defaced, his name was removed from the recently completed theatre and one gang went to the cemetery where his amputated leg was buried, dug it up and dragged it through the streets. The cry was now 'Death to the Cripple: long live Congress'.[63]

To what extent the 6 December coup was prearranged, thus fitting the pattern of other such events, is by no means clear. According to Herrera's biographer, 'It was a people's revolution against tyranny, accomplished with little bloodshed and was the most universal and spontaneous uprising of popular opinion since 1821'.[64] Other indications are, however, that it was far from spontaneous but rather was the result of a carefully prepared and well-executed plot. According to Rejón, who was Minister of Relations at the time, the government knew what was going on and that it was all being organized in the deputies' clubs: 'It was public knowledge that the centre of the revolution was in congress'.[65] On 5 December, Paredes wrote to his supporters urging them to act, and on the next day

60 *El Siglo XIX*, 7 December 1844.
61 Details in ibid., 25 December 1844. Carlos Bustamante was one of those carried back to the palace. He gives a vivid description of the day's events in *Apuntes*, pp. 362–4.
62 Ibid., p. 361. On 5 December, *barrio* leaders issued a pro-Congress statement: 'Acta levantada por los barrios de esta capital', in *El Siglo XIX*, 7 December 1844.
63 Details from press reports and Bankhead's report of 31 December 1844, P.R.O., F.O. 50, 177, fols. 147–59. Santa Anna's leg was rescued by an army officer and reburied later.
64 Cotner, *Herrera*, p. 106.
65 M. C. Rejón, *Justificación de la conducta de Manuel Crescencio Rejón desde octubre de 1841 hasta la fecha* (New Orleans, 1846).

one of them immediately replied to tell him of their success. On 9 December, General Pedro García Conde, who became Minister of War in the new administration and who had in October promised to back Paredes, also wrote to say, 'I have fulfilled exactly my undertaking to you and constitutional order is now re-established in this capital'.[66]

The triumphant deputies reopened their sessions on the evening of 6 December amid an atmosphere, to use Carlos Bustamante's words, of 'utmost joy'.[67] After the euphoria of the day had subsided and the crowds of people who had poured into the palace had left, they began to consider the future. Moves were started to impeach Santa Anna and his executive, and four new ministers were selected. They were García Conde (War), Pedro Echeverría (Hacienda), Luis Cuevas (Relations) and Riva Palacio (Justice). On the next day, 7 December, the Senate voted by 38 votes to 1 – the latter thought to have been cast by Canalizo's brother, Rafael – to make Herrera provisional president. Former acting president Canalizo was already under arrest and a search was ordered for the four ministers, who had fled. Haro had gone to join Santa Anna and Basadre was later picked up on the Querétaro highway disguised as a friar.[68] Baranda and Rejón remained in hiding for the time being. Finally, a new city council was elected, including, significantly for the future, the liberal federalists Olaguíbel, Otero and Lafragua.

The victory seemed complete and overwhelming, but Santa Anna was not a man to give up easily and the Herrera government knew it. Over the next few weeks, it adopted a dual policy of trying to persuade him to give up peacefully and at the same time preparing to defend the capital against what they believed would be an attempt by him to besiege or attack it. The day after the coup, García Conde wrote to Santa Anna to say that he was relieved of his command and ordering that he appear before Congress to answer the charges against him. Santa Anna replied that he would defend his constitutional rights, and in a letter to Herrera on 18 December he insisted that he was still the legal president.[69] He instructed Herrera to relinquish his office, warning that he had twelve thousand men and had every intention of coming to the capital to restore his government. More letters were exchanged over the next few days, with Santa Anna repeatedly denouncing Herrera and the coup (he said he had irrefutable proof that it was organized in Congress) and claiming that it was Canalizo and not he who had issued the 29 November decree.

66 Paredes correspondence in García Collection, Paredes y Arrillaga Papers, 141/420, 431, 445.
67 Bustamante, *Apuntes*, p. 363.
68 Published in *El Siglo XIX*, 13 December 1844.
69 The letters to and from Santa Anna over the next few weeks referred to in following paragraphs were all published by the government in the collection entitled *Corespondencia entre el Supremo Gobierno y el General D. Antonio López de Santa Anna*.

Herrera knew that he had to take Santa Anna's belligerent threats seriously. First, Congress voted to refuse to recognize him as president, and then a series of steps were taken to defend the city. New military units were authorized to be called 'volunteer defenders of the laws' and weapons were distributed to them. Bravo was summoned to take command of the defence, and until his arrival from the south, Valencia was put in charge. He had been noticeably silent in recent weeks, but on 15 December he issued a statement saying that illness had prevented him from partic- ipating.[70] True or not, the government accepted his explanation and appointed him second-in-command to Bravo. All taxes on foodstuffs brought into the capital were lifted. When Bravo arrived on 24 December with his own military forces, there were said to be nine thousand regular army personnel and nine thousand volunteers ready to face Santa Anna. On 26 December, a state of siege was declared, and two days later Valencia announced that Santa Anna was approaching the city. He called on all citizens to fight from the rooftops and balconies if necessary. While there was no panic among the public, and life proceeded as normal as the outbreak of hostilities was awaited, there was an atmosphere of great tension in the city. The ringing of church bells was forbidden, meetings in the streets were prohibited and hotel owners were instructed to tell the authorities of any new guests who might be Santa Anna infiltrators. For three days, the population waited for Santa Anna to begin his assault. Finally, on New Year's Eve, it was announced that he had gone around the capital and was heading south for Puebla.

The details of Santa Anna's movements need not concern us, and it is not known why he decided not to attempt an attack on the capital, but despite his bravado and increasingly intemperate language, he must have realized the weakness of his position. Declarations of support for the coup had poured in from all over the country, and in an almost hysterical outburst of pent-up resentment, his entire career and personality were dissected and ridiculed by the press and pamphleteers. He was now de- scribed as the 'Evil spirit, Devil of ambition and discord'; 'that accu- mulation of inconsistencies and vices, that ungrateful, disloyal man'. He was no more than a despicable bandit, an 'aspiring dictator', 'nasty and immoral', who at San Jacinto and elsewhere had demonstrated his 'military ineptitude'.

In possession of large sums of money seized by his men from the mint at Guanajuato and from other places, Santa Anna brought his army, which he claimed to be twelve thousand strong (government agents put it at five thousand) down to Puebla, where he arrived on 3 January 1845. At 4 p.m. on that day, he sent a note to the commander general of the city,

70 Valencia's statement is in *El Siglo XIX*, 18 December 1844.

Ignacio Inclán, ordering him not to oppose his entry. Inclán replied at 5:30 p.m. that he would fight to defend the city. The next day, Santa Anna gave Inclán two hours to surrender or face an attack with no quarter given to any military of any rank. Again, displaying considerable courage, Inclán repeated his refusal, telling Santa Anna that although he might have more men, he, Inclán, had right on his side.

Santa Anna apparently opened fire on the city, but after a few days with no surrender in sight, his men began to desert in droves, and knowing that Bravo and Paredes with several thousand reinforcements were heading towards him, he decided on 9 January to open negotiations. Haro y Tamariz and General José María Mendoza, acting as his envoys, were allowed to travel to the capital to deliver a note to Herrera.[71] In this note Santa Anna offered to resign the presidency provided that he and his officers were allowed to leave the country, retaining their salaries, and provided that there was no persecution of his supporters. García Conde replied the next day, telling him plainly that the government would not negotiate. He must surrender himself and stand trial before Congress.

On receipt of this rejection and with hundreds of his men deserting, Santa Anna concluded that he was trapped and prepared to escape. On 10 January, he sent a note to Herrera to tell him that he was going to Veracruz, where he would embark as soon as possible. At dawn on the next day, he climbed into his carriage and, with an escort of five hundred men, set out for the coast. He reached the village of Vigas, where he dismissed most of his escort, and with just five personal servants, he left for the final leg of the journey to El Encero, where he hoped to collect his baggage. He had already made arrangements to have his wife and children brought to him, but at 9:30 p.m. on the evening of 15 January, near the village of Jico about ten miles south of Jalapa, a small group of locals came across him and his servants and detained them, refusing a bribe of 2,000 pesos which Santa Anna offered for their help. He was taken back to the village and handed over to the military commander. According to the latter's report, Santa Anna was 'very ill-treated' and therefore allowed to rest the night. Then he was taken to Jalapa, where he was placed in the town jail.[72]

From jail, Santa Anna at once composed an angry letter to Herrera. He was not being allowed to see his wife and children, people had insulted him in the streets, he had no privacy, no servant and 'I cannot sleep because of the thoughtless noise of the guards'. Over the next few weeks, he wrote many such letters complaining of his treatment, particularly after he was transferred to the prison at Perote. In a bizarre mixture of

71 For details of Haro's reception in the capital, see Bazant, *Haro y Tamariz*, pp. 38–9.
72 All details are from *Correspondencia*.

appeals for clemency, better food and the return of his wife's wardrobe, which had been confiscated, he inserted demands that his record of service to the nation be acknowledged, that his rights as a citizen be respected and that he be allowed to keep all his assets as well as his salary. Indeed, he maintained that the government owed him 89,000 pesos and he wanted it paid. At the same time that he sent these demands to the capital, he tried secretly (the letters were intercepted) to arrange for some of his funds to be transferred abroad. In four letters on 18 January, he told his agents to transfer his funds to the English firm of Manning and Mackintosh, which had an office at Veracruz, to give them the protection of the English flag and 'to save them from being confiscated'.[73]

Throughout this correspondence, and despite Santa Anna's attempts to appeal to old friendships and solidarity among army officers, the Herrera government remained inflexible, refusing to give in to any of his demands and rejecting his complaints that he was being left to starve in prison. Congress formally indicted him for treason and ordered him to stand trial, but as the weeks passed while the case was being prepared, other issues more important than the disgraced hero of Tampico began to take priority. In May 1845, an amnesty was declared for all political offenders with the exception of Santa Anna, Canalizo and his four ministers. Santa Anna was sentenced to lifelong exile in Venezuela, but retaining half a general's pay, and the others were condemned to ten years' foreign exile.

Santa Anna began his preparations to leave, offering his several estates for sale at less than half their value, although apparently without immediate success, and, as always, he composed an emotional farewell manifesto to defend his record, his conduct and his patriotism. Finally, he embarked at Antigua, near Veracruz, on 3 June 1845, his career, it seemed, truly over. He was never a man to be easily forgiven or forgotten, but the words of the editor of *El Siglo XIX* well sum up the surprise and relief of the Mexican *hombres de bien* at the way things had turned out: 'What have we done? Overthrown the despot. What has it cost us? Nothing'.[74]

73 Ibid.
74 *El Siglo XIX,* 11 December 1844.

11

Herrera and the rise of Paredes y Arrillaga

> We saw the patriot tumblers
> The twenty-third of May;
> They met in merry Mexico
> To dance their country away.[1]

The 6 December coup was an oddity in the gallery of Mexican *pronunciamientos*. Although almost certainly prearranged and not the spontaneous event sometimes depicted, it was not a party political affair and did not have ideological motives. It was not staged, for example, by federalists, centralists, monarchists or any other group intent on constitutional reform. Nor did its perpetrators represent any particular interest group such as merchants or clergy, and while Paredes definitely had personal ambitions, it was not a conventional coup involving army officers seeking advancement or political power. In contrast – and this feature is unusual, if not unique – it did reflect a rare consensus of opinion among the myriad political, social and economic groups. Without exception, they came to agree, coincidentally or by arrangement, on one common objective and that was to remove Santa Anna from power. In short, Santa Anna had alienated *hombres de bien* in general, and by his conduct had brought about an unprecedented alliance of all the rival forces on the political stage. For the time being, they were willing to forget their differences and unite in the movement against him.

This anti–Santa Anna alliance, however, was a strictly temporary phenomenon; once its objective was achieved, it disintegrated and the various rival factions rapidly began to work to fill the vacuum left by the dictator's departure. Within days of 6 December, the politicians began to discuss their future strategy. The conservatives naturally wanted to retain the centralized form of government and the pre-eminence of the upper echelons of *hombres de bien,* and they found, perhaps to their surprise, that the moderates led by Gómez Pedraza shared their hopes, at least for the

---

1 Verse published in English in *La Voz del Pueblo,* 24 May 1845, referring to a ball hosted on the night of 23 May by British ambassador Charles Bankhead.

immediate future. This brought them into renewed conflict with the radical federalists, who saw an opportunity for the immediate restoration of federalism. As Lafragua put it, 'Tyranny was destroyed and division followed'.[2] Such divisions in the political spectrum, of course, were not unexpected and were simply a continuation of the argument conducted for the past decade. Rather more surprising, if not astonishing in the circumstances, was the rapid recovery of a pro–Santa Anna faction. We do not know the identities of its spokesmen – it may be assumed that Tornel was involved – but even before the end of December and before Santa Anna's capitulation, the editors of *El Siglo XIX* warned that *santanistas* were already actively trying to corrupt the army and to discredit the government.[3] Even more significant for the future, there were persistent rumours of secret negotiations between federalists and *santanistas*, with the latter allegedly offering to restore the 1824 constitution in return for support for their leader.[4]

All the parties looked to the new provisional president to support their cause. Herrera was known as a moderate liberal federalist, and over a long career since independence, he had always been identified with that position.[5] Born at Jalapa in 1792 to a family of above-average financial means – his father was an official in the postal service – he joined the Spanish army in 1809 and over the next few years participated in several campaigns against the insurgency. Then in 1820 he retired from the army and opened a drugstore at Perote but soon began to make contact with insurgent leaders. Like so many others of his generation, he joined Iturbide and the Plan of Iguala, thus resuming a military career. Quickly promoted to brigadier-general, he was a member of the first Congress, participated in the opposition to Iturbide and was jailed by him. After the emperor's fall, he was made military commander of Mexico City and later Minister of War. Over the decade of federalism, he occupied several other senior military posts and again served in Congress as well as another spell as Minister of War in 1833. He retained his sound reputation when the centralists took control and was given several important jobs, including the presidency of the Military Tribunal, and his name was mentioned several times as a potential presidential candidate for the federalists. As a recognized federalist leader, he was persecuted by Santa Anna in the 1842 election period, but again he survived and kept his seniority to such

2 Lafragua memoir, Lafragua Collection, 398.
3 *El Siglo XIX*, 29 December 1844.
4 From his exile in Havana, Santa Anna suggested an alliance with Gómez Farías in July 1845; C. A. Hutchinson, 'Valentín Gómez Farías and the Movement for the Return of General Santa Anna to Mexico in 1846', in T. E. Cotner and C. E. Castañeda, eds., *Essays in Mexican history* (Austin, Tex., 1958), pp. 169–91.
5 For a good, full-length biography, see Cotner, *The Military and Political career of José Joaquín de Herrera*.

an extent that by 1844 he was president of the Council of Government. It was in that capacity that he became acting president of the republic for eight days in September until Canalizo had returned, and when the 6 December coup took place, still president of the Council, he assumed the presidential office, in which he was confirmed by Congress the following day.

In terms of political belief, therefore, Herrera was a moderate liberal federalist, and although by no means wealthy, he was a long-established member of the social elite of *hombres de bien*. Furthermore, he was one of the few army officers of the time who enjoyed an unblemished reputation as a man of integrity and personal honesty. He was universally respected, in Zamacois' words, as a 'man in whom were found honesty, modesty, good judgement and common sense'.[6] He was also, however, someone who 'lacked the type of dynamic personality necessary under the circumstances surrounding his term of office'.[7] Nevertheless, his elevation to the presidency was initially well received by all sectors, each of which expected to benefit, but in his early speeches to Congress, he revealed a perhaps unexpected firmness of purpose. To the anger of the radicals, he insisted that the Bases Orgánicas were to remain in force until such time as a full consultation procedure in the departments about constitutional reform could be conducted. He made no secret of his preference for federalism, but he gave priority to the importance of legal procedures, which inevitably took time. Again surprisingly, he announced that one of his first priorities was reform of the army and also of the civil bureaucracy, 'this impenetrable chaos', as he put it, especially in the area of public finances.[8] Finally, he promised to resolve the problem of Texas in an honourable and acceptable fashion.

With this manifesto, which also included the standard commitments to improve law and order, the administration of justice and the economy, Herrera confirmed his objective of steering a moderate course of change. His approach was well summed up by his Minister of Relations, Luis G. Cuevas:

In society, as in nature, everything is successive, and if the wish today is that the republic should preserve peace and order, we must first pay attention to the most urgent needs of the administration. Once the fundamentals of this are established, all the improvements implied by the existence of a constituted government and a contented nation in agreement with the system by which it is ruled will follow.[9]

6 Quoted in ibid., p. 110.
7 Ibid., p. 151.
8 Herrera's speeches to Congress, 15 December 1844 and 1 January 1845, in *El Siglo XIX*, 15 December 1844, 2 January 1845.
9 *Memoria de Relaciones* (1845), in ibid., 8–12 April 1845.

Hence, he promised 'gradual and prudent reforms' but only after due consideration and consultation within the existing constitutional framework.[10] While this consultation process was being carried out in the Congress and departments, he began to reward his allies or those whose support he needed. Valencia, for example, was made president of the Council of Government and Paredes became commander general of the Mexico department, an appointment it was soon clear he felt was not a proper reward for his services. Riva Palacio, now identified with the moderate liberals, was made Minister of Justice, and Pedro García Conde was acceptable to the army as Minister of War. Several of the more unpopular measures imposed by Santa Anna were quickly repealed. A whole range of taxes, including the head tax, were cancelled, as was the forced loan of August 1843, and on 1 March the government announced that Treasury creditors whose contracts had been signed during the Santa Anna regime would be paid only a legal interest rate of 6 per cent on what was owed to them.[11] Unsold temporalities were returned to the charitable institutional owners from which they had been confiscated, money was allocated to hospitals and schools and what was left of the Pious Fund of the Californias was returned to episcopal jurisdiction. Clearly reflecting Herrera's federalist inclination, Congress quickly began to discuss and later agreed to the reallocation of most tax revenues to the departments, and the government left no doubt that it favoured a decentralization of power away from the capital.

In this programme of reform, Herrera managed to remove some of the causes of popular discontent, particularly in the departments, several of which also abolished their own head taxes, but there were many other groups which saw an opportunity to promote their interests. The tobacco lobby was again prominent, with the growers of Orizaba complaining that they had not been paid for their tobacco. The government accepted their case and managed to borrow 100,000 pesos at 6 per cent interest to meet their claim.[12] In contrast, the former private tobacco monopoly shareholders, including Escandón and Rubio, bitterly protested against the suspension of payments due to them.[13] Rubio was also at the centre of a dispute concerning his ownership of the salt mines at Peñón (San Luis Potosí) which Santa Anna had sold to him. Rival local interests challenged the validity of his title, and he appealed to Herrera to confirm that he had acted legally and properly.[14] The different sectors in the cotton

10 Speech to Congress, 1 January 1845, in ibid., 2 January 1845.
11 Dublán and Lozano, *Legislación mexicana*, vol. 5, pp. 7–8.
12 Reports in *El Siglo XIX*, 1 and 6 February 1845.
13 'Representación dirigida a la augusta cámara de senadores por los antiguos empresarios del tabaco', 19 February 1845, in ibid., 21 February 1845.
14 Rubio published two long defences of his ownership, in ibid., 12 and 13 March 1845.

bloc were as vocal as ever. Puebla and Jalisco manufacturers asked for the ban on imported cotton to be relaxed, while growers from around the Veracruz region opposed the request, insisting that there had been a good harvest and that plentiful domestic supplies were available.[15] Both the Guanajuato and Zacatecas departmental assemblies wanted their local mints, which Santa Anna had rented to British companies, returned to public ownership, and Tabasco wanted all taxes on locally produced cocoa lifted as well as the repeal of measures they considered harmful to their local dye-wood industry.[16] Finally, the Dirección General de Industria, in a report signed by Alamán, pleaded for urgent reform of the general import–export tariff.[17] These and many other groups put pressure on the new administration, but Herrera was unable to satisfy all of them, and he and his ministers refused to act hastily or 'innovate without a plan or system'.[18] They referred some of the demands, that from Tabasco, for example, to the Dirección de Industria, which advised rejection; on others, like the Guanajuato and Zacatecas mints, it concluded that the private contracts were legal.[19]

Apart from these individual and departmental matters, Herrera had indicated that his government would concentrate its attention on several broader national issues. There were three of these in particular: the army, constitutional reform and Texas. As a former Minister of War, Herrera had already proved anxious to improve the army, and it was evident as soon as he took office that he still believed fundamental change was required. He promised in a speech on 2 January to publish his ideas, and a few weeks later he issued a pamphlet entitled *Breves ideas sobre el arreglo provisional para el ejército mexicano*. In this he advocated several radical changes, which included the complete separation of military and civilian authorities, the formation of a general staff, reform of the system of commands general and the creation of a militia force based in the de-

---

15 'Representación que se ha elevado a la cámara de diputados por las comisiones de los departamentos cosecheros de algodón', 3 April 1845, in ibid., 5 April 1845; 'Representación solicitando que las augustas cámaras del congreso no levantan la prohibición de algodón en rama extranjero', 11 April 1845, in ibid., 7 August 1845. The latter was from cotton growers in the Acapulco region. For further details, see Potash, *Banco de Avío*, p. 143; Thomson, *Puebla de los Angeles*, pp. 258–9.

16 The petitions from Guanajuato, Zacatecas and Tabasco are in *El Siglo XIX*, 7 April, 15 May, 7 August 1845.

17 'Representación que ha elevado la dirección general de industria al supremo gobierno, pidiendo se reforme el arancel vigente de las aduanas marítimas', 7 March 1845, in ibid., 18 March 1845. A new tariff was published on 4 October; see Dublán and Lozano, *Legislación mexicana*, vol. 5, pp. 40–92, and Potash, *Banco de Avío*, p. 144.

18 *Memoria de Relaciones* (1845).

19 'Memoria sobre el estado de la agricultura e industria en el año de 1844 que la Dirección General de estos ramos presenta al Supremo Gobierno' (Mexico, 1845), in Alamán, *Obras: Documentos diversos*, vol. 2, pp. 258–63.

partments.[20] Some of these proposals were quickly implemented. The military map of the country was redrawn, and in place of the twenty-two commands general, four military divisions and five general commands were created, with the latter concentrated on the border areas to the north and south. The union of political and military power in the departments was stopped, and it was made clear that henceforth civil governors and military commanders would be kept strictly to their respective jurisdictions. The prosecution of thieves and other felons, which had been transferred to the military courts in a vain attempt to reduce the crime rate, was also given back to the civil magistrates.

This reduction in the army's status and powers naturally concerned senior military officers, but they were even more incensed by Herrera's decision to establish a militia. In a decree of 4 June, much to the delight of the federalists, who had long resented the effective abolition of the civil militia in 1835, a new national militia was created. Known as Defensores Voluntarios de la Independencia y de las Leyes, it was obviously intended as a counterweight to the regular army. Enlistment was to be voluntary, with recruits receiving no pay and not enjoying the military *fuero*. The units were to be entirely under the command of the local civil authority and called to arms only in the event of a foreign invasion or 'by order of the supreme government'.[21] Finally, the government promised to introduce a promotion system in the army based on merit and to address the problem of surplus officers by whom, it was alleged, both the army and the Treasury were overburdened. According to *El Siglo XIX*, there were at least 532 infantry and cavalry officers on indefinite leave, including twenty-nine generals, and in total they were costing the Treasury 820,830 pesos in pay. Calculating that there were eighteen officers for every five soldiers, a 'truly monstrous proportion', the editor remarked, 'It is not the army which is devouring the Treasury but rather the multitude of officers'.[22]

Herrera's reforms of the army were, to say the least, controversial, provoking what must have been expected resistance from reactionary military officers. His attitude to constitutional reform was equally contentious, and his cautious step-by-step approach antagonized all the political parties. He had committed himself to sustaining the Bases Orgánicas for the time being on the grounds that they were the legal charter of the nation and therefore the 'only point of departure in our present social state'.[23] At the same time, his reputation, words and actions, notably his creation of the militia and the return of revenues to departments, appeared

20 Details of the changes are given in *Memoria de Guerra* (1845).
21 Dublán and Lozano, *Legislación mexicana*, vol. 5, pp. 19–22.
22 *El Siglo XIX*, 11 July 1845.
23 Speech to Congress, 15 December 1844, in ibid., 15 December 1844.

to confirm that he envisaged a return to federalism, and when Gómez Farías returned early in 1845, the pressure on him to act intensified. The problem was the nature of the federal system to be adopted, and the government chose to invite the departments to send in their ideas on how the Bases Orgánicas could best be reformed. Several departments used their submissions to argue for the return of the 1824 charter, others wanted an amended version of it and some kept strictly to their brief by concentrating on changes to the Bases.[24] Zacatecas, for example, stated that it would prefer a reformed 1824 system, but as far as comments on the Bases were concerned, many changes were needed. In particular, it suggested the abolition of the income qualifications for voters, pointing out that a large proportion of the population was made up of 'labourers, cowboys, shepherds and peons' who were lucky to earn 5 pesos a month and had been completely disenfranchised. Also, the minimum-income requirements on deputies and senators should be abolished on the same grounds that most of the population had been excluded from standing for election.[25] The Mexico department wanted assemblies increased in size, the power to elect a governor and a reduction in the executive power of veto over legislation.[26] Other departments, in what were mostly lengthy documents, produced a mass of other ideas. All their submissions were sent to Congress, where they were examined and evaluated in detail through the committee structure. Despite attempts by federalist deputies to push through the immediate reintroduction of federalism, the majority of the representatives preferred to follow Herrera's lead and take the whole process slowly, stage by stage.[27] By the end of the ordinary sessions in May, nothing had been resolved, and when extraordinary sessions were announced on 16 June, constitutional reform remained on the agenda.

As will be indicated later, Herrera's failure to act quickly or decisively on the matter of constitutional reform lost his government a great deal of support, but the main target or pretext for the opposition was his policy on Texas. He had witnessed the failure of Santa Anna's efforts to make reconquest a popular national crusade, and it may have been the public apathy which helped to persuade him that successful military action was impossible. At any rate, whatever the origin of his opinions, it was soon evident that he did not share his predecessors's jingoism. He told Congress on 1 January that he would present proposals in due course,

24 The departmental submissions were published in the press; see, e.g., ibid., February–March 1845.
25 'Iniciativa de la honorable asamblea departamental de Zacatecas, sobre reformas de las bases de organización política de la república', 1 March 1845, in ibid., 28 March 1845.
26 'Iniciativa que la Exma. asamblea departamental de México ha elevado al soberano congreso nacional sobre reforma de las Bases Orgánicas', in *La Minerva*, 10 April 1845.
27 *El Estandarte Nacional*, 21 May 1845, reports the defeat of a motion in Congress to restore federalism by 39 votes to 13.

and he asked his Minister of Relations, Cuevas, to prepare a report on the options that were still feasible. Cuevas presented his views on 11 March, telling the deputies that the nation had two choices: either it could try to maintain its aim of reconquest, which would certainly mean war with the United States, or it could recognize Texan independence and thus prevent annexation by the United States. The executive, he said, strongly advised the latter course of action.[28] Thus, Herrera and his cabinet concluded that negotiations based on the recognition of Texan independence was the best, if not only, policy, and with the encouragement of British and French diplomats, contact was made with the Texan authorities. They sent an agent to Mexico City, and British ambassador Bankhead conveyed his proposals to Cuevas. They were, in brief, that in return for recognition Texas would agree not to be annexed to the United States and that boundary questions and other matters should be settled by negotiation or, if necessary, by arbitration. On 21 April Cuevas reported these proposals to Congress and asked authority for the government to open negotiations. After a delay of about a month, Congress gave its approval, and on 17 May Herrera announced that he hoped to arrange a treaty which would be 'advantageous and honourable for the Republic'.[29]

Herrera's decision to abandon the hope of military reconquest in favour of negotiating a peaceful solution received support from the moderates, especially Gómez Pedraza, who was said to be his principal adviser on foreign policy, but it provoked a wave of protest from the radicals. They had already become disillusioned with his failure to press ahead with constitutional reform, and with several new radical papers on the streets both in the capital and in the provinces, a massive propaganda campaign was started. In countless articles and editorials, the case for federalism was restated, creating, as the editor of *El Siglo XIX* expressed it, a 'federative wave, each time bigger and more irresistible'.[30] Representations poured in from town councils and other bodies around the country, and in April Lafragua and Olaguíbel, who were both on the Mexico City council, started a public petition demanding a new Congress to reform the 1824 charter.[31]

As it became clear that Herrera would not respond to this pressure, the radicals increased their attacks on him, his cabinet and the Congress. When the policy of negotiation over Texas was publicly confirmed, they at once seized on it to condemn the administration as weak, vacillating and cowardly. Their press began to demand a belligerent policy towards Texas and the United States, and even the more moderate *El Siglo XIX*

28 Cotner, *Herrera*, pp. 123–4.
29 Decree of 17 May 1845, in Dublán and Lozano, *Legislación mexicana*, vol. 5, p. 17.
30 *El Siglo XIX*, 25 February 1845.
31 *El Estandarte Nacional*, 16 April 1845.

joined in, stating its position as follows: 'The struggle on which Mexico is today being obliged to enter is the most national cause since 1810. It is a fight to the death, a question of existence and nationality'.[32] *La Minerva* openly called for war on the United States, and *La Voz del Pueblo* proclaimed, 'Federation and war on Texas, that is the cry of the people'.[33]

The propaganda campaign in the press was not the radicals' only tactic. As already noted, as early as December 1844, there were rumours of secret deals being concocted with Santa Anna's few remaining loyalists, and these persisted in the early months of 1845. Then Gómez Farías returned from exile, arriving at Veracruz on 11 February and in the capital on 10 March. The documentation in his archive leaves no doubt that he had not lost his propensity for political intrigue or his determination to see the restoration of federalism. He immediately renewed his prolific correspondence with his friends and allies around the country, replying to the dozens of letters of welcome he received. Among those who wrote to him was the exiled former minister Manuel C. Rejón, who was in Havana, and he implied that deals were being discussed behind the scenes. He referred to the talks he had had with Canalizo, who had asked him to tell Gómez Farías that he remained committed to the promises he had made to him. Canalizo, Rejón said, was certainly a 'friend of freedom' who would help the federalists in their aims. He had also written to Yucatán to pass on the list of candidates Gómez Farías had given him for the forthcoming elections.[34] Described by one of his many admirers as the 'guardian Angel of national liberty', Gómez Farías thus resumed his position as leader of the radicals.[35] Nevertheless, Herrera, who almost certainly knew of his activities given that secrecy was virtually impossible to sustain at this time, nominated him as a senator early in May, and on 6 June he was declared elected.

By early June, Herrera and his administration were being assailed from all sides. The military hierarchy was making it clear that it did not approve of his army reforms, and the government was obliged to issue a circular to all departments denying that it intended the destruction of the army.[36] The creation of the national militia above all annoyed the generals, but it also ran into difficulties which, according to the governor of Guanajuato, should have been anticipated. He reported that despite extensive publicity in his department, not a single recruit had been forthcoming.[37] There

32 *El Siglo XIX*, 25 March 1845. There is a full examination of press opinion on the Texas issue in J. V. Márquez, *La guerra del 47 y la opinión pública (1845–1848)* (Mexico, 1975).

33 *La Minerva*, 27 March 1845; *La Voz del Pueblo*, 7 May 1845.

34 M. C. Rejón to V. Gómez Farías, 13 February 1845, Gómez Farías Papers, 1069.

35 F. Santoyo to V. Gómez Farías, 22 February 1845, ibid., 1085.

36 The circular is in *El Amigo del Pueblo*, 4 September 1845.

37 J. B. Morales to Minister of Relations, 29 August 1845, in ibid., 6 September 1845.

were also the usual difficulties with the regular army troops. Although the Minister of Relations claimed in his report to Congress in March that soldiers were receiving their pay, a month later it was reported that the commander of Veracruz had had to borrow cash from local merchants to buy food for his men.[38] The Minister also proclaimed that the fiscal situation was finally under control and that no loans had been sought from *agiotistas,* but soon afterwards the executive had to seek congressional approval for a national or foreign loan of up to 3 million pesos, promising a maximum interest rate of 15 per cent. In the same initiative, approval was also sought for a one-off import of foreign cotton from which it was hoped to derive substantial tax revenues. Prior to this breaking of the import ban, it was emphasized, agreement would be sought from domestic cotton producers.[39]

In addition to the discontent in the army, the renewed fiscal problems and the ever more vocal opposition in the press to his policies over Texas and constitutional reform, Herrera also had to contend with a major earthquake, which caused widespread damage. The first tremors began at 3:52 p.m. on 7 April and lasted about four minutes. Further shocks were felt over the next two days.[40] There was substantial damage to property – every building was affected, according to *El Siglo XIX.* The San Lázaro hospital was destroyed completely, several churches and the national palace were badly damaged and 'the magnificent chapel of Santa Teresa la Antigua no longer exists'. The city authorities took emergency powers to demolish dangerous buildings, and the council remained in permanent session for the duration of the crisis. Once it was over, the price of construction materials rose sharply in response to the sudden increased demand.[41]

Throughout these developments in the first six months of Herrera's government, there were constant rumours of plots to overthrow the regime. Such talk was commonplace and was part and parcel of daily political life in the capital. To what extent the rumours had any basis in fact or were simply fabricated by one faction to discredit a rival is always difficult to judge, and when a revolt did occur, it is usually difficult, if not impossible, to be able to trace the details of its preparation and organization because conspirators rarely committed their actions to paper. On 7 June, however, there was an attempted coup for which there are some unusually revealing sources. At 3 p.m. on that day, some of the palace guards led by Captain Ramón Othon mutinied. They ran quickly up the

38 *La Minerva,* 12 April 1845.
39 For the text of the initiative, see *La Voz del Pueblo,* 26 April 1845.
40 *El Siglo XIX,* 8 April 1845.
41 Ibid., 8–26 April 1845; *La Minerva,* 12 April 1845. The editor of the latter urged the government to inspect nearby volcanoes for any sign of activity, saying that 'Mexico mucho tiene que temer de esos gigantes de nieve que llaman volcanes'.

main staircase of the palace into the presidential quarters, where they encountered and arrested the Ministers of Relations and Justice, several officers who refused to join them and Herrera himself. Colonel Joaquín Rangel arrived shortly afterwards with more rebels and assumed command. Word spread quickly throughout the palace complex. Loyal soldiers began to resist, and for about an hour there was considerable firing along the corridors and in the courtyards, resulting in twenty-three dead, including Othon, and a number of wounded. While this fighting was under way, Herrera and his ministers remained under guard. Herrera refused to be intimidated and managed to persuade his captors of the error of their ways so successfully that they switched sides and released him. He then went along the corridors persuading other rebels to give up, and by about 5 p.m. the whole thing was over, with Rangel and his supporters fleeing the building. Herrera mounted his horse and rode out into the city to reassure the public that the coup had failed.[42]

Blame for the revolt was placed firmly on the *santanistas,* and according to some reports, the rebels did shout Santa Anna's name as they opened their assault.[43] In fact, it was a conspiracy organized by the radical federalists and involved Gómez Farías, Lafragua and other federalist leaders. In the days before 7 June, Gómez Farías wrote to several of his allies to warn them to be prepared. On 20 May, for example, he sent a letter, delivered by hand for the sake of security, to General José Vicente Miñón in which he advised, 'Be prepared and ready with our other friends to work at once and assure them that general Santa Anna will have no part in the struggle we are about to embark on'. Miñón replied from Puebla that all was ready but that he needed a copy of the plan. Also, he warned Gómez Farías that Bishop Vázquez considered him a personal enemy and that it would be politic to write a reassuring letter to him. Gómez Farías responded at once with a copy of the plan and a flattering letter for the bishop.[44]

The person who took the letter to General Miñón at Puebla was the son of former president Canalizo, with whom, Gómez Farías added, 'I am in agreement'. Canalizo was awaiting the result of his appeal against the exile to which he had been sentenced, and it seems that he had persuaded the radicals that he was on their side. His defence counsel was Lafragua – Olaguíbel was defending Basadre – who tells us that a deal

---

42 There are several detailed contemporary accounts of the coup; see, e.g., *El Siglo XIX,* June 1845; C. M. Bustamante, *El nuevo Bernal Díaz del Castillo o sea historia de la invasión de los anglo-americanos en México* (Mexico, 1949), pp. 17–21.

43 Carlos Bustamante was convinced the coup was staged by both *santanistas* and federalists. Santa Anna's farewell message was published in the press the day before; Bustamante, *El nuevo Bernal Díaz,* pp. 16–17. See also *El Siglo XIX,* 8 June 1845.

44 Gómez Farías Papers, 1179, 1187, 1189, 1189(2).

was struck with him to restore the federation and that Canalizo provided the money used to bribe the garrison. With the cash available, the main problem was the lack of a leader, and Lafragua and Olaguíbel approached Rangel, who agreed to take command.[45]

All that remained was to suborn the garrison, and how that was done is explained by Francisco Mejía in his autobiography.[46] One of the jobs of Mejía, who was aged 23 at the time, was as a foreman for Rangel, who despite his military rank was a prominent building contractor. The contract on which Mejía was employed involved the erection of a monument to independence in the central plaza, but when he turned up for work, Rangel told him he had another job for him. He was given two pistols and, accompanied by a servant, went in Rangel's carriage to the café del Cazador at the Portal de Mercaderes, where he was handed a draft for 10,000 pesos – he does not say by whom but it was probably Lafragua, who says in his own memoir, 'I myself handed over the money provided by Canalizo'. He took the draft to no. 4 Almacen del Empedrado, where it was cashed – again no details are given – and returned with the money to the café. Rangel was waiting for him and told him to take 4,000 pesos to the grenadiers' garrison in the palace and deliver it personally to Captain Othon. With that errand accomplished, he returned to the café and was ordered by Rangel to take another 4,000 pesos to the fourth infantry regiment garrison. On his return, Rangel ordered him to go back to the palace, find Othon, tell him that all was ready and to start the revolt. By the time he arrived there, Mejía recalled, the fighting had already started and he was arrested, although released soon afterwards.

The amount needed to attempt to overthrow a government, therefore, was 10,000 pesos, 4,000 per army unit and 2,000 for a leader, in this case Rangel. This particular plot was hatched by Lafragua, Olaguíbel and Gómez Farías in collusion with Canalizo, who provided the cash. Lafragua, knowing that his role would be discovered, went into hiding at a friend's house and then, with the connivance of the Minister of War, García Conde, who provided him with a safe-conduct pass and an escort, he left for Veracruz, intending to go abroad. He stayed at Jalapa for a few weeks until the furor subsided, and after receiving assurances from Herrera, he returned to the capital, resumed his seat on the council and was elected a deputy for Puebla, as if nothing had happened. Rangel also went into hiding but was soon caught and put on trial. Despite some demands for capital punishment, his military judges refused to impose the ultimate penalty and sentenced him instead to ten years in exile. As for Gómez Farías, his position was peculiar. The government issued orders for his

45 Lafragua memoir, Lafragua Collection, 398.
46 F. Mejía, 'Epocas, hechos etc. de mi vida', ms. in García Collection, G402.

arrest, but two days before the revolt, the Minister of Relations had notified him of his appointment to the Senate. Almost certainly deliberately, Gómez Farías had left the capital and hence did not receive the letter of appointment until the day of the revolt. Then the arrest order was issued, and he also went into hiding. Ten days later, he wrote back to the Minister, accepting the Senate post and claiming senatorial immunity, but as he had not taken the oath of office because of the arrest order, the Minister referred the matter to the Senate.[47] There the senators debated what to do and a jurisdictional dispute followed, with the senators demanding the antecedents of the arrest order and the government refusing to hand them over. In the meantime, Gómez Farías stayed out of sight but was soon allowed back into circulation. On 24 July he wrote to Mora to say that the coup would have succeeded 'if two confused and presumptuous young men had not anticipated the movement . . . haste caused the loss of everything'.[48] Another prominent suspect in the conspiracy, adding credence to the allegation that *santanistas* were involved, was Tornel. Lafragua says he was given the task of rousing support in the departments, but in a letter to the press on 8 June, Tornel denied any complicity and chose to move out of harm's way by accepting a military post with the army of the north.[49]

The 7 June revolt was not unexpected – *El Siglo XIX* had reported strong rumors two days before – and it was the product of the frustration felt by the radicals at Herrera's refusal to back an immediate return to federalism. For his part, Herrera whose undoubted display of personal courage in the palace had added to his standing, does not seem to have been unduly perturbed by what had happened, and he ignored the warnings in the press that other opposition forces were merely awaiting their opportunity. Instead, he appeared determined to pursue the policies on Texas, army and constitutional reform that he had already set out.

Again Texas was at the forefront of public debate. Early in June, the government had received confirmation that the United States had decided to admit the state into the Union, and the Texas Congress met on 16 June to vote for annexation, a decision that was confirmed by a special convention on 4 July. It seemed that Herrera's policy of prompt recognition to forestall annexation was in ruins, and in public he responded by taking a much more militant stance. In a circular released on 9 June, Cuevas called on all Mexicans to defend national independence threatened by the imminent usurpation of Texas, and Congress approved the executive's request for the 3 million loan. As far as the press was concerned,

47 Details in *El Amigo del Pueblo*, 28 June, 1 July 1845; *La Voz del Pueblo*, 28 June, 2 July 1845; *El Siglo XIX*, 27 June 1845.
48 Published in García, *Documentos inéditos*, vol. 60, pp. 548–9.
49 Tornel's letter is in *El Siglo XIX*, 8 June 1845.

war was now inevitable. *El Siglo XIX*'s editor wrote, 'The Mexican republic is today in a war which is absolutely inevitable but just', and while all papers appealed for national unity, some blamed Herrera and his 'imbecile cabinet' for the crisis.[50] When General Zachary Taylor moved troops to Corpus Christi in July, Herrera responded by sending his army units to the Rio Grande but with orders not to cross the river or to open hostilities.

The Texas crisis dominated the headlines throughout the latter half of 1845. It provided the opposition with ample opportunity, which they used to the full to attack Herrera, but it was not sufficient to make him lose all support among the *hombres de bien*. After the June coup, the politicians had turned their attention to the forthcoming elections for both the presidency and part of the Senate and Chamber of Deputies. In the less repressive atmosphere which Herrera encouraged, there was an unusually open and vigorous campaign, and Gómez Farías told Mora that 'Herrera, Pedraza, Cuevas and Almonte are in a constant state of excitement as they try to get the votes for the Presidency'.[51] Congress had decided that the presidential election should be held on 1 August, when the departmental assemblies were to cast their votes. Newspapers around the country began to nominate their favoured candidates, and by no means all opted for Herrera. The editors of *El Siglo XIX* conducted a nationwide survey which revealed that as far the press was concerned, there were four favoured candidates: Herrera had the support of fourteen papers; Gómez Pedraza, six; Gómez Farías, six; and Bravo, four.[52] When the results began to come in, it was soon clear that the views of the press editors were not far removed from those of the assemblies, but they had underestimated Herrera's popularity. Eventually, his victory proved to be overwhelming, with all twenty-two departments which participated voting for him. None of the other candidates received more than a handful of votes from individual assembly members. Congress duly declared Herrera elected on 14 September, and he was sworn in two days later.

By 16 September, when Herrera's formal presidency began, the congressional campaign was already in full swing, with the rival parties campaigning and intriguing as vigorously as ever. Four main groups were active: radical federalists led by Gómez Farías; moderate federalists led by Gómez Pedraza, who was now labelled by his rivals 'the philosopher' (his supporters were 'the philosophers'); the *aristócratas* or *serviles* allegedly led by the former minister Cuevas; and the military or *santanistas*, whose leaders were not named though again one may assume Tornel was involved. In the run-up to the primaries, which were due on Sunday, 10 August,

50 Ibid., 20 July 1845; *El Amigo del Pueblo*, 17 July 1845.
51 García, *Documentos inéditos*, vol. 60, pp. 548–9.
52 *El Siglo XIX*, June–July 1845.

the main federalist demand was for reform of the electoral law and especially the removal of the high-income qualifications for both voters and candidates.[53] On 3 July, Deputy Atristaín introduced a motion in Congress to the effect that Santa Anna's electoral law of 10 December 1841 should be reinstated. After discussion, an amended version of that law was approved as the basis for the elections, but the income requirements for voters (200 pesos), electors (500 pesos) and deputies (1,200 pesos) stipulated in the Bases Orgánicas were retained.[54]

In addition to their press campaign, the federalists kept up their pressure in other ways. On 14 June, General Ignacio Martínez pronounced at Tabasco in favour of the immediate restoration of the 1824 constitution, and a group of military officers at Juchitan (Oaxaca) were reported to have made the same demand.[55] Another round of profederal representations came in from several departments, including Zacatecas and California, and on 5 August there was an attempt in the Mexico City council to push through a motion for the return of federalism. This was put by José del Río, and in a heated debate fully reported in the press, the councillors voted 9 to 4 against the motion. Among those voting against were Otero and Espinosa de los Monteros, who argued that constitutional change must be achieved democratically and that the best mechanism for that was the elections.[56]

The primaries were held on 10 August and there seems to have been an unusually high turn-out, at least in the capital. Of the 241 sections into which the city was divided for electoral purposes, 236 chose primary electors. Among those reported elected were Bravo, Riva Palacio, Pozo and a newcomer on the political scene of whom much more would be heard, Benito Juares (*sic*).[57] The secondary stage took place on 7 September, by which time there were two lists of candidates in circulation, known as the red and the yellow.[58] Although we have scant details, the usual deals had been negotiated, with the moderate and radical liberal federalists (the reds) reaching an accommodation in opposition to the yellow *serviles* group. The result was an easy victory for the liberal faction, and when the electoral college met in the capital on 5 October, all of its candidates, with one exception, were chosen as deputies. The exception was Lafragua, now a 'puritanical federalist' in his words, who although

53 See, e.g., ibid., 21 June 1845.
54 Ibid., 4 and 10 July 1845.
55 The text of the Tabasco plan is in *Planes en la nación mexicana*, book 4, 287–8.
56 'Proposiciones que el Sr. Regidor D. José del Río presentó al Exmo. ayuntamiento de México', in *La Voz del Pueblo*, 6 August 1845. The record of the council debates was published in *El Siglo XIX*, 23 August 1845.
57 The full list of *compromisarios* elected is in *El Siglo XIX*, 12 August 1845. It is assumed that the Juárez named was the future president.
58 Lists in ibid., 7 September 1845.

he reached the final stage failed to be elected because, he claimed, of the personal intervention of Riva Palacio. He was, however, elected by Puebla. In the departments, the moderates seem to have predominated, and there were the usual complaints in the press of government-inspired intimidation and corruption. One of Otero's friends at Guadalajara, for example, reported that despite some success for the liberals in the early stages, government pressure resulted in all of its own candidates being elected.[59]

The Senate also had to be renewed, and as with the lower house, there was pressure to reform the electoral procedure, especially with regard to those senators chosen according to occupation and the minimum-assets rule of 40,000 pesos. Again, Congress agreed to a new set of regulations, but these introduced no significant change, keeping the corporate representation and income or asset qualifications. The new system, according to one paper, was worse than the one it replaced. Pointing out that there were scarcely a hundred men in the capital who were worth 40,000 pesos, the editor argued that the elite was guaranteeing its self-perpetuation. Lacking a titled aristocracy, it was creating one based on money as a preparatory step in the formation of a monarchy while the 'mass of the population' went unrepresented.[60] When the results were announced, while there was no clear political bias, it was evident that the Senate would again be dominated by well-heeled members of the elite. Riva Palacio and Neri del Barrio were among the landowner group, Francisco Fagoaga and Cirilo Gómez Anaya represented the mining industry and Couto, Cuevas and Francisco Elorriaga were businessmen or *capitalistas*. The general list included mostly well-known names from across the political spectrum – for example, Anastasio Bustamante, Almonte, Gómez Pedraza, Malo and Archbishop Posada y Garduño.[61]

During and after the elections, war fever dominated the press, but Herrera and his advisers were convinced in private that a negotiated solution was still possible. While on the one hand the government was still apparently preparing for war – the executive was given authority to raise a 15 million peso loan and there was talk of using Church wealth for the war effort – on the other, Herrera employed diplomatic channels to let it be known that he was willing to negotiate with the United States provided that it would pay an indemnity for Texas.[62] On receiving a favourable response, he indicated his willingness to receive a commissioner 'with full powers to treat upon the present question in a pacific, reasonable

59 R. Arce to M. Otero, 9 September, 7 October 1845, Otero Archive.
60 *La Voz del Pueblo*, 1 October 1845.
61 Bustamante had returned from Europe in 1844.
62 The Church continued to lend money to the government. *El Amigo del Pueblo*, 5 July 1845, gives a list of the loans made since 1839. The idea of the 15 million peso loan was floated in the press in October; see ibid., 25 October 1845.

and honourable manner'.[63] Eventually, John Slidell arrived at Veracruz on 30 November with the status of envoy extraordinary and minister plenipotentiary. His arrival seemed to confirm suspicions that Herrera was preparing to settle, and the press again launched intense attacks on him and his cabinet, accusing them of treachery and being willing to sell not just Texas but also much of northern Mexico. *La Voz del Pueblo* warned that the oligarchy of *hombres de bien* was leading the nation to ruin: 'Either the government disappears or the nation does. Mexicans, the government can see our imminent ruin and it is allowing us to perish'.[64] *El Amigo del Pueblo* was equally abusive: 'This vile gang of hypocrites and philosophers who baptise themselves with the name of government . . . it has degraded, debased even the name, Mexican government'.[65] Taken aback by the reaction, or perhaps having second thoughts, Herrera decided not to receive Slidell, but he ignored advice and travelled to the capital. There he was told that only Congress could decide whether to receive a fully accredited minister, which would imply the restoration of diplomatic relations and could be taken to mean Mexican acceptance of Texas annexation.

The most vitriolic attacks on the government were to be found in the pages of the radical press. Having failed to persuade Herrera or Congress to revive the 1824 charter and with the collapse of the June coup, the radicals, inspired by Gómez Farías and the absent but 'wise Mexican, Dr. D. Luis Mora', had concentrated their efforts on the elections and had had some success in the departments. Then, with daily diatribes against the government over Texas, they promoted their alternative leader; 'liberty and Sr. Farías are the same thing'.[66] Gómez Pedraza and the moderates who supported the regime were condemned as 'los equilibristas' who lacked an ideology and were concerned only with preserving the power of *hombres de bien*. Arguing that there was now a struggle between 'the aristocratic and the democratic elements', they openly called for revolution to overthrow the government before it was too late. Appeals began to be issued to the army to intervene:

Soldiers! If you have no shirt, if you are naked, if you have not been paid for days, it is not because there are no resources but because the present government is wasting Treasury revenues. Soldiers! May God free you from the hypocrites; only you can liberate yourselves from such bare-faced scoundrels.[67]

Such appeals to the military did not fall on deaf ears, but those who heard them were not those the radicals hoped would heed them. The

63 Cotner, *Herrera*, p. 143.
64 *La Voz del Pueblo*, 1 November 1845.
65 *El Amigo del Pueblo*, 1 November 1845.
66 *La Voz del Pueblo*, 15 November 1845.
67 Ibid., 21 May, 6 December 1845; *El Amigo del Pueblo*, 1 November 1845.

party political feuding and the turmoil in the capital had been watched passively by army officers in the departments, but there were indications of mounting anxiety. The reforms of the army, the creation of the militia, the intensification of the radicals' campaign, the likelihood of capitulation over Texas and the federalists' success in the elections were all causes for concern. Paredes in particular watched developments closely. His participation in the overthrow of Santa Anna had attracted once again, in his view, inadequate recompense, and while certainly not a forgotten man, he had not figured prominently in the early months of the Herrera administration. By the summer of 1845, he was at San Luis Potosí at the head of an army several thousand strong which was supposed to be enroute to Texas. He published a standard condemnation of the 7 June coup and repeatedly denied that he was planning to rebel, but nevertheless, as the government's popularity declined, people from all parties began to look to him as the most likely to intervene. General Mariano Arista, commander of the forces on the Texas border, wrote on 24 August that 'we command the armed forces, we are in entire agreement, united and ready to stifle any attempt at sansculottism'.[68] Herrera himself wrote a couple of weeks later, just before his inauguration on 16 September, to tell him that 'the revolutionaries in this capital have redoubled their activity these days. Last night a junta was surprised, but by the clumsiness of the police, only five men were arrested. . . . Public opinion and different channels of information reveal that Valentín Gómez Farías is at the head of it all'.[69] Even Gómez Farías thought it worthwhile to approach Paredes for support, writing on 4 October to suggest that they might correspond and exchange ideas.[70] More and more of Paredes' correspondents, however, urged him to act quickly. Tornel, for example, wrote to warn him of the 'very violent state of society' and that people were looking for a 'saviour'. Both Bravo and Valencia, he added, sent their regards.[71] Another anonymous writer told him that public opinion was ready for the fall of Herrera and that 'the eyes of the public are turned towards you'.[72]

Although the timing of his decision is unclear, the evidence of his archive leaves no doubt that Paredes had resolved to attempt to overthrow the government. The delay was caused by several factors. In the first place, he always moved cautiously and he spent much of the period from September to December sounding out opinion, especially among fellow army officers and departmental governors around the country. Second, he also

68 Quoted in Hutchinson, 'Gómez Farías and the Return of Santa Anna', p. 176.
69 Ibid.
70 Ibid., p. 178.
71 J. M. Tornel to M. Paredes y Arrillaga, 19 November 1845, Paredes y Arrillaga Papers, 143/406.
72 Ibid., 143/519.

engaged in a protracted correspondence with Alamán and the Spanish minister, Salvador Bermúdez de Castro, in which they discussed the possibility of setting up a monarchy headed by a European prince.[73] Alamán and Bermúdez de Castro forcefully pressed the idea on him, and Paredes seemed to go along with their proposals, partly because of their promise of financial aid to be supplied by their fellow monarchist conspirator, the Spanish merchant Lorenzo de Carrera. At the same time, Paredes had his own ideas on the future political organization of the country, which were not unlike those he had urged on Santa Anna in 1842, and in a letter of 29 August he stated that Mexico would never be a monarchy. He was clearly keeping his options open, and as Soto puts it, 'He made no definite commitment with any political position and he left many – perhaps too many – options open'.[74]

As always, the government and the press knew, or certainly suspected, that Paredes could not be trusted, and in August he was instructed to return to the capital to receive orders for the Texas campaign. When he ignored the instruction, Herrera sent General Vicente Filisola with a small military unit to San Luis Potosí. Again, Paredes ignored the orders and when some of Filisola's men mutinied on the grounds that the government was antiarmy and profederal, Paredes did nothing to reprimand them. It seemed to the press in the capital that a general revolt was about to start. Paredes was accused of wanting the dictatorship 'which has always slipped from his hands', and in Congress, Deputy Boves, a radical federalist, made an impassioned attack on his career record.[75] Paredes, he said, had been responsible for the death of General Moctezuma, the Santa Anna dictatorship, the abolition of Congress and the betrayal of Bustamante and had supported dictatorship while serving in the Senate. He demanded that the government bring him back to the capital to answer charges of insubordination. Rumours of the monarchist conspiracy were also rampant, and it was reported on 1 September that a revolt was imminent, which would be 'not only against the present order of things but also against the very essence of the institutions'.[76]

Paredes continued to deny everything and took it upon himself on 6 September to issue a circular to all governors and commander generals in which he rejected the allegations being made against him. He insisted that he had no intention of deserting the government: 'Nobody could

73 The monarchist conspiracy has been examined by a number of scholars. I have generally used the excellent account by M. Soto, *La conspiración monárquica en México, 1845–1846* (Mexico, 1988), from which these details are largely taken.
74 Quoted in ibid., p. 68.
75 *La Voz del Pueblo*, 27, 30 August 1845. Boves, who represented Yucatán, defended his views in a letter to *El Siglo XIX*, 21 August 1845.
76 *La Voz del Pueblo*, 1 September 1845.

speculate that there is any plan in my mind which tends towards disturbing public order'.[77] On the same day, he wrote to the Minister of War to reassure him of his loyalty and support. Although he continued his correspondence with him, it is unlikely that Herrera had any doubts about his aims, and if he did so, these were dispelled early in December when Paredes wrote to demand his resignation from the presidency.[78] The government began to take precautions. Several thousand rifles and cartridges arrived in the capital early in December, but by then, it was too late. Paredes' agents confirmed that Bravo and Valencia would cooperate, and they gave him details of the defensive preparations.[79]

At San Luis Potosí on 14 December, the *pronunciamiento* finally began, and it followed the conventional pattern. General Manuel Romero, commander general of the department, together with officers of his garrison, issued a statement in which they denounced the Herrera government and the Congress and made several charges against them.[80] They had, they claimed, brought the nation to the brink of a precipice by making concessions to the United States; they had created a militia of 'men who think least and who have least morality'; they had tried to abolish the army and refused it permission to march to Texas; they had admitted a commissioner with whom they were prepared to agree to the 'ignominious loss of our integrity'; and they were causing anarchy and chaos in society. Hence, the army demanded the immediate removal of the executive and Congress; the summoning of an emergency Congress with representatives of all social classes to reconstitute the nation; an invitation to Paredes to assume the leadership of the movement. On the next day, 15 December, Paredes accepted the command and published a manifesto to the nation. In this, he made the same basic charges as the garrison. The government had betrayed the nation over Texas, the army was being destroyed, chaos and anarchy prevailed. Emphasizing the prosperity of the nation in 1821, he condemned the demagogues who, masquerading as federalists, sought no more than to avenge their defeat in 1834. His objectives were fundamental change, to stop the dissolution of society, to stop radicals from gaining power: 'I am trying to return to the productive classes their lost influence, and to give wealth, industry, and work the part which corresponds to them in the government of society'. Finally, he confirmed that the new Congress he envisaged would have unrestricted powers and would include 'all social classes, the clergy and the military, the magistrate and

77 Circular of 6 September in ibid., 26 September 1845.
78 Herrera wrote to Paredes on 6 December to say that there was no point in further discussion between them; Paredes y Arrillaga Papers, 143/537.
79 Ibid., 143/529, 536.
80 *Planes en la nación mexicana*, book 4, 289–90.

the administrator, the literary professions and the merchant, industry and agriculture'.[81]

Obviously intended to appeal to *hombres de bien* and the upper echelons of the middle class, Paredes' ideas and promises met with a mixed reception. The monarchist conspirators were content with some of the implications, but criticized the apparent commitment to war over Texas, which Alamán had advised against. For the radicals, the whole thing was a poorly disguised attempt at military dictatorship, an accusation Paredes continued to deny, and Morales wrote from Guanajuato on 19 December to say that he could never support such a poorly conceived and presented plan.[82] Army officers in some areas also expressed their disappointment. Arista complained that 'you are going to destroy the focal point of our unity, to put us into anarchy, surely guided by some purpose you deem of greater interest', and Cortazar declined his support on the grounds that he now spent all his time looking after his extensive rural properties.[83] Some of the assemblies and municipal authorities in the departments – for example, Zacatecas, Tamaulipas, Jalapa and Veracruz – also declared their opposition.

Despite the early mixed reactions to the plan, Herrera knew that he faced a critical situation, compounded when most army garrisons began to announce their support for it. The Senate was told on 20 December that the government was determined to resist and that it was 'resolved to be buried under the ruins of the Bases Orgánicas', but there was virtual panic in Congress as some deputies – few now bothered to attend – bitterly attacked the military as a bunch of drunkards, no doubt referring to Paredes' known intemperance.[84] With officers alienated by these attacks, Herrera was forced to rely on the militia and on volunteers for whom recruiting centres were hastily established. Seven thousand rifles were distributed to the populace, and as armed vigilantes patrolled the streets, the mercantile community began to fear popular anarchy. The Junta de Fomento, which represented leading businessmen, advised its members to acquire weapons to defend themselves and their property, and families began to leave the city.[85] Opponents of the government were arrested, and police raids on the opposition press intimidated some papers into

---

81 The full text of Paredes' manifesto is in *El Amigo del Pueblo*, 20 December 1845, and there is a good summary in Soto, *Conspiración monárquica*, pp. 70–3.

82 Paredes y Arrillaga Papers, 143/572.

83 Letters in ibid., 550, 567.

84 Actas del Consejo de Gobierno, fols. 216–17, Archivo del Senado. There is an interesting day-by-day account of events in December onwards by José Fernando Ramírez, who was a deputy in Congress; J. F. Ramírez, *Mexico during the War with the United States*, ed. W. V. Scholes, trans. B. Scherr (Columbia, Mo., 1950). Bustamante also gives a detailed description in *El nuevo Bernal Díaz*, pp. 79–91.

85 Soto, *Conspiración monárquica*, p. 78.

closure. With Paredes approaching the city, most people concluded that the government was bound to fall.

The end of the Herrera regime in fact came in the bizarre manner which often characterizes such events in Mexico's eventful history. Valencia, like several other senior army officers, had chosen to leave the city with his entire family on 17 December. He returned five days later and had a meeting with Herrera but made no public comment. Then, on 30 December, the capital's garrison pronounced in support of Paredes' plan and invited Valencia to lead them. He accepted and again went to the palace to see the president. By now deserted on all sides – Anastasio Bustamante was one of the very few officers to remain loyal – Herrera knew that his cause was lost, and he quietly resigned his office, withdrawing to his private residence. Valencia immediately proclaimed himself president, and as head of the Council of Government, he was technically next in line for an interim presidency in the event of the office being vacant. It was promptly evident, however, that he did not see his tenure as temporary and that his motives were in fact to pre-empt the arrival of Paredes. He ordered Tornel and Almonte to go to Paredes, who was now on the outskirts of the city, to discuss his future role, but when they returned the next day, they reported that he was unwilling to recognize Valencia or to accept the additions he had announced to the plan of San Luis Potosí.[86] Furthermore, he demanded that Valencia travel in person to see him, and he made it clear that he was the sole head of the revolution. The meeting took place at the shrine of Guadalupe – we do not know what transpired – but although Valencia returned to the capital and for the next twenty-four hours tried to assert his authority, he failed to attract any support from the military or the politicians. Realizing his position was untenable, he resigned and offered to leave the country, a move Paredes decided was not required.[87]

Thus, Valencia's latest opportunistic attempt to win the presidency was frustrated, but for Paredes it was a case of third time lucky. Perhaps having learned from his experiences in the past with both Santa Anna and Valencia, he was determined not to be outmanoeuvred yet again, and on 2 January 1846, at the head of his troops, he entered the capital to take the prize he considered to be the just reward for his efforts over many years. He called a meeting of senior army officers, including Bravo, Almonte, Valencia, Filisola and Salas, and with Tornel acting as secretary, they agreed that a junta of two representatives per department should be appointed by Paredes. It would meet immediately to choose an interim

---

86 G. Valencia to M. Paredes y Arrillaga, 30 December 1845, Paredes y Arrillaga Papers, 143/607.

87 Soto, *Conspiración monárquica*, pp. 80–3.

president, who would within eight days of taking office announce elections for a new Congress. The next day, 3 January, forty-three members of the junta met. By unanimous vote, they elected Paredes interim president of Mexico. The general who had made no secret of his loathing of the proletariat and of his conviction that only the *hombres de bien* were equipped to govern had at last achieved his goal, and we may assume that he had more than one drink to celebrate.

12

Hombres de bien and the restoration of federalism

The rise of Paredes to the supreme executive power was an appropriate culmination of the centralist decade. Conservatives like Alamán were once again in control, and they saw in him the ideal candidate to represent their views. Unlike the weak Bustamante or the mercurial and unprincipled Santa Anna, Paredes represented unequivocally the values of the conservative *hombre de bien*. As indicated in previous chapters of this study, he was strongly proclerical and nostalgic for what he saw as the social and moral stability of the colonial era. Moreover, he shared the priorities of all *hombres de bien* regarding such matters as law and order and education. More than anything, however, he believed that only property owners, or the 'well-off classes', as he termed them, were fit to govern, and he despised both the proletariat and especially those renegades of his own social class who advocated popular suffrage or sovereignty.

Paredes seemed, therefore, ideally placed to carry out at last the conservative programme, which was once again restated in the press in an attempt to persuade the uncommitted *hombres de bien* where their true interests lay. A new daily paper, *El Tiempo*, appeared on the streets for the first time on 24 January, and while its main objective was soon admitted to be the creation of a monarchy, its early articles expounded the same ideology as its conservative predecessors had done in 1830–2 and 1834–6. With Alamán as its principal editor and contributor, it openly derided the fashionable concepts of equality and democracy: 'Whenever democracy is preached, a lie is told'. Equality of rights brought lack of respect for authority, 'awful elections' and the dangerous rise to political power of men from the 'bottom social classes' who were entirely unsuitable and incapable of occupying public office. In sum, 'equality has mixed up the wise man with the ignorant, the judicious and moderate with the restless and rowdy, the honourable and virtuous citizen with the unruly and perverse'. All of the country's problems since independence had stemmed from such puerile concepts and the radical liberal/federal philosophy which enshrined them. The only hope for the future was to recognize that Mexico was not as advanced as the United States or Europe, and the first step was to recognize the reality of Mexico's condition: 'The remedy for these ills cannot be other than to accommodate the political institutions to things as they are and not pretend that it is things which mould institutions'. It was essential that the full privileges of citizenship including the suffrage be restricted to men of property, who had an innate, vested interest in peace and order: 'What does that jargon of imprescriptible rights of social contract, rights of man, and that nomenclature of absurdities preached seventy years ago by visionary publicists matter to the proprietor, miner, businessman and agriculturalist if all that offers them no benefits and certain losses in their fortunes and in the means of advancement?'

In a rare use of colonial terminology, the paper insisted that the *castas* and *indios,* although corrupted by modern ideas to some degree, were still passive and retained their respect for the middle-class creoles. All *hombres de bien* were urged to support the government, not least because 'the *hombre de bien,* just for what he is, must be the target of the factions'. Political stability, it was emphasized, would enable the clock to be turned back, and all the moral values and social attitudes of the golden age of the colonial era would be restored. What Mexico once had and must recover were 'great talents, utmost respect for religion, innate docility of the people, bravery, morality in all classes of the State, patriotism, knowledge, submission, obedience and respect for the authorities; definite love of order, cordial union between families, genuine hospitality with the stranger. Here I have the moral portrait of the inhabitants of this happy land'.[1]

This prospect of future harmony painted in the columns of *El Tiempo* must have been tempting to many *hombres de bien,* and it was certainly music to the ears of Paredes, corresponding as it did to his personal ideology in almost every respect. He promptly set about trying to bring it to reality, and during the early months of his regime, he enacted a number of reforms in line with this restated and refined conservative manifesto. He tried to reduce nepotism and patronage in the civil bureaucracy, ordered another enquiry into the administration of the Treasury, made many changes in the organization of the army and repealed unpopular measures of the Herrera government such as a 25 per cent discount imposed on public salaries the previous October.[2] The usual lobbies also soon made their voices heard. Tobacco farmers wanted to extend their production, and departmental governors were told to give special en-

---

1 Quotations are from editorials in *El Tiempo,* 24, 26, 28 and 31 January, 12, 15 and 26 February 1846. A list of the main contributors to the paper is given by Soto, *Conspiración monárquica,* p. 104. Reyes Heroles gives a good analysis of the ideas; *El liberalismo mexicano,* vol. 2, pp. 340–8.
2 *El Tiempo,* 24 and 25 January 1846.

couragement to the industry.[3] Cotton manufacturers renewed their pleas for the ban on imported cotton to be lifted, and with Alamán once again influential at the centre of power, it was no surprise that Paredes agreed to their request, authorizing imports of raw cotton on 22 January.[4] Law and order also naturally received Paredes' attention, and yet another colourfully attired police force was established for the capital and its environs. Accused felons were again put under the jurisdiction of the military courts, and stricter antivagrancy laws were introduced.[5] Determined to clean up the capital in more ways than one, the government issued regulations in a vain attempt to persuade householders to keep the streets clean, instituted an organized refuse collection service and began a crack-down on the prostitutes to be found at every corner, although as Carlos Bustamante noted, those with connections in high places easily escaped.[6]

With these and many other measures, Paredes set about creating or restoring his vision of a well-ordered society based on the values of old, but as he and everybody else believed, the issue of paramount priority was the form of government. On 27 January Paredes published the *convocatoria*, or regulations, to govern the election of a new Congress, and in these he left no doubt that he shared the ideas expressed so eloquently in *El Tiempo* regarding the future role and powers of the *hombres de bien*.[7] The Congress was to be chosen exclusively on the basis of class, with each representative chosen by members of his own socioeconomic group. There were to be 160 deputies, representing and chosen by the following groups:

> Urban and rural property owners, 38
> Commerce, 20
> Mining, 14
> Manufacturers, 14
> Literary professions, 14
> Judiciary, 10
> Public administration, 10
> Clergy, 20
> Army, 20

For the most part, no precise income or asset qualifications were specified for either voters or candidates, but only those who had paid sub-

---

3 Circular of 31 January in ibid., 3 February 1846.
4 L. Alamán to Minister of Hacienda, 21 January 1846, in ibid., 27 January 1846; decree of 22 January in ibid. See also the letters from E. de Antuñano in Paredes y Arrillaga Papers, 144/192, 326.
5 Ministry of War to Commander General of Veracruz, 9 February 1846, Paredes y Arrillaga Papers, 144/187.
6 Laws in Dublán and Lozano, *Legislación mexicana*, vol. 5, pp. 104–5, 122; Bustamante, *El nuevo Bernal Díaz*, p. 107.
7 The full text of the *convocatoria* is in Dublán and Lozano, *Legislación mexicana*, vol. 5, pp. 105–19.

stantial amounts in taxation were eligible to participate. The amount of tax payment required varied according to each group and according to department, and while none was indicated for the judicial, military or clerical sectors, it was taken for granted that those to be elected would belong to the 'well-off classes'. Indeed, the clerical representation specifically excluded the lower orders by its restriction to the senior hierarchy, with all eleven bishops automatically in Congress, together with one representative of each cathedral chapter. Similarly, the lower ranks of the military were excluded, with no officer below the rank of colonel eligible to vote or stand for election. Only in the so-called literary professions category was there some concession to the lower levels of the middle class. Teachers, for example, with a salary of 200 pesos (300 in the Mexico department) could vote but unless they had paid high taxes, they could not be candidates.

These new electoral regulations confirmed that neither Paredes nor Alamán, who is said to have written them, had any intention of allowing any kind of popular franchise, or 'electoral farces' as *El Tiempo* put it.[8] The ballot box henceforth was for *hombres de bien* only and only the upper echelons of the elite would participate in the electoral process. Thus, the alliance between the army, clergy and the proprietor class which Paredes had long wanted would be achieved and the dangerous concepts of democracy and popular sovereignty eliminated from the political landscape.

The election of a Congress, however, had a purpose – to devise a new constitution – and it was here that Paredes was to hesitate. In the months leading to his revolt against Herrera, Alamán and the Spanish ambassador had tried to persuade him of the virtues of a monarchy, to which he responded by alternately encouraging and discouraging them but without making any commitment. Alamán and his allies kept up the pressure, and having set out their intellectual justification in the early issues of *El Tiempo*, they finally declared their real objective on 12 February. In an editorial headed 'Our Profession of Faith', they publicly confirmed for the first time that, in their opinion, the best form of government for Mexico was a hereditary, constitutional monarchy which would rest on the twin pillars of a strong Church and a strong army and in which 'there [would be] no aristocracy except that of merit, ability, education, wealth, military and civil service'. Rejecting all the forms of government tried so far since independence, from representative republicanism to military dictatorship, and all the associated ideas of liberalism, they called for a new era of conservative values, of protection for property owners and security for their persons and possessions: 'Conservatives by conviction and by character, we ask protection for all vested interests, whatever their origin'.

8 *El Tiempo*, 28 January 1846.

What Paredes' position was with regard to the monarchist lobby and their now categorical and well-argued case is by no means clear. He had reputedly said to Arrangoiz as early as 1832 that he believed only a monarchy could save Mexico from anarchy and the United States, but as a pragmatic politician, he well knew the extent and intensity of the public opposition which had been immediately aroused when Gutiérrez Estrada had made a similar suggestion in 1840.[9] He was also well aware that the opposition press was using his presumed monarchist sympathies, if not intentions, to whip up public anger and hostility towards him, especially in the departments. Once *El Tiempo* made its declaration, the tempo of the opposition attack was rapidly and substantially increased. Governors and other officials in the departments warned Paredes to disassociate himself from the monarchists. Morales, for example, wrote from Guanajuato on 16 February that 'it is asserted that it is now beyond doubt that efforts are being made in that city to establish a monarchist government and that the principal agents are yourself, the Archbishop, D. Lucas Alamán, and several other people'.[10]

Paredes responded to these pressures, as he had done previously, by trying to keep his options open while at the same time not alienating totally either the republicans or the monarchists. He issued several proclamations or manifestos to the nation in which he was very careful not to state his own position for or against a monarchy. On 10 January, for example, apparently at the prompting of Alamán, he defended his overthrow of the Herrera government on the grounds that anarchy had threatened and that 'the social revolution showed its head, after the political revolution'.[11] The future political organization of the nation, he said, was a matter for the next Congress, which would be free to decide as it wished, always sustaining the two immutable principles of independence and freedom. His promise to halt the progress of the social revolution was well received by *hombres de bien* like Carlos Bustamante, but for others the most significant aspect of his words was his deliberate omission of any promise to uphold republicanism. It was at once assumed that the omission confirmed the suspicions that he had opted for monarchism. A few weeks later, on 21 March, in response to a crescendo of antimonarchist sentiment in the republican press, Paredes again addressed the nation, promising this time to defend republicanism but again in an oblique and qualified way: 'The nation will sustain the republican system, as long as it wants to sustain it'.[12]

9 Arrangoiz, *México desde 1808 hasta 1867*, p. 389.
10 J. B. Morales to M. Paredes y Arrillaga, 16 February 1846, Paredes y Arrillaga Papers, 144/220.
11 *El Tiempo*, 25 January 1846.
12 Ibid., 25 March 1846; *El Contra-Tiempo*, 7 April 1846.

At no point in the first few months of his regime, therefore, did Paredes come out openly in favour of the monarchy for which Alamán and others were campaigning, but equally, until Congress opened in June, he failed to give any credible assurances that he would defend the republican system. This indecisiveness was certainly calculated, but it was a tactical error which left him exposed to attack from all sides. With or without foundation, it was his presumed support for monarchism which quickly alienated politicians from all parties, and Alamán and his allies were soon irritated by his equivocation. In the departments, especially after the publication of the *convocatoria,* which was taken to be a preparatory step on the road to monarchism, several governors and assemblies refused to continue in office. At Veracruz, Coahuila, Nuevo León, Jalisco, Oaxaca, Michoacán and elsewhere, the assemblies protested and Yucatán once again declared its independence.[13] Marcos de Esparza wrote from Zacatecas on 6 February to tell him that the *convocatoria* had been a mistake and had lost him popular support because 'the Nation has not been convoked but rather those classes which represent wealth'.[14] Domingo Echagaray reported from Jalapa that the assembly there had condemned the *convocatoria* and approved an initiative demanding a popularly elected congress.[15]

These private warnings and symptoms of discontent from around the country were accompanied by what was probably the most concerted and clamorous press campaign since independence. Several new papers appeared in the capital and in the provinces – there were at least three entitled *El Contra-Tiempo* – to challenge and refute the monarchist ideas of *El Tiempo* and, by its association with them, the Paredes government.[16] In the capital, *La Reforma, Don Simplicio, El Republicano, La Epoca, El Monitor Republicano* and *El Contra-Tiempo* waged a daily defence of republicanism accompanied by a barrage of criticism of Paredes, his ministers and their alleged predilection for monarchy. Faced with this onslaught in the press, Paredes tried at first in private meetings with hostile editors to persuade them to moderate their criticism, and when this failed to have any effect, he ordered the authorities to enforce the provisions of Santa Anna's press law of 8 April 1839 whereby so-called subversive authors, editors and printers could be prosecuted.[17] This threat did not work, and in March, attempting to calm the monarchist–republican polemic, he ordered that there be no more discussion in the press of the

13 The Oaxaca assembly, including Benito Juárez, was dismissed. For the protest it issued, signed by Juárez, see Paredes y Arrillaga Papers, 144/161.
14 M. de Esparza to M. Paredes y Arrillaga, 6 February 1846, ibid., 144/158.
15 D. Echagaray to M. Paredes y Arrillaga, 29 April 1846, ibid., 145/299.
16 Soto, *Conspiración monárquica,* p. 148.
17 P. Santoni, 'Los federalistas radicales y la guerra del 47', Ph.D. diss., El Colegio de Mexico, 1987, p. 211.

form of government, warning that those who disobeyed would be liable to severe penalties.[18] The republican papers were still defiant, publishing an unusual joint declaration under the title 'Protest of the Republican Press' in *El Contra-Tiempo* on 17 March. Individual editors and printers were again summoned to the presidential palace, where they were cajoled and threatened. Vicente García Torres, one of the country's leading publishers, was one such victim of the president's wrath. He was told by Paredes that he was a traitor and a rebel and that, if he did not desist, he would have him sent to the Ulúa prison or even shot.[19] Finally, on 18 April another press law was published, banning criticism of the authorities and threatening those 'who assist any change in the established order'.[20] Almost immediately afterwards, the police began to raid newspaper offices, García Torres was arrested and, despite defiant attempts by his wife to keep their business going, some papers were forced into closure.[21]

The press campaign was by no means the only problem Paredes had to confront. Despite early optimism that he could get the fiscal situation under control – he was widely reputed to be an honest man – he soon found that the Treasury was virtually empty. Much to the anger of businessmen and speculators, he suspended payments on all types of credits owed by the government, and on 7 May he was obliged to reintroduce the cut of 25 per cent on public-sector salaries and pensions over 300 pesos a year, excluding salaries of military on active service. The Church was once again approached to consider a loan of several million pesos, and in June the executive was authorized to raise funds in any way it could, except through the seizure of private or corporate property.[22]

The shortage of revenue, of course, was nothing new, but it was seriously exacerbated by what seemed to be the inevitable approach of war with the United States. Paredes had, at least in part, achieved power by berating the Herrera government for its apparent unwillingness to go to war over Texas. Against the advice of Alamán, he had adopted a jingoist stance, but once in office he hesitated, perhaps realizing the weakness of the army, despite all the expenditures on it. The U.S. envoy, Slidell, had returned to Veracruz after Herrera's fall, and although there was some renewed diplomatic activity, both sides were by then in entrenched positions from which neither could or would move. On 21 March, in a final

18 Decree of 14 March in *El Contra-Tiempo*, 17 March 1846.
19 V. García Torres to editors, 12 March 1846, in ibid.
20 Dublán and Lozano, *Legislación mexicana*, pp. 121–2.
21 See reports in *El Contra-Tiempo*, 21 April, 20 May 1846. García Torres was exiled to Nuevo León; Malo, *Diario*, p. 300.
22 The Minister of Hacienda asked the Church for a loan of 2.4 million pesos payable at 200,00 per month. The clergy declined to help. For the correspondence, see *El Contra-Tiempo*, 20 May 1846; Robertson, 'Paredes y Arrillaga', pp. 223–5.

exchange of notes, Slidell was sent his passport papers.[23] Orders had already gone out from Washington to General Taylor to move his force to the Rio Grande, and early in April the first skirmishes with Mexican troops took place. Paredes was faced with the decision whether to declare war formally. As with the constitutional question, he equivocated, preferring to maintain that such a decision belonged exclusively to Congress. On 23 April he published a manifesto in which, after condemning U.S. aggression, he announced that until Congress made a decision, he would defend the territorial integrity of the nation in what he termed a defensive war.[24] Two weeks later, war was declared by the United States, and more of its forces entered Texas, New Mexico and California while its navy began to blockade Mexican ports.

Other than negotiate a settlement which would have inevitably included a humiliating retreat by his government, there was nothing Paredes could do to prevent the outbreak of hostilities. Several authors believe that, like Herrera, he wanted a peaceful solution, but he had tied his banner to the jingoist cause and it was, in the context of domestic politics, impossible for him to retreat from that position.[25] Accepting the inevitable, therefore, he began to prepare for war and spent much of his energy in the first weeks of June trying to organize military units. Then it was announced on 20 June that he was to vacate the presidency to take personal command of the army.

Paredes' authority to lead the army was given by the new Congress, which had assembled early in June. The complex electoral process detailed in the *convocatoria* had been carried out in preceding weeks, and it is clear from Paredes' personal archive that he had directly intervened to ensure that only *hombres de bien* to his satisfaction were elected. He sent lists of names of those he wanted, particularly for the military group, to governors and commanders around the country, and they willingly co-operated. On 21 February, for example, Manuel Lombardini wrote from Querétaro to tell him that the election results were 'all in accordance with the list which I was sent; I am pleased to have been able to meet your wishes'.[26] Similar reports came in from Tlaxcala, San Luis Potosí, Oaxaca and other places, and from Morelia, Fernando Palacio wrote that his officers who were eligible to vote had simply signed the ballots, leaving blank the space for the name of the candidate to be filled in by himself from the list Paredes had sent.[27] In a couple of places, however, there was some

---

23 *El Tiempo*, 26 March 1846, has the text of the correspondence with Slidell.
24 'Manifiesto del Exmo. Sr. presidente interino de la república, a la nación', 23 April 1846, in ibid., 25 April 1846.
25 See, e.g., Santoni, 'Los federalistas radicales', pp. 200–5.
26 Paredes y Arrillaga Papers, 144/295.
27 Ibid., 145/160.

resistance, most notably at Veracruz, where Sebastián Camacho reported that no elections had been possible because electors had refused to participate.[28] Nevertheless, candidates were eventually chosen to represent their various classes. Most were familiar faces and long-standing members of the governing elite, although, it must be said, Carlos Bustamante refused to attend the opening ceremony of what he called 'that farce'.[29] The first priority for the new Congress was to elect an interim president and vice-president. To nobody's surprise, Paredes was chosen for the former office and Bravo for the latter. A week later, Paredes was authorized to lead the army.

It is quite possible that Paredes chose to vacate the presidency so soon after being elected because he recognized by June that his own position and that of his government as a whole were, if not on the brink of collapse, close to the edge. Despite finally disassociating himself from the monarchists, which he did in a speech on 6 June – *El Tiempo* ceased publication the next day – his identification with that group had cost him too much support, and his promises and appeals to the self-interest of property owners had not generated the backing he needed among the *hombres de bien*. The threat or prospect of monarchy had polarized opinion, and for the first time in the centralist decade, the liberal federalists of all shades of radical to moderate opinion had agreed to forget their differences for the time being to present a united opposition. Secret meetings had been held in January, during which Gómez Pedraza, Lafragua, Otero, Luis de la Rosa, Domingo Ibarra, and Juan Bautista Ceballos and others decided to co-operate in a campaign to bring down the Paredes government.[30] The press was the public forum, and there were the usual campaigns against individual ministers, their legislation and, above all, the monarchists. It was no surprise to anybody, and certainly not Paredes, whose agents kept him well informed, when *pronunciamientos* were reported from various places, including Mazatlán and Guadalajara. Among the most notable of these occurred in April when General Alvarez rebelled in the south, withdrawing his recognition of the Paredes government and demanding ratification of the republican system.[31] Although Paredes was told by one adviser that the revolt would attract little support, Bravo, who had been sent to Veracruz because of rumours of rebellion there, was less optimistic about his old rival. Denouncing Alvarez as 'despicable, of no importance, mean and cowardly', he cautioned that he was very dan-

28 Ibid., 146/2.
29 Bustamante, *El nuevo Bernal Díaz*, p. 177.
30 Santoni, 'Los federalistas radicales', p. 226.
31 Alvarez had recognized the government in a letter to the Minister of War on 27 January 1846; see *El Tiempo*, 5 February 1846.

gerous and must be captured in person if his insubordination was not to spread.[32]

One of the demands in the Alvarez plan was of supreme significance: that Santa Anna be recognized as president. Santa Anna was still in Havana, and although he had made indirect contact with Gómez Farías the previous year, he had remained on the fringe of the political turmoil which had brought about the fall of Herrera. The radicals had seemed to reject any idea of an alliance with the *santanistas*, but with memories of Santa Anna's extreme unpopularity just a year or so before fading remarkably quickly as memories of Santa Anna always seemed to do, and faced with the threat of monarchy, Gómez Farías and his colleagues began to reconsider their options. From January 1846 onwards, a stream of visitors made the journey to Havana, including some of Gómez Farías' children, and a regular correspondence flowed back and forth between Santa Anna and Gómez Farías or their respective spokesmen. Initially, but not exclusively, the former Minister Rejón, who was in Havana, seems to have been the main intermediary.[33] In several letters in January and February to Gómez Farías and other radicals, he let it be known that Santa Anna, with whom he met regularly, was changing his opinions.[34] By early March it was widely known that negotiations between the radicals and *santanistas* were taking place and then, on 8 March, in a letter to Manuel Teulet but clearly intended for Gómez Farías – there is a copy in Gómez Farías' hand in his archive – Santa Anna made it known that he now welcomed an alliance with the liberals.[35] Insisting on his determination to defend his lifelong commitment to republicanism, he promised that if he were able to return and Paredes were overthrown, he would ensure that the people would decide the form of government, and that having done so, he would retire to private life. Moreover, he now accepted that federalism was the popular choice, that democratic principles were dominant and that provincial liberties had to be respected. The next day, Rejón confirmed in a letter of his own that Santa Anna was committed to the democratic and federal principles and that he thought Gómez Farías to be the most important person 'to bring order to the affairs of the republic'.[36]

Over the next few weeks, many other letters went to and from Havana, and there was much discussion over the details of the plan that Santa

32 S. Camacho to M. Paredes y Arrillaga, 26 April 1846, Paredes y Arrillaga Papers, 145/164; N. Bravo to M. Paredes y Arrillaga, 27 April 1846, ibid., 145/283.

33 Rejón's defence of his conduct while a minister in 1844 entitled 'Justificación de la conducta de MCR . . . ' began to be printed in *El Contra-Tiempo,* 20 March 1846.

34 For this correspondence, see Gómez Farías Papers, 1363, 1369, 1384.

35 Ibid., 1377.

36 Ibid., 1381.

Anna should issue, where he should land and which town or city should pronounce on his behalf. In addition to Gómez Farías, Lafragua, former Minister of War Almonte, who had resigned from Paredes' cabinet in February to be replaced by the perennial Tornel, Boves and various others including Alvarez, who was also corresponding with Santa Anna, were directly involved in the plotting. For his part, Gómez Farías seems to have been very cautious about accepting the hand of friendship proffered by his political enemy of so many years, and it is unlikely that he believed Santa Anna's protestations of faith in liberalism and federalism. But an alliance had its obvious attractions, which Santa Anna put succinctly in a letter of 25 April: 'I will give you the affection of the army in which I have many good friends and you will give me that of the masses in which you have so much influence'. He added that an 'intimate union' between them was essential for the national interest because in addition to the U.S. threat, Britain and France were both preparing to invade the continent, starting with Mexico, to establish monarchies and secure their commercial interests. 'All this', he concluded, 'indicates that we should hasten to take power from the hands of the detestable party of the so-called *hombres de bien*'.[37]

Although Gómez Farías' replies to Santa Anna have not been located, it is clear that by early May agreement had been reached, at least on general principles. Writing on 9 May, Santa Anna commented that even though their letters were getting crossed on the ocean journey, there was a definite 'fortuitous convergence of feelings' between them, and he asked Gómez Farías to consult with his agents at Veracruz on the timing and place of his return. He was, he added, to have lunch tomorrow with his daughter and son-in-law.[38] Meanwhile, Gómez Farías kept up his correspondence with his own allies around the country, and by the end of May, through his son Fermín, he was able to tell Santa Anna that they were certain of victory because revolts had already started at Guadalajara and elsewhere, with others expected soon at Zacatecas, Durango, Guanajuato and Puebla.[39]

These negotiations between Santa Anna and Gómez Farías were certainly known, at least in general terms, to the Paredes government. Reports of them were mentioned in the press, and Carlos Bustamante noted the constant rumours of envoys and money being sent to Havana.[40] When Santa Anna chose to publish proclamations to the nation, which he did on 8 February and again on 20 May to defend his record and his patriotism,

37 Ibid., 1400.
38 Ibid., 1406.
39 Ibid., 1412.
40 Bustamante, *El nuevo Bernal Díaz*, pp. 189–90.

it was obvious that something was afoot.[41] Paredes' own agents in the departments confirmed this in letters in April and May, advising him of an alliance between 'santanistas y extra-liberales'.[42] At first Paredes tried to negotiate his own deal with the moderates. Early in April, he met with Otero, Riva Palacio and others – Gómez Pedraza was invited but did not attend – and offered to repeal the antipress laws and to revise the *convocatoria*.[43] No deal was struck, however, and Paredes decided to take a harsher line. Between 17 and 20 May, leading radicals and *santanistas* were arrested; these included former ministers Trigueros and Lombardo, Santa Anna's lawyer Sierra y Rosso, former rebel Rangel and, above all, Gómez Farías.[44]

The arrest of Gómez Farías, who was accused of being involved in the Alvarez revolt, merely served to hinder the planning of Santa Anna's return, because his sons, particularly Fermín, continued the correspondence to Havana and a congressional grand jury absolved his father, who was released from jail on 14 July.[45] There remained one problem to be overcome, and that was the means whereby Santa Anna could evade the U.S. naval patrols that were blockading Mexico's gulf ports. The story of Santa Anna's secret talks with the U.S. government has already been told by several scholars, and there is no need to repeat the details here.[46] In brief, using his agents, especially Colonel Alexander Atocha, Santa Anna persuaded President Polk that, if he were allowed to return to Mexico, he would ensure a peaceful solution to the conflict over Texas and that he would cede some of the northern territories in return for substantial cash compensation. Polk had given orders that he be permitted through the blockade on 13 May, but the arrest in Mexico City of Gómez Farías and his other allies delayed arrangements for both his departure and arrival. Nevertheless, it must be presumed that Gómez Farías knew that Santa Anna's re-entry to Mexico would not be a problem, although it is unlikely he knew the terms promised to Washington, and after his release from jail, he was able to continue his preparations for a final strike against the Paredes government.

The dénouement, or one might say the last gasp of centralism, came in the first days of August. Paredes had vacated the presidency and left

---

41 'El General Antonio López de Santa Anna a la nación mexicana', Havana, 8 February 1846, in *El Tiempo*, 22 February 1846. There is a copy of the manifesto dated 20 May in Paredes y Arrillaga Papers, 146/31.

42 See, e.g., V. Jiménez to M. Paredes y Arrillaga, 13 April 1846, ibid., 145/109.

43 Santoni, 'Los federalistas radicales', p. 238.

44 Ibid., p. 244; Malo, *Diario*, p. 298.

45 For the letters between Fermín Gómez Farías and Santa Anna, see Gómez Farías Papers, 1412, 1417, 1419. Santa Anna also enclosed a letter to Cayetano Rubio instructing him to ensure that Gómez Farías did not lack financial resources.

46 See, e.g., Jones, *Santa Anna*, pp. 100–7.

the capital with three thousand men on 1 August after Bravo, as vice-president, had assumed the office on 27 July.[47] Bravo appointed a new cabinet and promptly tried to forestall the coup which everybody knew was imminent. On 3 August, in effect disowning the now notorious *convocatoria* by which it had been elected, Congress decreed that the Bases Orgánicas remained the national constitution. The next day, 4 August, at 5:30 a.m., cannon fire was heard once more from the Citadel. Led by Commander General Mariano Salas, a long-standing enemy of Paredes whose drunken confrontation with him on the night of 7 March 1843 had never been forgotten, the garrison pronounced, demanding a new Congress elected under the 1824 procedures to reconstitute the nation and calling on Santa Anna to be made commander-in-chief of the army.[48]

Bravo hastily took defensive precautions, stationing troops on the roof-tops of the palace and adjacent buildings, but talks with Salas brought no solution, and the rebels gradually occupied the area around the central plaza. With almost no ammunition – Salas had removed it from the palace earlier – Bravo realized he could not resist. On 6 August he agreed to capitulate and allow the rebel forces to occupy the palace unhindered. Paredes, who had returned to the capital with a small escort, was promptly arrested.[49]

Salas assumed the presidency, but it was evident that he was no more than a figurehead. The promoter, organizer and inspiration for the revolt was Gómez Farías, who, after a decade of almost continuous but futile plotting, had finally achieved his come-back. In the last weeks of July, he had made the detailed arrangements, ordering five hundred copies of the plan at a cost of 24 pesos, hiring a carriage to transport them to the Citadel (cost: 3 pesos 2 reales) and generally raising the necessary funds from sympathetic financiers.[50] Immediately moving into the national palace, he took charge of the government of the republic. On 6 August the procedure for the election of a new Congress was announced, with electoral regulations based on those of 1823 and allowing for a vote unrestricted by income or property qualifications. The next day, all the previously enacted antipress legislation was declared void, and a week later, the salary deductions which Paredes had decreed were cancelled.

Only two things remained to bring the centralist decade to an end: the return of Santa Anna and the formal restoration of federalism. Both

47 Robertson, 'Paredes y Arrillaga', pp. 246–7.
48 The text of the so-called Plan de la Ciudadela is in Dublán and Lozano, *Legislación mexicana*, vol. 5, pp. 143–6, n. 1.
49 Robertson, 'Paredes y Arrillaga', p. 252.
50 As was usual during revolts at this time, the rebels kept detailed accounts of expenses; those of Gómez Farías are in his archive, nos. 1486, 1488. Ignacio Carranza seems to have been the banker, supplying 1,047 pesos in gold and silver between 29 July and 5 August.

occurred from 16 to 22 August. On the 16th, the hero of Tampico finally stepped onto Mexican soil, arriving at Veracruz at 1 p.m. Almost immediately, and probably even before setting out for his country estate of El Encero, he sent a note to Gómez Farías, saying, 'I think the 1824 constitution should apply until the new one is published'.[51] Three days later, Gómez Farías replied. 'O.k., o.k.', he said, 'the 1824 constitution is the one we must have because it alone has any legitimacy'.[52] With this agreement between the army and the populace, to use Santa Anna's phrase, on 22 August the restoration of the 1824 charter was decreed. The departmental assemblies were abolished and governors of what were once again to be known as 'states' were to govern according to their respective state constitutions. The decade of centralism was finally over.

51 Gómez Farías Papers, 1545.
52 Ibid., 1577.

13

Conclusion

The centralist decade was an eventful period in Mexico's always eventful history. Ten individuals had occupied the presidential office – eight army officers and two civilians – and there were several hundred ministerial changes as the various administrations came and went. The 1836 constitution, or Siete Leyes, had lasted four and a half years until its replacement by the Bases de Tacubaya in 1841, which in turn was removed in favour of the Bases Orgánicas in 1843, which survived, if only on paper, until the restoration of the 1824 federal charter in 1846. *Pronunciamientos* had been declared more or less continuously, and Mexico City had witnessed the human and physical devastation of warfare in 1840 and 1841 as well as the comparatively bloodless coups of 1844, 1845 and 1846. Two presidents – Bustamante and Herrera – had been arrested in person inside the walls of the national palace, and apart from the interim occupants of the presidential quarters, every president had been driven unwillingly from office as a result of armed rebellion, with the unique exception of the peaceful coup by Congress against the Santa Anna–Canalizo regime of 1844. Texas had been lost forever, Yucatán was virtually independent for much of the decade and war had been declared, if not actually fought to any degree, against France in 1838. There had been congressional elections in almost every year, and seven elected assemblies plus two appointed bodies – Junta de Representantes (1841–3) and Junta de Notables (1843) – had met in the capital. At the regional and local levels, there had been *pronunciamientos* in most major towns where there were army barracks and commander generals, and there had been frequent elections for the departmental assemblies and local offices as each change of regime at the national level was followed by the removal of incumbent representatives or officials who were out of favour.

The list of these statistics and events provides a graphic demonstration of the fact that the aims of the *hombres de bien* and their hopes for a highly centralized form of government had failed. In 1835 centralist republicans, with the reluctant acquiescence of Santa Anna, had gained control of the national Congress. In their manifesto, they had promised to suppress radical liberalism and its supporters by creating a constitutional framework which effectively guaranteed that access to political power at all levels from Congress to municipality was firmly vested in the ranks of what they considered to be the middle-class *hombres de bien*. Their propaganda had emphasized the benefits to be derived from their new order. They promised an end to party factionalism, as well as economic reform, the protection of the status and privileges of the military, the reconquest of Texas and a halt to the rising rate of crime against both person and property. They offered a strong, reinvigorated Church, which would once again command the respect and obedience of the populace and which would ensure that the spread of increasingly fashionable radical ideas that were corrupting the nation's youth would be stopped. Above all, they promised to restore the 'morality of society' by ensuring that what they saw as traditional civic virtues and personal morality were again pre-eminent. They would remove the threat of social dissolution and guarantee progress with order in a society in which every man knew and accepted his place.

All of these things, they had argued, were wholly dependent on achieving the constitutional framework of a highly centralized system with the exercise of power removed from the regions and concentrated in the centre. They well appreciated that the State was weak and that, given the difficulties of distance, topography and communications, there were no fully effective means of enforcing national policies or priorities on distant and diverse regional interests. Their solution, therefore, was to design the electoral process to ensure that *hombres de bien* who shared the same aspirations and values regardless of where they lived were in full control of every level of government. Social status and values were to supersede political differences, and *hombres de bien* of all shades of the political spectrum could differ on the means to achieve progress with order provided that they did not threaten or jeopardize the power and status of their class. Those renegades, the so-called anarchists, demagogues or sansculottes, who did threaten that power with their talk of democracy, popular sovereignty, redistribution of wealth, reduction of Church influence and army privileges would be suppressed.

On every count, the centralists had failed. Their experiments in constitution making had not provided the political stability required to implement or achieve any of the social, economic or cultural reforms they had envisaged. Their first constitution, or Siete Leyes, had been ridiculed from the beginning, and within a couple of years the structure of government it provided had almost collapsed with open and public conflict among the four branches of government. Loud and increasing demands for reform were heard, and after the hostile reception of Gutiérrez de Estrada's monarchist proposal, merchant interests had turned their thoughts to autocracy and to the dictator-in-waiting, Santa Anna. But even with his dictatorial powers under the Bases de Tacubaya, Santa Anna was no more successful in establishing order with progress. Similarly, the Bases Orgánicas achieved no improvement, and ultimately brought Alamán and his allies to their own monarchist solution.

In every other area of the conservative manifesto, things seemed to have become worse rather than better. In foreign affairs, relations with Britain, France and the United States were deteriorating. Texas had not been reconquered despite all the rhetoric and all the cash taken largely from the pockets of the hard-pressed *hombres de bien*. A ruinous war with the United States, which most Mexicans accepted could not be won, was about to start. In the area of social policy, crime remained a daily preoccupation for all property owners and businessmen, and the administration of justice was universally seen as inefficient and corrupt. Despite commissions of enquiry and grandiose programmes of reform, little change had been made in educational provisions for the majority, and while some progressive provincial authorities had managed improvements, the overall picture remained bleak. The army still absorbed the major proportion of national revenues and yet, again despite many paper reforms, it remained plagued by desertion, indiscipline and insubordination. In many areas, regional chieftains retained their power independent of any central military or civil authority. Respect for the Church and indeed the faith, according to the bishops, was still diminishing; people refused to pay their tithes, read prohibited books, profaned the sanctuaries and increasingly resented the apparent wealth of the clergy. With only one or two exceptions, notably the textile industry, the economy continued to be depressed, and while some structural changes may have been occurring and there may have been some recovery of land values and investment in some sectors, what the ordinary *hombre de bien* saw was the critical poverty of the national Treasury and the rising demands on his purse which that poverty engendered. The middle class had suffered from increased taxation on its properties and incomes, forced loans and increases in the price of the imported goods it favoured. Bureaucrats had rarely been paid all their salaries, and their tenure and modest rents on their Church-owned homes had been threatened by property speculators. As for the poor, especially in the cities, hard hit by the copper money devaluation, there was a growing number of destitute and unemployed on the streets, above all in the capital, where those without full-time work comprised probably as much as 50 per cent of the population. In the rural areas and those small communities in which most Mexicans lived, there may have been little deterioration in the people's already impoverished life-style, but centralism had done nothing to improve their situation.

Nothing seemed to have been achieved, therefore, in the decade of centralism, and the same issues dominated the political agenda in 1846 as in 1835. Even more striking is the fact that the personalities who had fought the military, political and ideological battles remained largely the same. Most of the centralists and conservatives who had been instrumental in creating the centralized republic in 1835 were still prominent in the corridors of power at the end of the decade, and when Paredes had announced the membership of his temporary junta in January 1846, the names of those he selected were all familiar. Included were Archbishop Posada y Garduño and Bishop Pardío (Yucatán), Almonte, Tornel and his brother-in-law, Díez de Bonilla, Carlos Bustamante and Alamán. In June 1846 the newly elected Congress had opened its sessions to reveal an even more noticeable continuity of people. The conservative author of the Siete Leyes and its fourth power, Sánchez de Tagle, reappeared, as did the ultramontanist cleric Basilio Arrillaga, and altogether, approximately 60 per cent of the congressmen had served in earlier Congresses, some since the early 1820s and a significant proportion from 1830 to 1832. Several were senior generals whose names reappear time and again throughout the Age of Santa Anna – for example, Bravo, Michelena, Cervantes and Valencia. Similarly, those who opposed them were basically those who had done so in 1835. There were, for example, and to cite only a few, Gómez Farías, Gómez Pedraza, Riva Palacio, Morales, Couto, Herrera and, of course, the man who could never be forgotten, Santa Anna.

There was clearly a notable continuity of 'issues and people', to use the contemporary phrase, with the issues and personalities much the same in 1846 as they had been in 1835. There are several other notable features of the decade. The basic issue of the form of government was the pretext for much of the political conflict and instability as the federalists campaigned and fought to regain the supremacy they had lost in 1834. While the federalist case rested in general on such arguments as regional diversity and needs, however, they were seriously divided between moderates like Gómez Pedraza and radicals like Gómez Farías. What divided them was not just what may be said to be the standard issues such as the status and powers of Church and army but also the more controversial questions of civil rights and access to political power. The moderate liberal federalists shared many social assumptions with their conservative and centralist counterparts, firmly believing that only the middle-class property-owning *hombres de bien* were equipped to govern. Even though Gómez Farías did not dissent from that view, he nevertheless became the symbol of genuine radicalism, of a desire to institute universal male suffrage, the abolition of all forms of personal and institutional privilege, the redistribution of wealth, especially land, and, in commercial policy, free trade rather than protectionism. Above all, he was associated with populism and with threatening the social and economic dominance of the elite by mobilizing the mass of urban poor. In short, he, and particularly the radical press, seemed to threaten what every conservative and moderate *hombre de bien* feared, social dissolution.

The political and military turmoil of the decade was also fought amid a background of changing social values. Lack of research into the social history of the time makes this a problematic area for any historian, but there is no doubt from this study of the centralist decade that changes in social attitudes and morality were a cause of great concern for the *hombres de bien*. It is difficult to define precisely what these changes were, but those aspects mentioned constantly in the conservative press and clerical literature included lack of respect for all authority and for those who exercised it, including parents and the Church; immorality with a significant growth in prostitution and the circulation of so-called obscene literature or works which good Christians should not read; disregard of social conventions and etiquette; lack of respect for property and property owners, the law and legislators; and, in general, refusal of the young to conform to accepted patterns of behaviour within and outside of the family. Finally, the traditional scholastic education, which was considered to have inculcated the 'proper' values in the young, was losing its appeal and more fashionable but dangerous progressive, utilitarian ideas were being introduced.

Where these changes appear most evident is in respect of the Church. At the beginning of the decade, the clergy had certainly expected to be strengthened, if not restored to their once protected, superior position, but despite their exceptionally strong presence in the 1835–7 Congress and their proclerical allies in the executive and other government agencies, they promptly found that sympathy did not translate into action. Hence, they failed to have all the reform laws of 1833–4, notably those on tithes, repealed, and more important, the new conservative administration refused to give up national claims to ecclesiastical patronage. Then, as the crisis in the Treasury deepened, more and more demands were made on Church wealth and clerical institutions were required to contribute to the multiple taxes on property and rents as well as to the forced loans. Even more alarming for the senior clergy was renewed talk of the nationalization of all Church assets, and there had even been an occasional mention in Congress and often in the radical press of the dreaded freedom of worship. Recruitment of clergy continued to be a problem, and many parishes remained without a priest, as did some of the dioceses and cathedral chapters, which could no longer afford to fill their complement of canons. All of these practical problems were accompanied, according to numerous sermons and pastoral letters, by a change in public attitude towards the Church. Neither it nor the faith any longer commanded the automatic respect and obedience of the people, and it was not only the mostly propertied former tithe payers who were indifferent to appeals to their conscience. One parish priest in the remote and largely Indian diocese of Chiapas bemoaned his loss of influence over his indigenous flock. He reported that they had previously made an annual contribution to their church with the money earned from a communal maize crop. They now refused to do this because 'they say they are free citizens and they do not want to do it'.[1]

The other institutional pillar of the centralized regime was the army, and it may also be said to have had mixed fortunes during the decade. On the negative side, it had been humiliated in Texas and at Veracruz against the French, even with Santa Anna's claimed brief moment of glory. There had been a mass of new ordinances and reorganization, not to mention uniforms, and vast sums of money had been poured into the military coffers. But again all the indications are that public respect for the army was diminishing and that it had lost or was losing the over-whelming support it enjoyed in the years immediately following inde-pendence. There was growing resentment against the cost, especially when set against performance, and the visible condition and quality of recruits were matters of public scandal. On the other hand, the officer corps had done rather well. Generals Barragán, Bravo, Bustamante, Canalizo, Paredes and Santa Anna had occupied the presidential chair, and except for the interim presidents, there had been no serious challenge in any presidential election from civilian candidates. In control of the executive these general-presidents had liberally dispensed money, promotions and favours to maintain support, and in personal terms they, most of all Santa Anna, had done very well financially. But as Hamnett has aptly noted in a recent article, 'The Mexican military was not a monolith but a series of mutually antagonistic fragments aligned with factions or leaders'.[2] In their most obvious manifestation, those fragments were the regional com-manders, most of whom proved to be uncontrollable by political or mil-itary superiors in the centre or provinces. They ruled their domains as autocrats, and the more successful, like Paredes, were able to build a constituency of support and network of allies which enabled them to challenge the presidential power. All were willing to seek the backing of the political factions when convenient, and those like Valencia changed their allegiances almost at the drop of a hat or a few pesos. It was the volatility of those senior army officers and the lack among them of any

---

1 F. Orozco y Jiménez, *Colección de documentos inéditos relativos a la Iglesia de Chiapas* (San Cristóbal Las Casas, 1911), vol. 2, p. 123.
2 B. Hamnett, 'Benito Juárez, Early Liberalism, and the Regional Politics of Oaxaca, 1828–1853', *Bulletin of Latin American Research*, 10 (1991), 7.

loyalty to people or policies which proved to be a major problem for every president, including Santa Anna.

The name of Santa Anna obviously dominates the period, even though his physical presence in the national palace was relatively brief. After he left the presidency on 27 January 1835, he held the office on four more separate occasions, but his total residence over the eleven years amounted to less than twenty-six months. His longest stay in the capital was almost exactly one year – from late September 1841 to early October 1842 – and that seems to have been the maximum he could tolerate of life in the city, always longing to return to his beloved rural retreat. Nevertheless, even though absent, sometimes in disgrace after San Jacinto, his shadow was always present, and every political faction believed that he retained the influence and power to overthrow any government. The source of that influence lay in several factors, which have been indicated in earlier chapters of this study. Given his record of achievement on the battle-field, or rather nonachievement, it is remarkable that he managed to retain his prestige as a military commander. He did so because he was a master of propaganda and of the cult of his own reputation. There is also no doubt that he was a supreme political manipulator, articulate and persuasive, able to convince men as diverse as Alamán and Gómez Farías that he could be trusted or controlled. Time and again throughout his long career, he suffered defeat and humiliation, only to recover as both conservatives and liberals tried to use him or his reputation in their own interests.

Yet Santa Anna may also be said to have failed in the centralist decade. He had been forced from power in 1844, but his failure was even greater on a personal level. All the signs are that he expected and wanted to become the dictator of Mexico after his removal of the 1833–4 regime, that he considered himself the equal of Bolívar or Napoleon or certainly Rosas and other dictators to the south. He failed in that ambition, and there are at least two principal reasons why he did so. The first concerns his reputation and influence in the army. While his popularity with junior ranks cannot be questioned, his influence over his peers was much less reliable. Men like Paredes, Valencia, Canalizo, Bravo, Cortazar and many others used Santa Anna to further their careers in the same way that he used them to promote his own, and they had no compunction about removing him from office whenever a pretext or opportunity arose. Some like Arista, Inclán and Alvarez seemed content to rule their provincial domains, probably because they lacked the support to gain national success, but all displayed the same characteristics as the mercurial Santa Anna, changing sides and loyalties whenever it suited them. Hence, Santa Anna, while he gained the presidency with their support, was also driven from it when he lost it by the same rival and ambitious generals who had put him there, and he was never able to build any enduring military constituency.

Santa Anna, however, was not frustrated in his dictatorial ambitions solely by the rivalry of fellow army officers. He also failed to build any significant support among civilian politicians. It may certainly be argued that these years in Mexico's history were a time of militarism, but one outstanding feature of the centralist republic was the resilience of the civilian political opposition to military dominance. That opposition was to be seen mostly in Congress, which always had a large civilian majority, and in the press. Every general-president found himself soon after taking office in open conflict with the elected assembly, and although attempts were always made to influence or control elections, they invariably failed in the sense that those chosen were prepared, sometimes at considerable personal risk, to defy their military patron. Even those assemblies hand-picked or appointed directly by Paredes or Santa Anna, for example, refused to toe the line on every issue. The best illustration of this military–civilian antagonism came in 1844 when, despite his autocratic powers, Santa Anna was directly challenged time and again by the Congress, which refused to be intimidated into closure and ultimately inspired the successful and peaceful 'three-hour revolution' against him. Santa Anna and all the other general-presidents failed, therefore, to establish any form of totalitarian military rule or even to consolidate the military domination of the country. Thus, as we have seen, myriad political factions with their associated press and pamphleteers operated continuously regardless of the frequent exile or imprisonment of their leaders, the closure of their newspapers and the frequent behind-the-scenes threats and intimidation.

Just as influential as professional politicians like Gómez Farías, Lafragua and Otero were the organized interest groups. Ranging from mine operators and owners, cotton plantation owners, textile manufactures, tobacco farmers and so on to small-scale trade associations of tanners and bakers, these groups were always vocal and exerted considerable pressure on every administration. At times situated across several regions, they used their collective influence and money to gain the backing of departmental governors or military commanders, and often they sent representations and petitions to the national authorities in attempts to defend their interests or to change policy decisions. As indicated in earlier chapters, the textile and tobacco lobbies were especially active, and with public figures such as Alamán, Tornel and Santa Anna among their allies, they were able to exert substantial pressure on economic policy. Even more prominent were the entrepreneurs and financiers, usually but not always based in the capital. They became the bankers to the Bustamante government, and as the fiscal deficit mounted, so did their influence in the offices of the national palace. Some, but not all, made fortunes from their speculations in government stocks, and those who were favoured by the always corrupt Santa Anna benefited from their multiple deals and contracts. Opinion soon turned against them and their ostentatious affluence, which contrasted so sharply with the public poverty, but the main victim of this hostility turned out to be Santa Anna, whose personal venality in 1844 seems to have exceeded even the accepted level. Many of the *agiotistas* were also investors and entrepreneurs involved in agriculture, commerce, mining and transport, and they included in their number the so-called *comerciantes,* or merchants. Mostly anonymous in terms of their political role but definitely including a number of foreign nationals involved in the import–export trade, they seem to have been very active in using their contacts and financial resources to influence, if not determine, national policy. There is no doubt that the 1841 revolt which removed Bustamante and restored Santa Anna was very largely organized and financed by rich merchants in the capital and probably at Veracruz and Guadalajara.

All of these factors illustrate why the attempt to establish a centralized form of national government based in Mexico City and under the control of *hombres de bien* failed. The pressures arising from regional diversity, ideological division, social change, economic problems, institutional conservatism, traditional values in conflict with new and personal ambitions were simply too great to control. The *hombres de bien* were forced to concede, at least for the time being, that the form of government best suited to Mexico's needs was federalism. The causes of conflict and the tensions behind it which have been identified in this study were to continue for many more years, but the generation which had taken control in 1821 soon began to disappear. They were simply growing old, and with a handful of long-lived exceptions such as Santa Anna, Gómez Farías and Alvarez, many of them died or retired from public office soon after the end of the centralist decade. Sánchez de Tagle and Bishop Vázquez died in 1847; Carlos Bustamante and Valencia in 1848; Paredes in 1849; and by 1854, Anastasio Bustamante, Alamán, Bravo, Canalizo, Herrera, Tornel and many others of their time had gone from the stage. They were replaced by a new generation of conservatives and liberals who were to try to resolve in the midcentury Reform much the same issues that had dominated the centralist decade. Our fictional *hombre de bien,* however, with his desire for progress with order and the secure protection of his own social and economic position, had to await the arrival of Don Porfirio Díaz before his wishes were granted.

Sources and works cited

Manuscript sources

Full details of the archival references for the manuscript sources are given in the notes. The following archives and collections were used.

Great Britain
    Public Record Office (London), Foreign Office Papers, FO50/82–198
Mexico
    Archivo General de la Nación
    Archivo del Senado
    Biblioteca Nacional, Lafragua Collection
    Centro de Estudios Históricos (Fundación Cultural de Condumex)
United States
    University of Texas at Austin, Nettie Lee Benson Latin American Collection
      Genaro García Manuscript Collection
        Alamán Papers
        Anon. diario militar y político, 1836–7
        Correspondencia autógrafa de Santa Anna a M. M. Jiménez
        Documentos misceláneos, 1749–1860, 1842–59
        García, C., archive, 1810–35
        García Salinas, F., archive
        Gonzaga Gordoa, L., correspondence
        Gómez Farías, V., archive
        Gómez Pedraza, M., 'Prisión de los sres. Pedraza, Riva Palacio, Lafragua y Otero
        Justin Smith Papers
        López Escudero, M., correspondence, 1821–80
        Manning and Mackintosh Papers, 1825–94
        Mateos, J. A., segunda época, 1820–87
        Mejía, F., 'Epocas, hechos y acontecimientos de mi vida y de los que fui actor y testigo, 1822–1878'
        Mora, J. M. L., correspondence, 1794–1844
        Moreno, A., correspondence, 1841–7
        Paredes y Arrillaga, M., archive
        Peñasco, conde del, correspondence, 1789–1844
        Sánchez, A., correspondence, 1831–78
        Santa Anna, documentos relativos a . . . 1825–1876
      Riva Palacio, archive

Hernández y Dávalos Papers
Archivo de Mariano Otero (microfilm copy)

Newspapers and periodical publications

I have used a large number of contemporary newspapers, which are indispensable for any study of the Age of Santa Anna. For the sake of brevity, the list that follows is restricted to those cited directly in the text. They are located in various libraries, most notably, British Library (Colindale); Benson Collection, University of Texas; Bancroft Library, University of California; Library of Congress (Washington, D.C.); Hemeroteca Nacional (Mexico City); and Archivo General de la Nación (Mexico City). The dates are for issues I have used rather than the complete run of the publication.

La Abeja, 1844
Aguila Mexicana, 1843
El Amigo del Pueblo, 1845–6
El Anteojo, 1835–6
Aurora: Periódico científico y militar, 1835–6
Boletín de la Ciudadela, 1841
Boletín Oficial, 1841
El Cardillo de los Agiotistas, 1837
El Contra-Tiempo, 1846
El Cosmopolita, 1835–43
El Crepúsculo (Puebla), 1842
El Defensor de la Integridad Nacional, 1844
El Defensor de las Leyes, 1845
Diario del Gobierno, 1835–46
La Enciclopedia de los Sansculottes, 1835
El Estandarte Nacional, 1845
El Fénix de la Libertad, 1833
El Imparcial, 1837
El Independiente, 1839
El Investigador Mexicano, 1837
La Lima, 1834
La Lima de Vulcano, 1835–8
El Lucero de Tacubaya, 1844
La Luz, 1835–6
El Mercurio Poblano, 1843–5
El Mexicano, 1839
La Minerva, 1845
El Momo, 1838
El Mosquito Mexicano, 1834–43
El Nacional, 1836
La Oposición, 1834–5
El Restaurador Mexicano, 1838–9
El Santanista Oaxaqueño, 1836
El Siglo XIX, 1841–6
El Sol, 1835
El Telégrafo, 1834
El Tiempo, 1846
La Verdad Desnuda, 1833

El Voto Nacional, 1836
La Voz de Michoacán, 1843–4
La Voz del Pueblo, 1845

Books and pamphlets

The following list contains those works cited in the text together with a few others which have pertinent information. There is a vast range of contemporary pamphlets, but I have used mainly the G. R. G. Conway Collection (University of London); Benson Collection; Sutro Pamphlet Collection (University of San Francisco); British Library Collection; and Lafragua Collection. For the sake of brevity, I have again included only those cited directly in the text.

Alamán, L. *Obras: Documentos diversos.* 4 vols. Mexico, 1945–7.
    Historia de México desde los primeros movimientos que prepararon su independencia en el año 1808 hasta la época presente. 5 vols. Mexico, 1969.
Alpuche e Infante, J. M. *Exposición o sea satisfacción que el que suscribe, hace al Supremo Gobierno de la república contra el despotismo del alto clero yucateco y metropolitano.* Mexico, 1837.
Amador, E. *Bosquejo histórico de Zacatecas.* Zacatecas, 1943.
Anna, T. E. *The Mexican Empire of Iturbide.* Lincoln, Neb., 1990.
Aranda, D. *Carta pastoral.* Guadalajara, 2 January 1837.
Archer, C. *The Army in Bourbon Mexico.* Albuquerque, N.M., 1977.
Arnold, L. *Bureaucracy and Bureaucrats in Mexico City, 1742–1835.* Tucson, Ariz., 1988.
Arrangoiz, F. de P. *México desde 1808 hasta 1867.* Mexico, 1968.
Arrillaga, B. *Examen crítico de la Memoria del Ministerio de Justicia y Negocios Eclesiásticos.* Mexico, 1835.
Arrom, S. *The Women of Mexico City, 1800–1857.* Stanford, Calif., 1984.
Bancroft, H. H. *History of Mexico.* vol. 5. San Francisco, 1887.
Barker, N. N. *The French Experience in Mexico, 1821–1861.* Chapel Hill, N.C., 1979.
Barrera, M. *Exposición que acerca de la contrata de vestuarios para los cuerpos del ejército hace el que suscribe.* Mexico, 1837.
Bazant, J. *Historia de la deuda exterior de México (1823–1946).* Mexico, 1968.
    Alienation of Church Wealth in Mexico: Social and Economic Aspects of the Liberal Revolution, 1856–1875. Cambridge, 1971.
    Cinco haciendas mexicanas: Tres siglos de vida rural en San Luis Potosí (1600–1910). Mexico, 1975.
    Antonio Haro y Tamariz y sus aventuras políticas. Mexico, 1985.
Benson, N. L., ed. *Mexico and the Spanish Cortes.* Austin, Tex., 1966.
Bocanegra, J. M. *Memorias para la historia de México independiente, 1821–1841.* 2 vols. Mexico, 1892–7.
Brachet de Márquez, V. *Población de los Estados Mexicanos en el siglo XIX (1824–1895).* Mexico, 1976.
Bravo Ugarte, J. *Periodistas y periódicos mexicanos.* Mexico, 1966.
Buisson, I., et al., eds. *Problemas de la formación del estado y de la nación en Hispanoamérica.* Bonn, 1984.
Bullock, W. *Six Months' Residence and Travels in Mexico.* London, 1824.
Bushnell, C. G. *La carrera política y militar de Juan Alvarez.* Mexico, 1988.
Bustamante, C. M. *El nuevo Bernal Díaz del Castillo o sea historia de la invasión de los anglo-americanos en México.* Mexico, 1949.
    Continuación del cuadro histórico de la revolución mexicana. 4 vols. Mexico, 1953–63.

Continuación del cuadro histórico: El gabinete mexicano durante el segundo período de Bustamante hasta la entrega del mando a Santa Anna. 2 vols. Mexico, 1985.

Apuntes para la historia del gobierno del general don Antonio López de Santa Anna. Mexico, 1986.

Calderón de la Barca, F. *Life in Mexico.* London, 1970.

Callcott, W. H. *Santa Anna.* Hamden, Conn., 1964.

Cárdenas, E. *Some Issues on Mexico's Nineteenth Century Depression.* Mexico, 1983.

Cárdenas de la Peña, E. *Tiempo y tarea de Luis Gonzaga Cuevas.* Mexico, 1982.

Cardoso, C. F. S., ed. *Formación y desarrollo de la burguesía en México.* Mexico, 1978.

Carr, R. *Spain, 1808–1975.* Oxford, 1982.

Carreño, A. M., ed. *Jefes del ejército mexicano en 1847.* Mexico, 1914.

Castañeda, C., ed. *Elite, clases sociales y rebelión en Guadalajara y Jalisco: Siglos XVIII y XIX.* Guadalajara, 1988.

Catálogo de la Colección Lafragua, 1821–1853. Mexico, 1975.

Colección de los documentos más interesantes relativos al préstamo de medio millón de pesos ofrecido por el venerable clero secular y regular de este arzobispado. Mexico, 1839.

Correspondencia entre el Supremo Gobierno y el general D. Antonio López de Santa Anna. Mexico, 1845.

Costeloe, M. P. *Church Wealth in Mexico.* Cambridge, 1967.

La primera república federal de México (1824–1835). Mexico, 1975.

Church and State in Independent Mexico: A Study of the Patronage Debate, 1821–1857. London, 1978.

Response to Revolution: Imperial Spain and the Spanish American Revolutions, 1810–1840. Cambridge, 1986.

Cotner, T. E. *The Military and Political Career of José Joaquín de Herrera, 1792–1854.* New York, 1969.

Cotner, T. E., and Castañeda, C. E., eds. *Essays in Mexican History.* Austin, Tex., 1958.

Cue Cánovas, A. *El federalismo mexicano.* Mexico, 1960.

Cuevas, L. G. *Porvenir de México.* Mexico, 1954.

Cuevas, M. *Historia de la nación mexicana.* Mexico, 1967.

Delgado, J. *La monarquía en México, 1845–1847.* Mexico, 1990.

Díaz y Díaz, F. *Caudillos y caciques: Antonio López de Santa Anna y Juan Alvarez.* Mexico, 1972.

Diccionario Porrúa: Historia, biografía y geografía de México. 3d ed. Mexico, 1970.

Dictamen de la comisión y acuerdo del Illmo. Cabildo metropolitano de México sobre hipotecar los bienes eclesiásticos para el empréstito que solicita el supremo gobierno. Mexico, 1837.

Dictamen de la comisión especial de la cámara de diputados, nombrada para darlo sobre las manifestaciones relativos al cambio del sistema de gobierno. Mexico, 1835.

Dictamen de la comisión especial de la cámara de senadores sobre cambio de la forma de gobierno y voto particular del señor Couto. Mexico, 1835.

Dictamen de la comisión revisora de los poderes conferidos a los Sres. diputados al congreso general de la unión para reforma de la constitución federal. Mexico, 1835.

Dublán, M., and Lozano, J. M., eds. *Legislación mexicana,* vols. 2–5. Mexico, 1876.

Los dueños de los ingenios de azúcar representan los enormes males que han sufrido. Mexico, 1837.

Estudios de historia moderna y contemporánea de México. Mexico, 1972.

Exposición dirigida de la capital del departamento de Puebla al Exmo. Sr. Presidente general Don Anastasio Bustamante, pidiendo el restablecimiento del sistema federal. Mexico, 1837.

Florescano, E., ed. *Orígenes y desarrollo de la burguesía en América Latina, 1700–1955.* Mexico, 1985.

Fuentes Mares, J. *Santa Anna: Aurora y ocaso de un comediante.* Mexico, 1967.

Galván Rivera, M. *Guía de forasteros*. Mexico, 1842.

García, G., ed. *Documentos inéditos o muy raros para la historia de México*, vols. 56, 59, 60. Mexico, 1974–5.

Garza Villareal, G. *El proceso de industrialización en la ciudad de México*. Mexico, 1985.

Gayón Córdova, M. *Condiciones de vida y de trabajo en la ciudad de México en el siglo XIX*. Mexico, 1988.

Gilliam, A. *Travels in Mexico during the Years 1843 and 1844*. Aberdeen, 1847.

González Navarro, M. *El pensamiento político de Lucas Alamán*. Mexico, 1952.

Gutiérrez Estrada, J. M. *Carta dirigida al Exmo. Sr. Presidente de la república sobre la necesidad de buscar en una convención el posible remedio de los males que aquejan a la república y opiniones del autor acerca del mismo asunto*. Mexico, 1840.

Hale, C. *Mexican Liberalism in the Age of Mora, 1821–1853*. New Haven, Conn., 1968.

Hamnett, B. *Roots of Insurgency: Mexican Regions, 1750–1824*. Cambridge, 1986.

Harris, C. H. *A Mexican Family Empire: The Latifundios of the Sánchez Navarro Family, 1765–1867*. Austin, Tex., 1975.

Herrera Canales, I. *El comercio exterior de México*. Mexico, 1977.

Hutchinson, C. A. 'Valentín Gómez Farías: A Biographical Study'. Ph.D. Diss. University of Texas, 1948.

Jones, O. L. *Santa Anna*. New York, 1968.

Katz, F., ed. *Riot, Rebellion, and Revolution: Rural Social Conflict in Mexico*. Princeton, N.J., 1988.

Kicza, J. E. *Colonial Entrepreneurs: Families and Business in Bourbon Mexico City*. Albuquerque, N.M. 1983.

Knapp, F. A. *The Life of Sebastián Lerdo de Tejada, 1823–1889*. New York, 1968.

Knight, A. *The Mexican Revolution*. 2 vols. Cambridge, 1986.

Landazuri Benítez, G., and Vázquez Mantecón, V. *Azúcar y Estado (1750–1880)*. Mexico, 1988.

López Rosado, D. G. *Historia y pensamiento económico de México*. 6 vols. Mexico, 1968–74.

Ludlow, L., and Marichal, C., eds., *Banco y poder en México (1800–1925)*. Mexico, 1985.

Malagón Barceló, J., ed., *Relaciones diplomáticas hispano-mexicanas: Documentos procedentes del Archivo de la Embajada de España en México. Serie 1. Despachos generales*. 3 vols. Mexico, 1949–66.

Malo, J. R. *Diario de sucesos notables*. Mexico, 1948.

Márquez, J. V. *La guerra del 47 y la opinión pública (1845–1848)*. Mexico, 1975.

Mecham, J. L. *Church and State in Latin America*. rev. ed., Chapel Hill, N.C., 1966.

Memorias de Guerra. Mexico, 1835, 1836.

Memorias de Hacienda. Mexico, 1837–1841.

Memoria de Justicia. Mexico, 1835.

México a través de los informes presidenciales: Los mensajes políticos. Mexico, 1976.

Mora, J. M. L. *Obras sueltas*. Mexico, 1963.

La nación no quiere diezmos. Mexico, 1835.

Noriega Cantú, A. *El pensamiento conservador y el conservadurismo mexicano*. Mexico, 1972. *Las ideas políticas en las declaraciones de derechos de las constituciones políticas de México (1814–1917)*. Mexico, 1984.

Noriega Elío, C. *El Constituyente de 1842*. Mexico, 1986.

Observaciones que sobre el proyecto de bases orgánicas hacen a la h. junta legislativa el obispo y cabildo de Guadalajara. Mexico, 1843.

Olivera, R. R., and Crété, L. *Life in Mexico under Santa Anna, 1822–1855*. Norman, Okla., 1991.

Olveda, J. *Gordiano Guzmán: Un cacique del siglo XIX*. Mexico, 1980.

Olveda, J., ed., *Cartas a Gómez Farías*. Mexico, 1990.

Orozco y Jiménez, F. *Colección de documentos inéditos relativos a la Iglesia de Chiapas*. San Cristóbal las Casas, 1911.

Otero, M. *Ensayo sobre el verdadero estado de la cuestión social y política que se agita en la república mexicana*. Mexico, 1842.

Planes en la nación mexicana. Books 2–4. Mexico, 1987.

Pletcher, D. M. *The Diplomacy of Annexation: Texas, Oregon and the Mexican War*. Columbia, Mo., 1973.

Portugal, C. *Pastoral*. Mexico, 2 February 1835.

Potash, R. A. *Mexican Government and Industrial Development in the Early Republic: The Banco de Avío*. Amherst, Mass., 1983.

Prieto, G. *Memorias de mis tiempos*. 2 vols. Mexico, 1948.

Proceso del general Santa Anna. Mexico, 1836.

Ramírez, J. F. *Mexico during the War with the United States*, ed. W. V. Scholes, trans. B. Scherr. Columbia, Mo., 1950.

Ramírez Cabañas, J. *Las relaciones entre México y el Vaticano*. Mexico, 1928.

Randall, R. W. *Real del Monte: A British Mining Venture in Mexico*. Austin, Tex., 1972.

Rejón, M. C. *Justificación de la conducta de Manuel Crescencio Rejón desde octubre de 1841 hasta la fecha*. New Orleans, La., 1846.

Reina, L. *Las rebeliones campesinas en México (1819–1906)*. Mexico, 1980.

Representación que los dueños y administradores de las casas de matanza hacen al Supremo Congreso pidiendo que se derogue la ley que previene se paguen los derechos de la Hacienda Pública con dos terceras partes de plata y una de cobre. Mexico, 1836.

Reyes Heroles, J. *El liberalismo mexicano*. 3 vols. Mexico, 1961.

Estudio preliminar a las obras de Mariano Otero. Mexico, 1967.

Riva Palacio, V., ed. *México a través de los siglos*. vol. 4. Mexico, 1962.

Rivera Cambas, M. *Historia antigua y moderna de Jalapa y de las revoluciones del estado de Veracruz*. vols. 5–8. Mexico, 1959.

Los gobernantes de México. vols. 4, 5. Mexico, 1964.

Robertson, F. D. 'The military and political career of Mariano Paredes y Arillaga, 1797–1849'. Ph.D. diss. University of Texas, 1955.

Rodríguez, J. E. *Down from Colonialism: Mexico's Nineteenth Century Crisis*. Berkeley and Los Angeles, 1983.

Rodríguez, J. E. ed., *The Independence of Mexico and the Creation of a New Nation*. Berkeley and Los Angeles, 1989.

Rodríguez Puebla, J. *Tres días de ministerio*. Mexico, 1838.

Salado Alvarez, V. *Episodios nacionales mexicanos. De Santa Anna a la Reforma: Memorias de un veterano*. Mexico, 1984.

Salvucci, R. J. *Textiles and Capitalism in Mexico: An Economic History of the Obrajes, 1539–1840*. Princeton, N.J., 1987.

Samponaro, F. N. 'The Political Role of the Army in Mexico, 1821–1848'. Ph.D. diss. State University of New York, 1974.

Sánchez de Tagle, F. M. *Discurso del Sr. Francisco Manuel Sánchez de Tagle en la sesión del 15 de diciembre (1835) sobre creación de un poder conservador*. Mexico, 1835.

Sanders, F. J. 'Proposals for Monarchy in Mexico, 1823–1860'. Ph.D. diss. University of Arizona, 1967.

Santa Anna, A. López de. *Manifiesto que de sus operaciones en la campaña de Tejas y en su cautiverio dirige a sus conciudadanos el Sr. general Antonio López de Santa Anna*. Veracruz, 1837.

Santoni, P. 'Los federalistas radicales y la guerra del 47'. Ph.D. diss. El Colegio de México, 1987.

Semblanzas de los representantes que compusieron el congreso constituyente de 1836. Mexico, 1837.
Shaw, F. J. 'Poverty and Politics in Mexico City, 1824–1854'. Ph.D. diss. University of Florida, 1975.
Sierra, J. *Evolución política del pueblo mexicano.* Mexico, 1948.
Sims, H. D. *The Expulsion of Mexico's Spaniards, 1821–1836.* Pittsburgh, Pa., 1990.
Soto, M. *La conspiración monárquica en México, 1845–1846.* Mexico, 1988.
Stevens, D. F. 'Instability in Mexico from Independence to the War of the Reform'. Ph.D. diss. University of Chicago, 1984.
   Origins of Instability in Early Republican Mexico. Durham, N.C., London, 1991.
Tena Ramírez, F. *Leyes fundamentales de México, 1808–1971.* Mexico, 1971.
Tenenbaum, B. *The Politics of Penury: Debts and Taxes in Mexico, 1821–1856.* Albuquerque, N.M., 1986.
Thompson, W. *Recollections of Mexico.* New York, 1846.
Thomson, G. P. C. *Puebla de los Angeles: Industry and Society in a Mexican City, 1700–1850.* Boulder, Colo., 1989.
Tornel y Mendívil, J. M. *Breve reseña histórica de los acontecimientos más notables de la nación mexicana desde el año de 1821 hasta nuestros días.* Mexico, 1852.
Tutino, J. *From Insurrection to Revolution in Mexico: Social Bases of Agrarian Violence, 1750–1940.* Princeton, N.J., 1986.
Valadés, J. C. *Alamán, estadista e historiador.* Mexico, 1938.
Vázquez, J. Z., and Meyer, L. *The United States and Mexico.* Chicago, 1985.
Veliz, C. *The Centralist Tradition of Latin America.* Princeton, N.J., 1980.
Victoria, G. *Voto particular del senador Guadalupe Victoria sobre el proyecto de ley en que se declara que las actuales cámaras tienen facultad para variar la forma de gobierno.* Mexico, 1835.
Walker, D. W. *Kinship, Business and Politics: The Martínez del Río Family in Mexico, 1824–1867.* Austin, Tex., 1986.
Ward, H. G. *Mexico in 1827.* 2 vols. London, 1828.
Wilson, B. R. *Religion in Secular Society: A Sociological Comment.* London, 1966.
Wolcott, R., ed. *The Correspondence of W. H. Prescott, 1833–1847.* Boston, 1925.
Yañez, A. *Santa Anna: Espectro de una sociedad.* Mexico, 1982.
Ynsfran, P. M. *Catálogo de los manuscritos del Archivo de Don Valentín Gómez Farías.* Mexico, 1968.
Zamacois, N. de. *Historia de México.* vol. 12. Barcelona, 1880.
Zavala, L. de. *Obras.* Mexico, 1969.

Articles

Chowning, M. 'The Contours of the post–1910 Depression in Mexico: A Reappraisal'. Unpublished conference paper.
Coatsworth, J. 'Obstacles to Economic Growth in Nineteenth Century Mexico'. *American Historical Review,* 83 (1978), 80–100.
Costeloe, M. P. 'Federalism to Centralism in Mexico: The Conservative Case for Change, 1834–1835'. *The Americas,* 45 (1988), 173–85.
   'The Triangular Revolt in Mexico and the Fall of Anastasio Bustamante, August–October, 1841'. *Journal of Latin American Studies,* 20 (1988), 337–60.
   'The Mexican Press of 1836 and the Battle of the Alamo'. *Southwestern Historical Quarterly,* 61 (1988), 533–43.
   'A *Pronunciamiento* in Nineteenth Century Mexico: 15 de julio de 1840'. *Mexican Studies/ Estudios Mexicanos,* 4 (1988), 245–64.

'Los generales Santa Anna y Paredes y Arrillaga en México, 1841–1843: Rivales por el poder o una copa más'. *Historia Mexicana,* 39 (1989), 417–40.

'Generals versus Presidents: Santa Anna and the 1842 Congressional Elections in Mexico'. *Bulletin of Latin American Research,* 8 (1989), 257–74.

Cross, H. E. 'Living Standards in Rural Nineteenth Century Mexico: Zacatecas, 1820–1880'. *Journal of Latin American Studies,* 10 (1973), 1–19.

Gayón Córdova, M. 'Guerra, dictadura y cobre: Crónica de una ciudad asediada (agosto-diciembre de 1841)'. *Historias,* 5 (1984), 53–65.

Hamnett, B. 'Benito Juárez, Early Liberalism, and the Regional Politics of Oaxaca'. *Bulletin of Latin American Research,* 10 (1991), 3–21.

Hutchinson, C. A. 'Valentín Gómez Farías and the "Secret Pact of New Orleans'. *Hispanic American Historical Review,* 36 (1956), 471–89.

Mayo, J. 'Consuls and Silver Contraband on Mexico's West Coast in the Era of Santa Anna'. *Journal of Latin American Studies,* 19 (1987), 389–411.

Ortiz Escamilla, J. 'El pronunciamiento federalista de Gordiano Guzmán, 1837–1842'. *Historia Mexicana,* 38 (1988), 241–82.

Rives, G. L. 'Mexican Diplomacy on the Eve of the War with the United States'. *American Historical Review,* 18 (1912–13), 275–94.

Salvucci, R., and, Salvucci, L. K. 'Crecimiento económico y cambio de productividad en México, 1750–1895', *HISLA,* 10 (1987), 67–89.

Stevens, D. F. 'Economic Fluctuations and Political Instability in Early Republican Mexico'. *Journal of Interdisciplinary History,* 16 (1986), 645–66.

Tella, T. S. di. 'The Dangerous Classes in Early Nineteenth Century Mexico'. *Journal of Latin American Studies,* 5 (1973), 79–105.

Van Young, E. 'Recent Anglophone Scholarship on Mexico and Central America in the Age of Revolution (1750–1850)'. *Hispanic American Historical Review,* 65 (1985), 725–43.

Vázquez, J. Z. 'The Texas Question in Mexican Politics, 1836–1845'. *Southwestern Historical Quarterly,* 89 (1986), 309–43.

'Los Años Olvidados'. *Mexican Studies/Estudios Mexicanos,* 5 (1989), 313–26.

'Iglesia, ejército y centralismo'. *Historia Mexicana,* 39 (1989), 205–34.

Walker, D. W. 'Business as Usual: The Empresa del Tabaco in Mexico, 1837–1844'. *Hispanic American Historical Review,* 64 (1984), 675–705.

Wells, A. 'Family Élites in a Boom or Bust Economy: The Molinas and Peóns of Porfirian Yucatán'. *Hispanic American Historical Review,* 62 (1982), 24–253.

Index

Acajete, battle of, 153–4
Acapulco, 8
agiotistas, 83–4, 127, 130–1, 159, 164, 191–2, 243, 249, 270, 305–6
Alamán, Lucas, 32, 80, 224, 231, 301, 306, passim; correspondence of, 62, 82, 92, 106–7, 111, 145; influence of, 27, 89–90, 165, 225, 284; political views of, 17, 38–9, 44, 47, 73, 109, 265; as presidential candidate, 78, 116–19
Alamo, battle of, 52–3
Alas, Ignacio, 215
Almonte, Juan Nepomuceno, 161, 164–5, 175, 179–80, 276, 282, 294, 301
Alpuche, Wenceslao, 108
Alpuche e Infante, José María, 130, 140
Alvarez, Juan, 8, 27, 109, 165, 199, 203, 215, 222, 304, 306; revolts by, 112, 178, 292–4
Arago, Juan, 49
Aranda y Carpinteiro, Diego, 44, 232
Arista, Mariano, 89, 146, 153, 278, 304
aristócratas, 16, 32–3, 38, 274; *see also* political parties
army: commander-generals, 8, 33, 74, 154 passim; condition of, 6–7, 300; conscription, 168–9, 190, 242–3, 245; cost of, 75, 131, 242, 266; criticism of, 75–6, 169; declining prestige of, 168, 303; *fuero*, 77, 95, 110, 210–11, 226; officers, 5–7, 15, 167–9, 266, 303; popularity of, 5–6; powers of, 154; reform of, 31–2, 167–8, 265–6, 278, 285, 303; representation of, in Congress, 44, 74, 214; size of, 7, 167, 169, 237, 242; structure of, 8–9, 190, 237; under centralism, 110, 167, 303–4
Arrillaga, Basilio, 65, 67, 70–1, 96, 100, 215, 301
Atocha, Alexander, 295

Banco de Avío, 89, 209
Banco Nacional de Amortización de moneda de cobre, 81, 88, 130–1, 165, 194

Barajas, Pedro, 43
Barasorda, Pedro, 251
Barragán, Miguel, 50, 67, 78, 303; early career of, 55; legislation of, 63–5; presidency of, 55–65
Barrera, Ignacio, 232
Barrera, Manuel, 89–90, 123
Barrio, Rafael, 73
Basadre, José Ignacio, 140, 249, 257, 271
Bases Orgánicas, 216, 263, 266–7, 296, 298; details of, 225–7
Bases de Tacubaya, 179, 298; details of, 179
Bazo, Joaquín, 42
Becerra, José Luis, 43, 95
Bermúdez de Castro, Salvador, 279
Berruecos, José, 44, 152
Blasco, José Mariano, 79
Bocanegra, José María, 62
Bravo, Nicolás, 27, 55, 112, 178–9, 199, 203, 222, 258, 275, 282, 301, 303–4, 306; correspondence of, 199; as interim president, 155, 208–12, 214; as presidential candidate, 78, 116–18, 274; reputation of, 118; as vice-president, 292–3, 296
Bustamante, Anastasio, 21, 27, 32, 38, 282, 298, 303, 306; criticism of, 124–5, 141; during war with France, 144–8; early career of, 116, 121–2; election of, to presidency, 116–18; federalist sympathies, 124, 141–3, 180; ideology of, 116, 123–4; later career of, 182–3, 276; loss of support for, 135–6, 141, 153–4, 163–4, 163–7; military campaigns of, 148, 153–4; personality of, 121–5, 144, 182–3; policies of, 126, 158; rebellion against, 161–3, 172–83; and resignation of presidency, 148, 179; resistance of to rebels, 161–3, 172–81
Bustamante, Carlos María, 23, 27–8, 62–3, 67, 69, 94–5, 105, 123–5, 128, 141, 158, 162, 243, 292, 301, 306

Calleja, Félix María, 79
Camacho, Sebastián, 73, 99, 233, 292

Canales, Antonio, 227
Canalizo, José Rafael, 28, 43, 247, 257
Canalizo, Valentín, 28, 215, 269, 271–2,
303–4, 306; early career of, 234; interim
presidency of, 234
Cañedo, Juan de Dios, 242
Cardoso, Joaquín, 140
Carrera, Lorenzo de, 279
Castillo, Demetrio, 44
Ceballos, Juan Bautista, 292
Celaya, 28, 164
centralism: ascendancy of (1834), 38–45, 143;
campaign for, 38–45, 57–62; failure of,
121, 149–50, 160–1, 298–306; and
propaganda, 39, 57–62; trade policy of, 89–
91; weakness of, 158–9; *see also* Siete Leyes
Cervantes, José María, 84–5, 301
Cervantes, Miguel, 32, 231
Chiapas, 8, 95
Chihuahua, 8, 10, 158
Chilapa, 223
Church, 10–11; and anticlericalism, 11–12,
31–4, 129; decline of, 11, 25, 60, 67–8,
135, 300, 302; and freedom of worship
issue, 129, 192, 210–11, 302; *fuero*, 73,
95, 210–11, 226, 229; loans by, 127–31,
193, 224, 290; wealth of, 11, 17, 67, 83–
4, 127–30, 192–3, 204, 208, 229, 276,
302; *see also* clergy; ecclesiastical patronage;
Santa Anna; tithes
Cícero, José Mariano de, 41
civic militia, 33, 48, 56–7, 266, 269–70
clergy: in Congress, 43–4, 67, 69–71, 73,
119, 214, 232–3, 287; numbers of, 67–8,
302; relationship of, with Santa Anna,
50, 68–73, 84, 192–3, 204, 208, 229–30;
see also Church; ecclesiastical patronage;
tithes
Coahuila, 8, 28
Codallos, Felipe, 32
Comonfort, Ignacio, 115, 206, 236
Congress: closure of (1834), 35, (1842), 210–
12, (1844), 254–6; debates of, in 1842,
206–10; independence of, 52, 235–6, 239–
40, 252, 305; sessions of (1835), 46, 95–7,
(1842), 206–10, (1844), 252; *see also*
elections
conservatives, 11, 15, 207, 215, 227, 284,
301; ideology of, 12, 73, 150, 298–301;
manifesto of, 57–62; strategy of, 76–7,
109–10, 150
constitution of 1824, 95, 297
constitution of 1836, *see* Siete Leyes
constitutional reform: pressure for, 156, 170;
proposals in 1842, 207–10
continuity, thesis, 3–4; of people, 27–8, 301;
of issues, 27–8, 301

copper currency, 4, 164; crisis of, 27, 79–82,
193–4
Corro, José Justo, 126; early career of, 77–8;
election of, as president, 77–8; views of,
77–8
Cortazar, Luis, 28, 147, 151, 178, 184, 190,
281, 304
Cortazar, Pedro, 251
Cortes of Cádiz, 14
Cortina Chávez, Ignacio, 81
Cosío, Mariano, 224
Couto, José Bernardo, 36, 66, 92, 96, 112,
116, 142, 171–2, 207, 215–16, 233, 276,
301
crime: extent of, 59, 134, 237, 300; and
legislation, 64, 286; policing of, 64, 134,
286; as political issue, 59–60
Cuernavaca, plan of, 36
Cuevas, Luis Gonzaga, 257, 263, 268, 274,
276
Cumplido, Ignacio, 171, 195, 23

días festivos, 135
Díaz Guzmán, Antonio, 207
Díez de Bonilla, Manuel, 28, 49, 72, 85, 90,
231, 301
Dromundo, Ricardo, 49
Dublán, Manuel, 215, 232
Durango, 8, 68

ecclesiastical patronage, 68–71, 73–4,
302
Echagaray, Domingo, 289
Echeverría, Francisco Javier, 179–80
Echeverría, Pedro José, 81, 141, 257
economy: change in, 4, 9, 79; difficulties of,
4, 85–6; effects of war on, 4; and exports/
imports, 85–6, 228; inequalities in, 150–9;
policy towards, 9, 89, 191, 208–9;
products of, 85–7, 228; regional diversity
of, 9–10, 85–6; *see also* fiscal matters; textile
industry
elections: campaigns, 41–5, 198–200, 230–1,
274–6; congressional, 43–5, 111, 117–18,
198–200, 230–1, 274, 298; presidential,
116–18, 233–4, 247, 274; results (1834),
43–5, (1837), 118–19, (1842), 199–200,
(1843), 231–3, (1845), 274–6, (1846),
291–2, 301; *see also* Congress; electoral
regulations
electoral regulations, 100–3, 196–8, 226,
230–1, 286–7, 296; decrees, 111–12, 296;
electorate, 107–9; income qualifications,
17–18, 61, 100–3, 107–9, 196–8, 211,
226, 275–6, 286–7
Elizalde, Juan Manuel, 73
Elorriaga, Francisco, 233, 276

empleados: attacks on, 167; poverty of, 166–7; *see also empleomanía*

empleomanía, 14, 58

Envides, D. N., 140

Escandón, Manuel, 84–5, 89, 145, 190, 249, 264

Escobedo, Antonio, 173, 189

escoceses, 14, 55, 66, 73, 114, 236; *see also* political parties

Esparza, Marcos de, 289

Espinosa, José Ignacio, 126

Espinosa, Rafael, 243

Espinosa de los Monteros, José, 36, 142, 207, 232, 275

Fagoaga, José Francisco, 28, 73, 81, 85, 169, 276

Fagoaga, José María, 28, 73, 85

federalism: attack on, 38–45, 57–62, 97; campaigns for, 10–11, 141–2; end of, 45, 98–9; identification of, with radicalism, 39; restoration of, 293–7; revolts in favour of, 136–8; *see also* federalists; political parties; *pronunciamientos*

federalists: campaigns against, 145, 160, 222; campaigns by, 112–13, 138, 141–2, 195–6, 199–200, 227, 268, 274–5, 289, 292–7, 301; in Congress, 97, 156, 206–10, 215, 233, 267; organization of, 199–200, 301; petitions by, 138, 275; and press, 113, 195–6, 200, 216, 268; revolts by, 51, 112, 148, 153, 270–3; *see also* federalism; political parties; *pronunciamientos*

Ferdinand VII, 5–6

Fernández de Celís, José, 81

Filisola, Vicente, 231, 279, 282

fiscal matters: deficits, 4, 79, 131, 290; loans, 4, 270; problems, 127, 290; *see also* tariff regulations; taxation

Flores, Bernardo, 251

France, 6, 13, 294, 300, passim; peace treaty with, 154; war with, 145–8, 298

freemasonry, 12, 15, 114–15; *see also escoceses*; *yorkinos*

French Revolution (1789), 14, 22, 149–50

Furlong, Cosme, 28

Galindo, Pánfilo, 249

Garay, Antonio, 35, 85, 145

García, Francisco, 38, 51, 195

García Conde, Francisco, 76

García Conde, Pedro, 257, 264, 272

García Torres, Vicente, 231, 290

García Ugarte, Ramón, 137

Garibay, Miguel, 85

Garza Flores, 96

Godoy, Juan Ignacio, 233,

Gómez Anaya, Cirilo, 108, 155, 276

Gómez de la Cortina, José Justo, 170

Gómez Farías, Valentín, 17, 27–8, 31–4, 39, passim; arrest of, 140, 295; correspondence of, with rebels, 114, 139, 236, 271; dismissal of, 55–6; ideology of, 18, 25–6, 301–2; as leader of radicals, 139–41, 161–3, 277; negotiations of, with Canalizo, 269; opinion of, concerning A. Bustamante, 124–5; plotting of revolt by, 114, 139, 227–8, 269–73, 277, 296–7; as presidential candidate, 274; as rebel leader, 161–3, 296–7; relationship of, with Santa Anna, 18, 187, 189, 236, 269, 293–7; removal of, from vice-presidency, 55–6; as vice-president (1833–4), 31–5; in Yucatán, 160, 227; *see also* federalists; political parties; radicals

Gómez Pedraza, Manuel, 27, 162, 222–3, passim; break with Santa Anna, 197–8; in Congress, 199, 231–2, 233, 235–6, 244, 255, 276; early career of, 115; as government minister, 141–3, 195–8; as *moderado* leader, 38, 115–16, 140–1, 185, 195, 207, 249, 255, 261, 274, 277, 292, 295; political activities of, 140–3, 196–8; as presidential candidate, 115–17, 274; views of, 38, 73, 197

Gonzaga Cuevas, Luis, 126

González Angulo, Bernardo, 194

González Cosío, Manuel, 139

Gordoa, Luis G., 92, 112, 199

Gorostiza, Manuel Eduardo, 36, 177

Great Britain, 6, 13, 294, 300

Guadalajara, 13, 37, 218, passim; elections in, 200; revolts in, 37, 172–3, 249–51, 292

Guanajuato, 159

Guerra, José María, 36, 42, 129

Guerrero, Vicente, 19, 27, 32, 122

Gutiérrez Estrada, José María, 73, 185, 287, 299; and advocacy of monarchy, 170–2; correspondence of, with Mora, 170–1

Guzmán, Gordiano, 27, 112, 138, 160

Haro y Tamariz, Antonio, 232, 248, 252, 254–5, 257, 259

Haro y Tamariz, Joaquín, 215

Herrera, José Joaquín de, 27, 35, 162, 199, 298; attitude of, towards reform, 265–7; early career of, 262–3; and election as president, 274; and government of 1845, 262–83; as interim president, 247–274; as leader of revolt, 255–7; policy of, on army, 265–6; policy of, on Texas, 267–9; political views of, 263, 266–7; revolt against, 270–3, 277–83

hombres de bien: appeals to, 150; coalition of, 34–5, 38, 150, 211, 284–5, 299; definition of, 16–17; disillusion of, 91–4, 134, 151, 158, 249, 302; ethnic origins of, 18–19; ideas of, 17–27, 29; income of, 17; life-style of, 19–21; nostalgia of, 25, 151; political views of, 17–27, 34, 38, 46, 150–1, 189, 211, 298–306; prejudices of, 34
Huejotzingo, 210
Huerta, Nieves, 136

Ibarra, Domingo, 292
immigration, 13
Inclán, Ignacio, 259, 304
independence, effects of, 3–4
Iturbe, Francisco, 85, 193
Iturbide, Agustín de, 4–5, 10, 27, 51, 55, 122
Iturbide, Joaquín de, 69–72, 78

Jalapa, 13, 36
Jalisco, 8, 37, 51, 58, passim
Juárez, Benito, 5, 19, 112, 275
Junta de Notables, 214–15, 225–7, 298
Junta de Representantes, 195–7, 2
Juvera, Julián, 190

Ladrón de Guevara, Joaquín, 207
Lafragua, José María, 114–15, 124, 162, 196, 206–7, 222, 236, 249, 257, 268, 271–3, 275–6, 292, 294, 305
Landero, Antonio, 202
Lebrija, Joaquín, 126
León, Antonio de, 37
ley del caso, 32, 36, 39, 60
liberals: arrests of, 222; association of, with federalism, 39, 196; in Congress, 206–10, 215, 233, 236; divisions among, 140–1, 207, 301; electoral campaigns of, 226, 231–2, 274–5; leaders of, 140, 207, 257, 274; policies of, 31–5, 140, 207, 293–7, 301
loans, 83–4, 127–32, 155, 270, 273, 276; forced, 4, 84–5, 163, 223–4, 236; protests against, 85, 163; *see also* Church
Lombardini, Manuel, 231, 291
Lope de Vergara, Francisco, 47, 95
Loperena, Ignacio, 145, 229
López de Santa Anna, Antonio, *see* Santa Anna

Malo, Ramón, 207, 276
Mangino, Rafael, 78, 126
Martínez, Ignacio, 275
Martínez Caro, Ramón, 49
Mejía, Francisco, 272–3
Mejía, José Antonio, 35, 112, 114, 153

Mendoza, José María, 259
Michelena, José Mariano, 126, 301
Michoacán, 8, 37, 51, 68, 159, passim
middle class: 10, 22, 26; attitudes, 10, 23; definition of, 21–3; solidarity, 21–2, 28, 38, 60, 91–2, 110, 150; *see also hombres de bien*
Mier y Terán, Gregorio, 128
Miñón, José Vicente, 271
Moctezuma, Esteban, 114, 137, 279
moderates, 15, 40, 277, 292–7; in Congress, 207; leaders of, 38–41; policies of, 41; *see also* Gómez Pedraza, Manuel
monarchists: campaigns of, 170–2, 284–6; press, 171, 284–6; *see also* Alamán, Lucas; Gutiérrez Estrada, José María; Paredes y Arrillaga, Mariano; political parties
Montes, Ezequiel, 207
Mora, José María Luis, 17, 19, 28, 32, 36, 55, 57, 65–6, 277; political analysis by, 66–7
Mora y Villamil, Ignacio, 74
Morales, Angel, 70, 154, 199
Morales, Juan Bautista, 196, 206–7, 233, 235, 244–5, 281, 287, 301
Morphy, Francisco, 172–3, 181, 190, 193, 201–2
Muñoz Ledo, Octaviano, 207
Muría, Manuel, 93
Múzquiz, Melchor, 77, 126, 199, 236

Neri del Barrio, Felipe, 73, 85, 92, 95, 112, 145, 190, 276
newspapers, 12, 195–6, 216, 289; circulation of, 12; influence of, 12–13

Oaxaca, 8, 36–7, 71, 159, passim
Ocampo, Melchor, 207
Olaguíbel, Francisco Modesto, 140, 199, 206–7, 236, 257, 268, 271–2
Olarte, Mariano, 112, 138
Orbegoso, Juan, 180
Orizaba, 28, 36, 62
Ormaechea, Ignacio, 85, 232
Ortíz Monasterio, José María, 78
Otero, Mariano, 195–6, 207, 222, 231–2, 236, 257, 275, 292, 295, 305
Othón, Ramón, 270–2

Pacheco, Ramón, 56
Pacheco Leal, José, 96–8
Palacio, Fernando, 291
Palafox, Manuel, 138
Pardío, Manuel José, 301
Paredes y Arrillaga, Mariano, 28, 303–4, 306; appointments of, 74, 141, 190, 215, 220, 233, 250, 264; arrest of, 221, 296; attitude

of, towards monarchism, 279–80, 284–92;
control of elections by, 200, 291–2;
correspondence of, with Santa Anna, 110,
172–3, 200–12, 214, 233, 249–50;
correspondence of, with Tornel, 200–3,
219–21; disgrace of, 217–22; early career
of, 74, 137, 217–18; and government of
1846, 283–95; ideology of, 110, 201, 217–
18, 284; as member of Junta de Notables,
215, 219; personality of, 217–8; policy of,
on Texas, 290–1; rebellion of, at
Guadalajara (1841), 172–81, 203; rebellion
of, against Santa Anna (1844), 249–52;
rebellion of, against Herrera (1845), 278–
83; relations of, with Santa Anna, 184,
214, 217–22, 233, 249–51; revolt against,
290

Parres, Joaquín, 78
Peña y Peña, Manuel de la, 126, 155
Peón, Sebastián, 158
Pérez, Pedro Celestino, 41
Pesado, José Joaquín, 215–6
Poinsett, Joel R., 6
political parties, 2, 14–15, 23, 66–7, 274–5;
see also conservatives; *escoceses*; liberals;
moderates; politicians; radicals; *yorkinos*
politicians: characteristics of, 14–15, 23, 261–
2; families of, 27–8; occupations of, 15–16;
origins of, 15–16; see also *hombres de bien*;
political parties
Polk, James, 241, 295
popular protests, 26–7
Portugal, Juan Cayetano, 36, 41, 96, 215
Posada y Garduño, Manuel, 163, 215, 276,
301
Posadas, Manuel, 81
press, 12–13, 152–3, 171, 195–6, 277, 289;
attacks on, 152–3; freedom of, 12, 100,
153, 210, 226; restrictions on, 152–3,
216–17, 289–90; see also newspapers
Prieto, Guillermo, 115, 123–4
pronunciamientos, 2, 7–9, 29, 210, 249–51,
278–83, 298; centralist, 36, 44, 62, 96;
federalist, 112, 148, 275, 292–7; in Mexico
City, 160–63, 176–81, 270–3, 292–8
Puebla, 8–9, 28, 36–7, 41, 44, 68, 71, 159,
passim

Querétaro, 8, 43–4, 51, passim; resistance of,
to Santa Anna, 252–3
Quintana Roo, Andrés, 36, 215
Quirós y Medina, José Nicolás, 70

radical government (1833–4), 31–8
radicals, 15, 31–5, 115, 210, 227, 268, 274–
6, 281; alliance of, with *santanistas*, 262,
270–3, 292–7; programme of, 31–5, 210;

see also federalists; liberals; radical
government (1833–4); Gómez Farías, V.
Ramírez, José Fernando, 207
Ramírez, Mateo, 139
Ramírez, Pedro María, 57, 95, 112, 207
Rangel, Joaquín, 271–3, 295
regionalism, 9–10, 15
Rejón, Manuel Crescencio, 36, 74, 140, 206,
257, 269, 293
Requena, Tomás, 94
Reyes, Isidro, 248
Rincón, Manuel, 32, 78, 117, 146, 162, 233,
236, 247
Río, José del, 275
Riva Palacio, Mariano, 115, 199, 207,
222, 231–2, 257, 264, 275–6, 295,
301
Rodríguez Puebla, Juan, 36, 141–3, 195,
199, 207, 215–16, 232–3
Romero, José Antonio, 179
Romero, Manuel, 280
Romero, Vicente, 38
Rosa, Luis de la, 243, 248, 292
Rubio, Cayetano, 166, 190, 193, 246, 249,
264–5

Salas, José Mariano de, 220–1, 282, 296
San Luis Potosí, 8, 32, 37, 43, 52, 55,
passim; revolt in, 137, 280
Sánchez Hidalgo, Sabás, 192
Sánchez de Tagle, Francisco, 47, 65, 113,
301, 306; as advocate of SPC, 104–6; in
Congress, 44, 95–8, 104–6, 119–20, 301;
conservative views of, 73, 100; early career
of, 100; as member of SPC, 126, 155; *see
also* Siete Leyes; Supreme Conservative
Power
Santa Anna, Antonio López de, 15, 21, 26–9,
46, passim; attitude of, towards Church,
50, 68–73, 84, 192–3, 204, 208, 229–30;
autocratic aims of; 37, 47–8, 50–4, 62–3,
104, 110, 155, 174, 184, 201–3, 213,
300, 304–5; closure of congress by (1834),
35; (1842), 208–12; (1844), 253–5;
corruption of, 50, 186–7, 213, 246, 248;
coterie of, 48–9; cult of, 6, 47, 154, 188–
9, 225–6, 237; deals of, 54, 184–5, 190–
5; decrees of, 151–5, 193–4, 204–5, 208–
9, 216, 223–4, 228–9, 234; deposition of,
111, 213; description of, 47, 186; early
career of, 47, 188, electoral regulations of,
196–8, 230–1; fall of, 54, 111, 252–60;
government of (1833–4), 35–45; (1839),
151–5; (1841–4), 184–206, 208–12, 213–
47; marriage of, 213, 242; opposition of,
to liberals, 35–7, 206; personality of, 47,
186–9; political isolation of, 48–9, 305;

political principles of, 36, 44–5, 49–50,
  151–2, 187, 206; quarrels of, with Tornel,
  237; quarrels of, with Valencia, 222;
  reaction of, to elections (1842), 200–1,
  205; rebellion of, against Bustamante, A.,
  172–181; and reconquest of Texas, 51–5,
  230, 237–8, 240–7; regal ambitions of,
  205–9; and relations with Congress (1835),
  96, (1842), 205–6, (1844), 235–6, 239–
  60; relationship of, with Gómez Farías, V.,
  18, 35, 187, 293–7, relationship of, with
  Paredes y Arillaga, M., 184, 200–3, 249–
  50; restriction of by press, 152–3, 216;
  return of, 35, 143, 151, 296–7; and
  santanistas, 262, 274, 293–5; and support
  for army, 74, 154, 188, 190, 203, 214;
  and war with France, 144–8; wealth of, 7,
  186, 260, 303
Sierra y Rosso, Ignacio, 49, 205
Siete Leyes, 23, 298; analysis of, 99–109;
  background to, 94–100; basic principles of,
  98–9; clauses of, on Church, 73–4, 99;
  committee reports on, 94–100; demands
  for reform of, 156; main advocates of,
  95–8
Slidell, John, 277, 290–1
social change, 22, 38, 60–1, 135, 302
Solana, Luis, 254
Sonora, 8, 10, 68, 137–8, 236, 250,
  passim
Spain, 3, 9, 13, 126
Supreme Conservative Power, 23, passim;
  analysis of, 104–6; criticism of, 106–7,
  157–8; decisions by, 142–3, 147, 155–8,
  177; dispute of, with executive, 155–8;
  membership of, 126, 155; powers of, 106;
  see also Sánchez de Tagle, Francisco
Supreme Court, 32–3, 101–2, 157, 171,
  passim

Tabasco, 275
Tamaulipas, 159
Tampico, 9, 13, 137–8
tariff regulations, 89–91, 204, 228–9
Taylor, Zachary, 274, 291
taxation, 5, 82, 132, 242, 300; commercial,
  82, 132–3, 204, 223, 244; *derecho de
  consumo*, 164, 166, 173, 177, 191; general
  taxes, 132–3, 163, 204, 223, 245, 247,
  264; head tax, 133, 163, 177, 204, 245,
  264; property taxes, 82, 132–3, 163, 223,
  244; protests against, 163, 249
Texas, 6, 298, 300; campaign of 1836, 51–5;
  planned reconquest of, 75, 209, 223, 240–
  7, 273–4, 276
textile industry: imports of, 86–90, 164–5,
  192, 225, 270, 286; legislation on, 90–1,

126, 191, 204; lobby by, 9, 86–90, 164–5,
  204, 225, 264–5, 305; petitions by, 89–
  91, 164–5, 225, 264–5
Three Day Ministry, 141–5
tithes, 41, 67, 112, 193, 302; *see also* Church;
  radical government (1833–4)
tobacco industry, 87–9, 190–1, 264;
  alienation of, 165–6; farmers, 9, 285–6;
  influence of, 87–8, 165–6, 305; monopoly
  of, 87–8, 165–6, 190; petitions by, 166,
  264
Toluca, 43, 62
Tornel y Mendívil, José Julián, 28, 99,
  232
Tornel y Mendívil, José María, 19, 21, 26–8,
  49–50, 65, 89, passim, 224, 282, 301,
  306; accusations against, 113; as ally of
  Santa Anna, 49, 96, 105, 184;
  condemnation of monarchism by, 171;
  correspondence of, with Paredes y Arillaga,
  M., 200–1, 278; and criticism of army, 76–
  7; dispute of, with SPC, 156–7; as member
  of SPC, 155; as Minister of War, 76, 105,
  147, 154, 167–9, 195, 210, 216, 235–6;
  as presidential candidate, 78, 116; quarrels
  of, with Santa Anna, 237; and reform of
  army, 76–7
Toro, Francisco de Paula, 42, 49, 74
trade policy, 88–91, 204
Trigueros, Ignacio, 248, 295
Troncoso, José María, 42

Ulúa, San Juan de, 55
United States, 6, 13, 224, passim; relations
  with, 273–4, 276, 290–1, 295, 300; *see also*
  Texas
University of Mexico, 19, 36, 64–5
Urrea, José, 137–9, 148, 153, 161–3

Valencia, Gabriel, 21, 49, 77, 184, 200, 211,
  222, 224, 227, 301, 303–4, 306;
  appointments of, 77, 190, 204, 215–16,
  264; and attempt at presidency, 282–3; and
  desertion of Bustamante, 176–81, 203; early
  career of, 185; personality of, 185; as
  presidential candidate, 78; supports of, for
  government, 161–3, 171, 258
Valentín, Miguel, 98
Vázquez, Ciriaco, 49, 74
Vázquez, Pablo, 32, 36, 42, 67, 130, 135,
  271, 306
Veracruz, 6, 8–9, 13, 43, 49, 145–8, 166,
  175
Victoria, Guadalupe, 38, 55, 89, 97–8, 116,
  125, 145, 171
Villaurrutia, Eulogio, 74

yorkinos, 14, 38, 114–15, 138; *see also* political parties; radicals

Yucatán, 8, 37, 54, 230, passim; rebellion of, 158–60, 209, 223, 230; separation of, 9, 158, 160, 298; settlement with, 230, 236

Zacapú (Michoacán), 136

Zacatecas, 9, 33, 37, 48, 51, 56, 62, passim

Zavala, Lorenzo de, 22, 65

Zelaeta, Juan, 140

Zubieta, Pedro, 232

Zuñiga, Ignacio, 139

CAMBRIDGE LATIN AMERICAN STUDIES

3   Peter Calvert. *The Mexican Revolution 1910–1914: The Diplomacy of Anglo-American Conflict*
8   Celso Furtado. *Economic Development of Latin America: Historical Background and Contemporary Problems*
10 D. A. Brading. *Mines and Merchants in Bourbon Mexico, 1763–1810*
15 P. J. Bakewell. *Silver Mining and Society in Colonial Mexico: Zacatecas, 1546–1700*
22 James Lockhart and Enrique Otté. *Letters and People of the Spanish Indies: The Sixteenth Century*
24 Jean A. Meyer. *The Cristero Rebellion: The Mexican People between Church and State, 1926–1929*
31 Charles F. Nunn. *Foreign Immigrants in Early Bourbon Mexico, 1700–1760*
32 D. A. Brading. *Haciendas and Ranchos in the Mexican Bajío*
34 David Nicholls. *From Dessalines to Duvalier: Race, Color, and National Independence in Haiti*
35 Jonathan C. Brown. *A Socioeconomic History of Argentina, 1776–1860*
36 Marco Palacios. *Coffee in Colombia, 1850–1970: An Economic, Social, and Political History*
37 David Murray. *Odious Commerce: Britain, Spain, and the Abolition of the Cuban Slave Trade*
38 D. A. Brading. *Caudillo and Peasant in the Mexican Revolution*
39 Joe Foweraker. *The Struggle for Land: A Political Economy of the Pioneer Frontier in Brazil from 1930 to the Present Day*
40 George Philip. *Oil and Politics in Latin America: Nationalist Movements and State Companies*
41 Noble David Cook. *Demographic Collapse: Indian Peru, 1520–1620*
42 Gilbert M. Joseph. *Revolution from Without: Yucatan, Mexico, and the United States, 1880–1924*
43 B. S. McBeth. *Juan Vicente Gomez and the Oil Companies in Venezuela, 1908–1935*
44 J. A. Offner. *Law and Politics in Aztec Texcoco*
45 Thomas J. Trebar. *Brazil's State-Owned Enterprises: A Case Study of the State as Entrepreneur*
46 James Lockhart and Stuart B. Schwartz. *Early Latin America: A History of Colonial Spanish America and Brazil*
47 Adolfo Figueroa. *Capitalist Development and the Peasant Economy in Peru*
48 Norman Long and Bryan Roberts. *Mines, Peasants, and Entreprenrurs: Regional Development in the Central Highlands of Peru*
49 Ian Roxborough. *Unions and Politics in Mexico: The Case of the Automobile Industry*
50 Alan Gilbert and Peter Ward. *Housing, the State, and the Poor: Policy and Practice in Three Latin American Cities*
51 Jean Stubbs. *Tobacco on the Periphery: A Case Study in Cuban Labor History, 1860–1958*
52 Stuart B. Schwartz. *Sugar Plantations in the Formation of Brazilian Society: Bahia, 1550–1835*
53 Richard J. Walter. *The Province of Buenos Aires and Argentine Politics, 1912–1945*
54 Alan Knight. *The Mexican Revolution, vol. 1: Porfirians, Liberals, and Peasants*
55 Alan Knight. *The Mexican Revolution, vol. 2: Counter-Revolution and Reconstruction*
56 P. Michael McKinley. *Pre-Revolutionary Caracas: Politics, Economy, and Society, 1777–1811*
57 Adriaan C. van Oss. *Catholic Colonialism: A Parish History of Guatemala, 1524–1821*
58 Leon Zomosc. *The Agrarian Question and the Peasant Movement in Colombia: Struggles of the National Peasant Association, 1967–1981*
59 Brian R. Hamnett. *Roots of Insurgency: Mexican Regions, 1750–1824*
60 Manuel Caballero. *Latin America and the Comintern, 1919–1943*
61 Inga Clendinnen. *Ambivalent Conquests: Maya and Spaniard in Yucatan, 1715–1570*
62 Jeffrey D. Needell. *Tropical Belle Epoque: Elite Culture and Society in Turn-of-the-Century Rio de Janeiro*
63 Victor Bulmer-Thomas. *The Political Economy of Central America since 1920*

64   Daniel James. *Resistance and Integration: Peronism and the Argentine Working Class, 1946–1976*

65   Bill Albert. *South America and the First World War: The Impact of the War in Brazil, Argentina, Peru, and Chile*

66   Jonathan Hartlyn. *The Politics of Coalition Rule in Colombia*

67   Charles H. Wood and José Alberto Magno de Carvalho. *The Demography of Inequality in Brazil*

68   Sandra Lauderdale Graham. *House and Street: The Domestic World of Servants and Masters in Nineteenth-Century Rio de Janeiro*

69   Ronald H. Chilcore. *Power and the Ruling Classes in Northeast Brazil: Juazeiro and Petrolina in Transition*

70   Joanne Rappaport. *The Politics of Memory: Native Historical Interpretation in the Columbian Andes*

71   Suzanne Austin Alchon. *Native Society and Disease in Colonial Ecuador*

72   Charles Guy Gillespie. *Negotiating Democracy: Politicians and Generals in Uruguay*